Elementary Social Studies

A PRACTICAL APPROACH TO TEACHING AND LEARNING

SEVENTH EDITION

Elementary Social Studies

A PRACTICAL APPROACH TO TEACHING AND LEARNING

SEVENTH EDITION

ian wright
university of british columbia

david hutchison
brock university

Pearson Canada
Toronto

Ian Wright dedicates this book to his grandchildren, Joel Wright, and Nicola and Taryn Chaney. I.W.

Dedicated to my nieces, Kate-Lynn and Heather, who will soon embark on their study of social studies. D.H.

Library and Archives Canada Cataloguing in Publication

Wright, Ian, 1941–
Elementary social studies : a practical approach to teaching and learning / Ian Wright, David Hutchison. — 7th ed.

Includes bibliographical references and index.
ISBN 978-0-13-515322-2

1. Social sciences—Study and teaching (Elementary). I. Hutchison, David, 1968– II. Title.

LB1584.5.C3W75 2010 372.83'044 C2008-904205-0

ISBN-13: 978-0-13-515322-2
ISBN-10: 0-13-515322-0

Vice-President, Editorial Director: Gary Bennett
Editor-in-Chief: Ky Pruesse
Executive Acquisitions Editor: David Le Gallais
Marketing Manager: Loula March
Associate Editor: Megan Burns
Production Editor: Melissa Hajek
Copy Editor: Kelli Howey
Proofreaders: Melissa Hajek, Susan Broadhurst
Production Coordinator: Janis Raisen
Composition: Laserwords
Art Director: Julia Hall
Cover Designer: Anthony Leung
Cover Image: Veer Inc.

5 6 7 14 13 12

Printed and bound in Canada.

PEARSON

Contents

Preface

This book is not a textbook in the usual sense of the word. Textbooks usually require readers to absorb information first and then carry out certain activities, such as answering questions based on the text's content. Perhaps this is how you learned social studies in school. The assumption in most methods textbooks is that if beginning teachers read about the theory and practice of social studies teaching, they will assimilate the required information and become an effective teacher. However, this book is based on the assumption that if you are actually *involved* in social studies teaching and learning, you are more likely to understand and implement effective instructional practices in the elementary school classroom. In other words, as you read this book, you are encouraged to "learn by doing," and *reflect critically* on what you are doing.

The emphasis, then, is on the procedures and standards of critical thinking as they pertain to the intellectual standards and personal and social values in social studies. The philosophy behind this text is that students of all ages should be actively engaged in finding, applying, interpreting, analyzing, synthesizing, and evaluating information in order to make well reasoned decisions.

We hope this book challenges you to think critically about both what you teach and how you teach, in addition to providing you with many practical ideas.

ORGANIZATION

This book is divided into five parts. In Part 1 you will be introduced to the nature of social studies and some rationales for teaching it. You will learn that there is no one agreed-upon definition of social studies and that differing definitions are based on differing philosophies of what constitutes the educated person. These philosophies are based on different assumptions about what constitutes knowledge, how people learn, what defines a good person, what comprises the ideal society, and what is important to know in order to create an educated person. Throughout the book, you are asked to reflect on what you believe and what factors in your background may have contributed to your beliefs. You should begin to develop your own philosophy for teaching social studies as you continue to read this book.

In the second part of the book, you are introduced to the teaching of empirical and conceptual claims and the intellectual standards associated with them. Empirical claims are statements about what *was, is,* or *will be* the case. If they are believed to be true, then we call them facts. For example, stating, "This book has six hundred pages" is an empirical claim because it asserts that something is the case, even though it is not true. "Ottawa is the capital of Canada" is an empirical claim that also happens to be true. We want students to evaluate empirical claims so that they can determine which ones to believe. Therefore, we need to introduce them to some of the intellectual standards usually found in the skills or applications sections of social studies curricula guidelines. These standards include validity, reliability, logic, accuracy, precision, lack of bias, and having enough evidence to support a conclusion. Similarly, because we need to teach students to use language effectively and to be clear about the concepts they use, readers are introduced to ways of helping students develop conceptual clarity. As you read this book, you will be asked to think critically about empirical and conceptual matters so that you can help your students do the same.

We begin Part 2 with some very general ideas for instructional planning, followed by more in-depth considerations. Expository and story-based formats are explained. We include a chapter on concepts as concepts are vital for understanding the content of social studies. Concepts always precede the *understanding* of a particular piece of information. For example, one cannot make any sense of the statement, "Ottawa is the capital of Canada" unless one knows what the term "capital" means. Questions are also significant and are ubiquitous in social studies classrooms. Both student- and teacher-originated questions are meant to be answered. Two major approaches can be followed: having students find out the answers for themselves, or *telling* them the answers. The former is closely associated with inquiry learning, which is the focus of Chapter 8; the latter relates to expository or didactic methods, which are the subject of Chapter 5.

Knowledge of methodology makes no sense unless there is "content" to teach. General teaching methods are given disciplinary substance in the following chapters. Chapters 10 and 11 present the rationales, organizing principles, and teaching strategies for two key social science disciplines: history and geography. Both disciplines can in part be taught via field studies, which are the subject of Chapter 13. And geography is a key discipline in environmental education, which is the focus of Chapter 12. To help you teach students how to make connections between the information learned, whether in history, geography, or any other subject area, Chapter 14 is devoted to the ways in which students can create generalizations, cause-and-effect relationships, and syntheses.

Part 3 deals with matters of value through the medium of decision making. It outlines approaches to values education and explores the value questions that arise in citizenship, multicultural, global, human rights, peace, law-related education, and First Nations, Inuit, and Métis studies. We believe that value issues should comprise the central features of social studies. If we wish to develop responsible and rational citizens, then we need to help students deal with the myriad value problems they confront in everyday life, as well as those that we might expect to confront them in the future. Knowing about Canadian history or world geography is of little use unless it is applied to the real world in some way. Such knowledge is most worthwhile when it helps students create a better world for themselves and others and for future generations. We think that this may be the most significant role for social studies education in the new millennium.

Part 4 is devoted to helping you locate, use, and evaluate information. This chapter also has ideas that will help you and your students employ new media and technology in the classroom.

Part 5 provides a detailed framework for unit planning. Chapter 21 discusses and provides examples of unit rationales, the scope and sequence of a unit, and actual unit episodes, some of which involve value questions. We end with a chapter on assessment and evaluation and include examples of a variety of techniques.

We hope that you find this text to be both exciting and challenging. We wish you well in your chosen career.

SUPPLEMENTS

A **Text Enrichment Site** has been developed for the seventh edition of *Elementary Social Studies*, and includes resources such as an annotated list of highly recommended websites for Canadian elementary social studies teachers, and a document with over 1500 activity ideas that can be used in the social studies classroom. You can access the site at the following URL: www.pearsoned.ca/text/wright.

Technology Specialists. Pearson's Technology Specialists work with faculty and campus course designers to ensure that Pearson technology products, assessment tools, and online course materials are tailored to meet your specific needs. This highly qualified team is dedicated to helping schools take full advantage of a wide range of educational resources, by assisting in the integration of a variety of instructional materials and media formats. Your local Pearson Education sales representative can provide you with more details on this service program.

Acknowledgments

Ian Wright thanks David Hutchison, without whom this book might never have been published, for his significant contributions to this book. He also thanks all those who contributed to his work in this textbook including Nancy Stubbs, a volunteer at the Museum of Anthropology at the University of British Columbia and Laurel Smith Wilson, Executive Director and Curator of 'Ksan Historic Village in Hazleton, British Columbia, for their help in the history of grave houses. He especially thanks Carol for her support and love. He dedicates this book to his grandchildren, Joel, Nicola, and Taryn.

David Hutchison wishes to thank Ian Wright and Pearson Education Canada for the opportunity to contribute to the 7th edition of the text.

We both want to thank the following people: the reviewers who helped in the development of this edition: Dr. Wanda Cassidy, Dr. Linda Farr Darling, Carole L. Ford, Dr. Larry A. Glassford, William A. Timmons, Ruth Hay, Binda Kissonpersad, and Sharon Murray and the staff at Pearson Canada: Christine Cozens, Megan Burns, and Melissa Hajek.

CHAPTER 1

What Is Social Studies?

Imagine you are teaching a class of elementary school students (you can choose which age group) and are free to plan and implement your own one-year social studies program. What will you do? How you answer this question depends upon your thoughts related to several factors: what "social studies" means, what the goals of social studies instruction should be, the context in which you will be teaching, and the backgrounds and capabilities of your students. In answering these questions in preparation for teaching you will draw upon your background experiences, and these will likely affect your decisions.[1] According to an old adage, we teach as we were taught.[2] For example, if you were taught social studies in elementary and/or secondary school through reading a textbook and having teachers lecture you, then these methods will be very familiar—whether you liked them or not. If you disliked these methods, you might find yourself rejecting them outright without first considering the potentially beneficial results they can lead to if used judiciously. On the other hand, if you liked these methods you might reject other alternatives that can produce different kinds of meaningful learning. All of these factors are related. Suppose you decide that it is a worthwhile goal to teach your Grade 4 students about the Quebec conscription crisis during World War I: Then someone might legitimately ask if Grade 4 students could make much sense of the topic. (This does not mean, of course, that the topic is not worth teaching at another grade level, or that Grade 4 students could well be introduced to this topic in an age-appropriate way.) Or, because you enjoyed and were good at memorizing lists, you require your students to memorize the names of the last five lieutenant governors of Prince Edward Island. Or, you decide not to teach about climate change in social studies, as you consider it to be a topic for the science curriculum. All of these considerations (and, no doubt, many others) influence your approach to teaching social studies.

Let us first look at how you define social studies, for how you define the term "social studies" affects what you teach in its name.

Activity 1-A

1. What words, phrases, or images come to mind when you think of "social studies"? Write down one word or phrase, or draw an image, in each segment of the reaction wheel (on page 2).
2. Exchange your reaction wheel with a peer. Try to clarify what your peer means by his or her reactions. What experiences led to these reactions?
3. What do you remember studying and doing in social studies classes when you were an elementary or secondary school student?

   Did you enjoy social studies? Why or why not?

   Do you think you learned anything of importance? Why or why not?

   Do you want to teach social studies in the ways that it was taught to you? Why or why not?

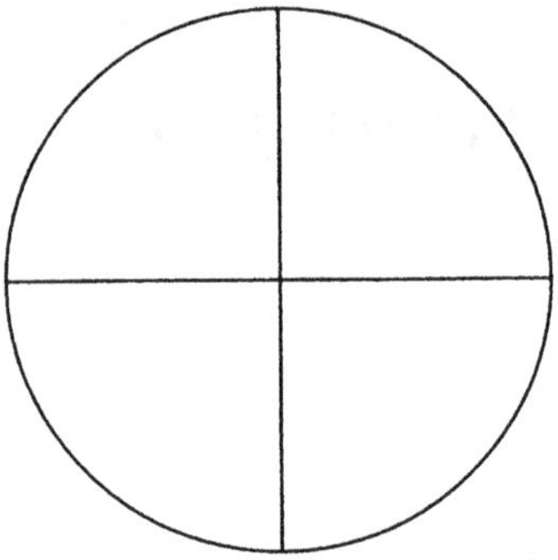

4. If necessary, rewrite or redraw your reactions so that they are clear and understandable.
5. In a large group (five or more people), collect all of the reactions. Try to classify the reactions into *the knowledge you learned, the skills you learned,* and *expressions of attitude*. Looking at just the knowledge classification, can you agree on what social studies is?

Knowledge: What One "Knows"	Skills: What One "Does"	Attitude: How One "Feels" (what evaluations one makes)

You may find that your group is able to agree on what the knowledge base of social studies is, at least in general terms. You have all studied some history and geography in social studies and may remember making models of Egyptian pyramids or colouring maps of Canada. There is not likely to be much disagreement that some activities, such as building models of the pyramids or colouring maps of Canada, could be construed as social studies activities. However, not all activities fall so clearly under the social studies label.

Activity 1-B

Read the following. Which of these situations would you consider to be social studies? Indicate your answers on the chart that follows, and then refer to the Answers to Activities section in the back of the book.

1. To teach a simple statistical procedure, the teacher has organized students to conduct a survey on people's attitudes toward litter in order to discover whether males and females differ significantly in their attitudes.
2. Students are creating a mural to display what they learned on a field trip to a farm.
3. Students are acting out the arrival of some of the first settlers in New France.
4. Students are listening to a nurse tell them how to apply a tourniquet.
5. Having read a story about the life of two children in Japan, students are answering comprehension questions in their notebooks.
6. To develop citizenship skills and attitudes, students are discussing how to welcome a new immigrant from India to their class.
7. Students are reading a fairy tale from China.
8. Students are learning songs sung by children in Israel.
9. Students are making scale drawings of their classroom.
10. Students are collecting food for the local food bank.

Situation	Social Studies	Not Social Studies	Not Sure	Reason
1.				
2.				
3.				
4.				
5.				
6.				
7.				
8.				
9.				
10.				

You will notice that in all the above situations students are engaged in some sort of activity. But it is not the activity itself that constitutes social studies; students could read, act, discuss, draw, and listen in any subject. Rather, it is the content of the activity and the reason(s) for doing it that lead us to conclude it is social studies. If the goal of reading a story about the life of two children in Japan is to develop students' abilities in phonics, then it is a language arts activity. If the goal is to teach students about the lives of children living in Japan, then reading a story in part constitutes a social studies activity. Finally, if the purpose of reading a story about children living in Japan is to teach both phonics and about life in Japan, then the activity is an integrated lesson (see Chapter 3) that crosses two or more subject boundaries.

DEFINITIONS OF SOCIAL STUDIES

It is unlikely that everyone in your class has arrived at exactly the same definition of social studies. Experts in the field who have articulated their own definitions of social studies also disagree.[3] The definitions that follow attest to this.

1. The social studies are the social sciences simplified for pedagogical purposes.[4]
2. A study of people and their relationships with their social and physical environments.[5]
3. The social studies are concerned exclusively with the education of citizens. In a democracy, citizenship consists of two related but sometimes disparate parts: the first socialization, the second countersocialization.[6]
4. Social studies is the study of people in relation to each other and their world. It is an issues-focused and inquiry-based interdisciplinary subject that draws upon history, geography, ecology, economics, law, philosophy, political science, and other **social sciences**. Social studies fosters students' understanding and involvement in practical and ethical issues that face their communities and humankind. Social studies is integral to the process of understanding who they are, what they want to become and the society in which they want to live.[7]
5. Social studies seeks to examine and understand communities, from the local to the global, their various heritages and the nature of citizenship within them. Students acquire knowledge of key social studies concepts including change, culture, environment, power, and the dynamics of the market place. They learn about Canada and the role of citizens within a culturally diverse and interdependent world.[8]
6. Social studies provides coordinated, systematic study drawing upon such disciplines as anthropology, economics, geography, history, political science, psychology, and sociology, as well as appropriate content from the humanities, mathematics, and the natural sciences. ... The social studies curriculum provides the multidisciplinary lens through which students examine issues affecting their lives from personal, academic, pluralistic, and global perspectives.[9]
7. Social studies is the study of people in relation to each other and the world in which they live. In Manitoba, social studies comprises the disciplines of history and geography, draws upon the social sciences, and integrates relevant content from the humanities. As a study of human beings in their physical, social, and cultural environments, social studies examines the past and present, and looks toward the future. Social studies helps students acquire the skills, knowledge, and values necessary to become active democratic citizens and contributing members of communities, locally, nationally, and globally.[10]
8. Social studies education can be defined as the study of people and their relationships with their social, physical, and technological environments.[11]
9. Social studies embodies the main principles of democracy, such as freedom, equality, human dignity, justice, rule of law, and civic rights and responsibilities. It provides opportunities for students to explore multiple approaches that may be used to explore their own world and the worlds of others. Social studies presents unique and particular ways for students to view interrelationships among Earth, its people, and its systems.[12]
10. Social studies should bring to the foreground the problems of knowledge, power, culture, and difference that have animated the humanities and social sciences over the past

20 years, and, along with them, the complex and theoretically rich tasks of teaching students how to read the texts that structure their lives, and write the ones that might restructure the world.[13]

Activity 1-C

What do the above definitions have in common? On what points do they disagree? Create a chart that outlines these agreements and disagreements, using the categories of "Disciplines included," "Other content included," "Rationales," and "Objectives." Then look at your own province or territory's curriculum guide and ascertain where, if at all, a few of these definitions fit.

Variations certainly exist in the above definitions. This is because disagreements exist about what disciplines make up social studies, what the major goals should be, and how citizenship is to be defined.[14] Yet, in spite of their differences, all these definitions either state explicitly that social studies includes the study of human beings in social and geographical settings, using knowledge drawn from (at least) the social sciences, or they imply that social studies requires this knowledge (e.g., to solve social problems). This is the *knowledge base* of social studies. But a definition does not tell us *why* we should teach social studies, or what the goals of teaching the subject should be. Nor does it tell us what we could or should teach from the vast array of possible social studies knowledge that has been accumulated over many centuries.

A BRIEF HISTORY OF SOCIAL STUDIES

The goals we aim for are those thought to be worth pursuing by makers of public policy; teachers make curriculum decisions on the basis of these goals. Some of the definitions above state what these goals should be. For example, several of them claim that the purpose of social studies is *education for citizenship*. The U.S. National Education Association—the association credited with the "invention" of social studies—identified this as the primary goal for social studies education in the United States in 1916. This same goal currently is espoused by the U.S. National Council for the Social Studies and by most of the ministries of education in Canada. Education for citizenship is thus viewed by most educators as the raison d'être for the social studies.

This goal has been the traditional one for the subject throughout its history in Canada.[15] Beginning in the western provinces in the 1920s and in Ontario in 1937, social studies was the name given to an interdisciplinary approach to the teaching of history, geography, the social sciences, and civics. Canadian social studies educators have been strongly influenced by their American counterparts and still are.[16] In the early days of the subject, in the 1930s and 1940s, there was an emphasis at the policy level on "child-centred" and "progressive" educational ideas, involving activity-oriented curricula in which children worked together on projects. These ideas relied heavily on the theories of the American philosopher John Dewey. Canadians also embraced the American expanding horizons model (see Chapter 3) for curriculum development. In the 1960s, Canadian educators were influenced by the "structure of the disciplines" movement in the United States. Here, curricula were structured on the various social studies disciplines, and students were taught to think and act like historians, geographers, political scientists, and so on. Another important influence was Hilda Taba (see Chapter 6), whose ideas on organizing curricula around key concepts were, and still are, supported by many curriculum developers.

The reliance on ideas from the United States was challenged in the late 1960s, especially by Hodgetts.[17] On the basis of his (somewhat flawed) research, Hodgetts concluded that civic education and the teaching of history needed a great deal of improvement. The Canadian Studies Foundation, created in 1970 as a result of his efforts, produced a profusion of curriculum materials. Provincial curricula began to focus more sharply on Canadian content, and Canadian publishers started to produce more materials on Canadian history and geography. Aspects of this movement can still be found in Canadian education, but the "structure of the disciplines" approach has given way to new concerns.

In the last 20 years, Canadian society has awakened to such problems as racism, sexism, environmental degradation, and the demand for First Nations self-government. Thus, new curricula have been developed, ranging from a focus on values issues to a renewed emphasis on history and geography. New themes such as multiculturalism, anti-racism, globalization, human rights, environmental and economic education, and First Nations, Inuit, and Métis studies have been included as the political climate has changed at the national and provincial levels. These changes have not always been put into widespread practice. There are many constraints on implementation and these have to be considered in any analysis of the history of social studies.[18] Yet, despite many changes over the years, the key concern of the social studies—**citizenship education**—has remained constant.[19] And this is despite the criticism that citizenship education is too broad an idea, as it is an overarching goal of schooling and there is no agreed-upon body of content that makes up citizenship education.[20]

Activity 1-D

Create a time line outlining the changes in Canadian social studies since the 1920s. Underneath this time line, draw another one indicating the political and social factors that you believe influenced the changes of the time in the social studies curriculum.

PROBLEMS OF DEFINING AND CONCEPTUALIZING SOCIAL STUDIES

There have been criticisms of how social studies is defined and put into practice. As long ago as 1932, Harold Rugg, an influential social studies educator, complained about a curriculum that, "Nothing short of genius on the part of a student could create an ordered understanding of modern life from such a compartmentalized arrangement of material."[21] In 1983, Kieran Egan claimed that, "the social studies curriculum has not worked, does not work, and cannot work."[22] And, more recently, Granatstein stated that social studies, with its themes, topics, or issues, was "a jumble sale with no focus."[23] Even though we may all agree on the broad knowledge base of the social studies, we may not agree on what the citizenship goals of social studies should be. Should social studies education develop passive citizens who do not criticize the existing social order? Or, as Engle and Ochoa ask, should its purpose consist of socialization and then countersocialization (by which the authors mean "a learning process designed to foster independent thought and social criticism"[24])? Other social studies experts may agree with Engle and Ochoa that education for citizenship should be the goal of social studies, but they have very different ideas on what constitutes a "good citizen." In Canadian social studies curricula, the notion of active citizenship has generally been de-emphasized, and where it has been included there may well be a gap between what is prescribed and what actually goes on in classrooms.

A similar problem arises when we consider other aspects of these definitions. Consider those that include a prescription for teaching history. What are the aims of this teaching to be? Are students to know only what great men, and a few women, did in the past? Are they to be taught to understand how historians work? Or is history aimed at raising important social and political issues to help students better understand how we got where we are, so they can make decisions about how they can get to where they want to go? Similar questions arise in defining the other disciplines included in the social studies and in conceptualizing multicultural and global education (see Chapters 17 and 18).

As we have seen, we may all agree, broadly speaking, on the knowledge base of the social studies, but what is actually taught will depend on our goals. Although it is a useful exercise to find out how other citizens, students, teachers, and curriculum developers define social studies, the definition question is not an empirical one (although we can find out empirically how others define it); it is a question of value. Thus, the question that is the title of this chapter—"What is social studies?"—might be better rephrased as "What *should* social studies be?"

Other Activities

1. Look at the social studies curriculum guidelines for your province or territory. How is "social studies" defined? Does the definition change according to grade level? What disciplines are included in the social studies curriculum?
2. Look at the social studies curriculum guidelines for another province or territory. How is "social studies" defined? Does the definition differ from the one in your province or territory? If so, what difference, if any, does this make to the objectives, content, and teaching methods outlined in the social studies guidelines?
3. Ask the students in an elementary school, as well as teachers, consultants, parents, professors, or school trustees, for their definitions of "social studies." Differentiate between what people say social studies *is* and what they say social studies *ought to be.* Compare your responses with those of another person who interviewed a different group of people. How do you account for the similarities or differences? How can you explain the differences between what people say social studies is and what they say it should be?
4. In discussing social studies with your peers, try to determine how their experiences have led them to form particular attitudes toward social studies.

Notes

1. A national study of elementary and middle school teachers in the U.S. revealed that 65 percent of respondents reported that "all the time" or "some of the time" their views on moral, political, and social issues influenced their approach to teaching social studies (J. Leming, L. Ellington, and M. Shrug, "The state of social studies: A national random survey of elementary and middle school teachers," *Social Education* 70:5 (2006), pp. 322–327). See also D. Hess, "How do teachers' political views influence teaching about controversial issues?" *Social Education* 69:1 (2005), pp. 47–48, and J. Chiodo and T. Brown, "Student perceptions of teaching: Assessing the mental images of teaching

social studies," *Journal of Social Studies Research* 31:1 (2007), pp. 12–26. Both of these articles demonstrate the influence of prior experiences and beliefs of teachers on their teaching of social studies.

2. N. Smith, "Challenges and choices facing elementary social studies teachers," in R. Case and P. Clark, eds., *The Anthology of Social Studies, Volume 1. Issues and Strategies for Elementary Teachers* (Vancouver: Pacific Educational Press, 2008), p. 3.
3. P. Seixas, "Review of research in social studies," in V. Richardson, ed., *Handbook of Research on Teaching* (Washington, DC: American Education Research Association, 2001).
4. E. Wesley and S. Wronski, *Teaching Social Studies in High Schools* (Boston: Heath, 1958), p. 3.
5. Saskatchewan Education, *Report of the Social Sciences Reference Committee* (Regina: Saskatchewan Education, 1984), p. 1.
6. S. Engle and A. Ochoa, *Education for Democratic Citizenship: Decision-Making in the Social Studies* (New York: Teachers College Press, 1990).
7. Alberta Education, *Alberta Social Studies K–12* (Edmonton: Alberta Education, 2005), p. 1. http://education.alberta.ca/teachers/core/socialstudies.aspx
8. Ontario Ministry of Education and Training, *Social Studies Grades 1–6; History and Geography, Grades 7 and 8*. (Toronto: Ministry of Education and Training, 2004), p. 2. www.edu.gov.on.ca/eng/curriculum/elementary/sstudies.html
9. Atlantic Provinces Education Foundation, *Foundation for the Atlantic Canada Social Studies Curriculum* (Atlantic Provinces Education Foundation, no date), p. 2.
10. Manitoba Education and Youth, *Kindergarten to Grade 8 Social Studies* (Winnipeg: Manitoba Education and Youth, 2003), p. 3. www.edu.gov.mb.ca/k12/cur/socstud/framework/index.html
11. Saskatchewan Education, *An information bulletin for the renewed middle level curriculum* (Saskatchewan Education, March 1999), p. 4.
12. Atlantic Canada, *Social Studies Curriculum, Grades Primary–2, Implementation Draft,* October 2005, p. 1.
13. P. Seixas, p. 561.
14. I. Wright, "What sort of question is 'What is social studies?' and how do we go about answering it?" *International Journal of Social Education* 13:1 (1999), pp. 66–76. See also P. Shield and D. Ramsey, "Social studies across English Canada," in A. Sears and I. Wright, eds., *Challenges and Prospects for Canadian Social Studies* (Vancouver: Pacific Educational Press, 2004).
15. P. Clark, "The historical context of social studies in English Canada," in A. Sears and I. Wright, eds., *Challenges and Prospects for Canadian Social Studies* (Vancouver: Pacific Educational Press, 2004).
16. P. Clark, *op cit,* p. 17.
17. A. Hodgetts, *What Culture? What Heritage? A Study in Civic Education in Canada* (Toronto: Ontario Institute for Studies in Education, 1978).
18. See C. Cornbleth, "What constrains meaningful social studies teaching?" *Social Education* 66:3 (2002), pp. 186–190.
19. G. Tomkins, "The social studies in Canada," in J. Parsons, G. Milburn, and M. van Manen, eds., *A Canadian Social Studies* (Edmonton: Faculty of Education Publication Services, University of Alberta, 1983).
20. A. Marker and H. Mehlinger, "Social studies," in P. Jackson, ed., *Handbook of Research on Curriculum* (New York: Macmillan, 1992).
21. H. Rugg, *American Life and the School Curriculum: Next Steps towards Schools of Living* (Boston: Ginn, 1936), p. 332.
22. K. Egan, "Social studies and the erosion of education," *Curriculum Inquiry,* 13:2 (1983), p. 195.
23. J. L. Granatstein, *Who Killed Canadian History?* (Toronto: HarperCollins, 2007).
24. S. Engle and A. Ochoa, p. 31.

Glossary of Key Terms

A glossary of key terms is provided at the end of each chapter. Please note that short definitions cannot always do justice to the complexity of some terms.

Citizenship education—A "contested" concept, with meanings ranging from inculcation of loyalty to the state to social activism.

Social sciences—Usually anthropology, history, sociology, cultural geography, political science, and economics are deemed social sciences.

CHAPTER 2

Social Studies: Why Bother?

Activity 2-A

Write down the most important issues facing you, your community, Canada, and the world. How many of them are included or could be included in the social studies curriculum? Which of these issues could elementary students deal with?

What is most important in a person's life may not be educationally significant. Look at your list and then decide which issues are significant enough to be included in the social studies curriculum. Given that social studies can be defined to include everything that is known about people and their interactions with others and their environments, this question arises: What should we teach? The answer will depend upon how we construe the purposes of social studies. What do you think the goals of social studies should be?

Activity 2-B

Indicate your degree of agreement or disagreement with each.

	Strongly Agree	Agree	No Opinion	Disagree	Strongly Disagree
The main task of social studies is to preserve and transmit the cultural heritage.					
Social studies should provide learners with an understanding of decision-making processes so that they may become effective decision makers.					
Social studies should teach about social phenomena; it should not manipulate students' attitudes and values.					
Social studies should help students understand the structure of the social sciences.					
Social studies should teach children to be good Canadian citizens by being patriotic and obeying the laws of the land.					

	Strongly Agree	Agree	No Opinion	Disagree	Strongly Disagree
Social studies should provide learners with an awareness of possible futures and the roles they might play in developing these futures.					
Social studies should teach history and geography so that students understand their place in the world.					
Social studies should teach a body of tested principles and generalizations about human relations and societies.					
Social studies should teach students to make rational decisions about personal and social issues and to act upon their decisions.					
Social studies should provide students with the skills necessary to solve problems and to become independent learners.					
Social studies should develop students' abilities to deal with questions of "What ought to be?" and "What can I do about it?"					

You may find that you agree with all the above statements to some extent. If you analyze the beliefs and value judgments that underlie each of the statements, however, you may find that some of them are incongruent. Can you strongly agree that students should both "obey the laws of the land" and "make rational decisions about personal and social issues and act upon their decisions" if a student's decision is to break a law? If you look at other statements with which you agree, you may find similar incongruities.

Whether differing aims are a result of differing definitions of social studies or vice versa is, perhaps, of little importance. What is important, however, is that each definition and its concomitant aim(s) are embedded in a larger conception of social studies. These conceptions will include beliefs about how students learn, what constitutes truth, what values are appropriate to hold, and so on.

CONCEPTIONS OF SOCIAL STUDIES

Look at the following four lesson plans. Even though the topic is the same in each, the objectives, instructional activities, and assessment methods are very different.

Activity 2-C

The following lesson plans are all for a Grade 4 class in a rural community. The class has 26 students with a variety of ethnic backgrounds: 21 students with various European backgrounds, three students of Indo-Canadian origin, and two Métis students. There are 13 males and 13 females. One ESL student has special lessons during language classes but is with the class for all other lessons. Another student is dyslexic. All students are engaged in a unit on the history of Canada. Having read all of them, decide what the key differences are and then carry out Activity 2-D.

Lesson Plan A

Objectives:

- Students will recall important facts about the explorations of Jacques Cartier.
- Students will work quietly and independently at their desks.
- Students will read the text for important facts.

Introduction: Ask students to tell you what they learned about Cabot as the first European explorer of Canada. Explain to students that they will now be learning about the second great explorer—Cartier.

Body of the lesson: Using a map, pictures of Cartier and his ship, and blackboard notes, tell students about Cartier's first voyage. Have students copy the notes into their books. Then ask students to read about Cartier's second voyage in their textbooks and answer the following questions:

- When did Cartier carry out his second voyage?
- Where did Cartier go on his second voyage?
- What happened to him and his crew?

Culmination: When students have finished answering the questions, collect their books and tell them that tomorrow they will be given a True/False test on what they have learned about Cartier and Cabot.

Assessment: Mark the notes and answers to the questions for neatness and accuracy.

Lesson Plan B

Objectives:

- Students will understand why Cartier explored North America.
- Students will write a diary of one of Cartier's voyages as if they were members of Cartier's crew.
- Students will empathize with the life of a sailor on one of Cartier's voyages.
- Students will comprehend, interpret, and analyze information to answer questions.
- Students will work effectively in groups.

Introduction: Remind students of what they discovered about Cabot and why he came to North America. Ask students to guess why other explorers would want to come to North America. List their responses on the board.

Body of the lesson: Students will get into their groups (equal number of males and females; one student helps the student with dyslexia, and the ESL student has special reading materials for the activity). Each group reads different materials, including some facsimiles of original documents, to determine whether their guesses about Cartier's motives were correct.

Invite students to share their findings on Cartier's motives and then draw their attention to the map on the blackboard of Cartier's two voyages. Briefly describe what Cartier did on the voyages. Have students pose questions about the voyages and then have them divide into teacher-chosen groups. Using materials provided, two groups study the first voyage and two groups study the second voyage. Each group works with materials developmentally appropriate for the group. Students who are at a concrete stage will have straightforward descriptive materials; those at a more abstract level will have materials that use metaphors and analogies. When students have answered the questions, have them put their findings into a diary format (group writing project) as though they were actually on the voyage.

Culmination: Have each group of students read one paragraph from their diary and then ask them how they would assess their work. Have students generate a list of criteria for diary assessment and then use these criteria to assess their work.

Assessment: Students will be observed in their groups, and a checklist will be used to assess participation and research skills based on the developmental level of each student. Diaries will be assessed on the basis of the criteria generated in class and the developmental level of the students.

Lesson Plan C

Objectives:

- Students will describe and evaluate the story of Cartier from the point of view of the French and the Native people.
- Students will analyze the relationships between the French and Native people, noting the colonizing mentality of the French leaders.
- Students will empathize with the Native people.
- Students will work in self-chosen groups or individually to create a chart noting the similarities and differences between the Native and French accounts.
- Students will use research skills to realize the first two objectives.

Introduction: Remind students about the last lesson, where they found out that Europeans carried out the exploration of North America for the purposes of obtaining power and wealth. Inform students that they will now be carrying out a case study of one explorer, Cartier.

Body of the lesson: Students choose to work in groups or individually. They read an account of Cartier's voyages written from the French point of view plus an account from the Native point of view. The readings have a lot of graphics, and there are audiotapes for those who learn best through listening. The student with dyslexia works with a partner, and the ESL student is given "simplified" reading material as well as an audiotape so that he can record his answers. Students determine what the similarities and differences are between the two accounts, note them on their charts, and hypothesize why they exist.

Culmination: Students share their findings with each other. Ask students whether it is possible to state that one account is more reliable than the other. Discuss why there can be many accounts of the same event and that it is impossible to tell which is true. Note that the stories of the people with the least power are often ignored. Have students give examples from their own experiences. Discuss how the power of the colonizing Europeans determined the treatment accorded the Native people. Ask students for other examples of colonization that they know about. Students then work on their charts to bring them up to a standard they think would warrant the charts being placed in their portfolios. Tell students they will be studying other explorers and their relationships with Native people and how these relationships, and other factors, contributed to the present marginalized state of many First Nations people.

Assessment: Students who wish to do so place their charts in their portfolios. Anecdotal records are kept of students who make significant comments in the discussion. For example, a student's comment that the French would view the Native people as "savages" because they were not Christians would be recorded.

Lesson Plan D

Objectives:

- Students either individually or in groups will decide upon a project related to the first explorers of Canada.
- Students will use provided sources to generate questions and decide how they will carry out their research and present their conclusions.
- Students will generate a list of criteria for assessing their work.

Introduction: Remind students that in the previous lesson they shared their ideas about and experiences of exploration, their own and others' motivations for exploring, and how they would react if they met people who looked and behaved very differently from them.

Body of the lesson: Tell students that now they are going to choose a project on the first explorers to what is now Canada. They can work in a group or on their own. They should first find out from the books, website URLs, pamphlets, and other resources who they will research. They must then decide what they think the important questions are, how they will carry out their research, how they will present their findings, and what criteria they will use to assess their work.

As the lesson progresses, one student decides to inquire into how the first explorers treated the natural environment and will draw and paint pictures; one group with the two First Nations students in it wants to study Cartier and how he treated the Native people, and then perform a TV interview between Cartier and Chief Donnacona. They then want to find out about relations between contemporary First Nations People and the Quebec and federal governments. Another pair of students decides to find out who the first explorers were and how they travelled from Asia; the ESL student and another student want to find out about navigation and to build and use a navigational instrument; another group decides to find out what effects (technological, cultural, etc.) occurred due to the interactions between the Native peoples and the explorers and evaluate these according to a list of criteria they generate. One student wishes to carry out some of her work at home with a friend in Grade 7 who is inquiring into exploration in Asia.

Culmination: Students present their work to each other and discuss their findings. They create a large chart showing how all their inquiries relate to each other and generate a list of the significant questions they think need to be answered.

Assessment: Students individually assess their own progress using criteria from the last project they completed and comparing their results.

According to Barr, Barth, and Shermis,[1] three traditions or **conceptions of social studies** can be identified:

1. social studies as *citizenship transmission*
2. social studies as *reflective inquiry*
3. social studies as *social science*

Social Studies as Citizenship Transmission

In this conception, the aim is to instill in students the knowledge and values thought necessary for good citizenship. Through the study of history, government, and the students' own community and country, students are to learn the virtues of being responsible, patriotic, loyal, and respectful citizens. The basic instructional approach is didactic: teachers pass on knowledge selected by an external authority (e.g., the province's ministry of education) through lectures and activities based on student reading of a textbook.

This **citizenship transmission** conception is based on several assumptions: that there are irrefutable societal values (such as respect for authority) students have to accept; that reality is objective (not based on the subjective views of individuals) and essentially unchanging; and that wisdom from the past must be transmitted to future generations. Presumably, children are born as *tabulae rasae*—their minds are "blank slates" on which the knowledge and values necessary for citizenship will be written. Alternatively, children are born with a propensity for being "bad" (the idea of "original sin" fits in with this view) and must be taught to be "good." This conception has received attention recently especially in the United States, where E. D. Hirsch[2] is promoting the view that there is a body of content (which he refers to as the "civil religion") that all students must learn if they are to be considered "good" Americans. Similarly, in Canada, various interest groups are calling for more "content" (especially Canadian history and geography) to be taught so that students become "good" Canadian citizens.

Social Studies as Reflective Inquiry

In the **reflective inquiry** conception the aim is to develop rational decision makers in the social–political context. The focus is on structured and disciplined inquiry into the problems and issues children face in their day-to-day lives—problems that have their counterparts in the wider world. In this conception it is not assumed that values are finite and absolute. Values can change. Similarly, knowledge is also changeable: it is constructed by the learner through the interaction of the content presented and the learner's developing mental powers. Children are not born "bad" or as "blank slates," but with potential that can be channelled in appropriate directions according to their developmental level. Further, it is assumed that if students are presented with relevant problems they can be taught to use their developing rational powers. They have the right to apply these powers in making their own decisions. This conception is child-centred.

Social Studies as Social Science

The aim in the **social science** conception is for students to become effective citizens by acquiring knowledge from the social sciences and the skills of social scientists. Thus, the content chosen for study consists of concepts and research methodologies that students are to apply to problems derived from these disciplines. The focus is on the academic aspect of the social studies. It is assumed that the social sciences best explain human behaviour and that students can use these explanations in becoming good citizens. Behind this conception lies the belief that knowledge can be organized into discrete disciplines and that truth can be determined through the use of social science research methodologies.

Social Studies as Critical Reflection

Barr, Barth, and Shermis do not consider one recent conception of social studies. Clarke[3] labels this the **critical reflective** approach, the goal of which is to empower people so that they can take action to solve societal ills. Clarke argues that students are currently socialized into holding the beliefs and ideologies of the dominant groups in society, and that opposing beliefs are ignored. Thus, students are taught to be non-critical and to accept the existing distribution of power in society. What students need to learn is to be critical, to participate in civic affairs, and to take the actions needed to bring about social justice. They must take into account the stories of those who are oppressed and marginalized. This conception assumes that knowledge is constructed by groups who share common interests. What qualifies as truth is relative to a group; there is no absolute knowledge. However, although some values are relative, underlying moral principles are not. Concerns for social justice, human dignity, and freedom are universal, even though the ways they are conceptualized and applied as a basis for action can be a matter of disagreement and debate. This postmodern conception (and variations of it) is receiving considerable attention in educational theory, although it is rarely found in curriculum documents or learning materials.

Social Studies as Part of Holistic Education[4]

Another conception of education not considered by Barr, Barth, and Sherman is that of **holistic education.** Miller states, "The focus of holistic education is on relationships: the relationship between linear thinking and intuition, the relationship between mind and body, the relationships among the various domains of knowledge, the relationship between the individual and the community, the relationship to the earth, and the relationship between self and Self."[5] Stemming from Rousseau's idea that children should be allowed to grow up naturally and learn on their own,[6] and borrowing from Gardner's work on multiple intelligences[7] and Bernstein's sagacious competence,[8] holistic educators focus on relationships, responsibility, and reverence for life. Holistic education integrates experiences and meanings into a broad conceptualization of human possibilities rather than the more narrow one used by progressive educators. Although there are many variations in how holistic education is conceptualized,[9] most agree that the goals are that students should develop all their potentials—artistic, creative, ethical, emotional, intellectual, physical, and spiritual (but not necessarily religious); learn about themselves; learn to be resilient; and construct their own knowledge at their own rates of progress. The teacher is a facilitator who practises flexible pacing and encourages integration of subject matter. Students assess themselves.[10]

Activity 2-D

Now that you are familiar with the five differing conceptions of social studies, identify the conception that would be congruent with each of the following statements. Then turn to the Answers section.

1. The content to be learned in the social studies should be determined by an authority and passed down to students by the teacher.
2. It is better to evaluate students on how they think rather than on the products of their thought.
3. By reading stories of great men and women of the past, students will learn the requirements for being good citizens.
4. By reading the stories of people who are oppressed or ignored in society, students will realize that there are differing realities.
5. Learning how historians arrive at their answers to historical questions will help students solve contemporary social problems.
6. Students should be tested on their knowledge of facts, and their performance should be compared against national norms.
7. The two most powerful psychological theories are behaviourism (human behaviour is a direct function of the environment, and learning is defined according to the quantity of information acquired) and social learning theory (learning is a gradual accumulation of patterns of behaviour through imitation and modelling).
8. If students are presented with problems that are relevant to them, they are more likely to be motivated to learn and to create solutions that are meaningful to them.
9. All knowledge is shaped by human interests. Dominant groups in society use their self-interested knowledge to subjugate other groups and individuals.
10. All knowledge is individually constructed and there are multiple truths.

The five conceptions are "ideal types"; rarely will you find pure examples of each. Rather, social studies curricula tend to incorporate aspects of more than one of them, although little evidence exists that the critical reflective or holistic views receive much attention. The other three conceptions receive varying degrees of emphasis. All elementary school social studies curricula in Canada (of which we are aware) include the study of history and geography and some study of the research methodologies used in these disciplines, such as oral history and field studies. All include the teaching of critical thinking. All incorporate the values thought necessary for being an effective citizen of Canada. Curricula vary in the degree of emphasis accorded history and geography, critical thinking, citizenship, and so on. There are other ways of categorizing conceptions of social studies (for examples, see Case,[11] who identifies categories of social initiation, social reformation, personal development, and academic understanding; the research of Goodman and Adler,[12] who found that elementary teachers held six different conceptions; and that of McKay and Gibson,[13] who identify seven orientations—cultural conservation, disciplines, inquiry, cultural transformation, personal development, diversity, and global). There are many similarities among these categorizations, and citizenship transmission, reflective inquiry, social science, critical reflection, and holistic education provide one useful way of looking at social studies.

DEVELOPING A RATIONALE

To answer the question as to which is the most appropriate conception, we have to develop a rationale. We have to argue that the aims of one particular conception of social studies are more appropriate than the aims of another. We must provide evidence that the assumptions of how children learn in one conception are more believable than those in another. We must decide between competing conceptions with respect to the nature of truth and how knowledge is constructed. These questions are not specific to social studies; they are relevant to the entire educational enterprise. To answer them, we need to develop our own philosophy of education. This is a complex endeavour. The example below demonstrates how one teacher (T) justifies teaching about the local community by answering questions posed by a pre-service teacher (PT).

T: I've decided to teach my Grade 2 students about the local community.

PT: What specifically will you be emphasizing?

T: Well, the role of people in the community and how they all have to work together to make the community work.

PT: Which people will you be focusing upon?

T: The mayor, police officers, firefighters.

PT: Aren't most of these people male?

T: Well, yes they are. But I will point out that women can be and are elected as mayor and can be and are firefighters and police officers.

PT: Why do you think students need to know this?

T: Students need to understand that women can contribute just as much to the community as men. And they need to learn that we are all interdependent.

PT: Why is this important?

T: Because we live in an interdependent world, and we all have to rely on each other if we are to have a better society. So students will have to think through how their community works and see if it can be improved.

PT: How do you think your study of the community will do this?

T: In a number of ways. Students will learn about different roles in the community and how they all relate; they will have to think through how the community might be improved; and they will see what their roles might be in bringing about these changes.

PT: Do you think your students can understand this?

T: Oh yes, by this age they can realize that they depend on people in the community for their food, shelter, safety, and so on. And they are able to understand the consequences if someone in the community does not perform their role. And they do have ideas about how their community could be made better.

PT: Do you have other reasons for teaching about the community?

T: I think students can begin to think about roles—and, as you pointed out, how males tend to dominate many roles. However, I will make sure that students can understand some of the reasons for this, and what changes women can make and have made. Anyway, girls ought to have the same opportunities as boys. In fact, I may persuade some girls to begin thinking about jobs as firefighters. *[T laughs]*

PT: And boys as secretaries in the mayor's office? *[PT laughs]*

T: Hadn't thought about that!

PT: How would you define "community"?

T: Well, I think as I have already said it is about people living and working together in interdependent relationships.

The above dialogue reveals that T has a number of reasons for including the study of the local community in the social studies curriculum. Notice that some of the initial reasons are supported with "higher order" reasons—for example, that understanding community roles can lead to an understanding of interdependence. T is also asked to clarify terms—to say what is meant by "community." T is also asked whether students are capable of understanding what is to be taught. Throughout, T has presented a series of arguments to justify the teaching of a particular topic. For example:

Conclusion: I ought to teach about the local community.

Reason: Through the study of the local community, students will understand the importance of interdependence.

Because T believes the reason to be a good one, T must also believe that learning about interdependence is significant. When asked to justify this belief, T presents yet another argument. You will find out more about arguments in later chapters.

Activity 2-E

Write a dialogue similar to the one above. Start with "I have decided to teach [state the topic] to my Grade [state the grade level] students." Then interrogate yourself or have a partner pose questions as to why you made this decision.

Now that you have some familiarity with the five conceptions of social studies and how to construct a rationale, try the next activity.

Activity 2-F

A committee has been formed in your school to look at the goals of social studies for your school. There are five people on the committee. In your class form groups of five people, each person representing one of the conceptions of social studies outlined above. They should argue their positions in their groups and arrive at a set of goals for their school. Then the entire class should compare each group's goals and note similarities and differences. Where there are more differences than similarities, can there be a class agreement? If there cannot, then what do you do?

Activity 2-G

Choose something—a topic, an ability, an attitude—that you think would be worthwhile to teach to a group of students. List your reasons for teaching it and, where appropriate, try to answer the following questions. (The questions are not in hierarchical order.)

1. What do I mean by "X"? ("X" is a key term in your reasoning, e.g., What do I mean by "respect," or "cooperation," or "history"?)
2. Do I believe that students don't already know what I intend to teach them? Have I any evidence for this?

3. Are students capable of learning what I intend to teach? Have I any evidence for this?
4. What value position am I assuming in giving a particular reason? Is this value defensible?
5. If students didn't learn what I intend to teach, would they be disadvantaged? Why or why not?
6. How is what I intend to teach relevant to students' lives? What does "relevance" mean in this case?
7. Do students really need to know what I intend to teach them? Why?

In synthesizing Chapters 1 and 2, we can see a number of significant goals.

- *Knowledge of the content of social studies.* It is clear that in all the definitions of social studies and the rationales for teaching it, subject matter knowledge is important. Even though the exact nature of what should be taught is disputed, no social studies educator would say that subject matter knowledge should not be taught.
- *The abilities and skills needed to obtain, process, and present this knowledge.* If students are to collect and use social studies information, then they need to be able to locate it, classify it, analyze it, and present it in reports, maps, graphs, or other formats.
- *The intellectual standards needed to evaluate this knowledge.* All social studies curricula in Canada call for students to be critical thinkers. **Intellectual standards** require that students examine information for its logic, plausibility, reliability, and accuracy. They also require students to be clear, coherent, open-minded, and fair-minded.
- *The personal and social values required to resolve issues and evaluate value claims and actions.* All social studies curricula also emphasize the resolution of social issues or call on students to be good citizens who will make responsible decisions. This will require students to understand and critically examine their own values and the values of society.
- *The citizenship-action competencies to put decisions into practice.* The raison d'être for social studies is citizenship. This entails that people take actions in democratic and responsible ways. To do this requires competencies such as making persuasive presentations, knowing where to obtain information, understanding how political institutions work, and evaluating how actions impinge on self and others.

We must remember that social studies is but one subject among many, that education is lifelong, and that the school can't "do it all." Further, although we may formulate what we consider to be a justifiable rationale for a particular goal of social studies, we need to keep open minds because our reasons and reasoning may change as we reflect upon our teaching practices. Rationale building is complex, but it can't be ignored. We should be able to give good reasons for what we do in the name of social studies.

Other Activities

1. What rationales are presented in your province's social studies curriculum? Are they based on the citizenship transmission, the reflective inquiry, the social science, the critical reflective, or the holistic conception of social studies?
2. Very often surveys are taken of public opinions on education. Commissions are convened to advise provincial governments on educational matters. Or assessments of students' knowledge about social studies are carried out by ministries/departments of education. If such information is available, which conceptions of social studies underlie

the results of the surveys or commissions, or the interpretations placed on the results? Are these conceptions consistent with those of your provincial curriculum?

3. Ask students in an elementary school why they think they have to study social studies. Compare their comments to rationale statements in your provincial curriculum.
4. According to the recommendations of the National Commission on Social Studies in the United States,[14] history and geography should provide the framework for social studies. Selective studies of the history, geography, government, and economic systems of the major civilizations should receive coverage at least equal to the study of the United States (substitute "Canada" here for purposes of answering the questions below). Integration of other subject areas with the social studies should be encouraged. Are these recommendations desirable? Are they feasible to implement?
5. In a more recent U.S. study,[15] one of the authors argues that the job of social studies is to "transmit the political vision of liberty and equality before the law that unites us Americans."[16] The report goes on to claim that, among others, gender studies, multicultural education, and global studies have ruined social studies and detracted from its goal of citizenship and history education. If this study were about Canadian social studies, would you agree? Why or why not?
6. Find out from other professional bodies (e.g., your provincial social studies organization) what they think the goals of social studies are and/or should be. Compare these goals with those in your provincial curriculum guide. How would you account for the similarities and differences?

Notes

1. R. Barr, J. Barth, and S. Shermis, *Defining the Social Studies* (Washington, DC: National Council for the Social Studies, 1977).
2. E. Hirsch, *Cultural Literacy: What Every American Needs to Know* (New York: Vintage Books, 1988).
3. M. Clarke, "A critically reflective social studies," *The History and Social Science Teacher* 25:4 (1990), pp. 214–220.
4. Holistic education is sometimes labelled as Wholistic Education but there is debate about whether the two terms are connected or separate.
5. J. Miller, *The Holistic Curriculum* (Toronto: Ontario Institute for Studies in Education, 1996), p. 8.
6. J. Rousseau, *Emile,* translated by B. Foxley, introduction by P. Jimack (London: J. M. Dent, 1993).
7. H. Gardner, *Intelligence Reframed—Multiple Intelligences for the 21st Century* (New York: Basic Books, 1999).
8. B. Bernstein, *Pedagogy, Symbolic Control and Identity: Theory, Research, Critique* (London; Washington, DC: Taylor and Francis, 1996). Sagacious competence includes freedom, good judgment, learning in one's own way, social ability, refining one's values, and self-knowledge.
9. S. Forbes and R. Martin, "What holistic education claims about itself: An analysis of holistic schools literature," AERA, San Diego, CA, April 2004. www.holistic-education.net/articles/research04.pdf
10. Informative websites on holistic education include www.holistic-education.net; www.emtech.net/construc.htm; www.infed.org/biblio/holistic_education.htm; en.wikipedia.org/wiki/Holistic_education; www.hent.org; and www.pathsoflearning.net/articles_Holistic_Ed.Introduction.php.
11. P. Clark and R. Case, "Four defining purposes of citizenship education," in R. Case and P. Clark, eds., *The Anthology of Social Studies, Volume 1. Issues and Strategies for Elementary Teachers* (Vancouver: Pacific Educational Press, 2008), p. 19.

12. J. Goodman and S. Adler, "Becoming an elementary social studies teacher: A study of perspectives," *Theory and Research in Social Education* 13:2 (1985), pp. 1–20.
13. R. McKay and S. Gibson, *Social Studies for the Twenty-First Century: A Review of Current Literature and Research* (Lewiston, NY: Edwin Mellen Press, 2004), pp. 5–19.
14. National Commission on Social Studies in the Schools, *Charting a Course: Social Studies for the 21st Century* (Report of the Curriculum Task Force of the National Commission on Social Studies in the Schools, Washington, DC, 1989).
15. J. Leming, Jr., L. Ellington, and K. Porter-Magee, eds. *Where Did Social Studies Go Wrong?* (Washington, DC: Thomas B. Fordham Institute, 2007). You can read the report at www.edexcellence.net/institute/publication/publication.cfm?id=317. For criticisms of the report, see *The Social Studies* 96:4 (2005).
16. C. Finn, Introduction, *ibid,* p. vi.

Glossary of Key Terms

Citizenship transmission—Teaching a decided-upon body of information via didactic means with the intent to socialize the student into the conventions of the society.

Conceptions of social studies—A set of assumptions about the major objectives of social studies and how they should be realized.

Critical reflection—Teaching students that there are many points of view and that all must be heeded, especially those of the disadvantaged and marginalized. The focus is on social justice.

Holistic education—Allowing students individually or in groups to pursue their own projects at their own pace using all their faculties in order to construct their own knowledge and build relationships with each other, the community, and the environment, and to become self-reflective.

Intellectual standards—Standards for judging the truth, reliability, validity, plausibility, clarity, and coherence of the knowledge we use and create.

Reflective inquiry—Teaching students how to inquire into problems that face them so that they can decide what actions to take.

Social science—Using the traditional disciplines to teach students how to be good citizens.

CHAPTER 3

What Should a Social Studies Curriculum Look Like?

It is clear that the content of social studies includes knowledge from many disciplines. As teachers can't teach all of this knowledge, they have to make curriculum choices. But on what criteria should these choices be based? In the previous chapter, we looked at some broad goals for social studies and some different conceptions of social studies. These goals and conceptions provide the framework for the development of a curriculum. So, if you view social studies as the teaching of the social sciences, then the curriculum you design is likely to reflect knowledge and skills that are drawn from these disciplines. If you are supportive of the reflective inquiry conception, your curriculum will likely be built around problems for students to resolve. But goals such as learning "the knowledge and skills of the social sciences," "solving problems," or helping students "become good citizens" are too broad to serve as specific guides to classroom teaching. How does one translate these goals into operational terms for a particular group of students?

How we translate goals into practice will depend upon a number of considerations. First and foremost, there are the curriculum guidelines that every province and territory produces. These either state in quite specific terms what to teach, or provide guidelines to follow. In both cases, teachers are contractually bound to follow what the curriculum guide stipulates. There may also be prescribed textbooks or other learning materials that a school or school board uses.

Activity 3-A

Turn to a particular section of the social studies curriculum guidelines for your province or territory. What does your social studies curriculum guideline prescribe that you teach? How much choice and flexibility do you have?

STUDENT CAPABILITIES

One key consideration in the design of curriculum guidelines and our own lessons will be the capabilities of our students at different grade levels. If what we intend to teach is beyond students' abilities, then there is no point in teaching it. Thus, we have to take into account the intellectual maturity of elementary students at various ages. We will not review learning theory; this is the task of educational psychology courses. Nor will we review the most recent research in social studies education.[1] However, we do refer to research on students' mapping abilities in Chapter 11 and their understanding of history in Chapter 10, and in other chapters we indicate relevant literature to substantiate our claims concerning theory and practice. Here, we draw your attention to two research studies that pertain to students' understanding of fundamental social studies concepts.

There has also been interesting research conducted in the U.S. pertaining to young students' knowledge of the fundamental concepts of food, clothing, and shelter.[2] Generally speaking, primary-level students in the U.S. study did not know why people lived in different kinds of housing or ate different kinds of food, although they could explain why people needed shelter and food. Many did not know where electricity, cloth, and several food products came from or how they were produced. For example, one response to the question, "How is cheese made?" garnered this response from a Kindergarten child: "You sit the melted cheese in the refrigerator for a really long time and let the cheese freeze." When asked where the melted cheese came from, the student replied that she did not know.[3] Also, students were generally not aware of the influences that geography and culture have on food and shelter. The authors argue that teachers must do a much better job of explaining why there are differences and similarities in food, shelter, and clothing around the world. The authors have developed materials to support teachers with this effort.[4]

These findings were based on a sample of 96 students, 24 in each of Grades K–3, in a small U.S. city. It would be interesting to replicate this research in different locations in Canada.

Peck and Sears[5] found with a sample of 19 Grade 7 students in a rural community in New Brunswick that students understood ethnic diversity in Canada in four ways, with some not understanding it at all. These perspectives were (1) the other as "weird," (2) the other as confusing, (3) diversity as following rules, and (4) diversity as emanating from world views.[6] The disturbing finding was that students' knowledge did not meet the expectations of the social studies curriculum. However these findings were based on a small sample and the research needs to be replicated, especially in locations where there is much ethnic diversity.

Activity 3-B

Obtain examples of students' work in social studies or interview students about their knowledge of social studies content. What conceptions do students have of the content they have studied? How do they conceive of time and space? What explanations do the students have for historical events, for weather phenomena, for social phenomena, and so on? Look at the maps drawn by students in Chapter 11 and the web related to Peru in Chapter 4 to infer those students' knowledge and abilities.

STUDENT AND SOCIAL CHARACTERISTICS

Activity 3-C

Write down the first things that come into your mind when you are told that in your class there will be:

1. Children from economically disadvantaged backgrounds
2. Children whose parents are very wealthy
3. A majority of girls
4. A majority of boys
5. Children who are recent immigrants from India, Vietnam, and Haiti
6. Two children with special needs.

Consider your responses and think about how they might influence your teaching.

Student characteristics such as class, ethnicity, and gender affect how the curriculum is developed and then implemented by teachers. There has been recent interest in gender learning differences and a call for boys and girls to be provided with different sorts of learning experiences. Based on brain research, Michael Gurian[7] claims that boys are more impulsive, single-task focused, spatial and kinesthetic learners, and are more aggressive. They thus require more physically active learning and the opportunity to make decisions about their classroom experiences. Girls' learning experiences must also be based on the latest research, with the provision of more female role models, concrete manipulatives in math- and science-related activities, access to technology, healthy competition, and encouragement.[8]

We should also consider the social makeup of Canada. According to Statistics Canada,[9] the population of Canada increased by 5.4 percent between the 2001 and 2006 censuses, with two-thirds of the growth rate being attributable to immigration: 1,109,980 immigrants arrived between 2001 and 2006. The 2006 census data reveal that of the 1,808,280 five- to nine-year-old recent immigrants, 258,175 first learned a non-official language and at the time of the census still understood it. Of the 2,078,130 ten- to fourteen-year-olds, 288,020 first learned a non-official language and at the time of the census could still understand it. Four out of five of all these new immigrants did not speak English or French as their mother tongue, with 11.9 percent speaking a non-official language at home. These new immigrants increased the number of foreign-born residents in Canada to 19.8 percent of the population, the highest proportion in 75 years. They represented more than 200 languages.[10] The multicultural nature of Canada has, and will continue to have, profound impacts on education, especially in the area of social studies where the focus is on citizenship education and learning about Canada and the rest of the world.

CURRICULUM ORGANIZATION

Another consideration in preparing to teach social studies relates to the way teachers *organize* the content of the social studies curriculum. The terms **scope** (what is to be taught, and the depth and breadth of what is to be taught) and **sequence** (the order in which knowledge, skills, and attitudes are taught) are frequently used to describe the organizational pattern of a curriculum. It should be noted here that ambiguity exists in the use of the term "scope." Sometimes it is used to refer to the topics (e.g., family, community, geography of Canada, etc.) and the skills and attitudes to be taught. Sometimes it refers to the depth and breadth of what is to be taught (e.g., the inclusion in Canadian geography of a detailed study of each of the regions of Canada and a section on interpreting topographical maps).

Roland Case[11] points out that a number of strands could be used in organizing a social studies curriculum.

1. A **disciplinary strand** consists of history, geography, and other social sciences.
2. A **dimension-based strand** involves topics that cross disciplinary boundaries. Examples include social phenomena such as conflict or peace; social roles such as citizen or worker; social institutions such as families or governments; and regional studies such as the Rockies or Southeast Asia.
3. Finally, there are **concern strands**—also known as **issue-based strands**—where the emphasis is on controversial topics. Examples include global, human rights, peace, multicultural, and environmental education where the objective is to suggest solutions to issues.

Using these strands entails having students obtain and present information. If we wish students to evaluate information, then we need to teach them the intellectual standards to do this. We need to teach them the standards of validity, logic, plausibility, relevance, and so on and how to apply these to the information they use. And, if we want students to consider issues and take action on them, then such personal and social values as equality, fairness, and respect need to be explored. Thus, using the major goals identified at the end of Chapter 2, a curriculum could be organized in the following way with the goals relating to whichever strand is emphasized:

Goals	Disciplinary Knowledge	Interdisciplinary Dimensions	Interdisciplinary Issues
Content knowledge			
Information gathering and reporting			
Intellectual standards			
Personal and social values			
Active citizenship			

Whatever strands are chosen, there needs to be a grade-by-grade sequence. Most elementary school curricula in Canada and the United States organize social studies programs on the basis of the **expanding horizons** model. This view of scope and sequence is based on the assumption that the curriculum should start with what children know most

Expanding Horizons

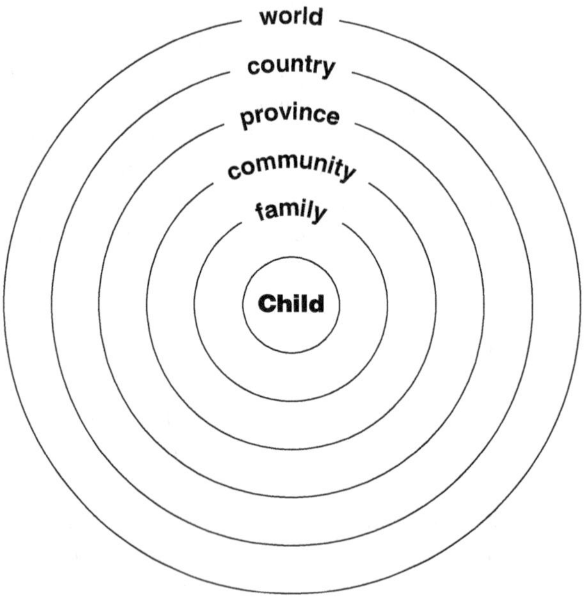

intimately—themselves and their families—and then gradually move outward in space to the community and eventually the world. Kieran Egan criticizes the expanding horizons view, arguing that what children know best are such concepts as "good" and "bad," and "love" and "hate," and that these, and the child's power of imagination, should be the basis for organizing the curriculum.[12] In his book *Teaching as Story Telling,* he outlines how his ideas could be put into practice (see Chapter 5).[13] Egan's concerns about the rigid and lock-step manner in which the expanding horizons approach has been implemented are arguably valid. For example, Grade 1 children *can* examine events that would be construed as beyond the boundaries of a study of the local community, and they *can and do* grapple with abstract ideas at their own levels of sophistication, either within a story format or through other activities.

Another way of organizing a curriculum is via a scope and sequence model based on **spiralling concepts**.

In this framework, chosen concepts are dealt with at increasing levels of sophistication as students move through the grades. Thus, at Grade 1 students might deal with concepts such as family, tradition, rules, and continuity at a Grade 1 level of sophistication, whereas Grade 5 students might return to these themes and deal with them at a Grade 5 level. In the spiralling concepts framework the concepts are often chosen from the scope of the expanding horizons approach; for example, in Grade 1 the concepts are related to the study of families, in Grade 2 to community studies, and so on. When this rigid pattern is followed, Egan's criticisms of the expanding horizons approach become clearer.

Another way of sequencing curricular content, applicable to historical content, is chronology. In this vein, students study their family history in Grade 1 and their community history in Grade 2. Then, starting at Grade 3 or 4, students learn about the history of Canada in chronological order beginning with the study of the first inhabitants followed by the arrival of the first European explorers and settlers, and so on. Then, at about Grade 6 or 7, students begin another much broader chronological sequence that begins with the study of the first humans and first civilizations and continues on in Grades 8 through 12 to follow a chronological history, usually of Europe and North America. For example, Ontario[14] organizes its curriculum following two distinct chronological sequences:

Grade	Heritage and Citizenship	Canada and World Connections
1	Relationships, Rules and Responsibilities	The Local Community
2	Traditions and Celebrations	Features of Communities Around the World
3	Early Settlements in Upper Canada	Urban and Rural Communities
4	Medieval Times	Canada's Provinces, Territories and Regions
5	Early Civilizations	Aspects of Citizenship and Government in Canada
6	First Nations Peoples and European Explorers	Canada's Links to the World

In the Grade 7 history half of the curriculum New France and British North America are studied with the major concepts being conflict and change; in the geography half, the themes are patterns of physical geography and natural resources.

A curriculum may be organized by amalgamating a number of different organizational models. In teaching Canadian history, for example, the expanding horizons model is often melded with spiralling concepts and a chronological approach. Further, the scope of the content may include topics that pertain to a single discipline or to topics that lend themselves toward a multidisciplinary or integrated disciplinary approach. The examples that follow reflect various provincial approaches to curriculum design.

The Atlantic provinces base their curricula on the Foundation for Atlantic Canada Social Studies Curriculum.[15] This curriculum is organized around several key concepts:[16]

Citizenship, Power, and Governance

Culture and Diversity

Individuals, Societies, and Economic Decisions

Interdependence

People, Place, and Environment

Time, Continuity, and Change

The topics are:

Kindergarten: Connections

Grade 1: Interaction

Grade 2: Change

Grade 3: Provincial Identity

Grade 4: Exploration

Grade 5: Societies

Grade 6: World Culture

Grade 7: Empowerment

The latter includes economic, political, cultural, societal, and national empowerment. Objectives, rather than being grade by grade, are listed at the end of Grades 3 and 6.

Quebec organizes the curriculum around key competencies sequenced in three cycles, with each cycle consisting of two elementary years:[17]

Cycle One Competency: To construct his/her representation of space, time, and society

Cycles Two and Three Competencies: To understand the organization of a society in its territory; to interpret change in a society and its territory; to be open to the diversity of societies and their territories.

Each of these competencies is fleshed out with specific content, techniques, and evaluative criteria.

Manitoba sequences the curriculum as follows:[18]

Kindergarten: Being Together

Grade 1: Connecting and Belonging

Grade 2: Communities in Canada

Grade 3: Communities of the World

Grade 4: Manitoba, Canada, and the North: Places and Stories

Grade 5: People and Stories of Canada to 1867

Grade 6: Canada: A Country of Change (1867 to Present)

Grade 7: People and Places in the World

Here, the organizing framework consists of the following concepts: Identity; Culture; Community; The Land; Places and People; Historical Connections; Global Interdependence; Power and Authority; and Economics and Resources.

Saskatchewan[19] organizes its curriculum as follows:

Grade 1: Families

Grade 2: Local Community

Grade 3: Community Comparisons

Grade 4: Saskatchewan

Grade 5: Canada

Grade 6: Canada and Its Atlantic Neighbours

Grade 7: Canada and Its Pacific Neighbours

Twenty major concepts are intertwined throughout the Grades 1 to 5 sequence, with some having more emphasis in one grade level and some in another. In Grade 6 the major concepts are location, interaction, identity, and interdependence; in Grade 7 they are location, resources, power, and change.[20] In both these grades, teachers choose the countries they study in order to realize the curriculum objectives.

Alberta[21] specifies topics in each grade:

Kindergarten: Being Together

Grade 1: Citizenship: Belonging and Connecting

Grade 2: Communities in Canada

Grade 3: Connecting to the World

Grade 4: Alberta: The Land, People, and Stories

Grade 5: Canada: The Land, People, and Stories

Grade 6: Democracy: Action and Participation

Grade 7: Canada: Origins, Histories, and Movement of People

The major strands are Time, Continuity and Change; The Land, Places and People; Global Connections; Power, Authority and Decision Making; Culture and Community; and Economics and Resources. This curriculum is to be fully implemented by 2010.

In British Columbia,[22] each grade is organized around five themes:

Skills and Processes of Social Studies

Identity, Society and Culture

Governance

Economy and Technology

Human and Physical Environment

The grade-by-grade content is:

K–2: Self, Family, School

Grade 3: Communities Past and Present

Grade 4: First Nations Cultures, Explorations, and Contact

Grade 5: Canada: From Colony to Country

Grade 6: Canada and the World

Grade 7: Ancient Civilizations

Activity 3-D

How is the scope and sequence of the social studies curriculum in your province or territory organized? Is any rationale given for the organizational scheme? If so, do you think the rationale is a good one? What skills are emphasized in the curriculum in your province or territory? How are they sequenced? Do you think the sequence is a realistic one? Is there any evidence that children learn these skills in the sequence outlined in the curriculum guide?

Activity 3-E

In your class in a group or on your own, debate, state, or write your reaction to the following statement, giving your reasons:

"Despite education being a provincial responsibility, there is a national social studies curriculum." Whether you agree or disagree with this statement, should there be a national social studies curriculum?

PRINCIPLES OF CURRICULUM ORGANIZATION

Whatever organizational pattern is used, it should be remembered that students learn best if the information is

- limited in amount
- structured around and related to a key idea or concept
- thought about in a critical way
- related to what students already know
- applied to new contexts

In choosing the scope and sequence for a curriculum, logical criteria must be considered. A student may have the capacity to memorize "15 degrees of longitude is equivalent to one hour of time," but to *understand* this the student must comprehend, at least, that the Earth rotates on its axis every 24 hours (approximately) and that there are 360 degrees in a circle. It is logically necessary to know some things before one can begin to understand other things. Therefore, in sequencing anything we have to ask, "In order to know X, what do students have to know prior to studying X?" Having ascertained this, we have to find out whether students actually have this prior knowledge. If they haven't got it, then we will have to teach it. For example, if students haven't grasped the concept of "capital," then teaching them Ottawa is the capital of Canada will be meaningless even if they could remember this fact. You may remember in school being required to memorize lists of facts that had no meaning to you, or being asked to perform tasks for which you had no background or instruction.

A further consideration is the number of objectives that can be realized through the study of a particular topic. It is usually better to strive for multiple objectives at the same time, as such a method is efficient (it allows, for example, teaching language arts skills as students write a report in social studies). Such a method can also be comprehensive (e.g., encouraging students to build up their knowledge at the same time as they develop skills and attitudes).

Another question is whether every student has to know the same information about X. Suppose students were studying Mexico. Why does every student have to know the same details about Mexican food, celebrations, and so on? If students worked in groups each studying a specific topic, and then each group shared its information with the other groups, all students could be assessed on the material by, for example, being required to give examples of how geography affects culture and culture affects geography. Those students who studied food might be expected to give many examples about food but fewer examples about the other topics.[23]

Your own knowledge, abilities, and interests are important in curriculum development. If you have recently visited another country, and the curriculum calls for the study of another culture, you are probably going to be more enthusiastic about studying the country you visited than one you haven't. Moreover, you are likely to have up-to-date information about that country's culture. Having current information about the topic being studied is another key criterion for choosing to study X rather than Y.

School and community pressures may also be an issue. Does the school administration require the teaching of certain topics? Does the community want particular controversial issues avoided? The mere mention of "values education" may raise the ire of some people in some communities. Factors such as the social makeup of the community and the students' cultural backgrounds need to be considered. If there is evidence of prejudice in the community, it has to be dealt with. If a political event occurs—a strike, a government action that divides the community, a war—it has to be dealt with in a way that is sensitive to both the educational goals of the school and the needs of students. This is especially true in light of recent phenomena such as terrorism, climate change, privacy and security concerns related to the Internet, school violence, and so on, all of which can impact students' lives. Some of these phenomena have become a focus for curriculum change (e.g., anti-bullying programs).

Yet, despite the fact that many people may have provided input for curricula decisions, the most important people—the students—are rarely consulted. No one in Canada, so far as we know, has ever carried out a systematic research study to find out what elementary school students would like to learn, or think is important to learn, in social studies.

Activity 3-F

What would you guess elementary school students would like to study or think would be important to study? Now go and ask two or more students. Have a class discussion on the findings.

1. Were your original hypotheses correct?
2. Are there any specific topics that a majority of students would like to study? Do these differ according to gender or another variable?

3. Are any of these topics included in the current provincial curriculum guidelines or textbooks?
4. Should topics that students like to study be included in the social studies curriculum?
5. If there is a vast discrepancy between the actual curriculum and student choices, should you as a teacher do anything about it? Why or why not? If you think something ought to be done, how would you go about taking action?
6. Are resource materials available to teach the topics chosen by students?

CURRICULUM INTEGRATION

Activity 3-G

Indicate which of the following vignettes serve as examples of integration. Then look at the Answers section.

a) The teacher looked at the objectives of the Grade 4 social studies curriculum and related them to the planning of her Grade 5 curriculum.

b) The teacher planned a unit on games. Students researched games played in their own society as well as games in other cultures. They played the games in their social studies classes and physical education classes; by so doing, they met some physical education objectives.

c) The teacher planned a unit on games. Students drew pictures of games; they learned to spell words related to games; they sang songs about games; they completed math problems involving games; they wrote stories about games; and in science class, they carried out experiments to determine how much force was required to throw and kick different sorts of balls (e.g., baseball, soccer ball) a certain distance.

d) Students were allowed to choose a topic related to their personal interests.

e) The school was dedicated to multiculturalism but had no firm policies. Teachers in all grade levels formulated policies and objectives related to multiculturalism. They then planned activities to realize those objectives and to include multiculturalism in whichever subject areas were deemed most appropriate.

f) The students studied the history of Canada for 10 weeks, and then they studied the geography of Canada for 10 weeks. They finished the year with a study of a First Nations group.

g) The students studied Peru. They learned about Peru's food, shelter, clothing, religion, government, education, celebrations, and so on and related these aspects to each other to formulate generalizations about Peru.

One major idea in contemporary social studies is **integration.** Of course, social studies has always functioned as an integrated subject as it draws on knowledge from many disciplines that are also integrated fields of study (e.g., historians study economic, social, cultural, and political events and ideas). In studying social studies, students use skills drawn from other subjects; they put their social studies skills to use in still other areas. One of the pressing debates in education today concerns the limits of integration and the question of what specific topics should and should not be integrated.

Curricular integration can include the

- joining of social studies and language arts into a humanities course
- teaching of something common to all subject areas (e.g., critical thinking)
- integration of student interests with what students must learn
- integration of all that is done in the school around a particular "philosophy," such as multiculturalism
- **vertical integration** of what is being studied now with what was learned in previous grades and what will be learned in the next grade

Thus, when integration is a focus it is necessary to determine what sort of integration should be or is being implemented and, especially, why it is desirable.

The following goals can be identified for integration:

- helping students deal with a complex and interconnected world
- helping students see that subject boundaries are artificial
- helping students learn more efficiently

For example, to understand the situation in Afghanistan today, one would need to have a good understanding of that country's history, geography, economics, religion, and anthropology. While teaching this topic, the goal of efficiency could certainly be met if students also learned and applied map-reading and other skills and compared what they learned about Afghanistan to their own lives.

According to Case,[24] there are four modes of integration:

1. **Fusion** refers to the joining of two elements, as in the example concerning social studies and language arts.
2. **Insertion** is the addition of part of another subject into an existing one. An example would be the teaching of statistics (for the purpose of designing survey research and interpreting the results of the research) in social studies.
3. **Correlation** refers to drawing connections between elements that are taught separately, for example learning about Japan in social studies and doing origami in art class.
4. **Harmonization** refers to a stress on common elements in all or several subject areas, for example when all teachers focus on the same critical-thinking competencies.

Whatever form integration takes, the results must make sense. *More* does not necessarily equal *better*. For instance, many of the so-called integrated units we have seen involve taking a topic and linking seemingly everything to it. So, in a unit on bears, students count bears, draw them, write about them, sing songs about them, and so on. In the end this risks performing no true integrative function.[25] A more sensible integrated unit on bears would draw on the knowledge needed to understand bear behaviour and habitats, and how humans have reacted, do react, and should react to bears. The degree to which the topic is integrated will depend upon the capacities of the students and on the objectives of the study. Forcing integration onto a topic can be counterproductive. Integration, like many other educational ideas, is complex and requires careful thought before it is undertaken.

Activity 3-H

To what extent does the curriculum guide in your province or territory integrate social studies into other subject areas? What subjects are integrated into social studies? What form does the integration take (e.g., fusion, insertion, etc.)?

Having looked at the range of factors that need to be considered in deciding what to teach, we will move on to the question, "How do I go about teaching social studies?" The rest of this book is devoted to trying to answer this question.

Other Activities

1. Choose a particular topic (e.g., law, climate change, multiculturalism, or the treatment of women) that you believe social studies should focus on. Show how you would modify the existing social studies curriculum to include this topic.
2. Suppose your major goal was to develop respect for others at a given grade level. How would you go about doing this, given the curriculum in your province/territory?
3. Choose a social studies topic at a specific grade level and, using the chart on page 26, show what you would focus on.
4. Using a curriculum guideline in another subject, choose a topic and a specific grade level and show how you could integrate social studies objectives and activities into this curriculum.

Notes

1. S. Gibson and R. McKay, *Social Studies for the 21st Century: Review of the Current Literature and Research* (Lewiston, NY: Edwin Mellen, 2004).
2. J. Brophy, J. Alleman, and C. O'Mahony, "Primary-grade students' knowledge and thinking about food production and the origins of common foods," *Theory and Research in Social Education* 31:1 (2003), pp. 10–50.
3. *Ibid,* p. 17.
4. J. Allerman, and J. Brophy, *Social Studies Excursions, K–3: Book One; Powerful Units on Food, Clothing and Shelter* (Portsmouth, NH: Heinemann, 2001).
5. C. Peck and A. Sears, "Uncharted territory: Mapping students' conceptions of ethnic diversity," *Canadian Ethnic Studies* 37:1 (2005), pp. 101–120.
6. C. Peck, A. Sears, and S. Donaldson, "Unreached and unreasonable: Curriculum standards and children's understanding of ethnic diversity," *Curriculum Inquiry* 28:1 (2008), p. 71.
7. K. King and M. Gurian, "Teaching to the minds of boys," *Educational Leadership* 64:1 (2006), pp. 56–58, 60–61.
8. M. Gurian, *Boys and Girls Learn Differently* (San Francisco: Jossey-Bass, 2001).
9. Statistics Canada: www12.statcan.ca/English/census06/data/highlights/ (accessed December 10, 2007).
10. Statistics Canada: www.statcan.ca/English/Daily/English/071204/d071204a.htm (accessed December 11, 2007).

11. R. Case, "Elements of a coherent social studies program," in R. Case and P. Clark, eds., *The Canadian Anthology of Social Studies* (Vancouver: Pacific Educational Press, 1999).
12. K. Egan, "What children know best," Social Education 43:2 (1979), pp. 130–139.
13. K. Egan, *Teaching as Story Telling* (London, ON.: Althouse Press, 1986).
14. *Ontario Curriculum: Social Studies, Grades 1 to 6; History and Geography, Grades 7 and 8* (Toronto: Ministry of Education, 2004).
15. Atlantic Provinces Education Foundation, *Foundation for the Atlantic Canada Social Studies Curriculum* (Halifax: Nova Scotia Education and Culture, 1998).
16. Atlantic Canada Social Studies Curriculum, Social Studies Grades Primary–2, Implementation Draft October 2005, pp. 5–6.
17. Gouvernement du Québec, Ministère de l'Éducation, Québec Education Program, 2001.
18. Manitoba Education and Youth, *Kindergarten to Grade 8 Social Studies* (Winnipeg: Manitoba Education and Youth, 2003).
19. Saskatchewan Education, *Elementary Social Studies: A Curriculum Guide for the Elementary Level* (Regina: Saskatchewan Education, 1995). www.sasked.gov.sk.ca/ branches/curr/evergreen/ social.shtml (accessed December 18, 2007).
20. Saskatchewan Learning: Social Studies, Grade 6, and Social Studies; A Curriculum Guide for the Middle Level, Grade 7 (Regina: Ministry of Education, 1999). www.sasked.gov.sk.ca/branches/curr/evergreen/social.shtml (accessed December 18, 2007).
21. Alberta Education, *Social Studies Kindergarten to Grade 12* (Edmonton: Alberta Education, 2005).
22. Ministry of Education British Columbia, *Social Studies K–7 Integrated Resource Package* (Victoria: Ministry of Education, 2006). www.bced.gov.bc.ca/irp (accessed December 18, 2007).
23. S. Thornton, *Teaching Social Studies That Matters* (New York: Teachers College Press, 2005).
24. R. Case, "The anatomy of curricular integration," *Canadian Journal of Education* 16:2 (1991), pp. 215–224.
25. *Ibid.,* pp. 215–224.

Glossary of Key Terms

Concern (or issue-based) strand—Using issues (e.g., human rights, global warming) to organize the curriculum.

Dimension-based strand—Using themes that cross subject boundaries (community or regional studies) to organize the curriculum.

Disciplinary strand—Using the traditional disciplines (especially history and geography) to organize the curriculum.

Expanding horizons—Basing the curriculum on the view that students first learn about themselves, then their families, their communities, their territory or province, their country, and eventually the world.

Integration—Organizing the curriculum in various ways that focus on relationships.

- **Correlation**—Drawing connections between elements that are taught separately (e.g., doing origami in art while studying Japan in social studies).
- **Fusion**—Joining of two elements, such as social studies and language arts.
- **Harmonization**—Stressing common elements in several subject areas, (e.g., multicultural education in social studies, language arts, art, and music).

Insertion—Adding part of a subject to another (e.g., using a mathematical formula to draw a map).

Vertical—Relating what has occurred in a previous grade or topic to the one at hand.

Scope—In a curriculum or lesson, how much is taught and to what depth.

Sequence—The order in which the curriculum or lesson is taught.

Spiralling concepts—Basing the curriculum on the progressive development of concepts.

Websites for Part One

Ministries/Departments of Education

Alberta:
www.education.gov.ab.ca

British Columbia:
www.bced.gov.bc.ca

Manitoba:
www.edu.gov.mb.ca

New Brunswick:
www.gnb.ca/0000/index-e.asp

Newfoundland and Labrador:
www.gov.nf.ca/edu

Nova Scotia:
www.ednet.ns.ca

Ontario:
www.edu.gov.on.ca

Prince Edward Island:
www.edu.pe.ca

Quebec:
www.mels.gouv.qc.ca

Saskatchewan:
www.sasklearning.gov.sk.ca

Teachers' Associations with Social Studies Websites

Alberta Social Studies Council:
www.ssc.teachers.ab.ca

British Columbia Social Studies Teachers Association:
www.bctf.ca/psas/BCSSTA

Nova Scotia Social Studies Teachers' Association:
http://ssta.ednet.ns.ca

Ontario Association for Geographic and Environmental Education:
http://oagee.org

Ontario History and Social Sciences Teachers' Association:
www.ohassta.org

Social Studies and Social Science Organizations

Canadian Council for Geographic Education:
www.ccge.org

Histor!ca:
www.histori.ca

National Council for the Social Studies:
www.ncss.org

CHAPTER 4

How Do I Get Started?

The broad goals of social studies, as well as the curriculum guidelines, students, and many other factors, all need to be taken into consideration when deciding what to teach. The goals for social studies education are likely to make direct reference to content knowledge; information gathering, processing, and presenting; intellectual standards; personal and social values; active citizenship; and the disciplinary, interdisciplinary, and issue strands that can be addressed in social studies (see Chapter 3). Taking these goals and strands into account, teachers can organize their lessons or units on a variety of bases, such as the following.[1]

THEME OR SURVEY

Organizing units on the basis of a **theme or survey** places the emphasis on (a) a historical or contemporary event or phenomenon, for example the expulsion of the Acadians, the building of the pyramids in Egypt, the fishing industry in Canada; (b) a place, for example my community, Newfoundland and Labrador, China; or (c) a particular time period, for example early exploration of Canada, Toronto in the early 1900s. Many curriculum guidelines and textbooks are organized around similar themes.

GENERALIZATION

The emphasis here is on a broad **generalization** that is developed through the study of one or more examples. "People in a community interact to provide goods and services" is one example of such a generalization. Another is "People adapt their environments to meet their needs, and they, in turn, adapt to their environments." See Chapter 14 for a discussion on how to teach generalizations.

CONCEPT

The focus here is on central **concepts** and how they are related to one particular example or to several. For example, a unit with "tradition" as its focus might look at what this concept means in the context of students' families, the community, and other places in the world. A unit with "equality" as its focus might examine this concept as it relates to the treatment of physically disadvantaged people in Canada, or male and female roles in a particular society. Chapter 6 will help you teach for conceptual understanding.

ISSUE

Another way to focus a lesson or unit is on an **issue** or concern where intellectual standards or personal and social values are applied. For example, deciding which account of a particular event is most plausible likely entails the use of intellectual standards (see Chapter 8). Deciding whether a shopping mall should be built in the community or what rights students should have in the classroom likely involve the use of personal and social values. See Part 3 for ideas on how to develop lessons or units on issues where social and personal values are developed.

INQUIRY

The organizer here can be questions related to answers that can be researched. Examples could include: What motivated Europeans to explore North America? What rules govern our community? How are the governments of Canada and Japan similar and different? Chapters 7 and 8 help you implement **inquiry** as an organizer.

PROBLEM

The aim of focusing on a **problem** is to suggest a course of action. How can we make a new immigrant feel welcome in our school? What can we do to clean up garbage in our community? What can we do to help other students become more globally aware? Part 3 focuses on ideas for using problems as an organizer.

PROJECT

If based on a **project**, a lesson or unit is built around the creation of a model (a Hudson's Bay fort), a newspaper article (about the Underground Railway), a drama (acting out the arrival of Irish immigrants in Halifax), a mural (showing how many of the goods we purchase are dependent on foreign sources), or a presentation (using a PowerPoint program and copies of old photographs to show what life was like for children in Winnipeg in the early 1900s).

NARRATIVE

The emphasis here is on a story or other **narrative**. Examples could be stories of another person (a biography or autobiography) or the story of the development of a city or of a particular invention.[2] Kieran Egan[3] has an approach to developing units based on the story form that you can read about in Chapter 5.

These organizers are not mutually exclusive. We could teach a unit using an identical knowledge base that involves several different organizers (see Chapter 21 for an example). However, each organizer requires some different objectives, teaching methods, and assessment strategies.

Activity 4-A

Look at the objectives for one grade level in your school's social studies curriculum and state how you could plan a lesson or unit based on each of the organizers listed above.

WEBBING

Whichever organizer is chosen, teachers need to map out what would be required to study the theme, answer the inquiry question, and so on. Here, **webbing** is a most useful tool.

The first step is to break down the topic into its constituent parts. Suppose we have a Grade 3 class and have been asked to teach about the Inuit in Nunavut using a thematic approach and focusing on the knowledge goals of social studies. What specifically do we teach? We could examine food, shelter, and clothing, but what else would we need to examine in order to build up as complete a picture as possible of the Inuit?

Activity 4-B

What aspects of Inuit life could be studied? Write down what you think ought to be studied to obtain as complete a picture as possible of Inuit life.

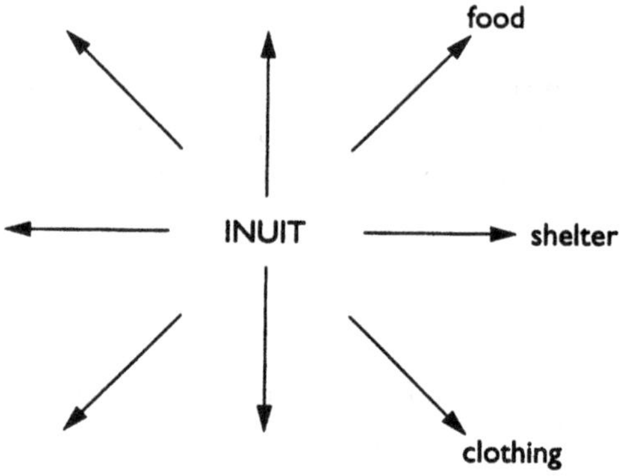

Depending on the objectives of the unit and student abilities, what might appear to be a simple concept like "food" can be broadened to include very powerful concepts that are food-related, such as ritual, community, conceptions of nature, power, cultural transmission, cultural change, exploitation, and needs. Thus, teaching the concept does not merely entail listing examples of Inuit food but also putting the concept in its wider social, political, spiritual, environmental, economic, and historical contexts. Similarly, depending on student abilities, other concepts can be related to more abstract and theoretically powerful concepts.

Activity 4-C

If the topic is ancient Greece, and our focus is on personal and social values and intellectual standards, what aspects might be studied?

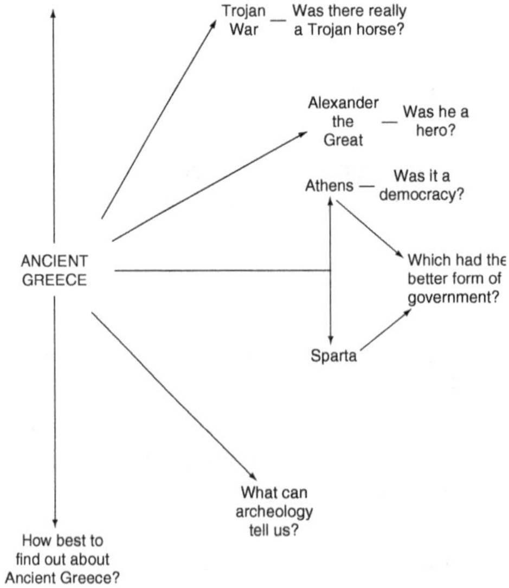

Activity 4-D

If our organizer is the issue of how violence in society should be dealt with, and our focus is on personal and social values and citizenship action, what aspects would have to be studied?

In the above activities, we have analyzed and broken down our topic into its component parts so that we can clearly see what might be taught. Of course, decisions will have to be made concerning what will actually be taught, especially as any analysis could be quite complex. If we mapped out a complete picture of the forest industry in Canada, it could include everything from chainsaws to types of trees, to conservation and international trade and tariff regulations. Specifically, what we focus on will depend upon such factors as the age and maturity of students, the time available to teach the topic, suitable resource materials, the curriculum guide, and our philosophy of social studies. But, in each case, a "map" of the territory we wish to cover will be necessary. Without a map we could become hopelessly lost!

This map is also useful to students if they are to derive meaning from what they are studying. Constructing meaning is an interactive process in which learners use their existing conceptual schemas (their knowledge and understandings) to make connections between what they already know and new information. Thus, students with rich background knowledge of a topic derive greater and deeper meanings from new information than do students with a poor background knowledge of the topic.[4] One of the ways teachers can help students use their prior knowledge to comprehend new information is to use a technique called **semantic mapping.**[5] Students draw a visual representation of the relationships between concepts and information that they already know. When completed, the map will look much like the one of Peru shown on page 42. Carried out at the beginning of a new unit, this activity allows teachers to determine how much students already know. If we wish to make our teaching meaningful to students, then we need to link it to how students make sense of the world and what they already know about it. As the topic is developed in class, students can add to their semantic maps and show how new information is linked to their prior knowledge.

Activity 4-E

Here is a web drawn by a student in Grade 6 during a unit on Peru.[6] What does she appear to know about the topic? How does she understand Peru? What else do you think she needs to know?

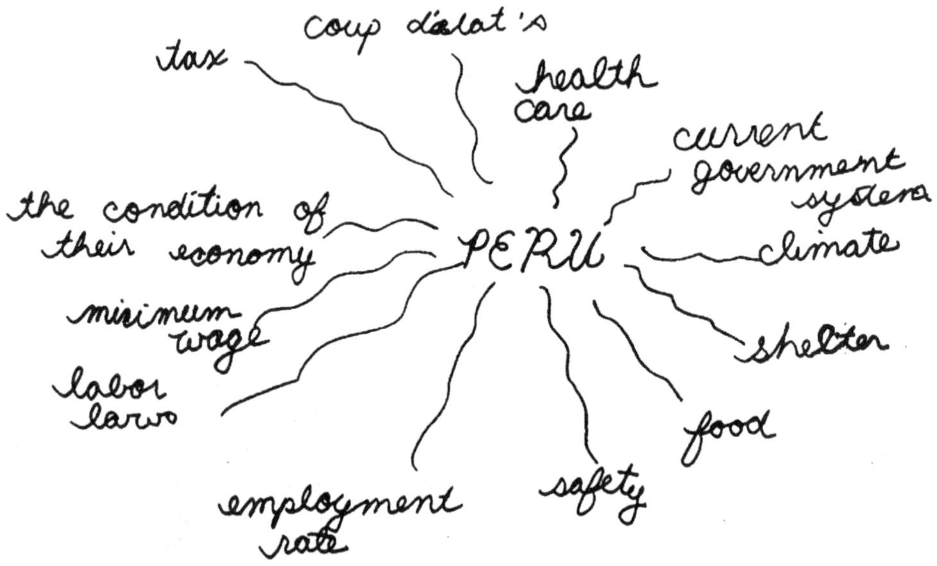

PLANNING A UNIT

From these maps and from the focus we choose, we then need to plan our unit. On the basis of our overall objectives, we would decide what aspects to teach and in what depth (scope), and what the sequence would be. Then we would choose our teaching methods and resources. We would also have to decide how to assess student learning. Although there is logic to developing a unit plan (there should be coherence among the objectives, what is taught, how it is taught, and how students will be assessed), we may find ourselves jumping around from one element to another as we plan. Eventually, we will develop a unit plan that provides a road map of where we are going and how we intend to get there—although it might be modified as we teach it. As you read further in this book you will find examples of lesson and unit plans that demonstrate how different organizing ideas can be implemented.

Other Activities

1. Create a web showing what *could* be studied about a topic at a grade level of your choice. Then decide which of these aspects you would wish a class of students to actually study. Give reasons for your decisions.
2. Develop a rough plan for a social studies topic of your choice. Will your goals focus on content knowledge, information gathering and presenting, intellectual standards, personal and social values, citizenship action, or a combination of the above? Will you organize your plan on the basis of a discipline, an interdisciplinary dimension, or an

interdisciplinary concern or issue? Will you organize your plan around a theme, generalization, concept, issue, inquiry, problem, project, or narrative?

3. Have a class of elementary school students work in groups to draw a semantic map related to a social studies topic they are studying in school. What concepts and information do the students provide? How are each group's concept maps similar or different? Compare the concept maps to determine whether students give the same meaning to the topic.
4. Some provincial and territorial social studies curriculum guidelines provide model unit plans. Review these to ascertain how they are organized. What goals are emphasized? What strands are focused upon? What organizing patterns are used? You could also look at one or more textbooks to see which organizational patterns are prevalent.

Notes

1. *British Columbia K–7 Integrated Resource Package* (Victoria, BC: Ministry of Education, 1998), p. 6.
2. For lists of suitable literature for history teaching, see Chapter 10.
3. K. Egan, *Teaching as Story Telling* (London, ON.: Althouse Press, 1983).
4. See K. Camperell and R. Knight, "Reading research and social studies," in J. Shaver, ed., *Handbook of Research on Social Studies Teaching and Learning* (New York: Macmillan, 1991).
5. P. Antonacci, "Students search for meaning in the text through semantic mapping," *Social Education* 55:3 (1991), pp. 174–175, 194.
6. Drawn by Vanessa Disler. Used with permission.

Glossary of Key Terms

Lesson/unit organization—Units or lessons can be based upon the following:

Concept—How a particular concept (e.g., equality) relates to a particular example (e.g., the treatment of disabled people in Canada).

Generalization—A broad relationship statement (e.g., people in a community interact to provide goods and services).

Inquiry—A question that is answered by students (e.g., what motivated the early explorers of Canada?).

Issue—Focus on an issue of concern (e.g., how should we clean up the community?; what should be done to deal with global warming in our community?).

Narrative—Organizing instruction around a story or other narrative such as a biography.

Problem—Focusing on courses of action concerning what oneself or others ought to do to solve a particular social problem.

Project—Organizing instruction around the creation of something tangible (e.g., a mural, video, newspaper, website, or drama).

Theme or survey—Organizing instruction around a historical or contemporary event (e.g., the Riel Rebellion, a provincial election), time period (e.g., the early exploration of Canada), place (e.g., my community, Newfoundland and Labrador, or China).

Semantic mapping—Diagramming the information and concepts students already know (similar to webbing).

Webbing—Diagramming the elements of a topic and their relationships.

CHAPTER 5

Telling It Like It Is: Exposition and Narrative

Once teachers have identified the objectives and content for a social studies topic they are teaching, they next need to decide on the most appropriate teaching methods. For reasons of familiarity, brevity, and efficiency, or because resource materials are not available, the only available teaching approach may be to present information to students directly. This does not mean that a teacher stands up in front of the class and reads from a prepared paper for 30 minutes. In the elementary classroom, teachers talk to students but they intersperse their presentation with questions, discussion, blackboard notes, and multimedia presentations. Here are some suggested guidelines:

1. Ensure students are familiar with the objectives for your presentation. Tell students at the beginning of the class what the presentation is about and what, in particular, they should listen for. Also, try to connect the presentation to any previous presentations you have given on the same topic. In other words, try to segue between presentations.
2. Consider beginning the presentation with some hook that grabs students' attention. A hook can be as simple as a noteworthy question that will intrigue students or a short activity that encourages students to think about the topic at hand.
3. Organize the presentation so that it contains the main points in a logical order. The planning you have done to prepare the presentation should focus particularly on this step.
4. Once some or all of the presentation content has been introduced, have students carry out an activity that focuses attention on the main points (e.g., filling in information on a worksheet or completing a herringbone; see p. 52).
5. At the end of the presentation, summarize the main points. Even better, ask students to summarize the main points.
6. Make your presentation as interesting as possible by directly posing questions to the students, encouraging discussion, and using visual materials. The use of multimedia materials to complement the verbal components of your presentation is absolutely critical when teaching young students.
7. Speak in a clear, interesting manner.
8. Maintain eye contact with the students and ensure they are facing you during the presentation.
9. If interest is slipping, ask a question or give the students an activity to complete. Also consider whether your presentation may simply be too long.
10. Prepare a cumulative activity in which students are asked to apply the information they have learned in the presentation.

Activity 5-A

Prepare a 10-minute presentation on a topic of your choice. Decide what the main points are and in what order you will present them. Choose suitable audio-visual aids. Prepare an activity for students to complete during or following your presentation. Give your presentation to a peer and have him or her evaluate it on the basis of the guidelines provided above.

The following is an example of an expository lesson plan. It is but one example of this kind of approach.

Grade 3: Rationale for Using an Expository Approach

Expository teaching offers a highly economical way of presenting information. It can synthesize quantities of information, eliminate the irrelevant, concentrate on the significant, and present information in a structured way. The presentation can be highly entertaining and interesting. It can include a variety of visual materials as well as other aids that reinforce important details. Changes in levels of abstraction can be included so that all students, whatever their cognitive capacities, can learn something.

Overall goals

Students will learn that people meet their needs in varying ways and are interdependent.

Students will respect the varying ways that people interact to meet their needs.

Students will actively listen.

Strand

Interdisciplinary, with a focus on social roles

Major organizer

The concept of community

Lesson objectives

Students will be able to list three basic needs of people (food, shelter, and clothing) and state how the Hutterites fulfill these needs.

Students will describe how the Hutterites' sense of community helps them meet basic needs.

Students will listen to the talk and correctly complete a worksheet based on the information contained in the talk.

Introduction

(In the previous lesson, students were introduced to the Hutterites and their history. In this lesson, students are looking at a picture of Hutterites eating a meal in the communal dining room.)

Looking at this picture, we can see that, like you and me, these people need food. What else do they need? At the end of this lesson, you will be able to tell me who these people are, what needs they have, and how they go about fulfilling their needs.

Main body of the lesson

These people are Hutterites *[reviews the term by writing the word on the board]*. This group lives in Alberta *[reviews where Alberta is on the map; relates location to where students live]*. Like you and me, they have certain needs.

(The needs are listed and explanations are given as to how the Hutterites fulfill these needs and their sense of community. Students are questioned about how their own needs are fulfilled and how these methods compare to the Hutterites' ways. Pictures of Hutterites farming, building, sewing, and so on are shown. Students fill in the worksheet.)

Synthesis

So we have seen that, like you and me, Hutterites need food, clothing, and shelter. They obtain them in their community in ways that may be similar to, or different from, the ways in which we obtain them.

Assessment

The worksheets are collected and assessed for accuracy.

The objective of exposition is for students to learn a body of information. Another way to achieve this objective would be to use a cooperative learning activity employing the "jigsaw" technique. For more information on cooperative learning, see Chapter 9. In the jigsaw technique, each student is assigned to a study group and a learning group. In the study groups, each member becomes an expert in a particular body of information. Students then go to their learning groups and teach the rest of the group the content they learned in their study groups. Finally, all students are tested on all the information. The steps in this procedure are as follows:

1. The teacher prepares a selection of research materials so that the content to be learned is divided into separate parts. For example, for a unit on pioneer life, the research material might be divided into information related to food, shelter, and clothing.
2. Students are assigned to research groups and each research group is assigned a number. Group 1 receives one body of information (e.g., food), Group 2 receives a different body of information (e.g., shelter), and so on.
3. All the students meet in their respective research groups. The members of each research group review, study, and make summary notes related to the research materials provided to their group until they are all experts on the material.
4. The students in each research group are numbered off.
5. Students form new groups according to the numbers they have been assigned. In each new group there will be a representative from each research group. Students use the notes they have taken in their research groups to teach the students in the new groups about what they have learned (e.g., pioneer food, shelter, or clothing). Students can also be asked to amalgamate the information they have collected as they complete a worksheet (e.g., about pioneer food, shelter, and clothing).
6. If students are assessed, then grades can be assigned on the basis of the average of each student's individual score and the team's average score. For example, if Rita's individual score was 90 and the learning group's average score was 86, then Rita would receive a score of 88. If students are informed at the beginning of this activity that their scores will be partially dependent on the score obtained by the rest of their group, they are more likely to stay on task and ensure the content is really understood.

To assess students, require that they submit the research notes they have taken in their research groups. Prior to completing this activity, remind students that in the second groups that are formed they will be the sole experts in a specific topic area (e.g., pioneer food, shelter, or clothing). The other students in that group will be relying on their knowledge of that topic.

EGAN'S STORY-TELLING APPROACH

Curricular content can also be imparted to students using a **story-telling approach**, similar to the one pioneered by Kieran Egan,[1] which is used by many teachers across Canada.[2] There are ongoing international projects where teachers are using the approach to design learning materials (some are available online); research projects, one of which involves First Nations students; and workshops, conferences, and a graduate program in imaginative education. Egan has also written a number of books in which his theory is explored in depth.[3]

Story-telling, or narrative, can involve fiction or non-fiction; the term refers to writing that is shaped in story form. If the content is fiction, then students should be apprised of this. A brief example follows, but you should study Egan's books for a full grasp of the theoretical basis of his approach and how best to apply it in your teaching. Egan argues that any social studies topic can be approached as a good story to be told, as well as a set of objectives to be attained. He suggests certain questions be answered so that a story unfolds.

Identifying Importance

What is most important about this topic? Why should it matter to children? What is engaging about it?

Suppose the unit is "multiculturalism" and the focus is on Japanese Canadians. In answering the questions above, we could argue that multiculturalism is vital to Canada (see Chapter 18), that it matters to children because they interact with people from a variety of cultural backgrounds, and that the stories of immigrants—their sorrows, their triumphs—can engage children.

Finding Binary Opposites

What powerful binary opposites best catch the importance of this topic?

A number of significant binary opposites can be addressed through story-telling: prejudice/tolerance, freedom/oppression, survival/destruction, cooperation/conflict, or unity/diversity. Given that many groups come to Canada to escape oppression and that young children find "oppression" to be a powerful idea (one author's children were always complaining that they were being oppressed!), the binary opposites "freedom/oppression" can serve as useful themes.

Organizing Content into Story Form

What content most dramatically embodies the binary opposites to provide access to the topic? What content best articulates the topic into a developing story form?

Many incidents could be used to show how "freedom/oppression" applies to the history of Japanese Canadians. They were denied the right to vote, excluded from certain jobs, and discriminated against in the fishing industry. But perhaps the most telling content concerns their evacuation from the British Columbia coast during World War II. One of the best ways of telling this story is by relating the tale of Joy Kogawa's *Obasan*[4] through the eyes of Naomi, who, with her family, experiences evacuation and subsequent internment. Students could carry out a number of activities based on the story: role-playing particular incidents; discussing the rightness or wrongness of the internment; or writing a diary from the point of view of one of the internees.

Conclusion

What is the best way of resolving the dramatic conflict inherent in the binary opposites? What degree of mediation of these opposites is it appropriate to seek?

In the story, there is a resolution. When the Canadian government ordered the deportation of Japanese Canadians, a decision that was upheld in the courts,[5] the resulting public outcry led to the repeal of the deportation orders on January 26, 1947. Recently, the survivors of the evacuation were granted both financial compensation and a formal apology from the Canadian government.

To extend this activity, we could clarify the two concepts to show, for example, that freedom does not mean licence, and that having to do what you're told does not necessarily mean oppression. We could show how oppressed people have taken political action and have sometimes gained particular freedoms (e.g., in Eastern Europe in 1989). We could look at the lives of immigrant groups and find out how they attempt to get control over their own lives. We could discuss relevant incidents in children's lives in which they see a conflict between freedom and oppression.

Evaluation

How can one know whether the topic has been understood, its importance grasped, and the content learned?

One of the best ways to evaluate student learning would be to have students write a story from the perspective of a member of the Japanese-Canadian community in 1941, telling of the evacuation, life in an internment camp or on a farm, and the deportation orders. Finally, students could state their feelings about freedom and oppression in this context. Other evaluation techniques can be found in Chapter 22.

Here is another example using a different topic.

Topic: First Nations peoples of Canada

Binary opposites: Survival and destruction

1. Begin with a vivid example of the concepts—tell a story of what would happen if buffalo could not be found before Plains people ran out of food, or depict the onset of an early winter for the Cree nation.
2. Link each aspect of the lives of First Nations peoples to the concepts: the importance of shelter as protection from the elements, the cycles of food gathering, and the impact of changes on these cycles. Survival relationships with other aspects of the cultures studied would be included here.
3. Introduce the impact of the Europeans on First Nations peoples. Show how, in many respects, the survival techniques of the First Nations peoples could not cope with European influences. Neither could the first explorers survive without the help of the local inhabitants. Study the destruction of the Beothuk, and the residential schools that were designed to destroy First Nations cultures.
4. Show how First Nations peoples have met the challenge of survival and destruction.
5. Assess students on their understanding. Have them give examples of survival and destruction. Ask students to explain how the challenges of survival and destruction were and are now being met.

Activity 5-B

Create a lesson plan using Egan's story-telling approach on a topic for a grade level of your choice. The lesson should contain your objectives, an "opener," a brief description of what you will say, activities students will carry out, and a method of evaluation.

1. Identifying importance
   What is most important about this topic?
   Why should it matter to children?
   What is engaging about it?
2. Finding binary opposites
   What powerful binary opposites best catch the importance of this topic?
3. Organizing content into story form
   What content most dramatically embodies the binary opposites to provide access to the topic?
   What content best articulates the topic into a developing story form?
4. Conclusion
   What is the best way of resolving the dramatic conflict inherent in the binary opposites?
   What degree of mediation of these opposites is it appropriate to seek?
5. Evaluation
   How can one know whether the topic has been understood, its importance grasped, and the content learned?

Egan's story-telling approach is a powerful one for teaching history, as it builds on students' experiences with stories, fairy tales, and myths. The major themes in these narratives are typically conflicts between bravery and cowardice, good and evil, and so on. Students are already familiar with these themes from stories, watching television and movies, and their own experiences. This eases the task of capturing their imagination and imparting some historical information. As stories consist of causes and effects within a temporal sequence, children can also begin to develop their concepts of historical time and causation. Chapter 10 provides you with other ideas for teaching history.

USING THE TEXTBOOK

Many jurisdictions recommend the use of particular textbooks.[6] Textbooks are a mixed blessing. They can certainly make our lives easier and, if used throughout a particular educational jurisdiction, they provide continuity for students and educators and a common basis on which to evaluate student learning. Most textbooks contain carefully organized and constructed information with plenty of aids for student readers, along with exercises to help them apply the information they are learning to new contexts. Most also come with teacher's guides. However, if textbooks are the only source of information for social studies, students' access to other points of view and primary sources of information may be limited. As well, textbooks do not always provide a close match with curriculum objectives as publishers cannot always afford to publish textbooks to suit each province or territory's curriculum.

Your Analysis of the Textbook

We pose the following questions to help you familiarize yourself with social studies textbooks. Consider browsing through one of the social studies textbooks your school is using as you answer these questions.

1. What are the backgrounds of the authors? What criteria would you apply to judge the authority of the authors? Do these authors measure up to your criteria?
2. What is the content of the book? Given the topic of the book, what content *could* be included? What in your view would be worth knowing about this topic? What content is excluded? What places, people, issues, ideas, events are given prominence? How much space is devoted to each? How are women, children, the aged, the challenged, the rich, the poor, minorities, people with particular occupations, people of different cultural backgrounds, etc., treated, referred to, referenced, and contextualized? What sorts of biases are present? What keywords are listed in the index and glossary? What biases, if any, do they reflect?
3. What visuals are included? Who is depicted (e.g., age, gender, ethnicity)? What are they doing? What does this say about the status of the people and the activities depicted?[7] What evidence is there of stereotypes? Of bias? What sorts of graphs, charts, and tables are included? What do they show? What importance is attached to them? Do the visuals distort the data in any way? If so, how? (See Chapter 19 for details of how to look at images critically.)
4. Is evidence presented for the claims made in the textbook, e.g., through phrases such as "research states. . . ," "according to (a source). . . ," or "there is evidence that. . . "? If no evidence is presented, how might readers go about determining the believability of the claims made? Locate at least one major event, person, idea, or place that is covered in the textbook. Look at the statements made and identify whether any evidence is presented to support their believability. If no evidence is presented, how would you go about determining the credibility of the claims made? Would the credibility differ according to who was telling the story or presenting the evidence? If so, how? If the story or evidence was likely to differ, is there any way we could determine "truth"? If there is more than one story and the textbook presents only one of them, how would you go about presenting the other stories? In what situations would it be really important to do this? Why?
5. What key concepts would a student have to grasp to understand the information presented? Are these concepts defined? Are the definitions adequate? If the concept is a contested one (people can legitimately differ in the way they define the term), then is this pointed out to readers? How would you go about determining the most appropriate definition?
6. Are there value claims in the textbook, e.g., this is good/bad, this is better/worse, or this should be done? Are arguments presented to support the value claims? If not, what sort of arguments would be required?
7. Is there any content you would regard as controversial? If so, how is it dealt with? In your view, how should it be dealt with? Where you know a controversy exists, is it mentioned? If not, why do you think it is not raised? Are opposing points of view identified? Are differing viewpoints mentioned? If not, which viewpoints receive attention?

Why these only? Is it merely stated that there are opposing points of view or do the authors of the text take a position? If so, what is that position? On what is it based? Are questions posed to the student? If so, what are they? Are they appropriate? Would it help the student resolve the controversy if the questions were answered?

8. Is cause and effect dealt with? If so, how? Are the cause-and-effect relationships believable? Viewed as complex? Seen as problematic? Choose one event about which you are familiar. Review the text and analyze the cause-and-effect reasoning. Is the reasoning sound?
9. Are there any generalization statements? Are these supported with evidence? What sorts of generalization statements are there (see Chapter 14)? What is the evidence to support the generalization? Are there enough instances to justify the generalization? Does the generalization fit into a larger body of knowledge that is believable? Have any fallacies been committed—for example, hasty generalizations (just because one A is a B doesn't necessarily mean that all As are Bs) or fallacy of division (just because a group generally has a certain characteristic doesn't mean necessarily that each individual member of the group has that characteristic)?
10. How was the textbook written, produced, and chosen for student use? Whose vision of education and truth does the textbook represent?

Helping Students Use the Textbook

Students should know how textbooks are written,[8] as this can help them use textbooks well. When the textbook is first introduced to students, you might want students to address some of the following questions and activities:

1. Who are the authors? What are their credentials?
2. When was the text published? If the text had been published some years ago, would there be any difference in the information presented?
3. Have students look at the title and hypothesize what they think they are going to learn. Then look at the table of contents and chapter headings and check their hypotheses. If the book is a history textbook, have students look at the index for people's names and categorize them in various ways (e.g., male/female; rulers, politicians, military, religious leaders, scientists, artists). Review the list and discuss the results. For instance, there are likely to be far more males than females mentioned in most history texts. Why might this be? If the text is geographical in focus, ask students what areas have received attention and why the areas that are addressed might be considered important by the authors. What areas receive no attention? Why? Here it is important to tell students that textbook authors have to make decisions about what to include. They have to consider the curriculum, the students, and the various guidelines that provinces and territories use to determine which textbooks will be recommended.
4. Have students look at the illustrations. What is emphasized? Why?
5. Who receives the most attention? Ideas on interpreting visuals can be found in Chapter 19.

Depending on the text, we might want to take several approaches.[9] We could ask students to make a web of what they already know or expect to learn when they first read a chapter title. On reading the chapter, they then fill out the web or check their hypotheses. If the text is in the form of a story, then we should ensure the story flow is maintained. But we should point out that a story is not fact, although it might be based upon facts. We have to ask students how they might check out the "truth" about the events, places, or persons in the story and check other sources. If the text consists of factual accounts, the first thing to do is ensure the context is clear and that students understand the key concepts in the titles or headings. For example, texts may well provide "openers" or chapter previews that introduce students to the topic and link it to what they have previously learned. You may have to flesh this out so that the new topic is comprehensible to students. For example, if the account is about a particular place, you might want to go beyond finding it on a map by asking the kinds of questions outlined in Chapter 11. As writers often begin paragraphs with summary statements, have students write these out and then use a diagram linking the other information in the paragraphs to the main ideas. An idea here is to use a "herringbone" activity. Here is an example:

Herringbone Activity

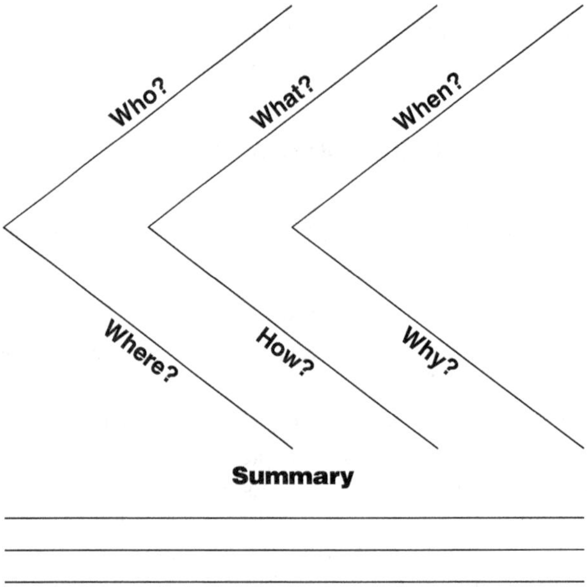

Another idea would be to have students write the summary statement for the chapter after having read that chapter.

If any of the text is in chronological order, such as an account of a historical event, have students transfer the information onto a timeline (see Chapter 10). Then have them look at the sequence and note what the causes and effects might be. Sometimes the text writer will identify these, but sometimes the writer will not. In other cases, where there are cause-and-effect claims, have students create a web showing these (see Chapter 14). Where there are comparisons, have students make a chart noting similarities and differences. Point out to students the importance of glossaries and other aids to understanding the material, such as sidebars. Point out the relationships between the visuals, printed text, captions, and so on.

Any chapter or part of a chapter can be studied as follows: Divide the class into learning groups and assign each group a portion of the text. Have each group then teach the content they are responsible for to the other learning groups. What is to be learned can be phrased in question form so that student attention is focused on the relevant content. Another technique, which is ideally used by pairs of students, is labelled **SQ3R**. SQ3R stands for the following:

Survey—read heading(s).

Question—create questions from the heading(s).

Read—read orally to find answers.

Recite—discuss answers to the questions.

Reread—to check answers and write them down.

In pairs, one student acts as the reader, the other as the recorder. The recorder asks the questions and listens as the reader reads the relevant materials. Both discuss the answers, and the recorder writes down the ones the two agree on. Roles are then switched for the next section of the materials.

Whenever we ask students to read materials, we should have a purpose in mind and a framework that can help them understand the information. For example, we could ask students to identify the major concepts, issues, or perspectives in the passage. We can also interrogate the text by asking why the passage was written, what information could have been presented but was not, the perspective of the author, and the biases present (e.g., how much content is devoted to women in a particular textbook?).

Other Activities

1. One way to teach students social studies content is to play games such as Twenty Questions or Word Bingo. Design a game for a group of students to play that reinforces information they have previously been taught.
2. Modify a board game such as Snakes and Ladders or Monopoly to teach social studies information.
3. Evaluate a textbook that is used in the jurisdiction in which you will be teaching. Use the questions posed earlier in this chapter as a guideline.
4. Evaluate a textbook passage. Does it constitute good social studies curricular material for the intended grade level?
5. Choose a textbook passage and design an activity that will help students better understand it.

Notes

1. K. Egan, *Teaching as Story Telling* (London, ON: Althouse Press, 1986).
2. For information about teachers who use this approach, see http://ierg.net. There are lesson and unit plans using Egan's approach, information about projects, and a newsletter.

3. K. Egan, *Primary Understanding: Education in Early Childhood* (New York: Routledge, 1988); K. Egan, *Romantic Understanding: The Development of Rationality and Imagination, Ages 8–15* (New York: Routledge, 1990); K. Egan, *The Educated Mind: How Cognitive Tools Shape Our Understanding* (Chicago: University of Chicago Press, 1997); K. Egan, *Children's Minds, Talking Rabbits and Clockwork Oranges: Essays on Education* (New York: Teachers College Press, 1999); K. Egan, *An Imaginative Approach to Teaching* (San Francisco: Jossey Bass, 2005); K. Egan, M. Stout and K. Takaya, eds. *Teaching and Learning Outside the Box: Inspiring Imagination Across the Curriculum* (New York: Teachers College Press, 2007).

4. J. Kogawa, *Obasan* (Harmondsworth, UK: Penguin, 1981).

5. I. Wright, "Social studies and law-related education: A case study of the Japanese in British Columbia," *The History and Social Science Teacher* 22:4 (1987), pp. 209–214.

6. A variety of textbooks are designed to support social studies. The following sites contain information: Appleseed Publishing (www.appleseedpublishing.com); Pearson Education (http://cf.pearsoned.ca/school); Nelson Education (www.nelson.com); Oxford University Press Canada (www.oupcan.com). Other resources can be found in provincial curriculum guides or on Ministry/Department of Education websites. For example, the Atlantic provinces' curriculum guides contain unit plan outlines complete with accompanying resource material suggestions. The British Columbia Ministry of Education has a regularly updated website of resources to support the BC curriculum at www.bced.gov.bc.ca/irp_resources/lr.

7. P. Clark, "Between the covers: Exposing images in social studies textbooks," in R. Case and P. Clark, eds., *The Canadian Anthology of Social Studies* (Vancouver: Pacific Educational Press, 1999). For an examination of how women and First Nations people are depicted in textbooks, see P. Clark, "A nice little wife to make things pleasant: Portrayals of women in social studies textbooks," *McGill Journal of Education,* 40:2 (2005), pp. 241–265; and P. Clark, "Representations of Aboriginal people in English Canada history textbooks: Towards reconciliation," in E. Cole, ed. *Teaching the Violent Past: History Education and Reconciliation* (Lanham, MD: Rowan and Littlefield and Carnegie Council for Ethics in International Affairs, 2007), pp. 81–120.

8. J. Parsons, "Helping students learn how textbooks are written," *Canadian Social Studies.* www.quasar.ualberta.ca/css/CSS_35_1/classrom_tips.htm

9. P. McCabe, "Working with the textbook: How to enhance student motivation," *Social Education,* 67:5 (2003), pp. 274–277.

Glossary of Key Terms

Expository teaching—Imparting information to students in didactic ways (e.g., by lecturing).

SQ3R—An activity in which pairs of students *survey* **(S)** what is read, create *questions* **(Q)**, *read* **(R)** to find answers, *recite* **(R)** (discuss) answers to questions, and *reread* **(R)** to check answers before writing them down.

Story-telling approach—A procedure designed by Kieran Egan in which the important element in a topic is identified, binary opposites are found that capture the importance of the topic, content is organized into story form, and a conclusion is arrived at that attempts to resolve the conflict between the binary opposites.

CHAPTER 6

What Does This Word Mean? Concept Teaching and Learning

When we use expository methods, either we tend to assume that students understand key terms or we provide definitions. We do this because we realize that concepts provide the lenses through which we view and understand our world. They are classification devices we use to bring order to the myriad objects, ideas, and events that surround us. They are crucial to the understanding of any statement or question. We cannot answer the questions "Can this product be recycled?" or "Was that a fair decision?" unless we know what the concepts "recycle" and "fairness" mean. Of course, we would also need to be familiar with the concept of "decision," and we need to have information about the product. Building a solid understanding of a particular question or statement is one important reason for teaching concepts. There are also other reasons for emphasizing concept formation in social studies.

RATIONALES FOR TEACHING CONCEPTS

Teachers need to be clear about the concepts they are using. In our teaching, we want to use words clearly so that our students understand exactly what we're trying to say. Suppose we want to teach students about democracy as a political system. To communicate with our students, we have to be as clear as possible about the concept of "democracy," since it is a term that can be used to describe several slightly different political systems.

Clarity is also needed when we attempt to interpret what someone else means in a statement or question. Suppose the headline in a newspaper reads, "Toronto to grow over the next 10 years." We would need to read the article to know whether the headline is referring to growth in population, land area, or something else before we can understand it.

To demonstrate an understanding of a concept, it is not always enough for a student to be able to speak the word or even to use it loosely in a sentence, neither of which means that the student has grasped the concept. The first author used to teach about the "customs" and "traditions" of various peoples and had a vague idea that these two terms were somehow different. However, it was not until one of his practicum teachers was asked to differentiate between these terms in teaching about the customs and traditions of people in Mexico that he seriously contemplated these concepts. You will see the result of the student's deliberations, and the author's own, later in this chapter (in Activity 6-H).

Although the difference between custom and tradition may not strike you as significant, in many contexts meaning is of crucial importance. For example, disagreements about what is "fair," whether someone was "cheating," or whether certain people are "poor" often revolve around the meaning attached to the terms. A recent example of this concerns "marriage." To some Canadians, this term, especially when used in a legal context, should apply only to the union of a male and female; others argue that it should also pertain to same-sex couples. Sometimes, cases that revolve around the specific meaning of a term are determined in court by judges. For example, in a 2007 Supreme Court of Canada case, the court was asked to decide whether a same-sex partner could obtain survivor benefits from the Canada Pension Plan when the other partner died—did this infringe on his "equality" rights? What was to count here as "equality"?[1] Was gender an attribute? Juries also have to decide if, in a particular case, a criminal is guilty of "murder" or "manslaughter." They have to decide if the facts of the case add up to the definition of one or the other. Are the attributes of "murder" present in the facts of the case, or are the facts more like the attributes of "manslaughter"? As teachers, we have to decide what "excellent" means when assessing a given assignment, or whether the performance of a student merely constitutes "good."

In the classroom, the teaching of any subject or discipline requires us to introduce students to the key concepts of that discipline. For example, to understand history, students need to grasp concepts such as "causation," "time," "change," "continuity," and "chronology." To understand anthropology we need to comprehend and apply such concepts as "culture" and "ethnic." We must remember, too, that disciplines often use specific concepts in a technical way. People who are immersed in a particular discipline will share a common understanding of certain terms that are used somewhat differently in everyday language. For instance, we may use the word "teaching" to refer to any activity that promotes learning. This could include encouraging and helping students to learn from each other. However, members of the public might use it only in the sense of imparting information to students by means of direct instruction. (Direct instruction is also a concept that has a specific meaning in education.) In teaching physics, the concept "work" is used very differently from its normal usage. So, in teaching concepts that are relevant to a particular discipline, we have to be aware of how a specific concept is used in that discipline and whether that usage differs from the concept's usage in everyday language.

We must also be on the lookout for words that can fool us. For example, advertisements that promise something for "free" may not give you anything that is really free. Ads for such items as computers and cars often try to persuade you to make a purchasing decision by bombarding you with lots of technical jargon. You may remember that during the war in Iraq, we were informed that the dropping of bombs on Baghdad had caused "collateral damage"—meaning that civilians had been wounded or killed.

Words have different connotations for different people. Even though a school is, by definition, a place where learning is intended to occur, to some people "school" may have a positive or negative emotive force, evoking pleasurable memories or feelings of loathing. So, in clarifying meaning, we have to be on the lookout for words where the meaning is surrounded by emotional reactions. Even if we loathed our elementary school, it was still a "school."

Most importantly, how words are used affects actions. For example, if certain human beings are regarded as "non-persons," then they will be treated differently from "persons" who have specific legal rights because they are defined as "persons." If taking candy from the local convenience store is not defined by a young "thief" as "stealing," then the action may not be deemed wrong by the taker. If someone is deemed not to be a "refugee," then we may not allow that person to stay in Canada. If we label students as "behaviour problems," then we tend to act toward them in particular ways.

Finally, it is crucial to understand that if we didn't each have a shared understanding of the concepts used in our language, we would be unable to communicate with one another. The most powerful symbolic tool of humankind is language. We use words to communicate information, to influence others, to plan, and to record what is happening. We shape words, and words shape us. Thus, an understanding of the language—i.e., the concepts—of social studies is vital.

Activity 6-A

Note the concepts that are emphasized in the curriculum guidelines for your province or territory. To which disciplines are these concepts related? Are the listed concepts vital to understanding a particular discipline? Can you tell whether these concepts are supposed to be used in specialized ways? If so, what are these specialized ways?

WHAT ARE CONCEPTS?

Before we can teach concepts, we have to know what they are. A **concept** is a mental construct that provides the rules for giving meaning to a word. It is, in one sense, a definition. Thus, if I say, "By 'school' I mean a place where it is intended that learning occurs," I am stating that one of the rules for saying that X is a school is that learning is intended to occur there.

Suppose, however, that we're not sure what a school is. Then two tasks face us. First, we have to find out what the attributes or characteristics of "school" are and how this term relates to other concepts, such as teaching and learning. Second, we have to know that the building on the corner of the street is a *school* and not a factory, or a store, or a house. We not only have to know what the word means, but also have to be able to point out examples of the word. Now, imagine a young child is told by a parent that the building on the corner is a school and that one day she will go to it. What does the child know? All she knows is that this building of a certain shape and size is called a school. She may notice that it has other characteristics, such as a playground, or that children go there, but how does she know it's a school, rather than a community centre, or a daycare facility, or another type of building that has a playground and children? She needs to learn that certain activities go on in a school that differentiate it from other buildings. Eventually, as her knowledge of the concept "school" grows more complex, she will realize that a school's key characteristic is not its particular structure (one can have a school under a tree, in an open field, or in the basement of a home), but rather the activities that take place therein. In this case, the child would probably learn about "school" through her own experiences and interactions with parents, teachers, peers, and others. But, we cannot assume that all concepts are learned in this way. Often, teachers need to teach students directly the attributes that give a term its meaning. Sometimes this is fairly easy. For example, all the shapes below are examples of the concept "triangle."

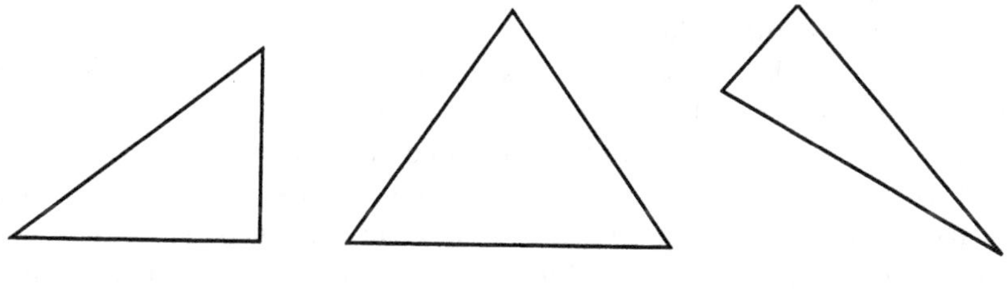

Even though each shape differs from the other two in some respect, they all share the same "triangle rules": closed plane figure, three straight sides. These characteristics or attributes are necessary for the pictured geometric shapes to be called triangles. Whether the triangle is blue and whether it has a dot in it are irrelevant attributes. A triangle must be a closed plane figure with three straight sides. Three sides alone do not make a triangle, nor does a closed plane figure *alone* make a triangle. A triangle must have *both* attributes. These are the **necessary** and **sufficient conditions** of a triangle.

Unfortunately, most concepts in social studies are not this easy to demonstrate, because most social studies concepts exist largely as abstractions that, unlike a triangle, cannot be drawn. It is not always possible to determine the necessary and sufficient conditions for a particular concept. There may well be fuzzy boundaries between one concept and a closely related one, even for seemingly simple concepts such as "family." Who constitutes a "family"? In a study in the U.S., primary-level students included grandparents as members of a "family," but did not always include aunts, uncles, and cousins, and found the concept of step-siblings very difficult to understand.[2] Even though all students will be familiar with "family," their meanings may be narrow and socio- or ethnocentric.

Activity 6-B

Which of the photos on the next page would qualify as examples of the concept of "family"? How do you know? What would you need to know if you are not sure whether the picture depicts a family? What does "family" mean? When you have answered these questions, refer to the Answers section.

TEACHING AND LEARNING CONCEPTS

From these activities, you have probably gained some idea of the difficulty that exists in teaching concepts. The idea that pointing at something and saying "That's an X" is all that is needed to teach a concept is inadequate. In the "family" example, merely pointing to a picture of a group of people seated around a kitchen table and saying "That's a family" would not be enough. Students have to learn that the concept is complex and can refer to different makeups of groups in which similar kinds of relationships exist. Different relationships pertain to different contexts. In some cultures, a family is always an extended one. In our society, a family can refer to a variety of social arrangements. In other contexts, "family" can refer to all members of a group, such as the cat family or the human family. Even though young students will have some understanding of "family" through their own experiences, this is often not enough. They need to be exposed to the various meanings of "family" and to realize that a "family" that is different from their own is still a "family."

The context in which a concept is used is significant. One colleague provides an example here. His son had learned the word "no" as a command, so "No, don't touch" made sense to him. When he began to read, he could point out the "no" at the start of certain signs, and when the rest of the sign was read to him, a message such as NO PARKING made perfect sense. NO THROUGH ROAD, however, was incomprehensible. While the words were no problem, the change in function from "no" as a command to "no" as information giving was something he didn't understand.

Photo 1

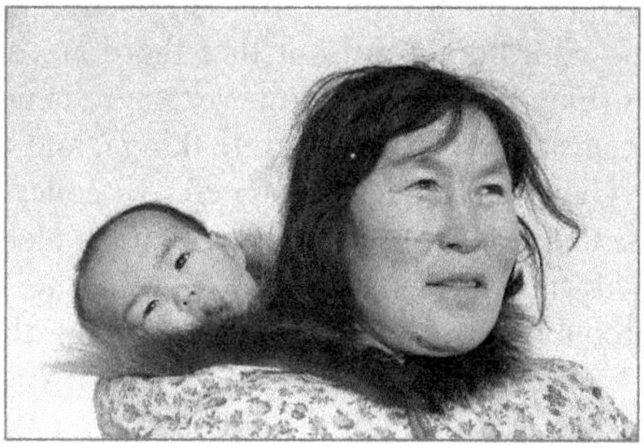

Photo 2

Photo 3

Photo 4

Photo 5

Photo 6

Another important matter is raised by the distinction between concrete and abstract. Some educators point out that there are concrete concepts (like "chair") and abstract ones (like "learning"). However, there is no such thing as a concrete concept. There are concepts that refer to concrete things, and there are concepts that refer to abstract ideas. The view that concepts that refer to concrete objects are easier to teach and learn than those that refer to abstract ideas can be also mistaken (the example of the triangle above notwithstanding). Teaching children the concept of "computer," a concrete object, is probably more difficult than teaching them the concept of "obey," a rather complex and certainly abstract idea. How would you define "computer" and "obey"? Which one is easier? True, children can become more sophisticated at using particular concepts as they acquire more experience with them, but this does not mean that concepts come in levels, with some more "simple" than others. The fact that some concepts must be taught in advance of others does not necessarily make these prerequisites simpler. And it must always be remembered that a new concept is easier to learn when students are familiar with concepts closely related to the new one and with the context in which the concept is being used.

As noted earlier, unlike "triangle," many concepts cannot be defined in terms of specific, necessary, and sufficient conditions unless we stipulate what these shall be. To return to the "marriage" example, in Canada, this term used to be applied only to the union of a male and a female who were deemed legally old enough to marry. The age limits had changed over time, but the one male and one female requirement had not.

Additional difficulties arise with value-laden concepts. As with other concepts, it may not be possible to define these in absolutely specific terms. The context in which they are used is crucial. The concept "good," for example, means different things when one is referring to a good person or a good painting. Although "good" is clearly a value term, not all value concepts are as easy to define. Concepts like "cheat," "discriminate," or "manipulate" are also evaluative in many contexts. In using them, we evaluate events, actions, and policies. We will examine value concepts in more depth in Part 3.

How, then, do we teach concepts? There are two procedures we can use. The first, **concept development**, helps students to classify information pertinent to a particular topic or question into relevant concepts. Using this procedure provides a conceptual structure for the study of a social studies unit or lesson. In some ways it is similar to a more formalized kind of webbing (see Chapter 4). The second, **concept attainment**, involves the direct teaching of one particular concept.

CONCEPT DEVELOPMENT

This procedure, developed by the late Hilda Taba,[3] consists of six steps that eventually lead to the testing of generalizations. We will concentrate on the first three steps and leave the last three until we discuss generalizations in Chapter 14.

Activity 6-C

1. List about 20 items you see in the following photographs of the Yukon.[4]
2. Select one item and see if any other items will go with it. If so, what could you call this grouping?

Photo 1

Photo 2

Photo 3

Photo 4

Photo 5

Photo 6

Photo 7

Photo 8

Photo 9

3. Continue this process until all of the items have been grouped into categories. It is permissible to have a category with only one item in it (e.g., there is only one example of the effects of permafrost, so this item could be in its own category). Create a chart showing your categories (see below). Explain why you have assigned each category a particular concept label. Review your categories and determine if any are too broad and/or encompass too much information. For example, a category labelled "geography" needs to be subdivided into other categories such as landscape and climate.
4. Look at your chart. Can any of the items in one group be placed into another group?
5. Can these items be classified in any other ways? Which concepts would be most appropriate for a study of the Yukon?
6. Get together with one or more of your peers and ascertain whether you agree on the labels. Does it matter if you disagree? Would different labels be equally useful for your purposes?

Category Label	Category Label	Category Label	Category Label	Category Label
[items]	[items]	[items]	[items]	[items]

This may appear at first to be a simple activity but, as we will see later in this chapter, the way items are classified differs according to the purposes of the classifier. Whether items are classified appropriately also depends upon the conceptual sophistication of the classifier.

IMPLEMENTING CONCEPT DEVELOPMENT

Students will need items to classify. Young children can classify actual objects or can be given pictures to manipulate physically. Older students can use pictorial or printed material. Students can form their own categories, or we can begin by asking them to state what they see and then list these items on the blackboard. Initially, we need to limit the number of items to between 10 and 20 so as not to overwhelm students. After the items are listed, ask the class to group and label them. We may have ideas as to how the items should be classified. Our students, however, may have different ideas, some of which reflect their unique way of seeing the world at their young age.

Activity 6-D

Below is a list of foods. In how many ways can you classify them?

Peach	Cheese	Pea
Egg	Meat	Milk
Melon	Eggplant	Carrot

1. If you were teaching beginning consonants, what classification scheme would be most appropriate?
2. If you were teaching about Canadian imports and exports, what classification scheme would be most appropriate?
3. If you were teaching about supermarkets/colours/vowel sounds/processed foods/ vitamin content/foods I like, what would be the most appropriate classification schemes?

Now write out a list of animals and have a number of students classify them in any way that makes sense to them. What classifications were applied? What reasons did students give for the schema they chose? Did any surprise you? (One author, when carrying out this activity, was presented with three schemas: bush meat, potential bush meat, and not bush meat. This student had lived in Kenya for many years.)

The classification scheme chosen will depend upon the purpose of the lesson and the perceptions of our students. If, using this list of foods, our purpose was to teach the concepts of "vegetable," "meat," "fruit," and "dairy," but our students wanted to instead classify the foods according to colour, our job would then be to encourage students to see that there are many different ways of classifying. We would then help them choose the one that is most useful in the context of our lesson.

When using the Taba Concept Development procedure, it is important to remember that even though the labels are concepts used to organize and classify information, the listed items are not necessarily attributes of the concept label. Clearly, in the above activity, a peach is not an attribute of the concept "fruit." A peach is an example of "fruit." The distinction should be kept clear. Students often give an example of the concept when asked for a definition. In using the Taba procedure, students may list items under a concept label when the items are not really examples of that concept label, but are related in some way. For example, if "climate" is the concept, items like "rain" and "snow" fit. "Umbrella" doesn't, even though umbrellas are linked to climatic conditions, since we can make inferences about the climate of a place if we see people using umbrellas.

Here is an example of a unit plan where Taba's concept development method is used.

Topic: Culture X

1. Show students a *representative* set of pictures (showing as many aspects of the culture as possible).
2. Have students list or draw items they see in the pictures. If students notice only major features, point out the details.
3. Have students tell you what they have noticed. List about 15 of the items on the blackboard. If students have drawn the items, collect the pictures and display them on a bulletin board.
4. Take the first item noted on the blackboard and ask whether anyone can see any item that would go with it, OR have groups of students classify the items and share their categories with the class.
5. Next, create a data-retrieval chart. For example, if the culture studied was that of the Tuareg, the chart might look like this:

DATA-RETRIEVAL CHART

Landform	Transportation	Climate	Dress	Daily Life	Other
Desert	Walking	Very hot during day	Long white robes	Children care for goats	

(*Continued*)

DATA-RETRIEVAL CHART continued

Landform	Transportation	Climate	Dress	Daily Life	Other
Oases	Camels	Sandstorms	Sandals	Worship each day	
Rolling sand dunes	Jeeps	Cold at night			
	Trucks	No rain			

6. Once a group of items has been identified, ask the students to label the group. When a concept label has been chosen, make sure that all the items are examples of the concept.
7. When the blackboard list has been classified, or groups of students have shared their concept labels and a common set of labels has been developed for the entire class, have the students copy the classification chart into their notebooks and/or make a large classroom display chart.
8. If students have collected other information derived from the initial presentation, have them fit it under the appropriate concept labels. Create new categories if an item does not fit the existing concepts. Ask students what information they think visitors from another planet would want to know about this culture. Would what they want to know fit into the categories above? Do the concepts developed help describe the culture of the people being studied?
9. Each student should now have a chart identifying the major concepts that are useful for the study of the culture. From this point forward, a number of different approaches could be taken. You could take each concept in turn and teach about it, or students could carry out inquiry activities (Chapter 8). The students themselves could choose a concept and questions for further study.
10. When students have completed their inquiries, collect their work, display it, and fill in the data-retrieval chart.
11. Ask questions that relate the various concepts to each other. ("What has climate got to do with dress?" "How is transportation adapted to the environment?" "What role do religious beliefs play in education, daily life, etc.?" "How and why do male and female roles differ?" "What roles do children play?") During this procedure, generalizations can be formulated (see Chapter 14).

CONCEPT ATTAINMENT

Concept attainment differs from concept development. Concept attainment is used to identify the attributes of a term (i.e., what the term means). Concept development is a technique for helping students to classify the myriad phenomena that are part of a place, event, institution, culture, and so on. Thus, in studying the Iroquois, students would list, group, and label what they saw in pictures and arrive at such concept labels as food, government, religion, and celebrations. If students were not clear about what their concept labels meant, then concept attainment would be used to give them a clearer sense of their meaning. For example, in studying Aboriginal people who live in Australia, students who have looked at pictures of what Aboriginals traditionally ate may fail to include wichiti bugs within their concept of food because they do not think bugs are food. Here, we would have to use a concept attainment method to show students that nutrition is one of the attributes of food, and wichiti bugs are very nutritious.

The Direct Teaching of Concepts

One obvious way to teach students the meaning of a concept is to give them a dictionary definition and have them apply this to the information they are learning. Or, students could instead look up the meaning of a word for themselves. Another direct and arguably more interesting method is to use a game. Here are some examples of game formats that can be used to teach concepts:

1. Two or more players identify examples of a concept drawn from the study of a particular culture or area of the world. Pictures provide the information.
   a) Players receive a matrix card with concepts identified at the top and letters of the alphabet running down the side.
   b) Players view a picture or series of pictures and attempt to place examples of the concept that begin with the letters of the alphabet listed on the matrix card.
   c) The winner is the player who can correctly complete the most matrix boxes. Here is an example:

SOUTH AFRICA

	Animals	Vegetation	Economic Activity	Landform
Letter A	Antelope			
Letter M			Mining	
Letter T				Table land
Letter D			Diamonds	

2. Another game involves the teacher stating a topic and a concept name. Students have to give an example of the concept; the example must be related to the topic. For example:

CANADA

Concepts	Examples
Vegetation	Douglas fir, maple
River	St. Lawrence, Saskatchewan, Thompson
Mineral	Gold, coal, nickel

3. In the Market Game, students learn the concepts of "supply," "demand," "profit," and "bargaining" and can learn other important economic concepts such as "surplus," "deficit," "profit/loss," and "monopoly." This is a simulation game, in that it simulates reality. Players make decisions within an economic system where their actions model what could occur in the real world.[5]

$5	$5	$5

$1	$1	$1	$1	$1

You will need to cut out the money and the "buyer" and "seller" cards. A collection of paper clips, erasers, pencils, and crayons will also be required.

	BUYER 1	BUYER 2	BUYER 3	BUYER 4
With $20 buy	Paper clips . . . 1	Paper clips . . . 2	Paper clips . . . 2	Paper clips . . . 1
	Erasers . . . 2	Erasers . . . 1	Erasers . . . 1	Erasers . . . 2
	Pencils . . . 3	Pencils . . . 3	Pencils . . . 1	Pencils . . . 1
	Crayons . . . 0	Crayons . . . 2	Crayons . . . 2	Crayons . . . 2
SELLER	SELLER 5	SELLER 6	SELLER 7	SELLER 8
	Paper clips	Erasers	Pencils	Crayons
	Sell 6	Sell 10	Sell 5	Sell 4
	Cost price $2 each	Cost price $1 each	Cost price $2 each	Cost price $2 each

a) Divide the class into four equal groups of buyers and four equal groups of sellers. Each group of buyers takes one buyer's card and collects $20 in money. Their objective is to purchase all the items listed on their card. Each group of sellers takes one seller's card and the requisite number of paper clips, erasers, pencils, and crayons. Their objective is to sell their products at a profit. Each sellers' group should set up a table and list the prices of the products. Prices can be changed at any time.

b) When the game has started, buyers go to the sellers' tables. Bargaining is permitted.

c) The game ends when a buyers' group collects all the items on their card. This buyers' group, and the sellers' group that makes the most profit, are declared winners.

d) When the game is over, ask the following questions:

Sellers:

- How did you decide what price to set for your products? (concept: profit/loss)
- Did you change the price during the game? Why or why not? (concept: profit/loss)
- Did you sell all your products? Why or why not? (concepts: supply/demand/cost/market)

Buyers:

- How did you decide what price you were willing to pay for each product? (concept: budget/needs/wants)
- Did you bargain with the sellers? Did bargaining result in lower prices? (concept: bargaining)

- Did you obtain all the items on your list? Why or why not? (concepts: supply/demand/need/want)

How could this simulation be adapted so that concepts of inflation, competition, and cooperation are introduced? To what student experiences could this game be related? Hughes presents an example that uses students' prior experiences to teach the concepts of supply and demand where both inductive and deductive methods are used.[6]

Teaching Concept Attainment

Activity 6-E

In order to fully grasp a concept, what must we be able to do? Read the following dialogue and try to ascertain what the teacher is doing to help the student fully grasp the concept of "(hot) desert."

TEACHER: Tell me, what is a desert?

STUDENT: A desert is a place where there is sand and it's hot.

TEACHER: Is this a desert? *[Shows a picture of the Sahara.]*

STUDENT: Yes.

TEACHER: Is this a desert? *[Shows a picture of a beach.]*

STUDENT: No, it's too small.

TEACHER: What about this? *[Shows a picture of Death Valley.]*

STUDENT: No. I can't see any sand.

TEACHER: Is the sandbox in the playground a desert?

STUDENT: No, it isn't big enough. A desert has to be big.

TEACHER: All of these are deserts. *[Shows pictures of deserts.]* Tell me what is the same about all of them.

STUDENT: They are all big and there's nothing growing. It's hot.

TEACHER: So, could this *[Death Valley]* be a desert?

STUDENT: Yes, I think so because there aren't any plants and it is very dry.

To understand a concept, students must be able to define the term (state the attributes that give the concept its meaning) as well as give examples of it (state what would qualify as an example of the concept). Thus, to understand the concept "island," students must know that a body of land is entirely surrounded by water, and that Newfoundland and Baffin are examples of this concept.

Simple diagrams can be used here.

A. Concept diagram:

WORD—Definition
    —Synonyms
    —Examples

B. Venn diagram.

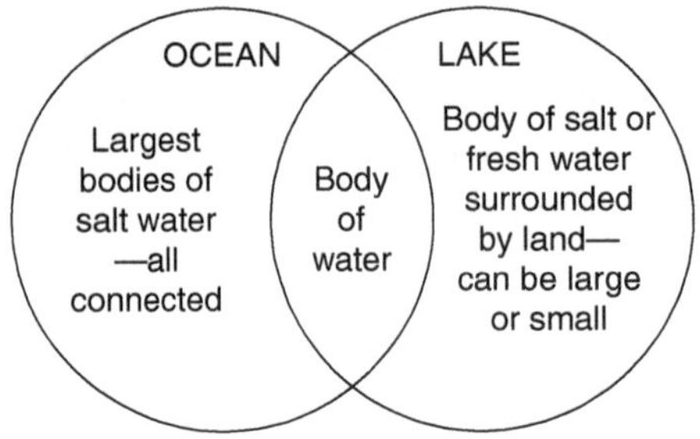

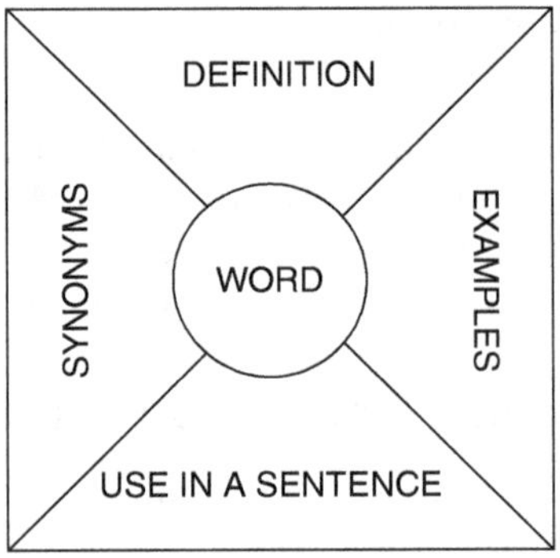

This diagram could be expanded to include ponds and seas.

As pointed out earlier, a simple way of finding out what a word means is to use a dictionary. Dictionaries, however, define words in their ideal form. Using a dictionary may be inadequate for the purposes of teaching concepts because (a) definitions are often circular (value = evaluation, and evaluation = judging on the basis of a value); (b) meanings in normal language are ambiguous or vague, and dictionaries cannot point out many of the complexities; and (c) dictionary definitions often lack precision. Using concept attainment procedures can help avoid these problems.

Activity 6-F

Below are three examples and one non-example of a particular concept. What might the concept be? After you have considered each of them, refer to the Answers section.

1. Jane Smith wanted to live in Canada. She went to the Canadian embassy in London, England, to apply to live in Canada. As she had the appropriate qualifications, she was accepted. Eventually, she became a Canadian citizen. Jane is an example of a/an ___________.
2. Liu Chan came to Canada as a graduate student. He liked being here and wanted to stay. However, he had to return to China in order to apply to live here. Eventually, he was accepted. Liu is an example of a/an ___________.
3. In the late 1880s, many families came to Canada to escape persecution and economic hardship in Eastern Europe. They intended to stay in Canada and create new lives for themselves. These families are examples of ___________.
4. Rajender Singh and his family came to Canada to visit friends and relatives. His family lived in Canada for nine months and then returned to India. Rajender Singh and his family are not examples of ___________.

Here are some suggested steps for teachers to follow when teaching concepts to students:

1. Having decided upon the concept to be taught, we must be able to define the term and know what would qualify as examples of the concept and what would count as

non-examples. The non-examples should be items that are closely related to the examples. It would be pointless to contrast "immigrants" with "skyscrapers"; rather, the first concept should be contrasted with examples of other people who come to stay in Canada—tourists, visitors, and diplomats, etc.—but who have no intention of settling here or becoming Canadian citizens. It would also help, where possible, to present a range of examples of the concept, some of which are more concrete than others, or more familiar to students. Examples and non-examples can be found in print, picture, or actual object form. We will also have to consider whether our students understand the concepts related to the one we plan to teach. If these concepts are not understood, we will have to teach them. Then we can teach the concept in an inductive way by proceeding as follows.

2. Show examples of the concept, and ask students if they can use one word (the concept) to describe all of the examples given (i.e., a guessing game). Ask, "Can you think of one word that would describe all of these?" Display non-examples and tell students that these are not examples of the concept. This may help make the game more interesting and may help students to make more reasoned guesses.
3. Once the students have guessed the correct concept name, ask them to state why the examples that have been given can be called by that name. This will lead them to note the attributes of the concept. Here, it is important to relate the concept to other concepts that are part of the students' prior experience.
4. Show the students additional examples and non-examples of the concept, and have them differentiate between them and state why they are examples or non-examples.
5. As an assessment procedure, the students could list the attributes of the concept, find examples and non-examples of the concept, and state why they are examples or non-examples.

Or we could use an expository method whereby we display the examples of the concept, state that these are examples of concept X, and present a definition. Ask the students what is similar about all of the examples given and help them to identify the attributes of the concept. Then carry out steps 4 and 5 above. For example:

Show students pictures of urban scenes. State, "All of these pictures are examples of the concept 'urban.'" Ask, "What have they all got in common?" Once the attributes of "urban" are listed, introduce some non-examples (e.g., a village and a house in the country) and tell them that these are not examples. Have the students state what attributes of "urban" are missing. Show the students some more pictures of urban and non-urban scenes and ask them to identify which are urban and which are non-urban. Have them give you their reasons. The students should list the attributes of the concept "urban." Finally, they could be given old magazines and be asked to cut out examples and non-examples of "urban" and paste them onto paper. Or, using a textbook, they could tell you on which pages pictures of urban scenes are depicted. Reasons for believing these pictures are examples of the concept "urban" could be discussed.

Older students can be introduced to more sophisticated examples, such as of "suburbs." Point out that the term "urban" has been modified to describe a phenomenon that is neither urban nor rural, but somewhere in between. We could ask students to think of other words that have been modified to describe situations in which the original word was not quite appropriate. Examples might include "war" and "civil war," or "book" and "booklet."

To help young students learn key concepts, we can pose the following types of questions:

- Can you name a kind of ___________?
- Can you give an example of a/an ___________?
- How are a/an ___________ and a/an ___________ alike?
- How are a/an ___________ and a/an ___________ different?
- How are ___________ all the same?

To help you clarify the meaning of the concept you wish to teach, ask yourself and your students the following sorts of questions:[7]

- With what terms is X (the concept you wish to teach) synonymous?
- Can X be classified as a kind of ___________?
- How does the meaning of X differ from the meaning of ___________ (which seems to be similar in meaning)?
- What are the attributes of X? Is ___________ a characteristic of things to which X refers?
- What different kinds of X are there? Is ___________ a kind of X?
- If I say something is an X, am I ascribing a positive or negative value to it?

Guidelines for Concept Attainment

A few key guidelines should be followed when leading concept attainment activities. First, research evidence suggests that it is better to present examples of the concept first and then have these examples remain in view (either in pictorial form or as printed statements) during the activity.[8] Second, the optimal number of examples presented simultaneously should be about four. Third, concepts having few critical attributes are easier to learn than those that have many. Finally, presenting examples and non-examples in verbal form increases the ease of concept attainment. This is because critical properties can be emphasized more easily through verbal means than pictorial ones.

Two major problems occur in concept learning: one is **overgeneralization**, and the other is **overdiscrimination**. Although young children may overgeneralize ("Anything that flies is a bird"), they are more likely to overdiscriminate ("That's not a bird, it's a sparrow"). There is evidence to suggest that a child's ability to determine differences among concepts develops earlier than the ability to determine similarities. While the tendency to overdiscriminate tends to decline with age, the tendency to overgeneralize does not.[9]

Although the ability to understand and use concepts increases with age, this does not mean that young children cannot deal with abstractions. Young children routinely use words such as "fair," "good," "cheat," and so on. Moreover, they understand the concept of "climate" in terms of hot/cold and wet/dry. Older children may be able to discuss wind force and air pressure. They understand these terms at their own developmental level and can be helped to develop conceptual abilities and knowledge through concept attainment activities. What follows are some variations on these activities.

Other Concept Attainment Activities

Another way to have students learn and demonstrate that they have grasped a concept is to have them use a concept map.[10] You can provide some of the information and have students fill in other boxes

Activity 6-G

Fill in the boxes and then share your work with others. Did you agree on the examples and description of war?

Concept Web

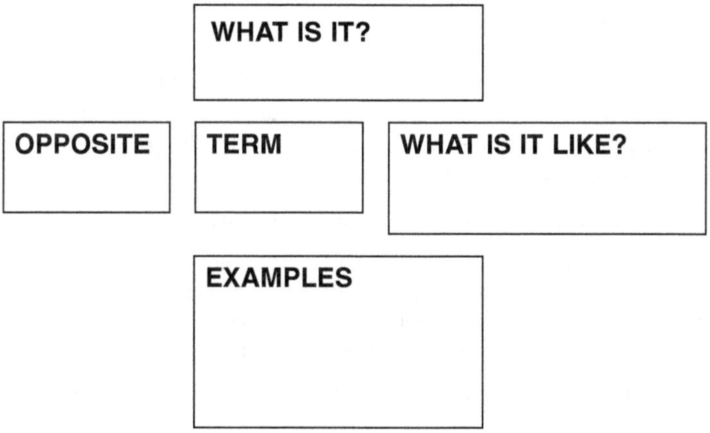

Activity 6-H

What one word could most appropriately be used in each of the following blanks? For a discussion of the concept, see the Answers section.

It is a __________ in this culture to make reed baskets. For centuries, mothers have taught their daughters to weave. When it appeared that modern technology would lead to the loss of this ancient craft, a revival of interest in this __________ occurred.

There has been a longstanding __________, based on a strong belief in male supremacy, of excluding women from important roles in Iranian society. When this __________ is flouted, there are serious repercussions.

Every year on October 3, the Smith family has held a birthday party for Grandma Smith. There is always a cake and presents. This family __________ has been practised for 82 years and is part of a larger cultural __________ of having parties on birthdays.

Every night John watches the television news. He does not expect his wife or children to do this, and he knows that he can change his behaviour at any time. This practice is not a __________.

Activity 6-I

Which of the following are examples of the exercise of "power," and which are examples of the exercise of "authority"? Once you have decided, turn to the Answers section.

a) The teacher tells the students to line up.
b) The captain of the baseball team says that Catrina can't pitch because she isn't as good as Rachel.
c) Some older children tell Billy to get out of the park.
d) Joel says, "If you don't give me your chocolate bar, I'll get you after school."
e) Mrs. Chan tells her daughter to take out the garbage.
f) A police officer tells Mr. Brown to pull his car off to the side of the road.
g) The school principal says that the teacher must attend the workshop on the new social studies curriculum.

From this activity you can see that agreements about meaning may not always be possible. As was pointed out earlier, we may argue about what a particular term should mean. When the meanings are in dispute, we can use critical thinking activities to help students figure out an appropriate meaning. Here is an example:[11]

Question: Was (David Thompson, Laura Secord, Louis Riel, Chief Dan George, etc.) a hero?

In groups, students discuss the characteristics of a hero. They identify people, both real and fictional, whom they think are heroes, and they list their characteristics. The lists are then shared and a class synthesis is created. Where there is disagreement, the characteristic is starred so that when the activity is completed, students can reconsider it.

Students then apply the characteristics to their hero by researching that person's life.

Characteristics of a hero	Hero's actions
Performs an amazing feat	
Possesses special abilities	
Overcomes obstacles	
Etc.	

From these activities you can see that although you and your students may use such words as "power" and "hero" in speech and may recognize them in print, mere use or recognition does not necessarily mean that the concepts are understood. As teachers, we have to ascertain whether our students have grasped necessary concepts and teach them if they have not. Note that many of the activities in this chapter can also be used to assess students on their understanding of a concept.

Other Activities

1. Design an activity to teach a primary-, junior-, or intermediate-level class a concept that you consider important to learn in the context of social studies. Give your reasons for choosing this particular concept. State in what context you will be teaching the concept and list the examples you will use and the questions you will ask. Try out your activity on a partner.

2. Formulate a lesson plan to teach the concept of "ceremony" to a primary-grade class.
   a) Define "ceremony."
   b) Choose examples that would be meaningful to primary-grade students.
   c) State how you would use these examples and how you might differentiate between "ceremony" and such closely related concepts as "celebration" and "ritual."
3. Write a lesson plan for a grade of your choice on a topic or concept that uses the Taba Concept Development procedure or a concept attainment model. Include the following:
   a) a rationale: Why teach concepts?
   b) objectives: What specifically do you want students to know and do?
   c) the materials you will use
   d) how you will begin the lesson
   e) the main body of your lesson: what you and the children will do and in what sequence; how the children will be organized (e.g., at individual desks or in groups)
   f) how you will end the lesson
   g) how you will evaluate student learning
   h) how you will follow up on the lesson; what you will do next
4. A teacher is using the Taba Concept Development procedure to introduce a unit about Japan. The students have viewed a video about the lives of a boy and girl in Tokyo and have listed what they saw. In groups, students are now categorizing and labelling the items. The teacher is working with one group. Critique the teacher's approach. For our assessment, see the Answers section.

TEACHER: I see you have *fish, noodles*, and *chopsticks* in one group. What is similar about these?

STUDENT: They all have to do with eating.

STUDENT: They're all food.

TEACHER: Well, what is the best label?

STUDENT: I think fish and noodles should go under *food* and the chopsticks should go somewhere else.

TEACHER: [To another student] What do you think?

STUDENT: Guess so. I wouldn't want to eat chopsticks.

TEACHER: So, what's similar about the food grouping?

STUDENT: They are all things you eat. They're good for you.

TEACHER: Where will the chopsticks go?

STUDENT: We've got a group here of pots, pans, knives, and stuff like that. It could go with them.

TEACHER: Do you remember in the videotape that the chopsticks had beautiful designs on them? Could they go with the group of items labelled *art?*

STUDENT: They could, but I think they fit better with the pots and things. They aren't like paintings.

TEACHER: Do you think your labels are OK?

STUDENT: I think so. If I were in Japan, I'd want to know about their food, how they cooked and ate it, and their art.

STUDENT: I think so too. If a Japanese person came here, she'd want to know what we ate.

Notes

1. *Supreme Court of Canada, Canada (Attorney General) v. Hislop,* 2007 SCC 10, 1.S.C.R. 429.
2. J. Brophy and J. Alleman, "Primary-grade students knowledge and thinking about families," *Journal of Social Studies Research,* 29:1 (2005), pp.18–22.
3. H. Taba, M. Durkin, J. Fraenkel, and A. McNaughton, *A Teacher's Handbook to Elementary Social Studies* (Reading, MA: Addison-Wesley, 1971).
4. For more photos go to the Yukon Government tourism website, www.yukoninfo.com/photogallery, and the Yukon First Nations Tourism Association website, www.yfnta.org.
5. A variation on this game can be found in D. Brozik and D. Zapalski, "Interactive classroom economics: The Market game." *Social Education,* 90:6 (1999), pp. 278–282, in which students have a variety of livestock to barter for other livestock that they require.
6. A. Hughes, "Getting the idea: An introduction to concept learning and teaching in social studies," in A. Sears and I. Wright, eds. *Challenges and Prospects for Canadian Social Studies* (Vancouver: Pacific Education Press, 2004), pp. 241–242.
7. Adapted from J. Coombs, "Critical thinking and problems of meaning," in I. Wright and C. LaBar, eds., *Critical Thinking and Social Studies* (Toronto: Grolier, 1987).
8. P. Martorella, "Knowledge and concept development in social studies," in J. Shaver, ed., *Handbook of Research on Social Studies Teaching and Learning* (New York: Macmillan, 1991).
9. H. Klausmeier and F. Hooper, "Conceptual development and instruction," in F. Kerlinger and J. Carroll, eds., *Review of Research in Education 2* (Itasca, IL: Peacock, 1974).
10. R. Schwartz and T. Raphael, "Concept of definition: A key to improving students' vocabulary," *The Reading Teacher* 39:2 (1985), pp. 198–203.
11. For an example of how this could be used at the upper elementary level, see J. Brien and S. White, "Students explore their conceptions of the heroic," *Social Education* 63:4 (1999), pp. M7–9.

Glossary of Key Terms

Concept—A mental construct that delineates the rules for giving meaning to a term.

Concept attainment—A procedure in which students use examples and non-examples of a concept to identify the concept's attributes.

Concept development—A procedure in which students list, group, and label information to develop concepts useful for organizing the study of a particular topic. Eventually, this leads to the development of generalizations.

Necessary conditions—Those attributes, characteristics, or rules of a concept that are required to give the term its meaning (e.g., two necessary attributes of a triangle are that it has three sides and that these sides are straight. However, these two attributes are not sufficient to give "triangle" its meaning.). (See **Sufficient conditions**.)

Overdiscrimination—Treating a member of a class of things as if it did not belong to that class (e.g., "That's not a dog; it's a poodle.")

Overgeneralization—Concluding that because A is a B, that all As are Bs, when the data do not warrant it.

Sufficient conditions—The required attributes of the concept that give it its meaning. Thus, to say that a triangle, in the geometric sense, has three straight sides and is a closed plane figure is sufficient to establish the shape as a triangle. These are the sufficient conditions for a shape to be called a triangle.

CHAPTER 7

What's the Right Question? Questions and Questioning

"Why should I read this chapter? Surely it is easy to ask questions; I ask questions all the time."

Questioning is an integral part of life and especially classroom life. It is estimated that teachers ask hundreds of questions every day.[1] We do so to assess student knowledge (Is it possible to assess students without asking questions?),[2] to encourage participation and thinking, to allow students to express themselves, and to keep students focused on a lesson. But this does not mean that every question is significant, interesting, asked appropriately and clearly, adapted to the students' level of understanding, sequenced logically, or posed in a way that encourages students to think critically or ask their own questions.

Activity 7-A

List 10 questions that could be asked about this photo of a grave marker in Atlin, BC.

Presumably, you are familiar with *what?, why?, where?, when?,* and *how?* questions. These are the questions with which we are most familiar and they are very useful questions. But in your list above, did you include any of the following types of questions? (Note that the first question in each category relates to the photo of the grave marker in Atlin, BC; the others may not.)

TYPES OF QUESTIONS

Empirical Answers are in the form of statements about what *is, was,* or *will be* the case. This does not mean that the statements will *necessarily* be true or correct. We may never know the truth about some matters. Descriptive:

- How did Charley William Rudolf die?
- How many of them are there? Is it raining?
- How does S use the term X?
- What does S value?

Comparative:

- How is this grave marker different from or similar to ones in your local graveyard or cemetery?
- Has X changed?

Historical: These questions are similar to descriptive questions, but they concern the past. Chapter 10 provides examples of significant historical questions.

- What was happening in Atlin in the 1940s?
- When did the first people inhabit North America?

Causal/Correlational:

- Why are the majority of grave markers made of wood?
- What caused that? Why did X happen?
- What has the climate got to do with the vegetation?

Predictive:

- What is likely to happen to these grave markers in the future?
- What would happen if . . . ?

Methodological:

- How can we find out more about Charley William Rudolf?
- Where can we locate the answer? How can we tackle this problem?

Relevance:

- What has this grave marker got to do with me? How does this relate to my life?

Conceptual Answers are statements about what X means.
- Does A mean the same as B? (Does "grave marker" mean the same as "tomb"?)
- Is A an example of B? (Is this landscape an example of a prairie?)
- Is A an attribute of the term B? (Is a peak an attribute of a mountain?)

Value Answers are in the form of a judgment where intellectual standards are applied.

- Are our observations about this photo reliable?
- Are the data believable?
- Is concept X used appropriately?
- Have we got enough evidence to justify this conclusion?

Or, answers are in the form of a judgment where other values (ethical, environmental, religious, aesthetic, prudential) are applied. These will be addressed in Part 3.

- Should grave markers be preserved for future generations?
- Is X good?
- Is A better than B?
- Should S do X?
- What should be done about X?

Activity 7-B

Now pose one question for each category above using the following picture.

We can ask questions to get students to state what they already know and also to stimulate further learning and thinking, as illustrated by this next set of questions. (Again, note that the first question pertains to the photo; the others may not.)

Questions to introduce discussion: Would you like to attend this school? What do you see here? If this picture had been taken 10 years later, what do you think might have changed? What solutions are there to this problem?

Questions to help analyze human behaviour: Why are these students sitting with their hands behind their backs? What are these people doing? Why are they doing this? Have you done anything like this? How is it done?

Questions to help identify human feelings: How do these students feel? Why do they feel this way? Have you ever felt this way? When? Do all people have the same feelings in this situation?

Questions to provoke further research: What questions about this photo could be asked? How could answers be found? Is there a problem here? What could be done to solve it? What would we need to know? If you had this problem, what would you do? Why? Are some problems easier to solve than others? Why?

Questions to encourage geographic inferences: What can we say about the location of this classroom? Is it hot or cold? Wet or dry? Is it similar to our own neighbourhood, province, or country? How have people adapted to the environment? How have people adapted the environment to suit themselves?

Questions to encourage historical inferences: What do you think this classroom would have looked like 50 years ago? Would people have done things differently 100 years ago? What events in the past caused this situation/scene to appear as it does today?

Questions to introduce sequential relationships: What happened before this photo was taken? What do you think will happen next? Why?

Questions to encourage the making of connections: Is the wearing of uniforms related to an authoritarian society? How is the new well in the village related to changes in the villagers' way of life? What change in your community has affected how you live?

Questions to broaden understanding and encourage summarization: What conclusions can we draw from this photo? Can you make up a sentence to summarize this? If ___________ occurred, what might happen? What does this tell us?

Questions to encourage clarity: Can you say more about the wearing of uniforms? What do you mean by X?

You will notice that just as there are different types of *questions,* there are also different types of *reasoning* required to answer those questions.

Activity 7-C

Go back to your list of questions in Activity 7-B.

1. Which questions would be easiest to answer? Why?
2. Which questions would be most difficult to answer? Why?
3. What types of reasoning would be required to answer the easiest and most difficult questions? (Reasoning consists of inferring, analyzing, evaluating, interpreting, comparing, conceptualizing, and the like.)
4. What intellectual standards (accuracy, plausibility, weight of evidence, clarity, logic, fair-mindedness) would you need to apply in order to answer both the most difficult and the easiest questions?

LEVELS OF QUESTIONS

Clearly, those questions to which we already know the answers are easy. If we want to find out what students know, then questions of recall are important. Frequent questioning can lead to gains in student learning.[3] But recall questions don't require any of the reasoning skills identified above. And questions should generate student thinking, not just the recall of specific information.

Many educators use **Bloom's taxonomy**[4] to identify different levels of questions and the thinking abilities necessary to answer questions at each level. Sanders,[5] who adapted Bloom's taxonomy, lists the following categories. (We use **Sanders's classification** because it divides Bloom's Level 2 into two separate categories, and we find it useful to differentiate Translation and Interpretation. Bloom places both of these under Comprehension.) A typical question is included for each of the categories.

1. **Memory**
   The student recalls previously learned information.
   "Who is the prime minister of Canada?"
2. **Translation**
   The student changes information into a different symbolic form or language.
   "What is the point the artist makes in the cartoon?"
3. **Interpretation**
   The student discovers relationships among facts, generalizations, and concepts. Interpretation involves a reordering or rearrangement of material. It makes use of comparative and cause-and-effect relationships.

   "Prior to European contact, what were the differences and similarities between the shelters of the Haida and Huron peoples? What might account for these?"
4. **Application**
   The student performs a task or solves a problem that requires the application of previously learned information.

   "Use your inquiry skills to answer the following question."
5. **Analysis**
   The student solves a problem by analyzing it into its constituent parts.

   "How did Wolfe's troops defeat those of Montcalm in the Battle of the Plains of Abraham in 1759?"
6. **Synthesis**
   The student solves a problem that requires original, creative thinking. Synthesis is the assembly of elements and parts so as to form a whole. Synthesis questions encourage students to engage in imaginative, original thinking.

   "How would you solve the problem of litter in the school playground?"
7. **Evaluation**
   The student makes a judgment of good or bad, right or wrong, according to particular criteria or standards such as the intellectual values of

   a) **empirical** accuracy
      "Have we got the correct measurement?"

b) **conceptual** appropriateness
"Are we using 'equal treatment' here to mean 'exactly the same treatment'?"

c) **logical** relationships and internal consistency
"Is the evidence that constitutes this explanation consistent?"

d) other **value** principles or standards (e.g., ethical or environmental)
"Should Canada give aid to people who are starving in Darfur?"

McComas and Abraham[6] provide an extra dimension to this taxonomy. They divide each category into questions that are convergent (requiring little or no thinking, such as the recall of a single piece of information) and divergent (requiring information to be applied so that the questions are broader and lead to multiple answers and thus more thinking).

An example of a convergent question would be, "What is the image on Canada's flag?" A divergent question would be, "Is the maple leaf the best symbol for Canada's flag?"

Activity 7-D

State whether each of the following examples is an empirical, conceptual, logical, or value question. Specify its level according to Sanders's categorization. Answers are in the Answers section.

a) In what year did Cartier build a settlement in what today is Quebec?
b) What are the major goals of your provincial or territorial social studies curriculum guidelines and what reasons are given for them?
c) What were the causes of World War II?
d) What is the population of Toronto? (Use the graph provided to answer the question.)
e) Do equity and equality mean the same thing?
f) How is the government of Canada similar to and different from that of the USA?
g) How could Canada help to alleviate starvation in Sudan?
h) Should First Nations people have the right to operate their own schools?
i) Should you hit someone whenever you feel like it?
j) If you believed killing was wrong and that capital punishment was a form of killing, would you then believe that capital punishment was wrong?

While Sanders's adaptation of Bloom's taxonomy can be useful in focusing attention on different levels of questions, there are some problems with it. First, it should not be assumed that it is more difficult to answer "higher-level" questions than "lower-level" ones. The question "Should you hit someone whenever you feel like it?" is an evaluation question, yet is easy to answer for anyone with any moral sensitivity. Second, recall questions can vary in their level of difficulty. Some require recall of a specific fact; others require recall of complex bodies of information. Third, merely stating that a question is at a particular level says nothing about the significance of the question. Fourth, just because we ask a higher-level question does not mean that students will reply with higher-level answers.[7] Fifth, the taxonomy does not mean that we should start with lower-level questions and then work up the hierarchy to evaluation questions. It might be perfectly sensible to start with an evaluation question, especially if students know the basic facts. In our view, rather than relying solely on Bloom's taxonomy or Sanders's adaptation of it to tell us something about what will be required to answer a question, we should instead use the following Question Checklist. And we should do this because we ought to plan the questions we ask just as we plan other aspects of a lesson. Note that not every checklist question is appropriate for every question you pose.

1. What type(s) of questions are most relevant and important for the lesson (i.e., empirical, conceptual, or value)?
2. Can I ask a number of different kinds of questions?
3. How many recall questions am I asking?
4. Is the question significant enough to be asked?
5. Will the question attract students' attention and engage them?
6. Will the question encourage student participation?
7. Will the question encourage students to ask their own questions?
8. Will the question challenge the students to think?
9. Is the question clearly worded?
10. Is the question sequenced so that the previous or next question is logically related to it?
11. Is the question adapted to the students' level of understanding?
12. Can the students who will be attempting to answer the question answer it in a satisfactory way?
13. What information will be needed to answer the question?
14. Is the information needed to answer the question available? If so, where?
15. What concepts (included in the question statement and in the information needed to answer it) will have to be understood to answer the question?
16. What sorts of procedures could be used to answer the question? Do students know how to carry out these procedures? Which is the best procedure?
17. What sorts of thinking tasks will students have to perform? Will they have to infer, generalize, and/or hypothesize? Are they capable of performing these tasks?
18. What would qualify as a good answer to the question? To what intellectual or other standards does the question appeal?

The last question will involve considerable critical reflection. Students should be introduced to some of the intellectual standards that pertain to evaluating the truth, or believing or accepting various types of claims. For example, some of the ways in which we can judge the appropriate use of a concept appear in Chapter 6. In Chapter 8, you'll find intellectual standards relevant to judging the accuracy and believability of empirical claims. In Part 3, some standards for justifying personal and social value claims are discussed.

Activity 7-E

Apply the Question Checklist above to a question of your choice or to one or more of the following questions, all of which are stated or based on objectives in recent provincial social studies curriculum guides.

1. What do people do in order to live together in groups peacefully? (Grade 1, British Columbia)
2. What does the word "respect" mean? (Grade 1, Atlantic provinces)
3. Is the product something people need or something they want? (Grade 2, Atlantic provinces)
4. How do the media influence your perceptions of people and places elsewhere in the world? (Grade 3, Manitoba)
5. To what extent do recreation and tourism foster appreciation of Alberta's natural regions and environment? (Grade 4, Alberta)
6. What global factors influenced the fur trade in Canada? (Grade 5, Manitoba)
7. Why do we need authority? (Grade 6, Saskatchewan)
8. How did the Catholic Church influence the life of First Nations people and French settlers in New France? (Ontario, Grade 7)

Activity 7-F

Now consider the following questions for a Grade 4 class that is studying the early exploration of North America. Decide which is the best question or, if you can't pick one, which are the better questions. State your reasons.

a) What was the sextant used for and how was it used?
b) Suppose you set sail from Europe to North America in the early 1500s. How would you know where you were?
c) Here is a picture (of a sailor using a sextant). What is he doing? What is the instrument he is using?
d) If sailors in the 1500s had a global positioning system, how would this have affected the exploration of North America?
e) Let's suppose you are sailing from Europe to North America in the 1500s, and you have a compass. What else would you need to determine the direction in which to sail, and how would you learn that information?
f) What's a sextant?
g) This is a sextant (show picture). What do you think it is used for?

CONSIDERATIONS IN POSING QUESTIONS

Several other important points are to be made about questions and questioning. It is clear that the sort of questions we ask will depend upon our objectives. If we want students to recall specific information, then a clearly worded recall question is needed. If we want students to generate a lot of different information, or pose many specific questions, then a broad general question is appropriate. For example, asking the question "What was life like in a fur-trading fort in 1750?" may lead not only to information being given by students but also to questions such as, "Where did people go to the bathroom?" (a serious question asked seriously by a Grade 5 student).

Asking Questions Orally in the Classroom

When we are orally asking questions in a classroom, there are basically two ways of operating:

Individual designated: "Saul, what is ___________?"

Group designated:

a) "Class, what is ___________? Saul, please answer."

b) "Class, what is ___________?" *[Student who is not designated by the teacher spontaneously answers.]*

c) "Class, what is ___________?" *[Whole class responds en masse.]*

Each of these procedures has its advantages and disadvantages.

Individual When a teacher poses a question directly to a student rather than to the whole class the rest of the class may not listen to the answer. A way of avoiding this is to ask another student whether the first student had the right answer.

Teacher: Raoul, when did Stephen Harper become prime minister of Canada?

Raoul: In 2006.

Teacher: Susan, is Raoul correct?

Susan: Yes.

Teacher: Joel, are you sure it wasn't 2007?

Joel: I don't think so. . . . I'm not sure.

Teacher: Who in the class is sure? Marie?

Marie: It was in 2006.

Then, to further the questioning, we could ask what responsibilities a prime minister has and have several students provide their answers.

A major disadvantage of individually asked questions is that favouritism can prevail if only certain individuals are called upon by the teacher. (This can be insidious if the favouritism is based on ethnicity, gender, class, or the presumed mental or physical capabilities of a student.) Exclusion of students in a question-and-answer session should be avoided at all costs unless there is a compelling reason for it (such as when a student is experiencing some emotional upset and needs to be left alone for a while).

Group The advantage here is that the entire class is involved initially—every student has the opportunity to answer. The disadvantages are that once a student is chosen to answer the question the rest of the class may not pay attention to the answer given, and, if an answer is to be given spontaneously, those who know the answer immediately will foreclose on those who need time to think. However, the procedure outlined above can engage more students.

When time is required for students to reflect, then the teacher should provide adequate "wait time" (sometimes referred to as "think time"). Morgan and Saxton[8] state that when we find it hard to wait it is because we are not used to silences, or because we think the question is too hard or not well posed. However, when we do pose questions that demand some thought and we do provide adequate time for students to formulate an answer, then students tend to give longer answers, more students volunteer responses, and student answers are more thoughtful.

One way in which students can be involved in a question-and-answer activity is to use the following cooperative learning strategy. The class is divided into groups of three to five, and each group member is given a number. Each group should be representative of the composition of the class (in ability, gender, ethnicity, etc.). Each group discusses the answer to a question. The teacher then calls upon all students with a particular number (e.g., all number 3s), and designates one of them to provide the answer. This procedure has several advantages. Higher achievers are willing to share their knowledge as they want their group to do well, and lower achievers are likely to listen carefully as they might be called upon to give the answer. Cooperation amongst students is also enhanced. Another simple strategy is Twenty Questions or Suchman's Yes/No technique (see page 295).

Children should be rewarded when their answers are correct. Avoid saying "good" or "OK" after every answer, as such a verbal cue will quickly become meaningless. Also avoid saying "No, you're wrong." Instead, say, "That's not quite right; can you clarify that a little more?" or ask for another student's help. When the correct answer is finally provided, ensure that the student who originally gave the wrong or incomplete answer is now aware of the correct answer. And watch your body language, as this can give students clues to how you are reacting to their responses.[9]

Student Posing of Questions

Young children are full of questions, but their inclination to ask them seems to fade away the longer they are in school. How can we encourage children to continue to be inquisitive as they grow older? Our attitude helps here, as does the classroom climate we foster (see Chapter 9). If we ask good questions and encourage students to ask good questions, then students are more likely to think about their own questions.[10] One way is to use the familiar questions "What do I already know about X?" "What would I like to find out about X?" and "What questions do I need to ask to find out about X?" Another idea is to have groups brainstorm questions about a topic, then share the questions and decide which ones would be best. In pairs, students could pose questions about a passage they have read, exchange questions, and answer them. They should then judge the questions they have asked using criteria they have generated (a list similar to the Question Checklist on page 81 could serve as the criteria). Having students interview others can also hone their questioning skills (see Chapters 10, 19, and 20), as can having them interview other students who role-play a particular character.

Assessing the Answers

Dantonio and Beisenherz[11] provide some criteria for assessing student responses. These include ensuring that the answer is clear, accurate, appropriate, supported with evidence where necessary, and shows awareness (where appropriate) that other points of view are possible.

Other Activities

1. Ask a number of questions about your classroom or a local parking lot, street, or other location. Take one particular question and list the ways in which this question could be extended. Evaluate your questions for their clarity and significance.

2. Pick a specific question from the social studies curriculum and analyze it using the criteria provided in this chapter.
   a) What sort of question is it (empirical, conceptual, value)?
   b) What concepts would students first need to grasp in order to answer the question?
   c) What information would students need to answer the question?
   d) What types of reasoning would students need to demonstrate?
   e) What would qualify as a reasonable answer? To what intellectual standards would you appeal to justify your claim that you had a reasonable answer?

Notes

1. W. McComas and L. Abraham, Asking more effective questions. www.edu/programs/cet/private/pdfs/usc/Asking_Better_Questions.pdf
2. It is possible to word assessment tasks in other than question form. For example, rather than asking, "What are the seven levels of Sanders's taxonomy?" we could ask, "State in your own words what the seven levels of Sanders's taxonomy are." Same task, just different wording.
3. W. Wilen, "Exploring myths about teacher questioning in the social studies curriculum," *The Social Studies* 92:1 (2001), p. 27.
4. B. Bloom, ed., *Taxonomy of Educational Objectives: Handbook 1—Cognitive Domain* (New York: David McKay, 1956).
5. N. Sanders, *Classroom Questions: What Kinds?* (New York: Harper and Row, 1966).
6. McComas, *op cit,* pp. 2–5.
7. W. Wilen, p. 28.
8. N. Morgan and J. Saxton, *Asking Better Questions* (Markham, ON: Pembroke Publishers, 1994), p. 83.
9. *Ibid.*, pp. 96–103. The authors also note other behaviours we ought to avoid, such as saying, "Yes, but . . . " or posing rhetorical questions.
10. *Ibid.*, pp. 112–114.
11. M. Dantonio and P. Beisenherz, *Learning to Question, Questioning to Learn* (Boston: Allyn and Bacon, 2001), p. 42.

Glossary of Key Terms

Bloom's/Sanders's Taxonomy:

Analysis—Breaking information into separate elements.

Application—Use of previously learned information to solve a new problem.

Evaluation—Judging information, plans, decisions, and objects.

Interpretation—The discovery of relationships between information.

Memory—The recall of information.

Synthesis—Assembling elements of information into a new whole.

Translation—Changing information from one form or language to another.

Conceptual—Statements or questions about what a word means.

Empirical—Statements or questions about what *was, is,* or *will be* the case.

Group designated question—A question posed to a group.

Individual designated question—A question posed to one person.

Value—Statements or questions about an evaluation of something, or about what *should be,* or what *should be done*. Example: "What sort of world would be best to live in? What should be done to bring about this world?"

CHAPTER 8

What's the Right Answer? Helping Students Answer Empirical Questions and Develop Intellectual Standards

Having students pose questions and posing questions lies at the heart of teaching. We could just tell students what the answer is to a question—and, in certain contexts, this may well be sufficient. But if we wish students to learn for themselves and think about what and how they learn, we also need to have students answer questions by hypothesizing what they think the answer is and then checking their **hypothesis** to ascertain whether it is supported. This procedure, called inquiry learning and teaching, is the focus of this chapter.

In the social studies literature, **inquiry** sometimes refers to any procedure whereby students find answers to questions. Thus, looking up the answer in a textbook to a simple and specific question could constitute inquiry. In this case, the defining attributes of inquiry are that the question is beyond the recall level, according to Sanders's taxonomy (see Chapter 7), and that the student has to find the answer by looking it up in resource materials or by asking someone. At times, this is a worthwhile activity, which we label as library research. In this chapter, however, inquiry will be used to denote a procedure in which students generate hypotheses about the answer to a question, and then test these hypotheses by locating, interpreting, analyzing, and evaluating information. The difference between library research and inquiry may be subtle. Rather than asking a question (and if students don't know the answer, having them locate it), students *hypothesize* what the answer is and then see if they are correct or not. This creates a more interesting activity as students ask themselves, "Am I right or wrong?" Usually inquiry is not used for single empirical questions; it is used for broader questions where there might be multiple hypotheses.

Sometimes answers will be known (Where did the stones used to build the pyramids in Egypt come from?). Sometimes there will be a partial answer (What toys did children play with in ancient Egypt?), but sometimes the answer can only be hypothesized, and some hypotheses will be more plausible than others (How were the pyramids built?). Sometimes a test can be performed to ascertain the answer (Could the pyramids have been built by using gigantic kites to lift the blocks of stone into place?). Sometimes there is no known test to prove or disprove a hypothesis (Did creatures from another planet build the pyramids?). Once a question has been posed that demands an empirical answer (that is, the answer will be a statement about *what is, was,* or *will be* the case), hypotheses are generated. Hypotheses are guesses about what the answer will be. We hypothesize that X is the answer and then we test this to see if it is supported.

RATIONALES FOR INQUIRY

Similar to all teaching methodologies, underlying the use of inquiry procedures are beliefs about how children learn, what constitutes knowledge, and what the aims of education should be. In Activity 8-A, you are asked to identify those beliefs that underlie inquiry procedures. In turn, these beliefs provide rationales for the use of inquiry procedures. For example, one of the assumptions on which inquiry learning is based is that students are more likely to take ownership of what they learn. If you believe this is a significant educational objective, then it provides a reason for using an inquiry procedure.

Activity 8-A

If you use an inquiry procedure, which of the following assumptions might you be making? When you have made your choice, refer to the Answers section.

a) All knowledge is absolute.

b) Children learn best when they are finding out their own answers.

c) In a democracy, people have to make decisions. Decision making necessitates the analysis and evaluation of conflicting evidence.

d) Children learn best when they are told the answer.

e) Children learn self-confidence when discovering knowledge for themselves.

f) Children by nature are inquirers.

g) Children learn to think by being taught the standards and procedures of good thinking.

h) Knowledge is a product of continuing inquiry and experimental testing, hence open to re-examination, renewal, and change.

i) Children remember what they've discovered for themselves better than what they've been taught directly.

j) Children need to be told what the right answers are so that they don't waste their time finding information. It is the teacher's job to know.

An Inquiry Method

Suppose you are interested in finding out what motivated your peers in your social studies methods class to become teachers. In that case, the following questions need to be asked as the inquiry procedure is implemented.

1. **Question:** What motivated my peers in my social studies methods class to become teachers? Is the question clear? Do you know what the terms used in the question mean?
2. **Hypothesis:** What do you think the answer(s) is/are?
3. **Organization and data collection:** How will you find out whether or not your hypothesis/hypotheses is/are supported? What information will you need? If you decide to ask your peers, how will you do this? What questions will you ask? How many of your peers will you question? Will you orally question them or use some kind of survey? How can you be sure that your data collection is reliable? Will you work alone or would working in a group be more efficient? If you work with others, how might various tasks be shared?
4. **Data analysis:** How might the information be classified, interpreted, and evaluated? What skills and abilities would you need to make use of the data?
5. **Checking the hypothesis:** Is the hypothesis supported by the information? What will you do if a) your hypothesis is not supported? or b) your conclusion is so tentative that you can neither accept nor reject your hypothesis?
6. **Conclusion:** How might you report your conclusion?

Activity 8-B

Carry out the above activity. Compare your conclusions and the way you went about carrying out your survey with your peers. Is there one right way of doing this survey?

In this inquiry procedure there are several important factors to consider.

The Question Make sure students understand the question, especially the concepts contained in it. For example, to answer the question "What motivated the first Europeans to explore North America?" students would need to clarify the term "motivation" and understand that various sorts of mental states—fear, greed, and curiosity—can motivate human behaviour. Without this clarification, the next step would be pointless.

Hypothesizing Once the question has been clarified, students should hypothesize what they think the answer will be. A simple way to start is to have students list what they know about the topic being studied. They can then use this list as the basis for their hypotheses. All hypotheses should be accepted, even if we think they're wrong. One of the reasons for using inquiry strategies in the classroom is that students find it more interesting and challenging to test hypotheses than to merely look up answers in a book—or to rely on a teacher.

Hypothesizing depends upon students' previous knowledge and experiences. It would be pointless to have students hypothesize about life in Mongolia if students had never heard of Mongolia, just as it would be pointless for them to hypothesize about "motivation" if they did not understand the term. The next activity is designed to show that the quantity and quality of background knowledge make a significant difference to the hypotheses that are generated.

Activity 8-C

Refer to the photograph below. Where do you think this structure is located? What is/was it used for? What does the art on the wall depict? When you are done, turn to the Answers section.

What previous knowledge did you use to arrive at these hypotheses?

Another way to introduce students to hypotheses is to use a game format.

Activity 8-D

Imagine you are a member of the British army in British North America in 1818. You are considering settling in what would eventually become Canada, but you'll need the help of the British government to do so. From the following list, decide what you think you will need and put a check mark in the "I would need" column. If you think the British government will give you this item, place a check mark in the "individual choice" column. In a group, decide what you think the government would give you and, if *you all agree on the item*, place a check mark in the "group choice" column.

WHAT WOULD THE BRITISH GOVERNMENT PROVIDE?

	I Would Need	Individual Choice	Individual Score	Group Choice	Group Score
free transportation					
radio					
land					
axe					
broadaxe					
money					
mattock					
Bible					
pickaxe					
furniture					
spade					
shovel					
hoe					
scythe					
drawknife					
hammer					
handsaw					
scythe stone					
panes of glass					
putty					
nails					
kettle					
bed tick (mattress)					
blanket					
cooking utensils					
TOTALS					

Check your responses in the Answers section at the end of the book. Also add up your individual and group scores, and consider these questions:

1. Were the individual and group scores the same or were they different?
2. If the scores were the same, what does this tell you about group decision making?
3. If the scores were different, what does this tell you about group decision making?
4. "Groups are more likely to arrive at better solutions to a problem because there will be more information available." Is this generalization warranted?

This game format can be adapted in several ways. For example, the question could be "What would you expect to find if you visited X *[another country, a museum, a farm, an industrial site, etc.]?"* Students list their individual hypotheses, decide in a group if their hypotheses are plausible, and then use resource materials, or actually visit the site, to find out if their hypotheses are correct. They can check if their individual hypotheses are more or less correct than the group ones and then answer the four questions above.

Data Gathering Ask students how they are going to find out whether their hypotheses are correct. Ensure they explore all possible sources. Depending upon the number of resources available and the skills of the students, we can either work with students in the library or we can provide all the materials in the classroom. All students could use the same materials, or groups could be formed. For example, one group could watch a video, another could look at pictures, a third could read print material, and a fourth could use the Internet. A variation on this is to use a webquest format.[1] (See Chapter 20 for how to conduct a webquest.) In cases where some sort of survey or experiment has to be conducted, ensure first that it is feasible.

Students will need to be taught the skills necessary to use the materials or conduct a survey. They should learn how to locate references in the library and on the internet, as well as how to use indexes, chapter headings, and subheadings to find specific information. By the intermediate grades, students should be able to use most reference sources and compare sources to see if they agree.

The reading level of resource materials may pose problems. Those students who have difficulties reading can be given simple print material, or another student can help them. Providing pictorial sources is another option for younger readers. Even in the intermediate grades, it may be necessary to paraphrase some reading material. Historical documents, for example, are often difficult for even older students to decipher.

The answers to some questions may involve conducting surveys, interviewing people (Chapter 19), doing historical research (Chapter 10), interpreting maps (Chapter 11), or going on a field trip (Chapter 13). In each case, students will need to be taught how to collect information by these means.

Analysis Once the information has been collected, the students will need to test their hypotheses. They may have to be taught how to classify, interpret, analyze, synthesize, summarize, and evaluate the information. Thinking critically about information and applying intellectual standards are dealt with later on in this chapter.

How the information is organized will depend on the question posed. One way information can be recorded is on an inquiry worksheet.

WHAT DID THE HAIDA EAT PRIOR TO CONTACT WITH EUROPEANS?		
Hypothesis	**Data Supporting**	**Data Rejecting and Additional Data**
Fish	Yes, salmon	Ate shellfish too
Beef		Didn't have cattle
Etc.	Etc.	Etc.

Making charts to display information is one way to prevent the student practice of copying word-for-word from the source and moving the text from one source to another. Another way is to use a note-taking format with a piece of paper divided down the middle. In the right-hand column, the students copy the information that supports or refutes a hypothesis. In the left-hand column, they rephrase the information in their own words. The copying problem can also be avoided if at the outset of the inquiry students know that their conclusion must be presented in a way that precludes copying. For example, if students use a **RAFT** writing strategy then they have to write

- in a particular **R**ole (e.g., historical figure, journalist, pioneer, world leader)
- to a particular **A**udience (e.g., government leaders, newspaper readers)
- using a particular **F**ormat (e.g., editorial, letter, poem, newspaper report)
- on a particular **T**opic

Checking the Hypotheses The conclusions derived from the information must be checked against the hypotheses. Are the hypotheses supported? Can we be sure we are right? Are the hypotheses rejected? Again, can we be sure we are right? Perhaps the evidence to support or reject a particular hypothesis cannot be found. In this case, we may be able to arrive at a tentative conclusion, or we may have to search further to see if we can find an answer. For example if, on the Haida question recorded on the worksheet above, students hypothesize that seagulls were eaten, and no evidence can be found that the Haida either did or did not eat seagulls, then this will have to remain a hypothesis. How will we know whether the conclusion is true or believable? What qualifies as a correct or reasonable answer to an inquiry question?

Here we have to think critically about the information and whether enough reliable evidence exists to support or refute a hypothesis.

Applying Intellectual Standards: Thinking Critically about the Information

Sometimes it is clear that a particular answer to an inquiry question is correct. There are a lot of facts about which we can agree. All the resources we check contain the same information. Checking other sources and seeing if they agree is one way we can check for accuracy. Our criteria include weight of evidence and consistency of that evidence. However, what do we do if sources are not consistent and they do not agree?

Authority Claims

Activity 8-E

Use at least three different sources to find out the date of Christopher Columbus's birth. Do these sources agree? If not, which source do you think is correct? Carry out the same procedure for the question "Where did Columbus first set foot in the New World?"

	Source 1	Source 2	Source 3
Date of Birth			

Generally, we rely on authorities to provide us with information. We accept that the information in a textbook is accurate; we believe what experts tell us. Most students will believe what we tell them. Despite this, it is obligatory for us to tell students why we believe that the information we impart to them is accurate; we should have reasons for saying that something is true or believable. We should teach students how to evaluate empirical claims. One way to do this is to focus on the types of information students are exposed to, not only in school but also in their daily lives, as we help them to judge reliability. Disagreements about which information to believe may be a result of authorities (i.e., experts on a subject) disagreeing, or people disagreeing about what they observed.

Activity 8-F

Suppose you were asked to teach the topics listed below. If you had to choose one reference, which would you consider the best? Why? When you have decided on your answer, refer to the Answers section.

1. Topic: Life in China today
   a) A *National Geographic* movie about life in China, produced in 2008 by two people who spent six months touring the country
   b) A book published in 2006 by the Chinese government extolling the virtues of life in the country
   c) Slides taken by a friend who recently spent two weeks in Beijing and Guangzhou
   d) A 2005 CBC documentary about the building of a dam on the Yangtze River in China
2. Topic: The internment of the Japanese during World War II
   a) A recent prescribed high-school textbook on the history of Canada in the 20th century, in which the history of the internment is discussed up to the granting of compensation by the Mulroney government
   b) The memoirs of a former politician who was instrumental in setting up internment camps
   c) A CBC television documentary made in 1990 about six families who were interned during the war
   d) The autobiography of a Japanese Canadian who, as a child, was interned

For the above activity, you should really choose more than one source because if authorities agree on something, there is a greater likelihood that it is accurate. However, by forcing you to choose only one source, our intention was to compel you to think seriously about the criteria you would use to determine what sources of information are likely to be the most reliable.

According to Ennis,[2] the following criteria should be applied. The authority or expert:

- has a good reputation
- is making statements that lie in his/her field
- has studied the matter using acceptable procedures
- is aware that his or her statements could affect his or her reputation

Applying these criteria is necessary not only when reading textbooks and other sources of information, but also when people are trying to convince us to believe something or to buy something. Suppose we see a television commercial in which a famous film star is telling us to buy Brand X toothpaste. While the star may be an expert on acting, there is little reason to accept the star's views on dental hygiene. If we did buy Brand X toothpaste because the star told us to, then we would be committing the fallacy of "appeal to authority."

Observation Claims We do not rely on authorities for all our information. The other major source is observations made by others or by us. These, too, need to be evaluated.

Activity 8-G

Which of the following would you consider a reliable observation? Why? After justifying your choice, turn to the Answers section.

1. a) The umpire in the baseball game said that Rachel was out.
   b) Rachel's mother said she was not out.
   c) The captain of the opposing team said that Rachel was out.
2. a) The driver of the car that hit the bus said the traffic light was green when he went through the intersection.
   b) The driver of a car that arrived at the intersection 10 seconds after the incident said he thought the light was red when the car went through the intersection.
   c) A cyclist who had stopped at the intersection said the car went through a red light.
3. a) Using a measuring tape, the police measured the skid marks of the car that crashed and said, "The car skidded for 20 metres."
   b) A witness to the crash paced out the skid and said, "The car skidded for 15 metres."
   c) Another witness to the crash, who had narrowly avoided being hit by the car, said, "The car skidded for at least 30 metres. It went right by me."

In assessing observation statements, the following criteria should be applied.[3] The observer:

- does not allow emotion to interfere
- has no conflict of interest

- has senses that function properly
- has a good reputation
- uses appropriate observation instruments
- was in a suitable position to observe
- makes statements that are confirmed by others, or are confirmable

Other Intellectual Standards

Students in elementary school can begin to grasp some intellectual standards by carrying out the following sorts of activities:

1. Compare two or more sources of information for answers to a particular question, or compare two or more newspaper/radio/TV/textbook accounts of a particular event. For example, ask students to find out the present-day population of Canada. Ask them to present their answers along with complete details about the sources they used.

POPULATION OF CANADA

Figure Cited	Title of Reference	Author	Where Published	Date of Publication	Date and Name of Original Source

2. Have the students witness a given event and write a description of it. For example, have them watch a news clip and then write a newspaper report. Compare their descriptions using the observation criteria listed above. Explore the reasons why people might have different points of view about the event. We all have our own biases, so it is important that students recognize their own and others' biases and judge when a bias leads to unfairness, distortion, prejudice, or closed-mindedness.

Activity 8-H

Which of the following accounts are biased in any of the senses above?

a) "Slugger" Smith hit 32 home runs for the Torpedoes in the 2002 season. "Hits" Wood of the Sharks hit 30, placing him second in the year's standings.

b) "Slugger" Smith was extremely lucky to hit 32 home runs last season. If you remember, most of these came against pretty poor teams and lousy pitching. Without a doubt, the player to praise is "Hits" Wood, who scored all his runs against top league teams and top pitchers.

c) "Slugger" Smith, who hit 32 magnificent homers last season, is probably the greatest ballplayer the Torpedoes have ever had. It was he, and he alone, who took the pennant away from the Sharks. He is so far ahead of "Hits" Wood in home runs that he is in a class all by himself.

3. Richburg, Nelson, and Reid[4] provide an interesting activity with regard to stereotypes in which they ask students to read an account of a person and then provide a physical

description of that person. One example they provide is about a freshman at Michigan State University who is studying calculus, chemistry, and analytical geometry. The person is expected to finish a Bachelor of Science degree and a medical degree in five years. To find out who this person is, consult the Answers section.

4. Help students distinguish between **primary** and **secondary sources.** Use a concept attainment method to teach students the difference by giving them examples of primary sources and then comparing these with secondary sources. Then hand out the following exercise.

Activity 8-I

Write the letter P beside those items that you think should be classed as primary sources and S for those you think are secondary sources. The answers are in the Answers section.

a) The *Canadian Charter of Rights and Freedoms*

b) *Obasan* by Joy Kogawa, a novel about the internment of Japanese Canadians in World War II

c) *Outlooks 3: Our Communities*, a Grade 3 social studies textbook published by Oxford University Press

d) Minutes of a meeting of the local town council

It must be remembered that there is not always a clear differentiation between primary and secondary sources. Dhand[5] provides an example in which a witness to an accident tells the story to his parents, who give the account to a newspaper reporter who writes the story. After some editing by the newspaper editor, the story appears. Is the newspaper story a primary source?

5. Encourage students to answer the following types of questions:
   - *Where* was the evidence found?
   - *When* was the evidence found?
   - *Who* reported the evidence?
   - *How* was the evidence found?
   - Can the evidence be *checked*? If so, *how*?

6. If inferences are made from information, then ask the students whether there is evidence for their **inference** or whether other **inferences** can be made that are just as plausible. For example, if a picture is shown of people lining up outside a store before it opens, it is plausible to infer that there is a sale. It is also plausible, however, to infer that there is a shortage of goods, and people are lining up to ensure they can obtain needed supplies, or that they are applying for work in the store. To discover which inference is true, we'd need more information.

Activity 8-J

Look at the sketch on page 97. Which of the statements that follow are inferences? Of these inferences, which do you think are plausible? Answers are given in the Answers section.

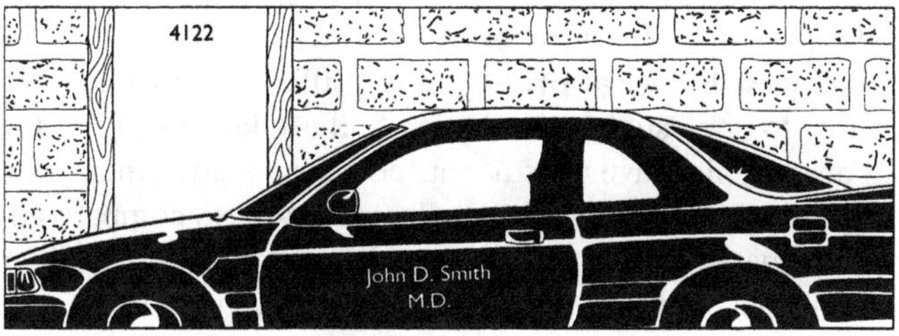

a) The colour of the car is black with white lettering.

b) The lettering on the car says John D. Smith, M.D.

c) Someone is ill in 4122.

d) The car belongs to John D. Smith, M.D.

e) The car is parked outside 4122.

f) John D. Smith lives at 4122.

g) John D. Smith is a doctor.

h) John D. Smith is economically well off.

7. To teach the differences between a descriptive claim, an inference, and a value judgment, we could play this game:
   a) One player (the leader) is given a picture and a number of statements identified as descriptions, inferences, or value claims.
   b) The other players are each given three cards. One card has "description" written on it, another has "inference," and the third has "value" written on it.
   c) The leader displays the picture and reads a statement about it.
   d) At a given signal from the leader, each player displays the card that she or he thinks correctly identifies the type of statement read.
   e) Players with the correct card receive a point or a token.
   f) The player with the most points becomes the winner and the next leader.

Help your students to avoid committing some common fallacies in their reasoning. One widely committed fallacy is overgeneralization, where it is argued that if one example of something has a particular characteristic, then all similar examples have the same characteristic. For instance, we cannot state that because one doctor is well off, therefore all doctors are well off (see Activity 8-J). Neither can we claim that because something is true of a group, then it is necessarily true for individual members of the group. The fact that Canadian doctors, on average, are near the top of the earning hierarchy doesn't mean that every single doctor is well off.

Another common mistake is called the **black-and-white fallacy**—seeing things only in black and white, ignoring possible shades of grey (e.g., "Either we stop all immigration or there will be no jobs left for people who already live here").

Other common fallacies include **appeals to tradition** ("We did X in the past, so we should do X now"); **appeals to large numbers** ("If the majority of people believe X, then

X must be right"); and reasoning that because one event preceded another, then the first must have caused the second. This unsupported assertion of a causal link between events in sequence is labelled **post hoc ergo propter hoc** ("after this, therefore because of this").

An excellent way to draw students' attention to these fallacies is to have them evaluate advertisements. For example, have the students critique advertisements for cars, especially ones that are endorsed by famous people. Students could also compare advertisements for similar products. Comparisons should be made about the intended audiences of each, the images created, the fallacies (if any) committed, the language used, the amount of information conveyed, and possible negative aspects of the product that are not mentioned.

Thinking critically about information takes time and effort, and depends upon having enough background information. Encouraging students to ask questions and gradually teaching them some of the intellectual standards of critical thought are important throughout our teaching, and they are essential when students are engaged in inquiry procedures.

Unless the information we use is as accurate as possible, we are likely to make serious mistakes that can affect our own lives and those of others. Consider the "simple" matter of being taken in by false advertising—and the far more serious consequences of hateful propaganda about minority groups.

TEACHING CRITICAL THINKING

We can incorporate critical thinking into the social studies curriculum in several ways. One way has been devised by Richard Paul and his colleagues.[6] They take popular lesson ideas and modify them to teach a particular component of critical thinking. Paul and Elder define critical thinking as

> that mode of thinking—about any subject, content or problem—in which the thinker improves the quality of his or her thinking by skillfully taking charge of the structures inherent in thinking and imposing intellectual standards upon them.[7]

These researchers argue that critical thinkers must view issues objectively from the various perspectives of those whose interests are involved. They state that most problems are "multi logical," as they cannot be resolved within a single frame of reference. To identify and define any problem "depends upon some arguable choice among alternative frames of references."[8] Thus, the frames have to be tested using such standards as clarity, accuracy, relevance, significance, completeness, precision, depth, consistency, sound logic, and fairness. Paul and Elder argue that these standards must be applied to the elements of critical thinking (purposes, questions, points of view, information, inferences, concepts, implications, and assumptions), within a framework of intellectual traits (humility, autonomy, integrity, courage, perseverance, empathy, fair-mindedness, and confidence in reason).[9]

Another approach is to use critical challenges. These are problematic situations that require critical thought. They are based on an approach developed by Sharon Bailin, Roland Case, Jerrold Coombs, and Leroi Daniels,[10] which was adapted for pedagogical purposes for the Critical Thinking Cooperative in British Columbia.[11]The following are examples of such challenges:

- **Concept:** Is Canada really a democracy?[12]
- **Inquiry:** What is the most plausible explanation for how the pyramids were built?

These questions indicate where facts or meanings (concepts) are in dispute and intellectual standards are used to see if we can say that this information is more reliable than other information, or that this meaning of a concept is more appropriate than another. Other critical thinking tasks involve the application of value standards (ethical and aesthetic, etc.). You will find examples of these in Part 3. Any critical challenge must meet certain criteria. These are that the activity (1) requires a judgment be made, (2) is meaningful to students, (3) is embedded in the curriculum, and (4) is focused so that it is not too difficult for students to tackle and students have or can obtain the "tools" necessary to tackle the challenge.[13] The tools required to tackle any critical challenge are as follows:[14]

Background knowledge: To answer any question requires that students already have or can obtain the knowledge required to answer the question.

Criteria for judgment making: A judgment requires the use of criteria. For example, in judging the reliability of observations made by witnesses, we would apply the criteria outlined previously. In judging whether a concept has been used appropriately, we would use the criteria outlined in Chapter 6. To judge an account of how the pyramids were built, we would appeal to such criteria as weight of evidence; feasibility (e.g., Could the ancient Egyptians have used this method? Did they have the technology?); archeological evidence; and the views of scholars.

Critical thinking vocabulary: To think critically requires that we use a variety of concepts such as conclusion, inference, and argument. Where answering a critical challenge entails students' using a critical thinking concept, then you have to teach them. For example, if you wished to teach the concept of "inference" you might use an activity akin to the one in Activity 8-J.

Thinking strategies: Many strategies can be used to answer a critical challenge. One of them, inquiry, is the subject of this chapter. Others include asking an expert, using graphic organizers such as a web, brainstorming, discussing with peers, and role-playing.

Habits of mind: Unless we are disposed to think critically, there may seem little point in doing it for its own sake. Thus, we need to foster in students **habits of mind**—attitudes such as open-mindedness, fair-mindedness, and respect for evidence. One way to do this is to ensure that we have a classroom climate that is conducive to critical inquiry, a classroom where students' ideas are treated with respect, where students are encouraged to ask questions, and where we model and teach critical thinking strategies and dispositions (see Chapter 9). This conception of critical thinking has been used to develop a series of critical challenge books.[15] There are other ways to teach critical thinking,[16] but the two mentioned above provide the most conceptually and pedagogically sound approaches.

Here is a critical thinking activity that asks you to examine the ways in which you make inferences about classroom interactions and how you would determine which inferences are most reliable.

Activity 8-K

Carry out an inquiry procedure to answer the question "What formal rules and informal conventions govern the interactions in this classroom?"

1. Is the question clear? What would qualify as a "rule"? What would qualify as a "convention"?
2. Generate a hypothesis about what rules and conventions you think govern interactions in the classroom. Write down your hypothesis.

3. How will you test your hypothesis? If you decide to observe interactions in the classroom, how will you observe whether a rule or convention is or is not being followed? For how long will you observe? How will you ensure that you observe all the likely situations in which your hypothesis could be tested? If you intend to ask people what rules and conventions they think they follow, how will you ascertain this? How will you record your data?
4. Collect your answers according to the decisions made in number 3 above. Decide what you're going to do with the answers—list all of them, classify them, graph them, or tabulate them in some other way.
5. Decide whether the evidence supports your hypothesis. Are you sure your results are reliable? Did you observe for a long enough period? Was your survey thorough enough? If your hypothesis was not supported, can you explain why? What conclusions can you draw? Do they fit in with your (or experts') theoretical understandings of the rules and conventions governing group interactions? Do the same rules and conventions operate in different contexts? What factors influence the creation of rules and conventions? What happens when they are not followed?

Questions about the reliability of information and what constitutes a best answer can be raised with young students as well as older ones. Here is an example where primary-level students inquired into the toys that their grandparents played with. They then questioned the validity of their findings. This lesson could well fit into family history projects as outlined in Chapter 10.

Question: What toys did my grandparents play with?[17]

This lesson would be within a history unit on the community. The teacher asks the class what a "toy" is. Answers are discussed and examples of "toys" are given. Students are asked how significant they think toys are in learning history. What do they tell us about children's lives? The students are then asked to guess the answer to the question. As guesses are forthcoming, they are written or drawn on the board or on chart paper. Students then draw one or more of the items they think children played with when their grandparents were children. Where possible, they interview their grandparents to see whether their hypotheses are supported. (They also use old Sears and Eaton's catalogues.) If a hypothesis is supported, the student puts a check mark against the toy. A student who finds a toy that nobody mentioned should draw that toy. Finally, the students share their findings. Other toys that students identified in their research are added to the list. If no evidence can be found for a toy listed by a student, students are asked whether it might have been a toy from another time period, and how they might check this hypothesis. The teacher asks the students whether their grandparents might have forgotten some of the toys they played with. The teacher also notes that catalogues may not show all of the toys that were available at the time. She asks the students about the toys they play with that are not necessarily available in toy stores—pieces of wood that are used to represent boats or spears, etc. She asks the students whether they think they have the complete answer to the inquiry question.

As further activities, the teacher can have students inquire into whether different cultural groups played with the same and/or different toys. If actual toys can be obtained, children can play with them and discuss such things as the level of technology involved in producing the toys; whether they are "good" toys; whether toys have changed since their grandparents' time and whether the changes have been good or bad; whether there were fewer toys available 50 years ago, and why; how economic status influenced the type and number of toys available to a child; whether there are, and should be, certain toys for boys and certain toys for girls; and how advertising was carried out in the past in comparison with the present and how it influences what children want. Students could also research what children were playing with in other parts of the world in their grandparents' era. They could carry out a project on the history of toys worldwide with students in groups looking at various parts of the world and then comparing their findings. This topic could culminate in a toy fair in which the work done by students is displayed, and other students in the school are invited to come and see the display and play with the toys.

Presenting Conclusions

Once the inquiry activity has been completed, students should present their conclusions. Rather than always writing them down, students could use a variety of methods. For example, in Activity 8-K, students could present their answers in the form of a graph (see Chapter 19), showing the number of times various rules and conventions appeared to be at play. The Haida inquiry (page 92) could be answered in the form of pictures or seasonal menus. Other ideas include:

- writing a diary, letter, poem, newspaper, story, guidebook, journal, travel brochure, or report
- creating a diorama, model, mural, or collage
- creating a play, skit, or radio or television show
- creating a wiki, podcast, blog, or video presentation (see Chapter 20)
- preparing a drawing, table, map, chart, diagram, graph, cartoon, painting, or computer graphic
- assembling a booklet
- creating an advertisement
- making a scrapbook
- preparing a menu or an actual meal
- making costumes
- simulating a ceremony
- taking a photograph
- displaying a collection of actual objects
- creating a game or a crossword puzzle
- creating a multimedia presentation on a computer

Students can present their work in a multitude of ways. Given that we want students to be excited about social studies, we should allow them to use the ways that appeal to them the most.

Helping Students Carry Out Inquiry Activities

Inquiry procedures have to be taught to students so that they can effectively perform the inquiry activities:

1. Identify a problem that is testable and suitable for their level of maturity.
2. Clarify the question by clarifying the words used in it, i.e., by defining words and/or by giving examples.

3. Hypothesize possible conclusions.
4. Select appropriate research techniques: e.g., survey, interview, library research, fieldwork, or actual experiment.
5. Select information pertinent to the question and show a willingness to look at all points of view. Locate information using card catalogues, bibliographies, or online data retrieval systems.
6. "Read" sources of information: skim to find specific information; use headings, topic sentences, and summary statements to distinguish between main and subordinate ideas; draw inferences from information; use and interpret maps, surveys, graphs, historical documents, and pictures.
7. Evaluate information: identify bias and faulty reasoning; use intellectual standards for judging the believability of information.
8. Organize information: use main and supporting evidence; formulate suitable classification schemes; create tables of contents; use appropriate bibliographic formats.
9. Synthesize information: formulate generalizations and cause-and-effect relationships; summarize main ideas; identify information that supports and does not support a hypothesis; recognize the need to change a conclusion when new evidence warrants it; show a willingness to re-inquire if necessary.
10. Present conclusions in a variety of forms: written and verbal reports, graphs, models, charts, diagrams, and so on.

The Problems and Pitfalls of Inquiry

Although the inquiry procedure has many major advantages, it also has potential pitfalls and problems:

- **lack of time:** Inquiry can be time-consuming; adequate time must be given so that students can explore on their own.
- **lack of resources:** Often resources are lacking, so teachers and students will need to search for pertinent materials.
- **teachers who want to be "in charge":** Teachers should refrain from imposing their "answers" on students. They instead need to be supportive and receptive to students' ideas.
- **questions that are too difficult:** Questions must be within the cognitive capacity of students.
- **rigidity:** Despite its many guises, if inquiry is the only method of teaching and learning, it can become boring for students.
- **particular student characteristics:** If students can't find answers or can reach only tentative conclusions, inquiry can have a paralyzing effect on them. Students need to know that there are some questions to which we can find answers, while also realizing that there are some questions to which answers do not come readily. The inquiry needs to be introduced gradually to students who are unfamiliar with it. You might start by finding answers to specific questions using one source, and then advance to posing questions requiring information from many sources. This process could lead to posing

more complex questions and, finally, to group inquiry in which questions are answered by groups of students who locate their own resource materials and make decisions about how the inquiry is to proceed.

- **possibility of gender bias:** The questions that are inquired into may be of more importance to males than females or vice versa; insistence on a particular answer may exclude other viewpoints, including feminist ones (see Maher[18]).

All these pitfalls can be avoided through careful teaching and by recognizing and taking into account possible negative biases. They should not dissuade us from using inquiry procedures that actively engage students, and sometimes even excite them, while teaching them many valuable skills. Students are more likely to remember what they learn through inquiry procedures than through more passive direct instruction methods. Their motivation for learning (not to mention their curiosity) is enhanced when it is their own questions that are the subject of inquiry.

Other Activities

1. Write a lesson plan that focuses on one of the following questions:
   a) Who works in my school and what jobs do they perform? (Grade 1)
   b) What role did the building of the Canadian Pacific Railway play in the history of Canada? (Grade 5)

   Include the following components:

   Opener: How will you motivate interest?

   Hypothesis/Hypotheses: How will you organize for hypothesis making?

   Organization and data collection: How will you organize the class? What data will you use?

   Data analysis: How will students use the data?

   Hypothesis check: How will this be carried out?

   Conclusion: How will students present their findings?

   Finale: How could you continue on this topic?
2. During a class discussion on clothing, the girls claim that they dress better than the boys. They say that boys wear dull-coloured clothing, whereas girls wear bright colours. The question arises, "Do boys in the school wear dull-coloured clothing whereas girls wear bright colours?" How would you use an inquiry approach to help students arrive at a conclusion to this question?
3. Get a picture of yourself as a small child (e.g., as a two-year-old) and as a ten-year-old. Formulate hypotheses for ages two and ten for each of the characteristics listed on the chart on page 104. Check the veracity of your hypotheses by consulting with parents, other relations, and friends.
4. Locate a letter to the editor of a newspaper, or a newspaper editorial, and critique it. What is the writer's conclusion? What reasons are offered for it? Does he or she present enough evidence for the reader to accept the conclusion? Is the evidence accurate? Are the concepts clear? Have any fallacies been committed? Do you agree with the conclusion? Why or why not?

HOW HAVE I CHANGED?

	Two-year-old	Ten-year-old	Today
Height			
Weight			
Usual Dress			
Hair Colour			
Favourite Food for:			
breakfast			
lunch			
supper			
Favourite Game			
Favourite TV Show			
Best Friend			
Favourite Book			
Hero/Heroine			

Notes

1. A. Milson and P. Downing, "Webquests: Using internet resources for cooperative inquiry," *Social Education* 65:3 (2001), pp. 144–146. For more on these, see Chapter 20.
2. R. Ennis, *Logic in Teaching* (Englewood Cliffs, NJ: Prentice-Hall, 1963), p. 393.
3. S. Norris, *The Dependability of Observation Statements: Rational Thinking Reports, Number 4* (Urbana, IL: Illinois Rational Thinking Project, 1979).
4. R. Richburg, B. Nelson, and J. Reid, "Jump-starting thinking: Challenging student preconceptions," *The Social Studies* 85:2 (1994), pp. 66–69.
5. H. Dhand, "The source method to teach Social Studies," in R. Case and P. Clark, eds., *The Canadian Anthology of Social Studies* (Vancouver: Pacific Educational Press, 1999).
6. R. Paul, A. Binker, and M. Charbonneau, *Critical Thinking Handbook: K–3, A Guide for Remodelling Lesson Plans in the Language Arts, Social Studies and Science* (Rohnert Park, CA: Center for Critical Thinking and Moral Critique, 1987).
7. R. Paul and L. Elder, *Critical Thinking: Tools for Taking Charge of Your Learning and Your Life* (Upper Saddle River, NJ: Prentice-Hall, 2001), p. xx.
8. R. Paul, "Dialogical thinking: Critical thought essential to the acquisition of rational knowledge and passions," in J. Baron and R. Sternberg, eds., *Teaching Thinking Skills: Theory and Practice* (New York: Freeman, 1987), p. 138.
9. R. Paul and L. Elder, *Critical Thinking*, p. 50.
10. S. Bailin, R. Case, J. Coombs, and L. Daniels, *A Conception of Critical Thinking for Curriculum, Instruction and Assessment* (Victoria, BC: Ministry of Education, 1993).

11. R. Case and I. Wright, "Taking seriously the teaching of critical thinking," *Canadian Social Studies* 32:1 (1997), pp. 12–19.

12. A Grade 4 class had an interesting time discussing this question. They first defined democracy and then considered whether they could vote and whether they had a say in important decisions in their day-to-day lives. They concluded that life for them was not democratic, so Canada was not democratic either.

13. R. Case and I. Wright, pp. 12–19.

14. *Ibid.*, pp. 14–16.

15. T. McDermid, R. Manzo, and T. Musselle, with R. Case, L. Daniels, and P. Schwartz, eds., *Critical Challenges for Primary Students* (1996), and J. Harrison, N. Smith, and I. Wright, eds., *Critical Challenges in Social Studies for Upper Elementary Students* (1999) (Burnaby, BC: Field Programs Faculty of Education, Simon Fraser University, and Richmond, BC: The Critical Thinking Cooperative). Other more recent titles in this Critical Challenges series can be found on the Pacific Educational Press website: www.pep.educ.ubc.ca

16. I. Wright, *Is That Right? Critical Thinking and the Social World of the Young Learner* (Toronto: Pippin Publishing, 2002).

17. Where grandparents cannot be questioned, students can use information from the resource materials provided to find out what children played with in the era when their grandparents were children.

18. F. Maher, "Inquiry teaching and feminist pedagogy," *Social Education* 51:3 (1987), pp. 186–193.

Glossary of Key Terms

Appeal to large numbers—Arguing that because many people believe something, therefore it is true.

Appeal to tradition—Arguing that because something was done in the past, therefore it is right today.

Authority claims—Statements made by experts.

Black-and-white fallacy—Assuming that there are only two positions on, or solutions to, a problem.

Habits of mind—Dispositions such as open-mindedness and fair-mindedness.

Hypothesis—A guess about an answer to a question; a statement about a predicted outcome that is tested by experimental means.

Inference—A statement that goes beyond the given data; to reason from some proposition(s) to another.

Inquiry—Sometimes referred to in the social studies literature as any procedure whereby students find answers to questions; often synonymous with problem solving and discovery learning. In this text, inquiry is defined as a procedure in which students test a hypothesis, or hypotheses, about the answer to a question.

Observation claims—Statements about what somebody saw.

Post hoc ergo propter hoc—Reasoning that as one event preceded another, then the first must have caused the second.

Primary sources—Reference sources produced at the time an event occurred (e.g., eyewitness accounts).

RAFT—An acronym from the words ***Role***, ***Audience***, ***Format***, and ***Topic***; a procedure in which students write in a particular *role* (e.g., historical figure, journalist, pioneer, world leader), to a particular *audience* (e.g., government leaders, newspaper readers), using a particular *format* (e.g., editorial, letter, poem, newspaper report), on a particular *topic.*

Secondary sources—Reference sources produced after the event; second-hand sources or those based on interpretations of the primary sources (e.g., a history textbook).

CHAPTER 9

Working Together: Cooperative Learning and Building a Classroom Community

In the previous chapter, discussion focused on how students could go about finding answers to questions using inquiry procedures. Sometimes an inquiry is best carried out by individual students; other times it is better to have groups of students work together in cooperative learning groups. The term **cooperative learning** is used to describe a variety of activities in which students work together on a task. These activities are designed with several objectives in mind: to develop communication skills; to create trust, acceptance, and sharing within the classroom; to lower the fear of failure; to develop a commitment to learning; to help develop conflict-resolution abilities;[1] and, especially, to foster individual and group accountability. Proponents of cooperative learning also point out that cooperative learning can help prepare students to work effectively with the range of people with whom they will interact in their day-to-day lives.[2] These activities are premised on the beliefs that students can learn from each other, that students construct meaning more readily through interaction with others, that students perceive their success as being linked to the success of others, and that cooperation is better than competition.[3]

Research evidence indicates that the objectives of cooperative learning can be achieved when cooperative learning is effectively used in the classroom. As achievement improves, students gain self-esteem and social skills. In addition, they develop positive attitudes toward school in general as well as toward particular subjects and other cultural groups.[4] Students are helped to make personal sense out of what they are learning by sharing information and teaching it to others.[5] It has also been found that teachers who use cooperative learning activities are more positive about their work than those who do not. They also see less need to discipline students.[6] Because these conclusions are derived from a compilation of results from different studies, it should not be assumed that any one cooperative learning activity will always lead to these outcomes. Nevertheless, there are many advantages in using cooperative learning activities. In whole-class instruction, a student has an approximately one-in-thirty chance of speaking. However, in a small group, every student has an approximately one-in-four chance. Students are able to help one another and learn from one another. In their lives, both inside and outside of school, students will find themselves in group situations at work and in the wider community; they need to learn how to interact with others in productive ways. Good group relationships are also rewarding and enjoyable in their own right.

Before launching into cooperative learning activities, we should ask ourselves the following questions:

1. Is the topic appropriate? Cohen[7] suggests that the questions posed should have more than one answer, that the task should allow different students to make different contributions, and that a variety of information should be required to carry out the task.
2. How will I ensure that all students can and do contribute? How will I avoid situations in which the high achievers either do all the work and learn more, or decrease their efforts so as not to be perceived negatively by the other students?
3. What behaviours should students exhibit, and how will I monitor these behaviours?
4. How will the group monitor its own progress?
5. How long should the cooperative activity last?

We cannot always expect students to be able to work together without some initial preparation.[8] Students need to be supported if they are to realize the benefits of cooperation. We may have to start off with simple partner activities and progress to more substantial group tasks. Depending on the activity, groups may be formed on the basis of prior friendships, common interests, or common abilities, or on a random basis. Groups should be small in size—three to five members is best. Rules for group learning should be followed: students should help one another; students should not "put down" anyone's contribution; students should encourage each other; students should monitor and evaluate their individual contributions to the overall group effort; and there should be equal participation. You might like to start with small-group activities in which students get to know each other, followed by activities that rely on the participation of all the group members (e.g., creating a collage, building a model). Carefully consider group membership. Ideally we want a fairly equal distribution on the basis of gender, ethnicity, and ability. However, we might want to avoid putting certain students together, at least initially, if we know that they do not get along well with one another. Be prepared to deal with the problems that arise when students work together. Some of these problems, such as "bright" students putting down those who are "less bright," can be avoided by assigning roles to each group member (see the ideas presented later in this chapter).

COOPERATIVE LEARNING STRATEGIES

The following activities are designed to help students begin to work together.

Production Line

Divide students into groups of six. Give each student a sheet of paper and give each group a pair of scissors, a red crayon, a blue crayon, a green crayon, a coin, a pencil (for drawing a circle), and a ruler with a pencil. Each group is to produce six of each of the items shown in the following diagram:

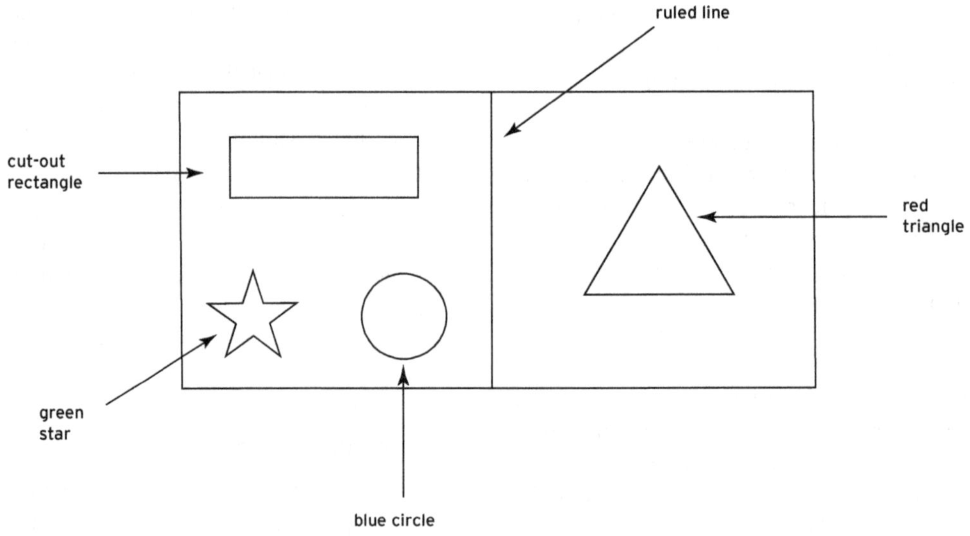

The first group to produce six of each item is the winner.

Usually, each student in each group will attempt to make his or her own item and will "fight" for the materials. The quickest way to produce six items is for each student to have one of the materials (e.g., crayon, ruler, or scissors). As the six pieces of paper are passed from student to student, one student draws a red triangle on each; another draws a ruled line on each; and so on. Specialization is required, with each specialist cooperating with the others to produce a finished product.

Partner Game

Cut out the following shape:

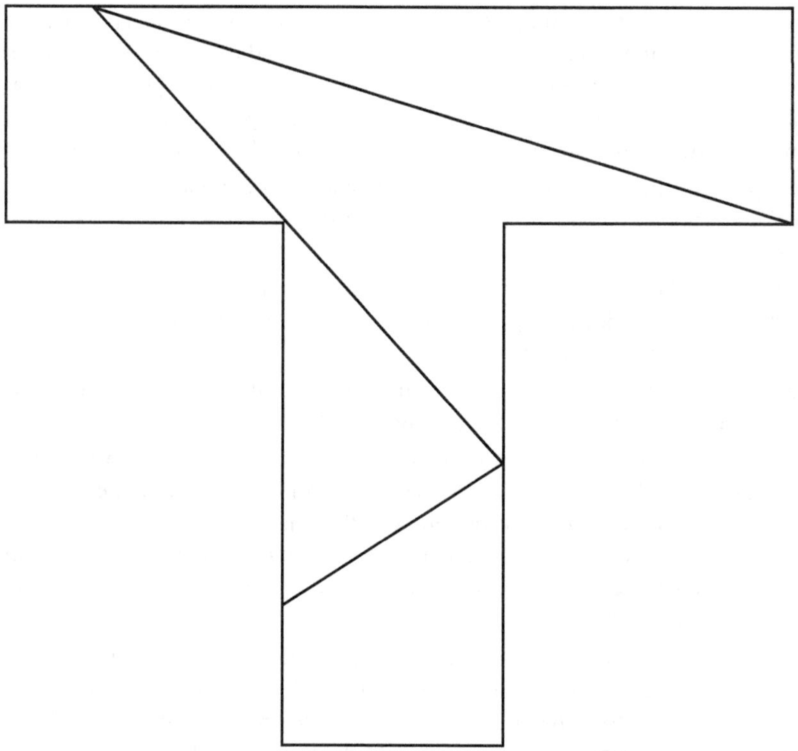

Divide the class into pairs, and give one member of each pair the cutout shape and the other the T diagram. The person with the T diagram tells the person holding the shapes how to put the shapes together in the form of the T. Try it—it's not easy.

Have each student create a list of likes and dislikes. Working in pairs, have each student share and compare their list with their partner, noting similarities and differences. Then have two pairs meet and do the same. Follow this by having groups of eight meet, and so on.

Two Facts, One Fiction[9] Each student states two facts and one fiction about themselves. Other students have to guess which statements are fact and fiction by asking questions to which the first student provides honest answers.

Implementing Cooperative Learning Strategies

Cooperative learning activities can be implemented in the classroom in a variety of ways.[10] All the ideas listed below can be used during inquiry activities, for example.

- Students in a group are given a topic, and then they identify a set of questions they think are worth investigating. These questions are ranked from most interesting to least interesting, then shared with the whole class, rank-ordered again, and classified. Groups are then formed to hypothesize answers to particular questions and to test the hypotheses.
- Within a group, certain students perform particular tasks—one acting as a scribe, another as a researcher, another as an illustrator. Broad questions on which a group is working can be broken down into more discrete questions and hypotheses, with one member of the group becoming a specialist on a specific question. The specialist then teaches the rest of the group, and the information is used to answer the broad question. If several groups are working on the same broad question, then specialists on a particular question from each group can work together. This **jigsaw technique** can also be used when students are required to learn larger bodies of information (see Chapter 5).
- If a group is working on a particular question, each member can use different resources to test their hypotheses, and the findings can be shared. The group can then formulate a final answer.
- If a group is working on a particular question, each member of the group can be given information that provides only part of the answer. The information can then be synthesized into a final group answer.
- If a group product is required (e.g., a report, a chart, a model, a mural), each student can be asked to make a particular contribution.
- If students are watching a video, they can be divided into pairs and a **think–pair–share strategy** can be used. The video is occasionally stopped and one of the students in each pair summarizes the information, tells the other student what is most interesting, identifies what was confusing, and tries to help the other student understand the information. When the video is stopped the next time, the other student takes on the role of summarizer and clarifier.
- If multiple groups are working on different aspects of the same broad question, each group can teach the rest of the class about their particular topic so that a class answer to the broad question is formulated. For example, if the broad question is "What motivated the first Europeans to explore Canada?" each group tests their hypotheses about a particular explorer. The groups then share their findings with the rest of the class, and the broad question is answered.
- If there are students who need help on a particular aspect of an inquiry procedure, then peer teaching can be used. For instance, if a student needs to be able to read the scale on a map, a classmate who knows how to do this can teach that student.
- If the objective is to help students listen to each other, then a **talking circle strategy** can be used.[11] A topic is discussed by students sitting in a circle. A talking stick is passed around the circle and only the person with the stick can speak. The other students must listen carefully. A person can decline to speak when given the stick and can pass it on to the next student. When speaking, no comments can be made about another speaker's comments.

- **Circle writing.** On a blank sheet of paper, each student writes one piece of information or one advantage of doing something and then passes this to the next student, who must add his or her contribution.
- **STAD.** Students study in groups for a quiz. They take the quiz separately and their scores are compared to the average of their past scores. If a student gets 100% on the quiz, the group receives 30 points; if one student gets a score of 10 points over his/her past average, the group gets 20 points; and so on.

Cooperative activities also are designed for students whilst they are using computers—creating crossword puzzles, timelines, digital maps, and perhaps even teaching keyboarding skills to a partner.[12]

Activity 9-A

Design a cooperative learning activity for a primary, junior, or intermediate class that is studying conservation. Choose one particular aspect of this topic that you consider appropriate for the grade level. Develop a lesson plan that includes your objectives and a detailed description of how the cooperative learning activity would be organized.

It should not be assumed that cooperative learning is designed to stifle conflict in debating issues. Rather, conditions can be created in which conflict is dealt with in rational ways. The following activity for upper elementary students illustrates one way to do this. It is consistent with Paul's[13] belief that critical thinkers are able to present arguments for all sides of an issue and to enter sympathetically into someone else's point of view.[14]

1. Groups of four are formed and then divided into twos. Each group of two is given a different side of an issue. The pairs then prepare a case to defend their side of the issue. Pairs can meet with other pairs on the same side of the issue to ensure they've got a strong case.
2. Each pair presents its case to the other members of their group of four; each pair is then given the opportunity to challenge the other pair's arguments.
3. Each pair then presents a strong argument for the side opposed to the one it was previously defending.
4. Finally, assigned positions are abandoned and the four students in each group work together to produce a report that summarizes the group's position. Consensus is not required. Each group member should be prepared to justify his or her individual decision to the rest of the class.

Before embarking on cooperative learning, we should carefully consider our objectives and the appropriateness of any particular strategy. Keep in mind that some educators advocate the use of cooperative learning activities for the purposes of competition with other groups; others, however, find this to be inappropriate. Is there any contradiction, for instance, in using cooperative activities in social studies and then emphasizing individual competition in spelling lessons? If cooperative activities are used in part to promote competition with other groups, will children believe that cooperation is just another way of getting ahead?

Whatever your answers are to the questions above, it is clear that group activities are worth pursuing in the classroom. Coupled with inquiry procedures, cooperative activities can provide valuable learning experiences for students.

BUILDING A CLASSROOM COMMUNITY

Cooperative learning strategies have the potential to create a classroom in which groups work well together, but they do not on their own engender the type of classroom where **intellectual virtues** are fostered. These virtues, such as reasonableness, trustworthiness, and empathic understanding,[15] ideally lead students to take responsibility for the questions they ask and the conclusions they arrive at. These virtues cannot be taught didactically; they have to be experienced and practised.[16] Sears and Parsons[17] argue that, as teachers, we need to embrace the following principles: that knowledge is subject to change; that any question can be asked; and that awareness and empathy for alternative points of view, tolerance for ambiguity, and skepticism of text are required. Thus, as teachers, we need to admit that we don't know everything and that we are prepared to change our minds when necessary. We also need to articulate alternative points of view and, whenever possible, tell students why the information they are learning is worth knowing and the reasons why we believe this information is believable. By modelling such behaviours we can begin to encourage students to adopt the same.

One of the best ways to foster these virtues is through critical thinking (see the previous chapter). This can be carried out through the use of a critical challenge,[18] the redesign of a regular lesson to emphasize a critical thinking problem or question,[19] or the insertion of a critical thinking activity into a lesson. For example, in a study of a particular geographic region, students could be asked to ascertain how the area has been affected by humans and what the benefits and disadvantages of this intervention have been. In a current affairs lesson, students could select an issue, research the arguments, and then take a position on the issue. Debating the issue is a good idea here so long as the debate is not viewed as a competition where the winner is assumed to have the right answer.

In any discussion or debate on issues, we need to persuade students that reasons matter. They cannot just say, "Well, that's just my opinion." Richard Paul has a set of questions that focus student attention on reasons.[20] These include "What evidence did I use?" and "How do I know that the conclusion is reliable?"

In open-ended discussions, teachers can ask students whether they agree with another student's response (see Chapter 7 for ideas about how responses to questions can be extended to involve several students). If different reasons are forthcoming, we can ask the students to decide which reasons are best. Students also need to learn to ask questions so that the discussion is student-focused rather than teacher-led.[21] Students should also question themselves—"How do I know this is true?" "Is this my best argument?" "Have I considered other points of view?" This encourages reflection and what Lipman calls "self correcting thinking."[22]

Asking students to consider and reason from different points of view can foster empathic understanding. In discussing an issue, students should become aware of all possible points of view and should be able to state what these are. For example, if one student disagrees with another, both students should be able to put into their own words the other's opinion. A wonderful way to consider different points of view is to read *The True Story of the 3 Little Pigs! by A.* Wolf, as told to Jon Scieszka.[23] In this story the wolf appears to have very good reasons for blowing down the pigs' houses and eating the inhabitants. Read the story to a class and ask the students to consider the story from the wolf's point of view and pass judgment on his behaviour. Role-playing can be a powerful strategy here. Literature can also enhance empathy. For example, reading stories of First Nations children can lead to increased understanding of their cultures.

As we teach, we should allow students to have a say in the rules that govern the classroom and, where possible, in the learning activities they pursue. However, we must build slowly. Students, generally speaking, are not always used to thinking critically; nor do they always seriously consider the viewpoints of others. It can be disquieting for them to realize that knowledge is very often tentative and that critical debate can be healthy.

Activity 9-B

Design an activity to foster one of the virtues outlined above; for example, one that would help students understand someone else's point of view, or one that would help teach students the rules of discussion so that all students' opinions are heard.

Other Activities

1. Organize a group issue discussion.
   a) Within a group of four, select a partner and then choose to defend one side of the following issue:
      X: You believe there should be no competition in social studies classes. You think that the social aspect of social studies should be emphasized, that working together will encourage respect, and that social problems should be solved through cooperative endeavours.
      Y: You believe competition should be emphasized in social studies because competition creates challenges that motivate students to work hard. Further, you know that to succeed in the world you have to be competitive.
   b) Get together with your partner and write down the three strongest arguments you can think of to support your position.
   c) Within your group of four, argue your case and try to refute the other side's position.
   d) With your partner, write down the three strongest arguments you can think of that support the other side's point of view, and present these to the other members of your group.
   e) See if your group of four can agree on a position. If you cannot agree, what is the basis of the disagreement? Is there any way it could be resolved if more evidence were available (e.g., the effects of cooperation or competition on students)?
2. Pick a topic at a grade level of your choice and design a cooperative learning activity that teaches or reinforces learning about that topic.
3. List some of the behaviours you could exhibit that would encourage students to work together cooperatively and think for themselves.

Notes

1. D. Johnson and R. Johnson, "Teaching students to be peacemakers: Results of twelve years of research." 2001. www.co-operation.org/pager/peace-meta.html
2. J. Myers, "Cooperative learning: Putting the 'social' into social studies," in I. Wright and A. Sears, eds., *Trends and Issues in Canadian Social Studies* (Vancouver: Pacific Educational Press, 1997). D. Johnson, R. Johnson and M. Stanne, Co-operative learning methods: A meta-analysis. www.co-operation.org/pages/cl-methods.html, 2000, accessed Feb. 11, 2008.

3. H. Margolis and P. McCabe, "Using co-operative learning to facilitate mainstreaming in the social studies," *Social Education* 54:2 (1990), pp. 111–114.
4. R. Slavin, "Research on co-operative learning: Consensus and controversy," *Educational Leadership* 47 (1990), pp. 52–55.
5. T. Morton, "Cooperative learning in elementary classrooms," in R. Case and P. Clark, eds., *The Anthology of Social Studies, Volume 1. Issues and Strategies for Elementary Teachers* (Vancouver: Pacific Educational Press, 2008), pp. 209–210.
6. S. Sharon, ed., *Co-operative Learning: Theory and Research* (New York: Praeger, 1989).
7. E. Cohen, *Designing Groupwork: Strategies for the Heterogeneous Classroom* (New York: Teachers College Press, 1986).
8. T. Morton, "Cooperative learning in elementary classrooms." in R. Case and P. Clark, eds., *The Anthology of Social Studies, Volume 1. Issues and Strategies for Elementary Teachers* (Vancouver: Pacific Educational Press, 2008), pp. 209–210.
9. G. Jacobs, M. Power, and L. Inn. *The Teacher's Sourcebook for Cooperative Learning* (Thousand Oaks, CA: Corwin Press Inc., 2002), p. 10.
10. T. Morton, *Cooperative Learning and Social Studies: Towards Excellence and Equity* (San Juan Capistrano, CA: Kagan, 1996).
11. J. Orr, "Teaching social studies for understanding First Nations issues," in A. Sears and I. Wright, eds., *Challenges and Prospects for Canadian Social Studies,* 2nd ed. (Vancouver: Pacific Educational Press, 2004).
12. L. Schwartz and K. Willing, *Computer Activities for the Cooperative Classroom* (Markham, ON: Pembroke Publishers, 2001).
13. R. Paul and L. Elder, *Critical Thinking: Tools for Taking Charge of Your Learning and Your Life* (Upper Saddle River, NJ: Prentice-Hall, 2001), pp. 15–17.
14. *Ibid.,* pp. 11–12.
15. *Ibid.,* pp. 4–19.
16. L. Farr Darling and I. Wright, "Critical thinking and the social in social studies," in A. Sears and I. Wright, eds., *Challenges and Prospects for Canadian Social Studies,* 2nd ed. (Vancouver: Pacific Educational Press, 2004).
17. A. Sears and J. Parsons, "Towards critical thinking as an ethic," *Theory and Research in Social Education* 19:1 (1991), pp. 45–68.
18. See, for example, T. McDermid, R. Manzo, and T. Musselle, with R. Case, L. Daniels, and P. Schwartz, eds., *Critical Challenges for Primary Students* (1996), and J. Harrison, N. Smith, and I. Wright, eds., *Critical Challenges in Social Studies for Upper Elementary Students* (1999) (Burnaby, BC: Field Programs Faculty of Education, Simon Fraser University, and Richmond, BC: The Critical Thinking Cooperative). For a complete list of the Critical Challenges series see the Pacific Educational Press website: www.pep.educ.ubc.ca
19. R. Paul, A. Binker, and M. Charbonneau, *Critical Thinking Handbook: K–3, A Guide for Remodelling Lesson Plans in the Language Arts, Social Studies and Science* (Rohnert Park, CA: Center for Critical Thinking and Moral Critique, 1987).
20. R. Paul and L. Elder, pp. 124–127.
21. L. Farr Darling and I. Wright.
22. M. Lipman, *Critical Thinking: What Can It Be?* (New Jersey: Institute for Critical Thinking, Montclair State College, 1988).
23. J. Scieszka, *The True Story of the 3 Little Pigs! by A. Wolf* (New York: Viking Kestral, 1989).

Glossary of Key Terms

Circle writing—An activity in which each student contributes to a collective writing task.

Cooperative learning—A variety of activities that help students learn together.

Intellectual virtues—Values that include reasonableness, empathic understanding, and the willingness to give reasons for one's conclusions, etc.

Jigsaw technique—An activity wherein groups of students have different pieces of information and have to work together to create a synthesis.

Talking circle strategy—Students sit in a circle to discuss a topic. A stick is passed around and the student who receives the stick can say something or pass it on to the next person. No positive or negative statements can be made about another speaker.

Think–pair–share strategy—Students in pairs summarize information and try to help each other understand it.

STAD—An assessment method in which groups of students are rewarded if one member of a group gets a perfect score or a higher one than in previous quizzes.

CHAPTER 10

What Was It Like in the Past? Teaching and Learning History

History and geography are the two major social science disciplines that make up most social studies programs in schools. While history continues to play a critical role in social studies, educators and historians[1] have recently argued that there is not enough history content in the social studies and wider curriculum, and that what there is, is often times poorly taught. However, efforts are being made to improve history teaching in many provinces.[2]

RATIONALES FOR TEACHING HISTORY

Intrinsic Value

People often find the past fascinating. Family histories are traced,[3] and movies and television programs about historical events and people receive much attention. Witness the large audiences for the CBC production *Canada: A People's History,*[4] as well as movies based on historical events and characters, the interest paid in various media to recent historical discoveries such as an unexplored tomb in the Valley of the Kings, and the popularity of the History Channel. Even quite young children are interested in historical sites, stories, movies, and cartoons about historical events and people, and in their family history. Teachers can build on this almost universal interest in history in teaching elementary students.

Building Pride in Heritage

Traditionally, history has been taught to instill national pride. This is why, in the past, textbooks have included stories of heroes and battles won. This is also why modern textbooks feature stories about the contributions of women and cultural minorities, as well as so-called "ordinary folk." From an international perspective, this is why textbooks in Iraq that extolled the virtues of Saddam Hussein and his Baath party are now being replaced by textbooks that cite the contributions of other people and groups in Iraq history.

Developing a Sense of Identity

History also provides us with a sense of identity as individuals and as members of a nation, or a cultural or ethnic group. Through the study of history, we know where we have come from and can decide where we want to go. Thus, history teaching at the elementary level focuses in part on family so that students can discover their roots. We now study the history of students' communities, and also the whole of Canada, so students can begin to understand their community and nation's history. As Levstik and Barton[5] state:

> Students who do not see themselves as members of a group who had agency in the past or power in the present, who are invisible in history, lack viable models for the future.

Avoiding Past Mistakes

History can lead us to reflect upon what occurred in the past so that we can try to avoid past mistakes. Consider, for instance, why we teach about some of the atrocities and harm imposed on people in the past (e.g., the Holocaust, the internment of the Japanese in World War II, and the residential schools for First Nations children). By teaching about these events, we can help students develop values that are antithetical to the mistreatment of others.

Teaching Inquiry Skills and Critical Thinking

Teaching history using inquiry strategies entails that students search for information, judge the reliability of sources, become aware of differing points of view, and decide if enough evidence exists to support a conclusion. For example, in the activity outlined in Chapter 8 where students identify their grandparents' toys, it is unlikely that printed sources such as catalogues or newspaper advertisements will indicate all the toys available, especially those not commercially produced. Thus, students can realize that their conclusions may well be incomplete. In the lesson plans in Chapter 2, one teacher has students compare French and Native accounts of Cartier's explorations, thus helping students understand that a historical account is rooted in someone's point of view.

Making Better Decisions

Students need not only to develop appropriate values about such events as the Holocaust, but also to make decisions about future actions. As history teaching helps develop critical thinking abilities (e.g., recognizing bias, identifying reliable information, and making plausible interpretations), students can apply these to contemporary problems and make more intelligent decisions. Thus, history education plays an important part in citizenship education. Osborne[6] says:

> The main advantage of history is that it enables us to think for ourselves about important issues bearing on the human condition. It makes it possible to see the world as it is (which means understanding how it came to be that way) and to see the world as it might be, while also helping us to think about how to get from one state of affairs to the other. This is what makes the study of history an ideal preparation for democratic citizenship.

Developing Historical Empathy

History can also teach us about the human condition and thus help develop each student's historical empathy. As pointed out above, by teaching about people's inhumanity we hope to develop values that are positive. By teaching about how people lived in the past, we try to encourage students to see different points of view and gain some understanding of what it would be like to live in a different time period, and thus develop empathy for those living now. Here, the use of literature can bring to life people who were famous, infamous, and "ordinary."[7]

However, all these rationales are contentious. Michael Bliss,[8] a well-respected Canadian historian, has argued that the purpose of history education should be the teaching of content about significant events and people in Canadian history. Peter Seixas,[9] in the same issue, puts forward a very different rationale—one based on the raising of historical consciousness.

Activity 10-A

What rationales for the teaching of history are presented in your provincial or territorial curriculum guide? Ask a number of elementary school students what importance, if any, they think learning history has, and what they think the study of history is all about.

ORGANIZING FOR HISTORY INSTRUCTION

To teach history in a meaningful and interesting way requires a set of **history concepts and questions.** Based on those developed by Seixas,[10] Denos and Case outline their application in history teaching.[11] Note that in any one history lesson or activity, more than one of the concepts outlined below may be useful.

Significance

In choosing what to teach, we decide what is **significant** for students to know. One criterion could be the people and events that have had the most dramatic long-term effects on us. In Canadian history, Sir John A. Macdonald and the building of the Canadian Pacific Railroad would certainly qualify here. Another criterion would be those people and historical events that connect us as individuals or groups to our present lives or illuminate issues that still face us. Thus, one author's experience of the Blitz (when England was bombed by the German air force in World War II) would count as historically significant both to him and in the wider social context. However, there may well be a disjuncture between what we consider significant for students to know and what is actually significant to students. Significance depends on one's perspective and varies over time. Seixas,[12] in his research, shows that students from diverse backgrounds cite immigration, living in countries other than Canada, and their initial experiences in Canada as being significant. Some students could link these experiences to what is being taught in social studies. One student related his growing up in a village in Portugal to the experiences of early settlers in Canada. Other students could not draw any such relationships. Some expressed dismay that they knew very little about their own family history and the history of the country of origin. To make history significant we can draw on students' family histories. If the topic is the development of communities in Canada then we could have students research a community in their country of origin by interviewing, where feasible, family and friends. As Seixas states:[13]

> Family history and family experiences had a profound impact on how many of these students understood the past. Unfortunately, their social studies classes have generally neglected these sources of historical understanding.

Seixas is talking about the secondary school students he interviewed, but his findings are relevant to elementary school students as well. One way, where feasible, is to have students research their family histories. If parents or guardians are willing, students could create family trees, collect artifacts from their relatives' lives and display these, create a family scrapbook, and link their relatives' lives to what was occurring in the communities in which they lived and the wider world. Here a time line can be used, as shown in an example later in this chapter. Then students could research the events pivotal in their relatives' lives. For example, if they were involved in the armed services, then which wars or actions did they serve in and what was Canada's role in these? Or if their relatives immigrated to Canada, then what was life like in their country of origin and what were the reasons for emigrating? Students could also collect images of the environments in which their relatives lived. Here, local archives and online archival photo collections may be useful (see pages 185–188 for a list of useful websites). Where feasible, relatives could be interviewed. Some might be persuaded to visit the class and talk about their lives. (See Chapter 19 for ideas about interviews and speakers.) Another idea is to have students collect family artifacts and put them in a box. Other students then have to identify the objects and place them in chronological order. Preparing a family history can also incorporate all the other concepts outlined below.

The following sorts of questions and activities can be used or adapted for particular grade levels.

1. List three significant events in your own life. Why did you choose these? Write an autobiography that links those three events. List three other significant events in your life. Write another autobiography linking them. How are the stories similar and different?
2. Draw a **time line** on which you place significant events in your family history. Why were these events chosen? Ask another family member to draw a time line. Compare the two. Why are there similarities or differences?
3. Create a time line for the history of or part of the history of a particular country or community. What categories of events (e.g., political, economic, military, religious, and recreational) or people (e.g., rulers, politicians, military leaders, media stars, and sports people) did you include?
4. Create a poster showing four significant events in the history of your community, province/territory, or country. Why did you choose these?

Activity 10-B

List what you consider to be the ten most significant events and people in Canadian history. You can limit your list by considering those who you think students should know about in a particular grade. What criteria did you use to select these? Are these incorporated in the social studies curriculum? If not, would you teach about them?

Evidence

What should qualify as a reliable account of a historical event or a plausible description of an artifact? Should students believe the history depicted in movies, textbooks, and the stories of the past as told by their families? For example, Seixas[14] has shown how students interpret the movie *Dances with Wolves,* and Justice[15] demonstrates the historical inaccuracies in the movie *Gangs of New York.*

One way to draw attention to **evidence** is through oral history projects. Arruda[16] states that students get deeper and more interesting information through talking to someone. They will also get better insights into people's lives—lives not always examined in textbooks. So, too, might students discover how accounts of the same event differ between interviewees. Elementary school students have carried out some very successful work interviewing people who have lived in the community for a long time.[17] Students can also visit historical sites and museums, and study old maps, letters, newspapers, and other documents to gain some understanding of the problems of, and criteria for, deciding what is the most reliable account of a given event or the best description of an artifact. If students are to interpret and evaluate evidence, they need to be taught some of the criteria for judging it (Chapter 8). They can be presented with two or more conflicting accounts of the same event and can begin to consider questions of historical interpretation. Many textbooks now present these sorts of accounts, describing, for example, how the First Nations people viewed European explorers, as well as the reactions of explorers to First Nations people.

Closer to home, students can be asked to describe what they saw in the playground at recess and to compare descriptions so that they realize that their vantage point and biases influence what they see. Students could also be asked to describe what they saw on a television program and to compare the descriptions. As a fun activity, have students select an everyday object and pretend that in the distant future an archeologist uncovers it in the year 4000. How would this archeologist likely describe it? Here is what could be said about a home entertainment centre:

> This huge artifact dominated one wall of the building, and all activities were directed toward it. It clearly had religious significance to the ancient Canadians. Although a large number of gods could be contacted from this altar, the favourites appeared to be TSN and MTV. There were impact marks on the top and sides of the altar, indicating that some communication consisted of hitting it. Communication was continued after death as a communicator box could be placed in the hands of the deceased. Below the glass face of the altar were spaces for offerings, and around the perimeter of the room were boxes that allowed the gods to communicate to the worshippers from all directions.

The realization that different points of view exist is an important lesson for elementary school students. As students mature, they deepen their understanding of this in the later grades. According to Lee and Ashby,[18] students progress through stages from viewing history as given—it is just "out there"—to thinking that history cannot be known as we were not there to see it, to history can be known only on the basis of available evidence, to later stages of realizing that the biases and choices of the historians create differences.

Questions

1. Examine a historical artifact and identify, where possible, when it was made and used, what it was made of, what it was used for, who made it, who used it, and what importance it had in its original context. How plausible do you think your conclusions are?
2. How could you find out what your community was like 100 years ago?
3. How could you write an account of the meeting between Cartier and Chief Donnacona that reflects each of their points of view?
4. Compare two history textbook accounts of the same event. Is one more reliable than the other?

Activity 10-C

Examine the following photograph. Do you think this is a realistic view of classroom life at the time or was the photo "posed" to achieve a particular purpose? What did the photographer want viewers to think when they viewed the photo? Give reasons for your answers. What other sources could you use to ascertain what schools were like a hundred years ago? Which would be the most reliable?

Continuity and Change

Change is a constant. Even though there is **continuity** in some ideas, roles, and institutions, these concepts change over time, and often entire ideas, roles, and institutions may be radically altered. Students must come to see how changes can affect many aspects of life. Consider, for example, a modern technological advance such as the computer. By tracing its relationship to work, education, leisure, male and female roles, industry, and economics, students can see the profound effects that technological change has on society over time. How students view change will depend upon their experiences. An economically disadvantaged refugee from a developing country will have a very different view of change from a student who has grown up in a fairly stable middle-class environment. When changes occur, we are likely to evaluate it in terms of the past. We sometimes talk about the "good old days" as if recent changes have been negative. We applaud technological inventions that result in us having to perform fewer tedious jobs. History textbooks often assume that history is about progress. Yet, there are those who argue that some changes have been for the worse—for instance, the "erosion" of family values, the decline in church attendance, and the possibility of human cloning. Students need to identify the criteria they believe should be used to judge changes. (Part 3 is devoted to helping students make value judgments.)

Questions

1. Examine a historical photo, picture, or account. What has changed? What has remained the same? Have matters improved or worsened since then? In what ways? For whom?
2. Decide whether a historical phenomenon (what was worn at a particular period of time, how people were governed or educated) has changed. Were these changes better or worse than that same phenomenon today?

3. Show how one change (e.g., human rights legislation or the abolition of slavery) has improved life.
4. Examine these three photos of the same scene taken at three different time periods. What is similar? What is different? Do you consider the changes to be a mark of progress?

5. Examine something that is no longer in use. Why is it not used anymore? What, if anything, has replaced it? How has the change affected our lives?
6. Arrange events, pictures, and photos in the order in which you think they occurred. Give reasons for your decision.
7. Have groups of students choose a particular phenomenon (e.g., clothing, household utensils, or education) in a particular area (e.g., a community or a whole country), trace its development, and identify the stimuli and impediments to the changes over time that occurred to the phenomenon. Groups could compare their findings and ascertain whether any stimuli or impediments to change can be generalized.
8. Draw a time line showing the development of an object over time (e.g., a bicycle, car, pen, or makeup).

Activity 10-D

Draw a diagram tracing the impact of one ancient or modern technological advance.

Cause and Consequence

What caused X to happen may be important because the same sort of causes may be present now and we may be able to predict events. For example, examining how the **causes and consequences** of climate change occurred in the past may help us deal more effectively with climate change in the present. Young children often find it difficult to understand the causes of a particular change, especially when it is divorced from their own experiences and when the causes are complex. Often they see a change as inevitable and not due to human agency.[19] Teachers can help students deal with causation by presenting them with simple situations such as a bicycle accident. What might have caused it? Historical events can be linked to things that students are familiar with so that analogies can be drawn. For example, in discussing why people were motivated to immigrate to Canada, we can ask students what might motivate *them* (i.e., the students) to move to a new location. We can study human **agency** and ask students what the causes and consequences were, for example, of the explorations of Franklin in the Arctic. In traditional history textbooks, it was often only the rich and powerful who were viewed as agents of change. Historians and, to an extent, history textbooks are now emphasizing the lives of "ordinary" people and the consequences of their lives on society as a whole. As well, stories of "marginalized" people demonstrate to students that it is not just the rich and famous who cause change to occur. Davis[20] makes this point well:

> If you spend most of your historical study learning about famous missionaries, explorers, kings and queens, politicians, financiers, writers and inventors, you pick up the message that the life of the average peon is unimportant. If, in addition, you are from a humble background yourself, you pick up the additional message that you and your folks are not that memorable either.

He goes on to conclude that history education should include the lives of ordinary people so that they receive the recognition they deserve as participants in history that impact on change. As young children are more interested in social history and know more about it than they do about political and military history, we can build on this interest to help students see that their ancestors were important.[21]

Questions

1. Choose a historical figure, famous or not, and inquire into his or her motivations and the consequences of his or her actions.
2. Draw a web diagram showing the causes and consequences of building a new arena, road, or shopping mall, etc. in the community.
3. Discover how the ancient Romans or Greeks explained a particular disease. How would we explain it now?
4. Do you think you have changed somebody else's life in a positive way? If so, what were the consequences of this change? If not, do you think you could do this in the future?
5. Which people have made significant changes in Canadian history? What conditions enabled them to bring about these changes?
6. Has the "ordinary" person in a historical picture (for example, a medieval farmer, a monk, or a seamstress) potentially made a difference to the path of history? If so, how?

Historical Perspective

When students read about people in the past, they realize that much was different in terms of the social conditions of society. Despite this, students may also believe that people reacted to their world in much the same way they do today. Yet, in many cases, people in the past had different belief systems and interpreted their world in ways far different from our own. Students need to realize this by understanding as clearly as possible the context in which a historical character acted. It is pointless to role-play the meeting between Cartier and Chief Donnacona unless we know that Cartier thought Native people were *"sauvages."* We cannot impose our own beliefs and motivations on historical characters even though this makes them familiar to us. Thus, we have to keep asking whether characters would really have felt this way, given the context in which they acted.

One way to help students develop a **historical perspective** is through role play and drama. Although young children find these difficult, as they tend to view the world from their own vantage point, there is evidence that older students can empathize with historical characters and see the world through their eyes and can become aware of other points of view.[22] One website[23] allows students to choose a character from the late 1800s or early 1900s. Students then decide which information from a series of information centres they will use to make a decision about moving to the prairies. Another way a historical perspective and **empathy** can be developed is through historical fiction.[24] For example, reading *Ghost Train*[25] to students can engender understanding, anger, and sadness about the plight of Chinese labourers in the building of the Canadian Pacific Railway (CPR). As pointed out above, however, any story should be chosen carefully so that students do not get erroneous information. Levstik and Barton[26] provide a set of criteria for selecting historical fiction:

- Does the book tell a good story?
- Is the book accurate and authentic in its historical detail, including the setting and the known events of history?
- Is the language authentic for its time?
- Is the historical interpretation sound?
- What voices are missing?
- Does the book provide insight and understanding into current issues as well as those in the past?

These authors also provide a structure for students to take on the perspective of another person.[27] Students pretend they are historical characters (real or imagined) and use the stem structure to write about the person:

- I am _______.
- I wonder _______.
- I hear _______.
- I see _______.
- I want _______.
- I am _______.

This is followed by I pretend, I feel, I touch, I worry, I cry, I understand, I say, and I dream.

Activity 10-E

On page 126 is a photo of William Miner, who was a train robber in Canada. He was captured during a bungled train robbery in 1906. This photo was taken after his capture. What did the photographer want to say about Bill Miner? How do you think Miner felt? Could he have felt pride in his accomplishments, exasperation at being caught, and at the same time apprehension about his future? Or do you think he dreamed of escaping?[28] See the Answers section for more details about Miner's life.

Questions

1. What did the author of a particular historical account think of (e.g., slavery, First Nations people, or the building of the CPR)?
2. Write an account of an event from the perspective of a particular person (e.g., a First Nations person in Dawson City during the Klondike gold rush or an immigrant from Ukraine arriving in Halifax in the 1800s).
3. How were the beliefs of a particular person or role (e.g., Egyptian priests) different from ours?
4. Use the stem structure outlined on page 125 and pretend you are a child who has just arrived in Canada from China in 1900.

Moral Judgment

We all make **moral judgments** about historical events and characters—Louis Riel, for example, was a traitor, a hero, and a misguided zealot. However, just because a historical character did what he or she thought right given the context of the times does not mean the action was in fact right from the perspectives of others. Even though slavery was an accepted practice in the past, that does not mean it was morally defensible, even in the past. Seixas[29] sums up this principle in the following way:

> As with the problem of historical empathy, our ability to make moral judgements about history requires that we entertain the notion of a historically transcendent human commonality, a recognition of our humanity in the person of historical actors, at the same time that we open every door to the possibility that those actors differ from us in ways so profound that we perpetually risk misunderstanding them.

Questions

1. What moral responsibility do you think the first fur trading companies ought to have had for First Nations people? Did they live up to these responsibilities? Should they be blamed if they did not?
2. Whom do you consider to be a hero in the history of your province or territory? Was this person a hero because of his or her moral characteristics?
3. Gladiatorial fights were considered to be acceptable in Roman times. Would you consider them to be acceptable now? Why or why not?
4. Do we bear responsibility for the actions of past generations? For example, should the government apologize to First Nations people for the establishment of residential schools and forcing First Nations children to attend them?

Activity 10-F

Using the picture below, generate at least one question from each of the categories above (i.e., significance, evidence, continuity and change, cause and consequence, historical perspective,

This is a photo of the first radio car on the CNR in 1924. Passengers could put on headphones and listen to the radio as they travelled.

and moral judgment) and suggest answers to each of them. Share your questions and answers with another person or group and discuss any differences. If the answers differ, how would you determine which answer is the best or most plausible?

TEACHING TIME AND CHRONOLOGY

In teaching a historical topic, it is necessary to locate it in time. The concept of "time" is a difficult one for young children in particular to grasp. Barton and Levstik[30] claim that by Grade 2 students are moving from a dichotomous characterization of time (e.g., long ago/close to now) to more complex temporal distinctions. Dates don't make much sense until Grade 3. However, research indicates that young children can and do understand historical time in several ways (see Downey and Levstik[31]). Young children conceive of time not only in terms of their daily lives—going to bed, watching TV cartoons on Saturday—but also in terms of "dinosaur times" or "when people lived in caves." They recognize the passage of time by identifying a number of sequential discrete points—for example, events in their own lives such as birthdays; important cultural festivals such as Christmas, Hanukkah, or Diwali; and times when they were in the hospital or when a sister or brother was born. So one way to teach children about historical time is to have them create a personal time line and then use this as a reference point for the **chronology** of historical events.

Other ideas include the sequential ordering of a series of artifacts. A faculty member at the University of British Columbia has a collection of money, postcards, and letters from an aunt. He asks his students to place them in sequential order and figure out the life history of his relative. Students really get involved in this activity, partly because they can *touch* the items. Students could also be given pictures of a particular phenomenon over time (e.g., costumes, implements of war, or kitchen utensils) and be asked to place them in chronological order. For other ideas on the teaching of time, see Muir,[32] Burlbaw,[33] and Alleman and Brophy.[34]

Time lines not only help students locate events in sequence, but also help them to "see" duration. Children have difficulty in understanding how long a year is, let alone a century or a millennium. Time lines can show duration in spatial terms. In Near Eastern and European prehistory, for instance, the Stone Age (approximately 1 million BC to 3000 BC) takes up more space on the time line than the Bronze Age (approximately 3000 BC to 1000 BC), which means it lasted longer. To help students understand the concepts of "BC" and "AD," it is necessary to tell them that in many Western cultures AD (Anno Domini) dates from the time that it is believed Christ was born. So the years 1 to 100 are in the first century AD (there is no zero century), the years 101 to 200 are in the second century, and so on. The publication date of this book is 2009, in the 21st century. Once this idea has been grasped, then the idea of BC becomes more understandable. Again, there is no zero century BC; we have to count backward from 1 BC. To find out how long ago something occurred "Before Christ," we have to add the AD and BC figures. So, if it is correct that the first people came to North America around 10 000 BC, then that was approximately 12 000 years ago.[35]

Activity 10-G

Create a time line for your own life. Underneath your time line, create another one listing important events that occurred in Canada during your lifetime. Compare this with a peer's time line. Did you mention the same events? Why or why not? Now, extend your time line into the future. What do you want to be able to place on your time line one year from now, 10 years from now, and 20 years from now? Do the same for the Canada time line. If possible, also create time lines for your parents and grandparents. Relate their lives to events in Canada and the rest of the world.

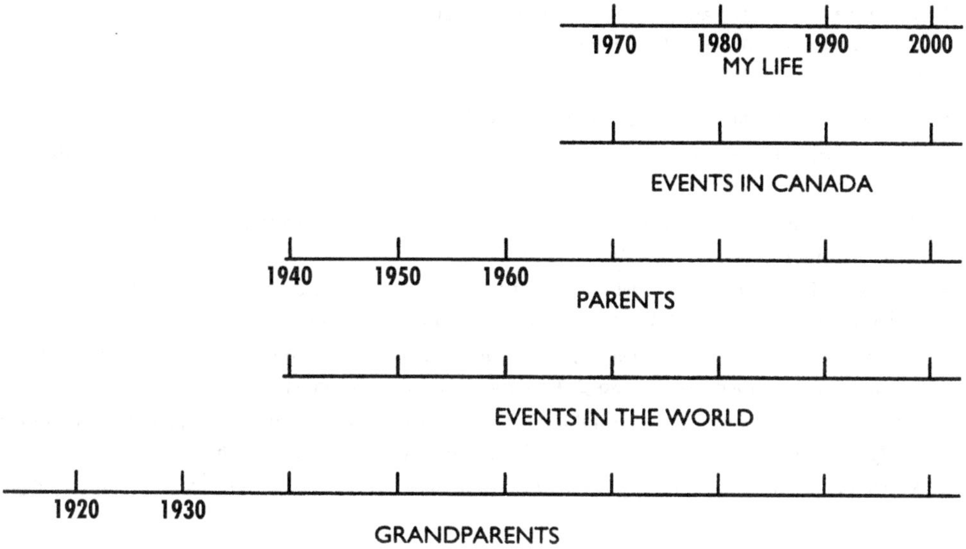

Other Activities

1. Choose a historical character with whom you are familiar and create a time line for that person's life. Underneath the time line, create another one that shows what other events were happening in the community or world during that character's lifetime.
2. Have a group of elementary school students of different ages construct time lines of their own lives. Compare the results and ask the students to explain why there are similarities and differences between the time lines.
3. In outline form, suggest what sources of information elementary school students could use to write a history of a community with which they are not familiar. What activities could students carry out to obtain this information?
4. Choose a topic in Canadian history from the social studies curriculum and find out what was occurring in another part of the country or world at that time. Suggest ways you could relate those events to the chosen topic in an effort to help your students gain a more global perspective on history.

Notes

1. J. Granatstein, *Who Killed Canadian History?* (Toronto: HarperCollins, 2007). For an excellent history of the teaching of history in Canadian schools, see D. Morton, "Teaching and learning history in Canada," in P. Stearns, P. Seixas, and S. Wineberg, eds., *Knowing, Teaching and Learning History* (New York: New York University Press, 2000).
2. For example, in February 2008 representatives of each province and history textbook editors met in Vancouver to discuss the incorporation of the historical concepts outlined in this chapter.
3. When the Church of Latter-day Saints placed its database on the internet, it was flooded with calls from people who wanted to trace their ancestors.
4. http://history.cbc.ca
5. L. Levstik and K. Barton, *Doing History* (Mahwah, NJ: Erlbaum, 1997), p. 2.
6. K. Osborne, "The teaching of history and democratic citizenship," in R. Case and P. Clark, eds., *The Canadian Anthology of Social Studies* (Vancouver: Pacific Educational Press, 1999).
7. P. Clark, "Literature and Canadian history: A marriage made in heaven," *Canadian Social Studies* 37(1). www.quasar.ualberta.ca/css/Css_37-1.htm
8. M. Bliss, "Teaching Canadian national identity," *Canadian Social Studies* 36:2 (2002). www.quasar.ualberta.ca/css/Css_36_2/ARteaching_canadian_national_history.htm
9. P. Seixas, "The purposes of teaching Canadian history," *Canadian Social Studies* 36:2 (2002). www.quasar.ualberta.ca/css/Css_36_2/ARpurposes_teaching_canadian_history.htm
10. P. Seixas, "Benchmarks of historical thinking: A framework for assessment in Canada," Centre for the Study of Historical Consciousness, The University of British Columbia, 2006.
11. M. Denos and R. Case, *Teaching about Historical Thinking* (Vancouver: The Critical Thinking Consortium, 2006).
12. P. Seixas, "Historical understanding among adolescents in a multicultural setting," *Curriculum Inquiry* 23:3 (1993), pp. 301–327.
13. P. Seixas, "Making sense of the past in a multicultural classroom," in R. Case and P. Clark, eds., *The Canadian Anthology of Social Studies* (Vancouver: Pacific Educational Press, 1999).
14. P. Seixas, "Confronting the moral frames of popular film: Young people respond to historical revisionism," *American Journal of Education* 102 (1994), pp. 261–285.
15. B. Justice, "Historical fiction to historical fact: *Gangs of New York* and the whitewashing of history," *Social Education* 67:4 (2003), pp. 253–256.
16. T. Arruda, "In their own voices: Exploring social history through oral narrative," in R. Case and P. Clark, eds., *The Canadian Anthology of Social Studies* (Vancouver: Pacific Educational Press, 1999).
17. See M. Hickey, "And then what happened, Grandpa? Oral history projects in the elementary classroom," *Social Education* 55:4 (1991), pp. 216–217.
18. P. Lee and R. Ashby, "Progression and historical understanding among students ages 7–14," in P. Stearns, P. Seixas, and S. Wineberg, eds., *Knowing, Teaching and Learning History* (New York: New York University Press, 2000).
19. T. Lomas, *Teaching and Assessing Historical Understanding* (London: Historical Association, 1990).
20. B. Davis. "Teaching the general level student: History and work—rewriting the curriculum," in R. Case and P. Clark, eds., *The Canadian Anthology of Social Studies* (Vancouver: Pacific Educational Press, 1999), p. 320.

21. R. McKay and S. Gibson, *Social Studies for the Twenty-First Century: A Review of Current Literature and Research* (Lewiston, NY: Edwin Mellen Press, 2004), pp. 33–34.

22. M. Booth, "A critique of the Piagetian approach to history teaching," in C. Portal, ed., *The History Curriculum for Teachers* (London: Falmer, 1987).

23. www.theclares.ca/prairies

24. For sources of such stories you might look at reviews of children's books that appear periodically in teacher journals and in Books, a supplement with the *The Globe and Mail*. Penney Clark also provides an extensive list of historical fiction suitable for elementary students in her article "Literature and Canadian history: A marriage made in heaven," *Canadian Social Studies* 37:1 (2002); www.quasar.ualberta.ca/css/css_37_1/ARliterature_canhistory_marriage.htm. She also discusses the use of graphic novels in M. Cromer and P. Clark, "Getting graphic with the past: Graphic novels and the teaching of history," *Theory and Research in Social Education* 35:4 (2007), pp. 574–593.

25. P. Yee, *Ghost Train* (Toronto: Groundwood Books, 1996).

26. L. Levstik and K. Barton, p. 95.

27. *Ibid.*, p. 130.

28. For more ideas about analyzing historical photos, see K. Barton, "Analyzing historical photos," *Social Education* 65:5 (2001), pp. 278–283. See also Chapter 19.

29. P. Seixas and C. Peck, "Teaching historical thinking," in A. Sears and I. Wright, eds., *Challenges and Prospects for Canadian Social Studies* (Vancouver: Pacific Educational Press, 2004), p. 113.

30. K. Barton and L. Levstik, *Teaching History for the Common Good* (Mahwah, NJ: Lawrence Erlbaum Associates, 2004).

31. M. Downey and L. Levstik, "Teaching and learning history," in J. Shaver, ed., *Handbook of Research on Social Studies Teaching and Learning* (New York: Macmillan, 1991).

32. S. Muir, "Time concepts for elementary school children," *Social Education* 54:4 (1990), pp. 215–218, 247.

33. L. Burlbaw, "An unfolding time line," *Canadian Social Studies* 26:4 (1992), pp. 158–160.

34. J. Alleman and J. Brophy, "Teaching young children about changes over time," *Social Education* 94:2 (2003), pp. 107–110.

35. However, there is purported evidence from Brazil that human habitation was much earlier—50 000 years ago. See E. Dewar, *Bones: Discovering the First Americans* (Toronto: Vintage Canada, 2001), and A. McIlroy, "Who were the first Americans?" *The Globe and Mail*, September 6, 2003, p. F10.

Glossary of Key Terms

Chronology—The order in which events occur.

History concepts and questions:

Agency—Seeing oneself as able to make changes and have an impact on history.

Causes and consequences—The reasons why events occurred (e.g., human agency and the intended and unintended consequences of the events).

Continuity and change—What has changed and what has remained more or less the same.

Evidence—What qualifies as a reliable account or plausible interpretation of a historical event or a person's actions.

Historical empathy—Putting oneself into the position of historical characters to try to understand their perspectives.

Historical perspective—Taking into account the different cultural, social, and religious perspectives of people who have lived in the past.

Moral judgment—How we judge past events and people.

Significance—What is important in a historical event, time period, or one's own life.

Time line—A visual portrayal of events in chronological order of a given time period.

CHAPTER 11

From Disciplinary to Place-based Education: Teaching and Learning Geography

Geography is considered to be one of the major disciplines in social studies, and all provincial curricula contain geography-related expectations.[1] However, there is great variation in how geography is taught. For example, in Ontario, geography is taught as a discrete subject area only beginning in Grade 7. Although geography expectations are featured prominently in all provincial K–6 social studies curricula, most students don't "take" geography per se as a separate subject until Grade 7.

Whether geography is taught as a separate subject or integrated into the broader social studies curriculum, there are many good reasons for its inclusion.

RATIONALES FOR TEACHING GEOGRAPHY

Intrinsic Value

The places we know are imbued with meanings: the school we attend; the home where we live; the place where we were born. Often we are also fascinated by places that we don't know, such as potential travel destinations or locations where major historical or contemporary world events have occurred. Rather like babies who explore their immediate spaces, often with great enthusiasm, we want to see what is around the corner or over the next hill. We are in awe when we see the Rocky Mountains, an Atlantic storm, or a prairie sunset. The geography of places appeals to the human spirit.

Life Skills

In our personal lives, we need to be able to navigate the world as we map a route from Point A to Point B through a city or as we plan a vacation. The ability to judge distances, to choose the most efficient (and cost-effective) route, and to read a map or use Global Positioning System (GPS) devices, geographic information systems (GIS),[2] GoogleMaps.com, or MapQuest.com are all rooted in geography skills learned in elementary school. Imagine how difficult life would be if you did not have, for example, even the most rudimentary understanding of maps.

Job Skills

Many jobs require either a direct or indirect knowledge of geography. These include urban planners, who design road systems, public parks, and the residential/commercial/industrial sectors of cities; real estate agents, who determine the property values of homes and businesses; truck drivers, who navigate their routes; and emergency service personnel, such as firefighters and police officers, who routinely use their geographic knowledge to help others in need. A variety of recreational and professional sports, such as cross-country skiing and mountain climbing, also rely on an intimate knowledge of geography. And there are many more examples.

Community Building

We employ geographic skills in our personal lives and in our jobs, but we also rely on them as we participate in the public commons. Our social identities are in part formed by geography—the country, province, and municipality where we live. So, too, is how we relate to the rest of the world (e.g., the United States) framed in part by our geographic identities as Canadians, as Albertans, or as residents of St. John's, for example. Every few years we are asked to participate in democratic elections in which voting districts are organized by geography. Many of us also participate more directly in enhancing the quality of life of our local communities. Our sense of place and commitment is rooted in large measure in our sense of belonging to a geographic community.

Each of the above rationales (and no doubt several others) form the basis upon which the expectations for the elementary geography curriculum are derived. Internationally, the Geography Education Standards Project[3] provides a comprehensive and significant list of educational objectives related to geography. For Kindergarten to Grade 4, teachers are encouraged to focus on:

- the characteristics and purposes of geographic representations and how to use and analyze them;
- the locations of major places in their community and the wider world;
- the physical and human characteristics of places and how they interact;
- the concept of region;
- the ways in which communities can be described from different perspectives and how people's perceptions of places vary;
- the major components of the earth's physical systems;
- the components of ecosystems;
- the distribution of populations and the causes and effects of human migration;
- how culture affects the way people live and how cultures change;
- factors influencing economic activities and settlement patterns; and
- the distribution of renewable and nonrenewable resources.

Activity 11-A

Browse through the social studies curriculum for your province or territory. Identify the rationales, if any, that are cited for the inclusion of geography in the elementary curriculum.

ORGANIZING FOR GEOGRAPHY INSTRUCTION

Having established the importance of geography as a subject area, great care should be taken to effectively organize for geography instruction. There are several approaches teachers can take.[4] One popular approach is widely referred to as the "expanding horizons model" (see Chapter 3), where students start with the places they know best and gradually expand their knowledge of the world "outward" to the wider community, province or territory, region, Canada, and the rest of the world.

Expanding Horizons Approach in Reverse

As will be noted in this chapter, the expanding horizons approach can also work in reverse. In this scenario, geography instruction starts big (by focusing young children's attention on the whole earth as a globe) and gradually moves inward to address a more detailed study of country, province or territory, region, local community, home, and self.

Study of Self

In the early grades, the focus should be less on places that are external to the child and more on the internal *meaningfulness* children ascribe to their immediate environments and the *sense of place* they feel in relation to home, their bedroom, a favourite playspace, or a fort or den they have built. The study of self in relation to place aims in part to directly address the intrinsic value rationale for geography instruction noted at the beginning of this chapter. As such, this focus remains an important touchstone throughout the elementary and secondary years, even as students begin to study the wider world in a more disciplined and objective way.

Study of the Local Community

The study of the local community builds on students' sense of place. As young students learn about their immediate neighbourhoods, they engage in a number of activities that teach fundamental geographic concepts and skills. For example, students may trace their route from home to school and create simple maps of the local community. (For a unit plan on interdependency in a community, see Chapter 21). From a systematic perspective, older students can conduct an in-depth study of the flow of goods and resources (and waste products) through the community and then map these. They can identify through maps the different types of areas (e.g., residential, commercial, and industrial) typically found in communities. As a cumulative task, after conducting a community study older students can draw up plans for a new community that affords residents the same amenities and quality of life a well-functioning community in the real world should have. Alternatively, they can brainstorm improvements to their own community and map these.

Activity 11-B

Using a specific location as a reference point, consider the following geographic questions:

1. What would you find at your location that is unlikely to be shown on a map of the area? Create a map that depicts these features.
2. How is this location different from where you live, work, or go to school?
3. Is this location suitable for a range of purposes (e.g., to build a factory, to grow food, to locate a park)?
4. If you were going to build something at this location (e.g., a house, retail store, factory, or park), where would be the best place to put it? Why?
5. What do you smell at this location? What are the sources of these smells?
6. How could you improve this location environmentally? Economically? Aesthetically?
7. Can you identify a particular landform feature that is distinctive to this location (e.g., a cliff, hill, or moraine)?
8. What sorts of transportation networks are situated at this location?
9. What did this location look like 100 years ago? Upon what did you base your conclusions?
10. What do you think this location will look like ten years from now? Upon what did you base your prediction?
11. What natural and human "hazards" can you find in this location (e.g., erosion, possibility of flooding, or fire)?
12. How does the landscape of this location influence the way people live?
13. How have people changed the landscape at this location? Which of these changes have been beneficial and which have not?

Study of Regions

In so far as the focus of community study is squarely on the relationships and intradependencies *within* a single community, the study of regions focuses on the relationships and commonalities existing between or across two or more communities that share a common geographic context. In elementary social studies, the regions of Canada are normally understood to refer to six physical geographic regions: the Appalachian mountains; the Great Lakes and St. Lawrence lowlands; the Canadian Shield; the interior plains; the Western Cordilleras; and the Arctic lowlands. Students can reinforce their learning about the location of these regions using modelling clay or Play-doh to create a 3D topographic map of Canada. A diversity of elevations and "textures" are among the most important characteristics that define differences between the six physical regions of Canada. The tactile experience of working with clay or Play-doh to recreate representations of the Western Cordilleras (i.e., Rocky Mountains), the interior plains, and the Canadian Shield can help students internalize at a tactile—even affective—level the diverse topography that makes up Canada's physical geography. Teachers can also discuss with students the merits of dividing Canada into different regions. What are the benefits of living in each region, and how does each region affect Canada as a whole? With reference to different types of maps, have students discuss what other features could be used to determine the different regions of Canada (e.g., ethnicity, voting patterns, average temperatures). Would maps of people's food preferences create interesting and, more importantly, meaningful regions?

Study of Nations

All students, regardless of the province or territory in which they live, are expected to become familiar with the political boundaries and capital cities of Canada. Students learn to identify Canada on the globe, and on a map of the world and North America. They learn that Ottawa is the capital of Canada and that the country is politically divided into ten provinces and three territories. Students learn (and memorize) the capital cities of each province and territory and where to locate them on a map of the country. In the upper elementary grades, students also learn how geography affects the economies, political systems, culture, and relationships among and between people in both Canada and other countries. We can make the memorization of facts about Canada interesting to students by having them create bulletin board–size maps of the country, by cutting out the provinces and territories to make a jigsaw puzzle, or by playing card games to help students memorize the names of the provinces, territories, and capital cities. Students can also learn songs to help them memorize facts about Canada.

Study of International Political and Economic Systems

As helpful as it is to focus on a single location, be it local, regional, or national, the study of geography is enriched when students look beyond specific regions to also study **global systems,** such as key international economic and political systems that allow individual countries to communicate with one another and work together to solve or manage global challenges (see the section on global education in Chapter 17). Students can explore the flow of natural resources (e.g., trade), capital (e.g., money), and people (e.g., immigrants and refugees) between countries and begin to more fully appreciate the complex relationships that exist between developed and developing countries and the effects that geography have on these. For instance, a topic could be organized around a particular product (e.g., chocolate or orange juice), and the influences of global economies, climate, and landform patterns on the manufacture, distribution, and consumption of this product could be ascertained. (For ideas about how to use webs to help students make connections among related factors, see Chapter 14.)

Study of an Issue or a Problem

The study of the local community, region, and nation are all rooted in location. It is the size and scope of the location under study that in large part determines the geography content students learn. Contrast this with a geography curriculum that begins with a critical social issue (e.g., global warming) and then asks students to study this issue from a variety of different **perspectives,** including the local community, the wider region, the nation, and the world as a whole. (Consider the environmental axiom "think global, act local" in this regard.) In this scenario, it is the issue or critical question that is posed to students (e.g., how can we stop global warming?)—and not the specific location under study—that drives the instructional program.

In studying social issues, the problem-solving or inquiry method can be effectively employed (see Chapter 8):

1. Identify the problem (e.g., global warming). Clarify any terms in the problem statement. Identify for whom it is a problem and why.
2. Collect information about the problem.
3. Identify the site(s) of the problem. In some contexts, such as a drought or earthquake, the exact location can be determined. With a crisis such as global warming, the location is impossible to determine so students should note the places that generate the majority of the pollutants that, in turn, create the warming conditions.
4. Where possible, describe the geography of the site(s).
5. Determine the consequences of the problem. Explore the intended and unintended consequences over the short and long term. For example, the clear-cutting of forests is an efficient manufacturing process for harvesting wood, but trees play a key role in reducing carbon dioxide (CO_2) emissions in the environment that lead to global warming. There are other environmental and economic issues to consider. Logging is a major industry and source of employment in Canada (and elsewhere in the world). However, the erosion of soil due to overlogging a site is an important downside. The resulting consequences of droughts or floods may have far-reaching effects. Crops grown in the area may no longer be plentiful, leading to price increases and product shortages, and global warming has long-term and worldwide consequences.
6. Identify possible solutions. Evaluate the effectiveness of each solution (for example, judge the effectiveness of one's personal lifestyle changes or the effectiveness of an international agreement such as the Kyoto Accord).
7. Decide on the most defensible solution.
8. If feasible, take action. Write letters to relevant organizations, publicize concerns through displays and letters to newspapers, and carry out activities such as recycling cans and bottles, cleaning up streams and parks, and reducing consumption of non-recyclable products.

Activity 11-C

Review the social studies curriculum in your province or territory to determine how the geography topics and expectations are organized. As a teacher preparing a long-range plan for geography instruction in a particular grade over the course of a school year, how would you go about organizing a curriculum for geography instruction?

As the above approaches clearly indicate, the discipline of geography focuses not only on the physical environment around us, but also on the cultural environment in which humans live and interact. Physical geography and human geography constitute the two major branches of geography. The study of physical geography focuses on topics such as climate, topography, natural resources, ecology, lakes, rivers, oceans, and water systems. The study of human geography focuses on topics such as human migration, economics and trade, international relations, multiculturalism, and city planning. A particularly important theme running through the study of geography is the ways in which physical and human environments interact. For example:

- the influence of Canada's natural resources on our trading relationships with other countries;
- the relationship between Canada's topography and human settlement patterns throughout the country over the last two centuries;
- the relationship between Canada's seasons (e.g., winter) and our popular sporting pastimes (e.g., hockey); and
- the impact of Canada's geographic proximity to the United States on the influence of American culture on Canada.

MAPS AND MAPPING

Maps and mapping skills are essential components of the geography curriculum. Maps are also a fundamental part of a geographer's toolset as they help us represent features of places throughout the world in ways that can be easily communicated and shared with others. We of course rely on maps to figure out how to get from Point A to Point B (especially when we are lost), but they also provide us with an enormous amount of information about specific locations. Indeed, no single map can hope to record all of the information that is relevant about a specific place, such as its longitude and latitude coordinates, topography, roadways, and many other details. Instead, geographers rely on a variety of different types of maps to record information about an area's climate, landforms, geology, demographics, economics, flora, fauna, history, and so on. Students need to learn how to "read" these kinds of maps and also how to create their own maps using the concepts and skills learned in geography and other subject areas.

Geography and Math—The Interdisciplinary Link

Teachers are always looking for ways to build interdisciplinary links among the subjects they teach, as this enriches the teaching and learning process and helps teachers simultaneously cover multiple expectations in different subject areas. Mapping skills are one example of the mutual benefits of linking geography and mathematics instruction. Mapping concepts such as measurement, scale, and distance = speed x time calculations cross both subject areas. Students can learn about measurement and scale in a math class and then apply what they have learned as they calculate the distance between two points on a map in a geography class.

Before students can use detailed maps to obtain information, they first need to experience and grasp basic topographical concepts such as open and closed curves, direction, continuity and discontinuity, boundaries and regions, points of reference, size, and area.[5] Young children comprehend these concepts at a basic level and then build on their understandings as they cognitively mature and work with a variety of different types of maps that gradually increase in their complexity.

Starting Small and Big

It may seem like a contradiction to suggest that teachers should start both "small" and "big" when introducing maps to young students, but this is precisely what the research on geography instruction in early childhood tells us.[6] On the one hand, children need a sense of the world and the Earth as a whole in order to have a context for learning about the specific places around them, as well as, for example, the day/night cycle and the seasons. It is for these reasons that we introduce young students to the globe and its basic features. We want to give students a sense of the full size of the planet we live on as compared to, say, the city or town they call home. We also want to give students a sense of where they live in relation to the rest of the world.

Yet we also want young children to have an intimate sense of and respect for their local community. After all, their home, school, and neighbourhood are the places that they know best and most closely identify with. So we start both small and big and work our way into the middle, so to speak, reading and creating maps of their community, Canada, and the world as a whole, and then the provinces, territories, and regions as the geography curriculum progresses.

Maps and the Fantasy Lives of Children

Most of the maps students work with in school are representative of real-world places, such as the local community and the provinces and territories of Canada. Yet, as we all know, young children have active fantasy lives, as evidenced by the popularity of the make-believe stories they tell and the fictional books they read. Teachers can tap into children's fantasy lives by having them read and design maps of the fictional places they are reading about (e.g., Hogwarts School in the *Harry Potter* books), or by encouraging students to create a fictional map of a make-believe city or country or a topographic map of a faraway place on another planet. In either scenario, the students are using the same geographic concepts and mapping skills they are learning about when reading and creating real-world maps. The benefit is that fantasy maps also tap into children's creativity and sense of wonder.

The Globe

The globe is one of the first geographic models teachers are likely to introduce to students. Young children, through direct teaching and incidental learning, should learn that the world is a sphere and that there are continents and oceans. They should be shown that the world rotates, which is why there is a day/night cycle, and that the world revolves around the sun. In the later grades, students should learn that the world is tilted on its axis, and that the Tropics of Cancer and Capricorn are where the noonday sun is directly overhead at the solstices. By knowing this, students can explain the seasons.

Activity 11-D

In the intermediate grades maps should be related to the globe, because a flat map cannot give an accurate representation of shapes on a sphere. Students can discover this principle for themselves by drawing a large perfect circle on the side of an orange and then seeing what happens to the shape of their circle when the orange is carefully peeled and the peel is flattened out. Try this activity yourself—as best you can, outline the continents on the orange and then peel the orange and flatten it out. How distorted are the continents?

Here are some additional activities that help students learn about the world as depicted on a globe.

1. Have students choose a place in the world where they would really like to go, then:
   a) calculate the distance to this place. In the upper elementary grades, students can be shown that a great circle route is the shortest distance between two distant locations.
   b) determine what, if any, bodies of water will have to be crossed.
   c) determine what countries will have to be travelled through.
   d) determine the easiest route to the destination, and decide on the form(s) of transport to be used.
   e) have students determine whether it is daytime or nighttime at their destination when it is daytime where they live in Canada.
   f) have students determine what season it is at the destination.
2. Challenge students to make their own globes by blowing up a balloon and adding the continents using papier mâché or cutouts glued onto the balloon.
3. Give students cutouts of the continents. Have them label each of the cutouts and then locate them on a globe.
4. Play a game in which students are divided into two teams. Have each team take turns locating a place on the globe. If a team answers correctly, it is awarded a point and given the first opportunity to answer the next question.
5. Have students study a globe in order to estimate whether there is more land or water on the earth.
6. Have students study a globe to determine the largest and smallest continents. Have students confirm their answer by creating a cutout of each continent.
7. Whenever places are mentioned in stories or in current events, have students locate these places on the globe.

This last activity is a useful way of informally teaching students where places are in the world. There is no need for formal lessons, as familiarity with the globe over time will help students learn where places are located. These informal methods need to be pursued, as students don't learn location by osmosis. This was borne out in an assessment in British Columbia[7] where it was clear that Grade 4 students had not been formally taught, and had not learned through informal means, where the Prairie provinces are in Canada. Only 58 percent of the students tested could correctly locate them on a map of Canada.

Maps

Students will probably be more familiar with maps than with the globe and, as a result, will have a distorted view of the shape, size, and relative location of the world's continents. To account for the disparity between a flat map's representation of the spherical earth, geographers rely on a variety of projections that accentuate certain ways of representing the globe. For example, maps that use the Mercator projection show Europe and South America to be relatively equal in size, even though South America has twice Europe's land mass. Africa appears smaller than North America, yet Africa is 50 percent larger. Furthermore, Eurocentric views are fostered because two-thirds of the Mercator map is taken up with the northern hemisphere, and Europe is shown to be in the middle. All maps distort, but some are arguably "more distorted" than others.[8] As they study geography, students should be exposed to a variety of map projections so they can learn to see the world from different perspectives. To start, have a class of students look "down" on a globe from the North Pole and then "up" from the South Pole. Have them also view maps where Canada, Australia, or another country or continent are centred on the map.

Activity 11-E

To help students begin to understand how maps represent spatial features, provide each student with a chocolate chip cookie and two pieces of paper. Have them place their cookie on one of the sheets of paper and use the other piece of paper to draw a detailed topographic map that depicts all of the ridges, crevices, and other topographic details on the cookie. For an added challenge, use an eye dropper to release a few drops of milk onto the chocolate chip cookie. Challenge students to also map the "water bodies" that are created.

In order for students to read and draw maps, they need to be taught specific concepts and skills. (Refer to the glossary of key terms at the end of this chapter for definitions of the terms highlighted in bold.) Students should learn to:

1. Locate a place on a map and determine its **grid location** (e.g., latitude and longitude).
2. Locate two places and determine the distance between them using a map's **scale.**
3. Locate two places and determine the compass bearing between them using a map's **compass rose.**
4. Locate various topographical features (e.g., mountains, forests, rivers, roads, and buildings) using a map's **key.**
5. Locate the highest and lowest elevation points using a topographic map's **contour lines.**

The concepts of location, distance, scale, direction, bearing, elevation, and perspective all develop over time as children's cognitive and spatial perception matures. However, there is disagreement among experts concerning when young students can grasp certain map skills.[9] The following chart indicates the mapping concepts and skills children typically "grow into" at various ages as they mature. It is based on a compilation of evidence from several sources.[10]

MAP SKILLS

Concepts	By Age 7	Ages 7–9	Ages 9–11
Direction	Follows directions of left, right, etc.	Uses compass to find NEWS.	States compass bearing in degrees. Aligns map by means of a compass.
Location	Describes location in terms of front, behind, etc. Uses globe to locate continents or countries.	Uses simple grids. Locates objects on the ground in approximate position on a map.	Uses latitude and longitude.
Symbols	Uses symbols and colour on picture maps.	Draws and recognizes some conventional map symbols. Understands the need for a KEY.	Uses KEY to locate objects on a map.
Scale	Sorts objects by size and shape. Measures distances using hands and feet.	Draws and uses large-scale maps. Measures large objects accurately.	Measures accurately. Realizes that as scale decreases, generalizations on a map increase.
Elevation		Uses colour to indicate elevation.	Reads simple contour maps.
Other	Draws routes between objects.	Draws route to school and plan of classroom. Finds countries in atlas. Understands purposes of different sorts of maps. Uses aerial photos of known areas. Compares map to globe.	Relates map to aerial photos. Aware of limitations of maps. Compares map scales. Uses Landsat maps. Infers climate from latitude, and economic activity, etc. from location in the world. Uses time zone map of North America.

Activity 11-F

Below and on the following page are two maps. They show how the ability to draw maps develops over time as children mature. One map is drawn by a Grade 1 student. The other is drawn by a Grade 4 student.[11] What sense of "place" do these students display?

Compare these two maps. What are the differences? Use a variety of mapping concepts, such as location, scale, and perspective, to express your answer.

The ability to see things from a top-down, bird's-eye perspective develops with age. By about eight years of age, most children will have this ability. To develop it further, try the following activities:

1. Have students look down at their shoes and draw what they see.
2. Have students look down at a collection of objects on a desk and draw what they see.
3. Use a large sheet of paper to create a top-down view of the classroom, complete with student desks. Have students locate each others' desks on the map.
4. Have students pretend to be helicopter pilots hovering over the school. Ask them to draw what they think they would see.
5. Obtain an aerial photo of the area in which your school is located. Have students draw a top-down map of the area by tracing the roads and buildings.
6. Have students pick an object on an overhead map or aerial photo and draw it as if they were standing on the ground.

Young children find it very difficult to imagine what something looks like from the perspective of a bird or a pilot flying overhead. Because their abstract spatial and cognitive abilities have not yet matured, they cannot easily imagine themselves in the place of the bird or pilot. Nor can they take another perspective on an object that is different from their current vantage point. If asked to draw an overhead map of their house, young children tend to draw it as they most commonly see it (i.e., straight on from the front at street level). They also have trouble orienting the house to other objects on the ground. The four maps on the next page show the sorts of mapping challenges young children typically have.

Aerial photographs (such as the photo on the following page) and stereograms can help students to visualize from a map what a landscape actually looks like. Students can be asked to compare aerial photos, for example, with maps of the same locations. Where possible, start with aerial photos of the town or city the students live in. Using Google Earth (earth.google.com), students can locate their neighbourhood and places of interest and also trace their routes to school and compare these to a map. (Be sure to align the map with the aerial view.) For aerial photos that are out of date, have students

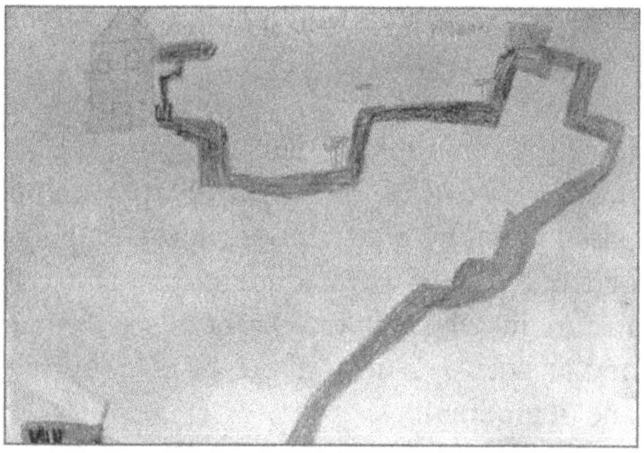

This map shows how a young child draws a straight road that goes up and down hills.

determine elements of the built environment (e.g., a new subdivision) that are not depicted on the aerial photo.

In addition to analyzing aerial photos, older students in particular can turn to computers to help them improve their mapping skills while working with the latest geographic information system (GIS) software from companies such as ESRI (www.esri.ca). Computer-based mapping programs such as GIS help students to visualize and interact with mapping data in different ways. Students can quickly create their own professional-looking maps that feature just the data they want to see. Students can also use GIS software to solve problems and answer questions about geography-related topics related to land use, traffic patterns, and demographics.

Activity 11-G

Produce a hand-drawn outline map of Canada without reference to an atlas, globe, or wall map. Can you locate the provincial and territorial boundaries, capital cities, major rivers, landforms, and other places you consider important? When your map is complete, compare it with a cartographic representation of Canada. Then answer the following questions:

1. If you live in the West, did you have problems mapping the eastern areas of Canada? Why?
2. If you live in the East, did you have problems mapping the western areas of Canada? Why?
3. What provincial and territorial boundaries, mountain ranges, major lakes and rivers, and capital cities did you include? Are they plotted at the proper locations?
4. Was your scale correct? Does the shape of your map roughly correspond to the shape of Canada?
5. Having reviewed areas where your map could be improved, draw it again. Also consider repeating this activity a few weeks later to see if the improvements to your map are retained.

We each view space in our own way, based on our age, background, and experience. Consider young children who live in a neighbourhood that is perceived to be unsafe. Their parents are concerned about the dangers lurking outside, so they do not allow them to venture very far from home. Now consider the increasing numbers of children who rarely leave their homes to play outside because they spend most of their playtime on the computer or watching TV. Both of these groups of children are likely to have a very limited view of the community in which they live (and the outside world more generally). On the other hand, children who regularly travel by car, bus, train, or airplane are likely to have an expanded sense of physical space that is bounded by roads and highways—or even national boundaries—instead of residential streets and back lanes. Now consider nomadic or migrant children who frequently move from place to place. Their view of home is not likely to be nearly as localized as a child who has lived in the same home for all of his or her life. Does your experience of place growing up match any of the above scenarios? Consider the places that were special to you in your childhood—for example, your home; your bedroom; the local playground; the local corner store; the route to school; a tree house, fort, or den you built out back; secret places where you could retreat for privacy; a sports field where you learned to play baseball or soccer, and so on. Do you have vivid memories of the places you visited far away from home as a child? Can you recall a moment when you became acutely aware of the cultural differences that exist between communities? In planning social studies instruction for young children, we should start with students' existing conceptions of space and then build on that knowledge as we gradually move them to a disciplinary understanding of geography.

Activity 11-H

Create a freeform map of a space that has special meaning to you (e.g., your immediate neighbourhood). What details did you include? Why? What details did you omit? Why? How does your map differ from one that a professional geographer might create?

We next take a closer look at a few of the major geographic concepts and mapping skills students should be introduced to in the elementary social studies program.

Direction Once students have grasped a sense of relative location and are able to properly use terms such as "left," "right," "in front of," and "behind," simple compass bearings can be introduced. To illustrate the relationship between compass bearings and relative location, quickly answer this question: If you are facing north, which compass bearings are to your left and right?

Many maps have north at the top. Unless corrected, students may believe that north and south are perpendicular, not parallel, to the earth's surface. This misconception has students saying, "up north" and "down south," and believing that rivers run north–south because water flows downhill. One of the authors' elementary students always had trouble conceiving of the Mackenzie River as flowing into the Arctic Sea, as this was toward the north and therefore "uphill."

One of the most useful introductions to directions is the "ME" diagram. In this activity, students draw objects along each axis that are situated relative to them in the environment.

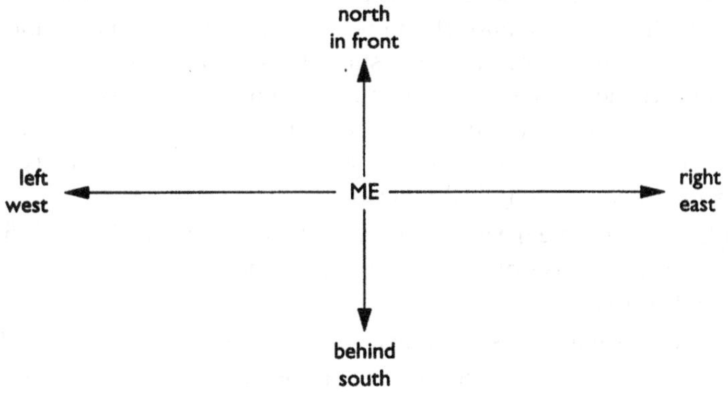

Modify this activity by having students also note the relative distance of nearby and faraway objects, as shown in the figure on page 148.

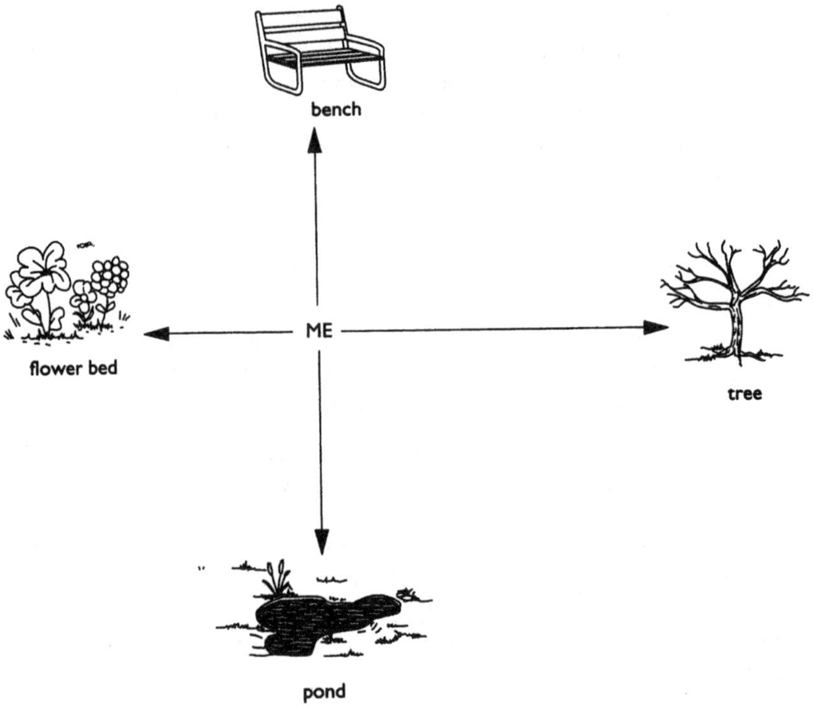

Here are a few other cross-curricular activities for teaching and reinforcing the concept of direction:

1. Divide the class into groups of five. One at a time, have each group come to the front of the class. Place one student in the centre of the group and position each of the remaining four students to his or her front, back, and sides. Designate that north is to the front of the student who is in the middle. Also have that student close his or her eyes. Point to one of the four students and have them clap once. The student in the middle is to call out the ordinal direction the clap is coming from. (Music)
2. In the school gym, divide the class into pairs and assign each pair a different start and end location. Place several obstacles in between the start and end locations. In moving between the two locations, have one student precisely follow the verbal directions given by the second student. For example, "Go three paces forward. Stop. Turn right. Take a big step to your left. Stop." If the student following directions seems ready, ask him or her to repeat the activity while wearing a blindfold. Keep safety issues in mind throughout this activity. (Physical Education)
3. Have students investigate the wide variety of strategies by which people have navigated direction throughout history (e.g., sundials, star navigation, compasses, global positioning satellites). (History/Science)
4. Locate direction using means other than a compass (e.g., the sun, stars). (Science)
5. Label the classroom walls with the correct compass bearings and give the students directions to follow (e.g., "Face the north wall. Go to the west door."). (Geography)
6. Hide an object in the classroom or playground and give the students directions on how to find it. (Geography)

7. Give each student an imaginary map. Then read a story and have students draw the route taken by a character (e.g., "John walked north to the big tree. He turned west toward the river."). (Language Arts)
8. Have students observe a slow-moving object (e.g., person or insect) and map the moves it makes. (Geography/Science)
9. Do simple orienteering. Give students a trundle and a map (such as the map below) marked with a number of locations where students have to go. The playground could be used as the orienteering course. For example:
   a) Start at A. Walk north for 80 m. Pick up a stone.
   b) Walk west for 70 m. What is located there?
   c) In what direction would you walk to arrive at the corner of the school?
   d) Walk south along the side of the school for 60 m. What is located there?

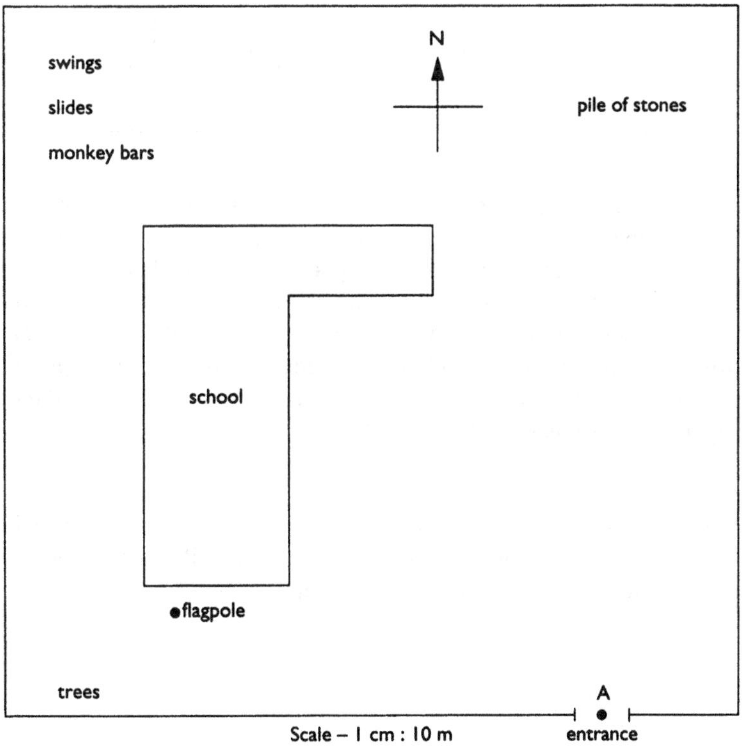

Grid Location Having a good sense of direction and a sound knowledge of relative location is important, but these are not the only location-related concepts and skills students need. They should also learn how to plot the absolute locations of places on maps that gradually increase in their complexity and specificity. Younger students typically learn to plot absolute locations using a grid map. Older students and professional geographers use latitude and longitude coordinates to plot the exact location of places.

For each of the grid maps below, answer the following questions:

1. Point to the grid coordinate B-3.
2. Which of the grid maps below is easiest to use? Why?
3. For the grid map on the left, how should one determine the grid coordinate where two lines cross?

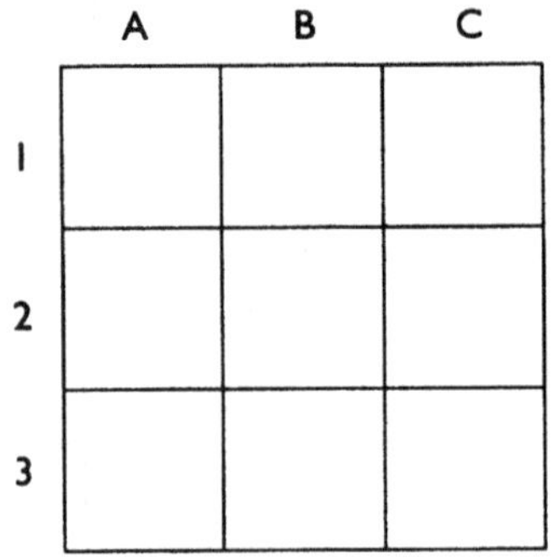

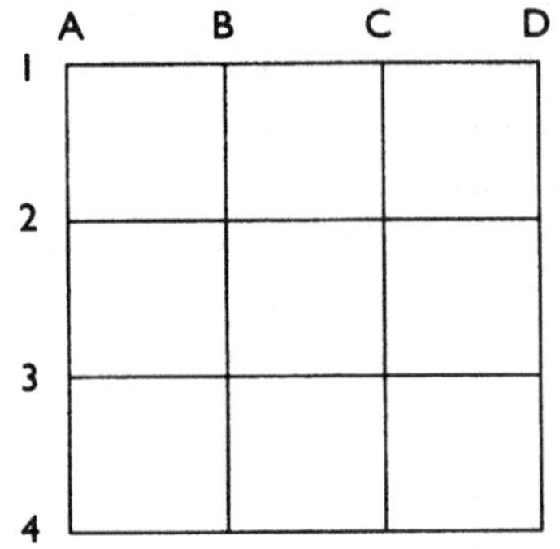

Activity 11-I

Form groups of four. Use a ball of string, a pair of scissors, some masking tape, a piece of paper, and a pencil to create a grid on a desk. (Use the masking tape to tape off the ends of the string.) Label the grid across and down using letters and numbers. Next, place a variety of objects (e.g., an eraser, stapler, and paper clip) on the grid and record the grid coordinates of each object on a separate piece of paper (e.g., paper clip: B-2). Once the above is complete, remove the objects from the grid and challenge another group to place the objects where they belong using the grid coordinates provided. Students can map their classrooms using tape, string, or chalk lines. Where feasible, they can also use the floor or ceiling tiles as coordinates.

Latitude and Longitude The conventional way of locating places on maps is to use latitude and longitude. These are quite complex concepts to fully understand, which is why most social studies teachers first introduce grid maps to younger students.

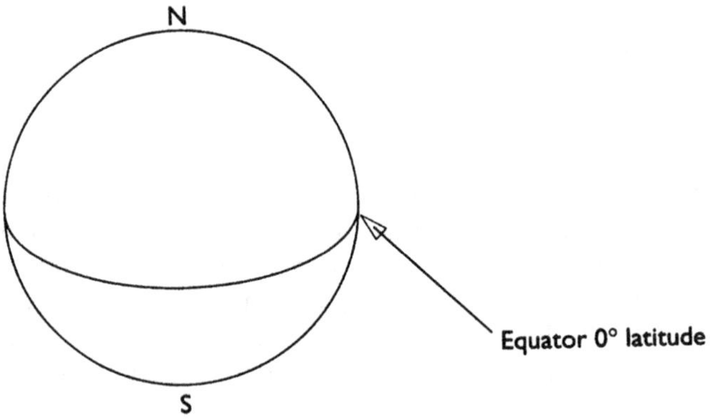

Before latitude and longitude are taught, students must know a few basic things about the globe (as noted earlier in this chapter). For example, they need to understand that the world is spherical, that there are North and South Poles, and that the equator divides the world into two hemispheres. (This last point is relatively easy to point out to students, as many globes are manufactured as two half spheres that are joined together at the equator.) Next, teach students that there are 360 degrees in a circle, and starting with latitude show how there are 90 degrees between the equator and the poles. Longitude is somewhat more difficult to conceptualize, as there is no physical divide on a globe to mark Greenwich and the **International Date Line (IDL).** So tell students that England "won" the right to place zero degrees at the Greenwich Observatory in London, England.

Once students have grasped the basic idea of latitude and longitude, they can begin to read and plot the locations of latitude and longitude coordinates. Students can use a world map or atlas to complete activities similar to the following:

1. Have students work in pairs to locate several major cities of the world using a list of latitude and longitude coordinates.
2. Have students determine the longitude of their community and ascertain which other communities in the world also have the same longitude. How are these communities the same or different in terms of climate, flora, and fauna?
3. On a wall map of the world, use thumb tacks to plot the fictional locations of several ships in distress. Time how long it takes for teams of students to determine and record the latitude and longitude coordinates for each ship in distress.
4. Teach students about the relationship between latitude and temperature and longitude and time. For a city close to the equator, have them use the internet or a reference book

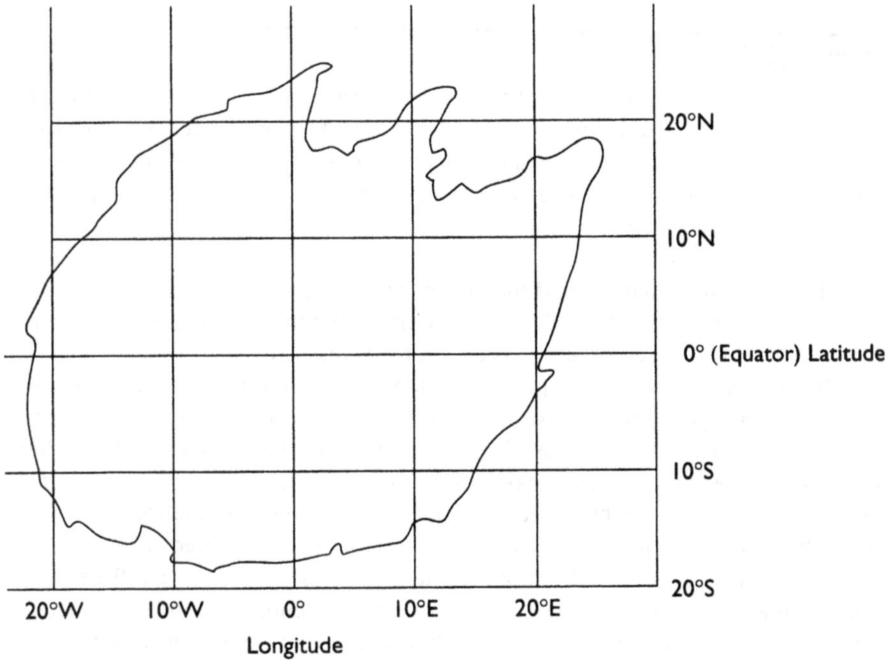

to look up the average annual temperature. For a city in a different time zone, have them use an atlas to ascertain the longitude coordinate.

5. Hand out a map of an imaginary island similar to the one shown on page 151. Now have students complete these tasks:

   a) Plot the location of a town at latitude 10° S and longitude 10° W.

   b) Plot the location of a lake at latitude 0° and longitude 10° E.

   c) Plot the location of a boat at latitude 20° N and longitude 20° E.

Time Zones and the International Date Line If you landed in Fiji on the morning of your birthday, stayed overnight, and then flew on to Samoa the following day, you would arrive in time to celebrate your birthday once again. This fact baffles most elementary school students (and many adults). And the same of course holds true for New Year's Eve parties. One could start in Australia and celebrate the arrival of the new year in multiple time zones while travelling west around the world.

To demonstrate **time zones** in the classroom, use a flashlight and a globe. Assume that it is noon when the sun is directly overhead any place in the world (Location A). Because lands to the east are ahead in time, and lands to the west are behind, it is afternoon to the east and morning to the west. To show this, shine the flashlight on the globe and rotate the globe 15° to the east (360° divided by 24 hours equals 15° for every hour). It will be noon at the new location (Location B) and 1 p.m. at Location A. If you were standing at Location A, you would see the sun to the west and eventually watch it "disappear" into the horizon. In reality time zones do not exactly follow lines of longitude, so students will have to refer to a time zone map to find out where time zones are actually located. Places that are located midway between 15° intervals often offset their times by a half hour from places east and west of them. One notable example of this is Newfoundland.

Activity 11-J

As a worthy cross-curricular math and geography exercise, solve this problem: "You are flying from Vancouver to London, England. Your flight departs Monday at noon, local time. The flight will take 10 hours. There is an eight-hour time difference between Vancouver and London. Calculate the local time at which your flight arrives in London. (See the Answers section for the correct answer.)

Symbols On the imaginary island map on page 151, students will have used symbols to show a town, a lake, and a boat. Although young children can sometimes be permitted to use their own symbolic representations on the maps they create, you should also introduce conventional map symbols in the primary grades. These symbols are not always simple to understand. Some symbols represent actual objects such as buildings. Others represent imaginary lines such as boundaries. (Young students may be surprised to learn that imaginary lines on maps do not actually exist on the ground.) Moreover, some symbols look like what they represent (e.g., a blue line for a river), while others do not (e.g., a red line for a road). When you ask younger students why some cities are coloured red, while others are black, they may tell you that the roofs in the two cities are made of different materials. Colours can also be confusing when they are used to denote elevation. Students' natural inclination is to associate colours with vegetation. They may mistakenly believe that green denotes lush vegetation and lots of rain, brown denotes little vegetation and not much rain, and white represents snow.

Here are some ideas to help students understand map symbols.

1. Make cards like those shown below:

   a) Fold a card in half and glue the two halves together so that a *picture* of a symbol is on one side of the card and the *name* of a *different* symbol is on the other.

   b) Divide the class into four equal groups, and seat each group around a table.

   c) Place a set of cards in the middle of each table. Shuffle the cards.

   d) The first person in each group finds the symbol for a bridge and hands the card to the next person in the group. This person reads the name of an object on the back of this card, puts the card back in the pile, and locates the card showing the correct symbol for the object name they have just read. This card is handed to the next person, who continues the matching game.

   e) With groups competing, play this game until one group arrives back at the symbol with which the game began.

   f) To extend the game, add more labelled cards with map symbols.

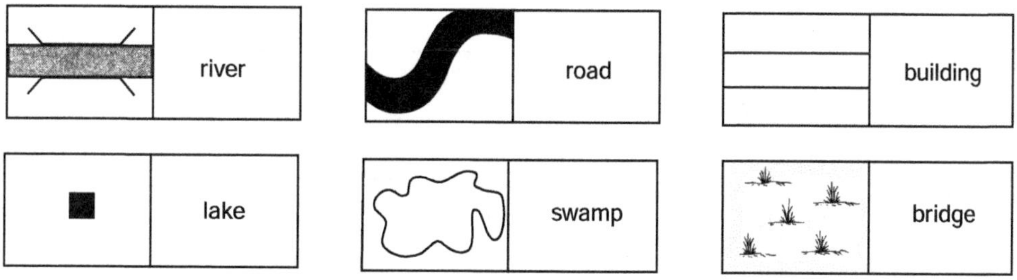

2. Make a set of cards. Label each card with a different geographic feature, such as a river, church, main road, and lake. For two students to play this game, you'll need about 20 cards with different labels. If you want the whole class to play, you'll have to make between 10 and 20 sets of cards.

   a) A pair of students is given a map (any suitable topographic map, real or imaginary, will do) and a pile of cards.

   b) Each student in turn picks up a card, reads the label, and, if the symbol for that label appears on the map, puts it on the map. If there is no symbol for the label, the student keeps the card. The student with the least number of cards kept wins the game.

3. Compare an aerial photograph of a location with a map of the same location. Note the map symbols and compare them with what the photograph shows.

4. Give out a blank map of the playground or part of the local community. Have students walk around the area and use symbols on the map to show what is there.

5. Give students a map and true or false statements (either in written form or stated orally)—for example, "There is a river on the map," or "There is a marsh." Have students identify which statements are true and which are false.

6. Have students make up imaginary maps and invent symbols to represent the objects they wish to depict on the maps.
7. For many objects, there are no universally recognized symbols. Have students make up symbols for such places as video stores, cinemas, parking lots, and so on.

Scale Young children usually grasp the concepts of "larger than" and "smaller than." But the concept of "exact scale" is difficult for young students to grasp, as it depends upon mathematical skills that aren't fully introduced until the junior and intermediate grades. Young children can practise using scales by working with "tools" other than rulers. For example, have students use their arm length, a paper clip, or their stride or pace to scale the distance between two objects.

Activity 11-K

Have students work with a partner. Give each pair a large sheet of paper that has a simple grid drawn on it. Have one partner lie down on the sheet of paper. Have the second partner trace his or her outline. Hand out another sheet of grid paper that is much smaller than the first. Have each pair copy the body outline on the larger sheet onto it. The following diagrams show how this activity can also be done using students' hands.

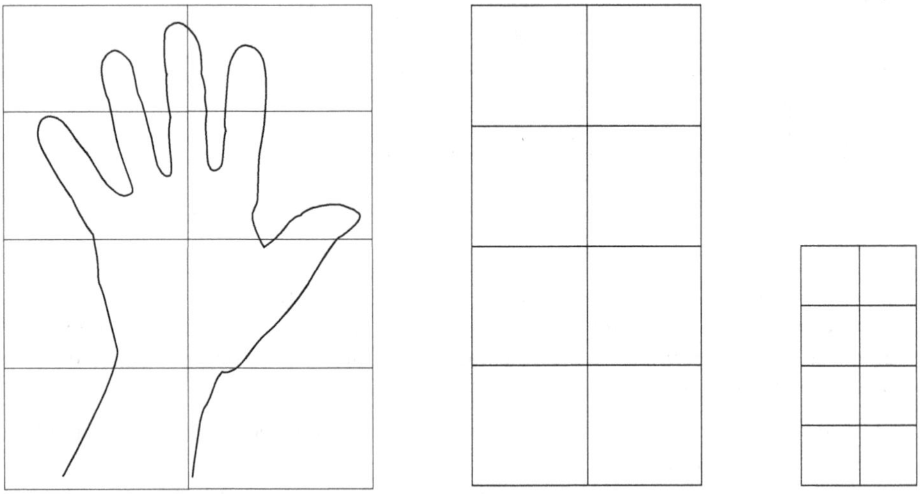

Young children find it quite fascinating to see themselves a tenth of their real size, and even more so to see themselves twice their own size when the original drawing is doubled. Another idea is to make a model of the classroom and have students create desk, chairs, tables, and so on to add to the model. They have to determine, for example, how much bigger the teacher's desk is than their own, and how much smaller a wastepaper basket is than a desk. Students could take photos of objects close up and far away and compare the amount of detail they can see.

Before working with maps of large areas, students should first learn to read large-scale maps of small areas. These show a great deal of detail because they cover small areas.

Small-scale maps (such as the ones found in atlases) do not show much detail because they cover large areas. To remember the difference between the two, think of *large-scale* maps as showing *large* details and *small-scale* maps as showing *little* detail.

Elevation In addition to scale and other details, many maps also represent elevation. Topographic maps use contour lines, but understanding what these lines represent is an advanced skill that is normally taught in the upper junior and intermediate grades. Nevertheless, the concept of **elevation** can still be introduced to younger students via 3D models that students can *feel* as well as see as they learn about the concept of elevation. (Papier mâché and Play-doh are good choices of materials for creating 3D topographic models.) Later, students can use atlases and colour keys (e.g., green for lowlands and white for the peaks of very high mountains) to locate various elevations. Ask students to locate flatlands on a map of the world or Canada. Then ask them to locate mountains.

To introduce a class of students to contour lines, provide them with sheets of paper and hand-made cones that can be drawn on. Then have them do the following:

1. Have students position the cones on the middle of the paper.
2. Have students draw an outline around the base of the cone.
3. Have students measure halfway up the cone. Then have them draw a circle on the cone around this halfway mark. Ask them to also plot on the paper a contour line that represents this elevation.
4. Also have students plot on the paper a contour line (or point) that represents the very top of the cone.

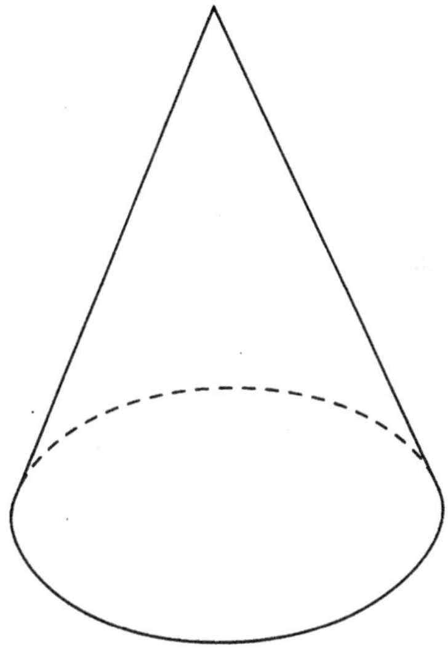

5. Next have students label the height (in cm) represented by each contour line on the paper. Have them colour in the area between the base line and the halfway mark, and also the halfway mark and the peak.

Activity 11-L

Draw a contour map for the following shape, using the same procedure as outlined above.

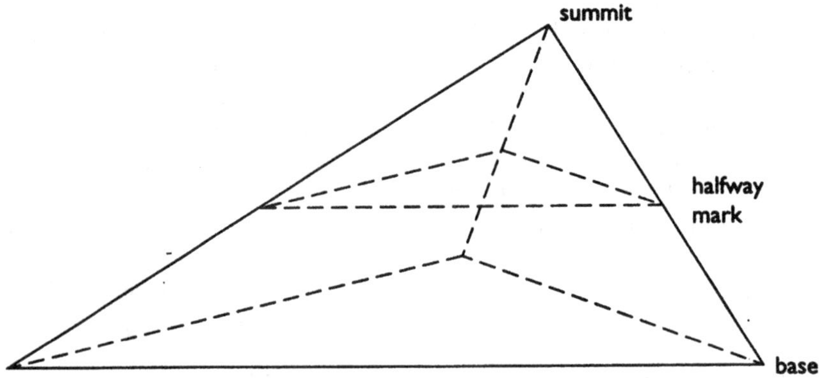

If you wished to climb this pyramid, which route would be the easiest? Which route would be the steepest? Give reasons for your answer.

Activity 11-M

On this map, draw contour lines linking benchmarks of the same height.

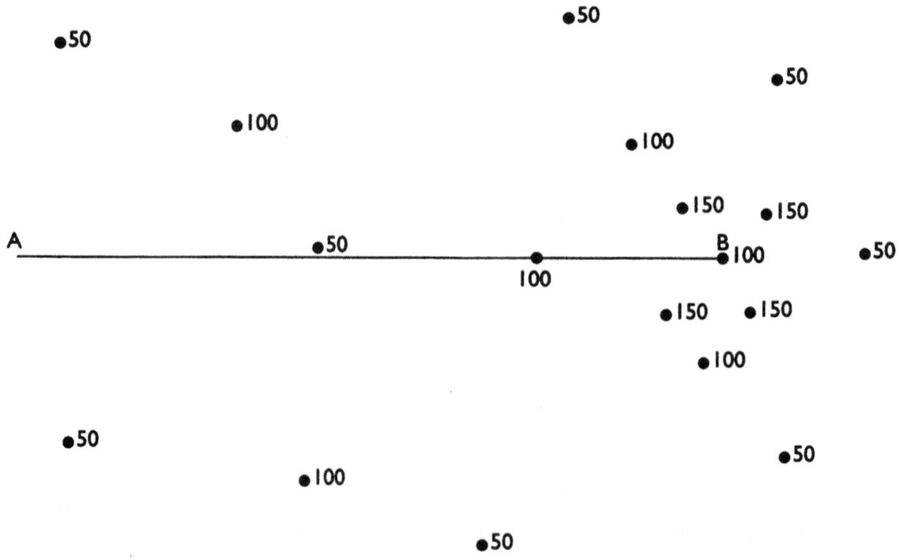

Cut out a piece of thick cardboard that would cover the area 50 m high or higher. Cut out a piece of cardboard to cover the area that is more than 100 m high. Cut out a piece of cardboard to cover the area that is more than 150 m high. Now build your hill.

1. In order to climb this hill, what would be the least steep routes? What would be the steepest route?
2. What might you expect to find along the A–B line? Explain your answer.

At a concrete level, elevation is not a very meaningful concept unless students can relate it to something they are familiar with. Prairie-town students will tend to think of grain elevators as being very tall, whereas urban students will relate to skyscrapers and office buildings. To help students better appreciate the heights of various objects, give each one a copy of a large protractor as shown below. Have them mount the protractor on stiff cardboard, attach a piece of wood (a ruler will do) along the top, and drop a plumb line from the centre of the protractor.

The students have now constructed a **clinometer.**

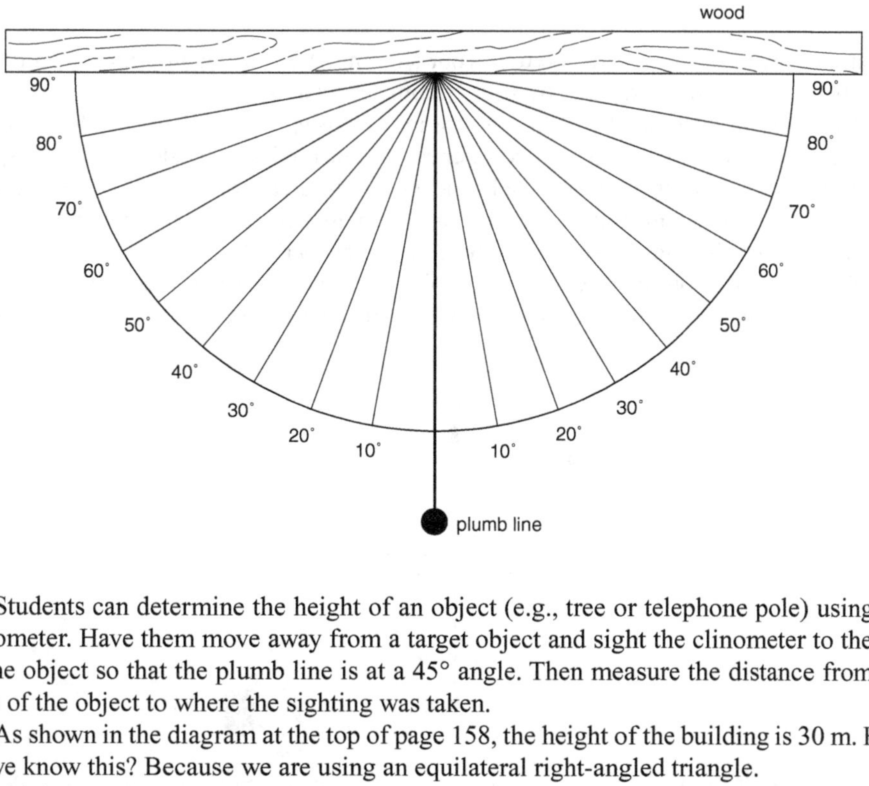

Students can determine the height of an object (e.g., tree or telephone pole) using the clinometer. Have them move away from a target object and sight the clinometer to the top of the object so that the plumb line is at a 45° angle. Then measure the distance from the base of the object to where the sighting was taken.

As shown in the diagram at the top of page 158, the height of the building is 30 m. How do we know this? Because we are using an equilateral right-angled triangle.

If it is not possible to get into a position where the clinometer indicates a 45° angle, then use the following procedure. Take a clinometer sighting and note the angle. Measure the distance from where the sighting was taken to the base of the object. On a sheet of paper, draw a large right angle and, using an appropriate scale, measure the distance from

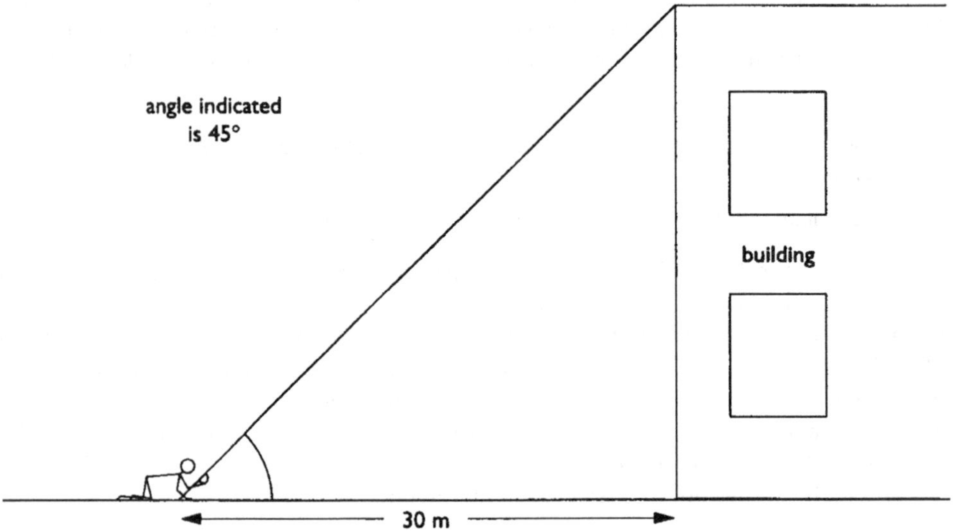

the base of the object to where you took your sighting. Now, using an ordinary protractor, draw the angle that was indicated by your clinometer reading.

Measure from the base of the object to the top. By using the scale, we can determine the approximate height of the object. A clinometer can also be used when students are making their own maps. Have students determine the boundaries of the area they wish to map and locate a sight line from which to measure angles. Replace the plumb line on the clinometer with a solid pointer. At a given location, have students hold the clinometer in front of them at eye level and sight the pointer at an object. Have them determine the angle of the object they wish to place on the map, measure the distance from their location to the object, and plot the object on the map.

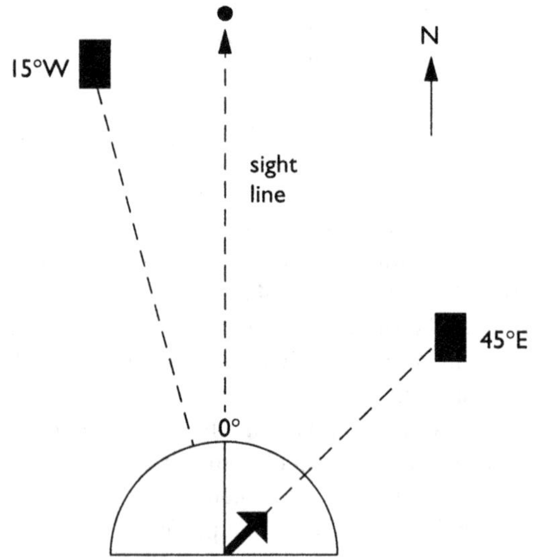

Other Activities

1. Browse through a Canadian school atlas. Write up a lesson plan that introduces the atlas to students who are seeing it for the first time.
2. Identify the mistakes this Grade 4 student has made in drawing the map shown below. (See the Answers section for a list of the mistakes.) How would you help this student to rectify his or her mistakes?

3. Have elementary school students of different ages draw maps of their routes from home to school. Compare the results. By looking at the maps, what can you glean about how students' map-making abilities develop over time?

Notes

1. Canadian Council for Geographic Education, *Canadian National Standards for Geography: A Standards-based Guide to K–12 Geography* (Ottawa: Royal Canadian Geographic Society, 2001).
2. Eui-Kyung Shin, "Using geographic information technology (GIS) to enhance elementary students' geographic understanding," *Theory and Research in Social Education* 35:2 (2007), pp. 231–255.
3. Geography Education Standards Project, *Geography for Life: National Geography Standards* (Washington, DC: National Geographic Research and Exploration, 1994).
4. *Ibid.*
5. C. Sunal and D. Sunal, "Mapping the child's world," *Social Education* 42:5 (1978), pp. 381–383.
6. For information, see Matthews, M. H. (1992). *Making sense of place: Children's understanding of large-scale environments*. Hemel Hempstead, UK: Harvester Wheatsheaf; and Sobel, D. (1998). *Map-making with Children: Sense of Place Education for the Elementary Years*. New York: Heinemann.

7. C. Bognar and W. Cassidy, *Social Studies in British Columbia: Technical Report of the 1989 Social Studies Assessment* (Victoria, BC: Assessment, Examinations and Reporting Branch of the Ministry of Education, 1991).

8. G. Rice, "Teaching students to become discriminating map users," *Social Education* 54:6 (1990), pp. 393–397.

9. J. Blaut, "The mapping abilities of young children: Children can," *Annals of the Association of American Geographers* 87:1 (1997), pp. 152–158.

10. T. Burley and G. Atkinson, "Geographic skills: A research-based sequence for grades one to nine," *History and Social Science Teacher* 22:2 (1986/87), pp. 101–105; S. Muir and H. Cheek, "Assessing spatial development: Implications for map skill instruction," *Social Education* 55:5 (1991), pp. 316–319; J. Bale, *Geography in the Primary School* (London: Routledge and Kegan Paul, 1987); S. Catling, "Environmental perception and maps," in D. Mills, ed., *Geography Work in Primary and Middle Schools* (Sheffield, England: The Geographical Association, 1988); P. Bailey, *Teaching Geography* (Newton Abbot, England: David and Charles, 1974); D. Milburn, "Children's conceptions of space and time," in R. Case and P. Clark, eds., *The Anthology of Social Studies, Volume 1. Issues and Strategies for Elementary Teachers* (Vancouver: Pacific Educational Press, 2008), p. 66; and R. McKay and S. Gibson, *Social Studies for the Twenty-First Century: A Review of Current Literature and Research* (Lewiston, NY: Edwin Mellen Press, 2004), pp. 43–44.

11. Drawn by Christina Disler. Used with permission.

Glossary of Key Terms

Clinometer—An instrument used to determine the height of objects.

Compass rose—A diagram that depicts the orientation of the cardinal directions on a map.

Contour lines—Lines on a map denoting elevation.

Elevation—The height of objects and landform features.

Global system—A network of relationships connecting a phenomenon (e.g., weather and trade) to more than one area in the world.

Grid location—A way of locating places on a globe or map; e.g., using latitude and longitude.

International Date Line (IDL)—An imaginary line at 180° longitude, east of which is one day earlier than to the west.

Key—A list of symbols that indicate how objects are represented on a map. A key is sometimes referred to as a legend.

Perspective—The position and angle from which an object is viewed (e.g., ground level, aerial, or bird's-eye).

Scale—A representation of the size of an object or the distance between objects, e.g., 1 cm:1 km.

Time zone—An area in which the time difference from Greenwich Mean Time is established, e.g., Pacific Time zone, Central Time zone.

CHAPTER 12

Environmental Education as an Organizing Theme for Interdisciplinary Learning

In the previous chapter, we identified the study of issues and problems as a viable strategy for organizing geography instruction in the elementary grades. In this chapter, we look at what has been identified by Al Gore, former vice-president of the United States and co-winner of the 2007 Nobel Peace Prize, as the most important challenge of our times: global warming and the environmental crisis.

We begin by briefly identifying the central issues and problems that lie at the heart of the environmental challenge from a historical perspective, and then move on to explore a variety of approaches to environmental education in the elementary grades. We also forge interdisciplinary connections between social studies and other subject areas by using "environmental studies" as an organizing theme for learning across multiple subject areas. Since the study of environmental issues crosses subject boundaries, no one subject can lay exclusive claim to environmental education. As with many other topics, the study of environmental issues is enriched through an **interdisciplinary approach** to teaching and learning.

THE 21ST-CENTURY ENVIRONMENTAL CHALLENGE

The environmental challenge the world faces—and the question of whether we even face an environmental crisis at all—emerged as a public policy issue in the mid to late 20th century. Since then, it has gradually evolved to become one of the most contentious social and scientific debates of the last half-century. Although climatologists and other earth scientists continue to debate the exact scope and severity of the environmental challenge, as well as its antecedent causes (particularly, whether humans are in fact partly responsible for the earth's changing climate), there is now wide-ranging agreement among scientists, and even politicians and business people, that the next several decades are likely to be marked by rapid environmental change the world over. This in turn requires the urgent attention of scientists, governments, corporations, schools and universities, and most other social institutions.

Differences of opinion over the antecedent causes of the environmental crisis do exist. Some social commentators see the environmental challenge in terms of a power struggle between humans and nature. They point to our continuing efforts to dominate, harness, and exploit the natural world as the chief cause of the environmental crisis and, in some cases, link problems related to environmental **sustainability** to other global issues, including racism and social justice.[1] Other social commentators view the environmental challenge from an ecofeminist point of view in terms of a historical power struggle between the forces of masculinity and femininity.[2] Still others look at the environmental challenge from a philosophical or even a spiritual point of view in terms of a crisis of humanity and our relation to the cosmos.[3] Despite these and other wide-ranging views, most social commentators would agree that at the heart of the environmental challenge is an economic system of industrialization that has offered the Western world, in particular, unprecedented growth over the last two centuries, but which has also strained and exhausted the very natural systems (e.g., the earth's atmosphere, forested areas, oil reserves, and wetlands) that we depend on for our sustenance.

Activity 12-A

Imagine you have been given the opportunity to teach a whole unit about environmental issues at the elementary level. In identifying the roots of the environmental problems we face, which of the above perspectives would you most likely wish to emphasize in the unit? Are there other environmental perspectives that you would also want your unit to address?

The process of industrialization ramped up significantly throughout the 20th century as the world's population increased and as industrial production processes (e.g., the assembly line) grew ever more automated and efficient, particularly in their effort to feed the consumptive lifestyles of Western nations. The industrial economies of the West became increasingly beholden to the need to produce ever-increasing amounts of goods, to urbanize increasing amounts of land, and to continue to exploit ever-increasing amounts of natural resources. At a cultural level, these same economic forces were largely seen to be synonymous with the notions of social progress, economic health and strength, and international competitiveness (e.g., GDP as a measure of a nation's standing within the world). In short, an ever-expanding economy was (and still is) seen to be the primary and most important indicator of social progress.

By the middle of the 20th century, a small number of scientists, economists, and social commentators had begun to highlight the problem of environmental degradation by equating social progress with economic growth. For example, in her seminal 1962 book *Silent Spring,* Rachel Carson documented the detrimental effects of pesticides on the environment.[4] In 1968, Paul R. Ehrlich published his controversial book *The Population Bomb*, which predicted mass famine throughout the world due to overpopulation.[5] Without environmentally sustainable technologies to rely on, an ever-expanding economy necessitated the ever-increasing exploitation of renewable and nonrenewable resources and the release of ever-increasing amounts of pollutants and waste products into the environment (i.e., as a by-product of ramped up industrial production and the ever-increasing consumption of packaged goods).

At the close of the 20th century, ever more populated countries, including China and India, were also increasing their production processes in an effort to grow their economies and compete with Western nations. The pressure of all of these and other developments on the world's biotic systems became increasingly apparent as study after study concluded that the earth's ecosystems were increasingly at risk of undergoing irreversible changes that could impact directly the prospects for future generations of humans—and other species.[6] The earth, some environmentalists concluded, was reaching a tipping point from which it might not be able to recover.

Activity 12-B

Consider the often-used axiom "Think global and act local." What does this phrase mean to you? How might it be relevant to a school? In what ways, environmental or otherwise, might teachers and students be encouraged to think global and act local?

The environmental challenge that most earth scientists agree the world now faces can be organized into several overriding issues, including the following. Keep in mind that these issues are all very much interrelated:

- *resource scarcity,* including sharp declines in the quantity and/or quality of renewable (e.g., water and trees) and nonrenewable (e.g., oil) resources, as well as lower agricultural yields due to global warming, deforestation, and other factors.
- *species extinction,* including the loss of animal and plant species and their associated habitats.
- *environmental pollution,* including the contamination of the air humans and animals breathe and the water we drink.
- *global warming,* in which the release of carbon dioxide and other "greenhouse gases" into the air contributes to the trapping of heat from the sun in the earth's atmosphere. This in turn causes the earth's atmosphere to warm. The anticipated effects of global warming include the melting and breaking apart of glaciers, rising sea levels, and more extreme weather events (e.g., hurricanes).

A number of schools in Canada include gardening as an activity in order to reconnect students with the natural world.

INTERDISCIPLINARY CONNECTIONS

As is clear from the above discussion, the environmental challenge is complex and multifaceted. Most environmentalists agree that it will require the efforts of all social institutions working together to ease the impact of humans on the natural world over the next few decades. Education is key among these social institutions as it is the current generation of children (and their children) who are likely to be most impacted by rapid environmental change, particularly the effects of **global warming.**

That said, the environmental challenge also presents schools with a unique opportunity to adopt the environmental topic as an organizing theme for instruction in virtually every subject area. Here, we briefly consider just a few of the interdisciplinary links that can be forged between social studies and other subjects when the environment becomes the focus of attention.

- *Environmental geography*: Ask students to consider the *quality* of the environments in which they live, play, and go to school. Do the students feel they have adequate contact with nature? Is this even important to them? Provide students with opportunities to study local landscapes, contrasting various topographies in the local community. Ask them to consider the ways in which nature is incorporated into the urban environment (e.g., city parks). (Chapter 13 provides ideas for studying a landscape, and includes an example of an environmental assessment that with some modifications even primary-level students could use.)
- *Environmental history*: Ask students to investigate the history of the local community, focusing particularly on the intersection of the natural and human environments. Have students research the topography of the land that existed before the first human settlements were established, the uses to which the land has been put over time (e.g., agriculture and industry), and the impact of humans on the surrounding natural world (e.g., waterways and forested areas). Show students top-down air photos of the local community over time, going back as far as possible. Have students look for patterns of urbanization, industrial growth, and human impact on the land over time. (See Chapter 10 for an example of how Vancouver changed over a 16-year period.)
- *Environment-themed mathematics*: Students can familiarize themselves with a plethora of statistics related to environmental issues as they study mathematics. For example, to demonstrate the problem of global warming, provide students with a data table that lists the average seasonal temperatures for the world for the last 100 years. Have students analyze the table, looking for patterns and trends, and perform calculations on the data.
- *Nature writing*: Ask students to focus closely on the natural world as an inspiration for their writing. Take students outside and have them write a descriptive paragraph that describes a natural space. Encourage students to express through words the perceptual, emotive, and visceral experience of "being in nature" or the sensation of walking through the grass barefoot, or to listen carefully for all the natural (and human-made) sounds they can hear.
- *Landscape painting*: Take students outside and provide them each with a large sheet of paper and a selection of drawing tools (e.g., pencils, pastels, paints, and charcoal). Have students find a quiet spot to work and then "frame" a landscape they wish to capture on paper. As they draw, sketch, and paint the natural world, encourage students to pay close attention to specific details such as shapes, textures, patterns, hues, lighting,

shadows, and depth of field. Once this activity has been completed, consider having students organize an environmental art show for other classes in the school to tour. (To see some examples of students' environmental art, visit the Paul G. Keough Earth Artist Program website: www.epa.gov/NE/students/gallery.html.)

Activity 12-C

Brainstorm a list of additional activity ideas through which the environmental topic could be addressed in other subject areas, including health and physical education (e.g., the study of environmental and community health), computers, drama, music, and science. Similar to social studies, the science curriculum in all provinces and territories provides students with plenty of opportunities to directly address environmental issues as they study biology, chemistry, and other scientific topics.

APPROACHES TO ENVIRONMENTAL EDUCATION

Although **environmental education** is not recognized in all provinces and territories as a core subject area, it is nevertheless a popular topic area in schools, especially as an organizing theme for interdisciplinary and applied learning and as a vehicle for teaching social action skills and care for the world. Below, we consider four ways in which environmental education is today infused into many Canadian schools.

Direct Instruction

Environmental topics are routinely taught directly to students as part of a traditional unit in social studies or science. At the secondary level, environmental science courses are on the books as electives in some provinces and territories. So, too, are environmental themes interspersed throughout the science, social studies, and geography curricula at the elementary level, as students learn about ecosystems, weather systems, natural resources, Canada's imports and exports, and other environment-related topics.

Activity 12-D

Conduct an "environmental audit" of the curriculum guidelines for your province or territory. Review the topic areas for each grade level to determine which topics focus directly (or, more likely, indirectly) on environmental themes. Pick one such topic and consider the ways in which environmental issues (e.g., resource scarcity, species extinction, overpopulation, environmental pollution, and global warming) could be addressed in teaching the topic to students.

Of course, each of these topics can be introduced to students without an overriding environmental message, but many teachers, well aware of the increasing attention environmental issues are receiving in the media, infuse an environmental ethic into their teaching that aims to nurture an awareness in students about the environmental challenges the world faces.

For example, the topic of climate change can be introduced in a unit on weather systems. Students can be asked to analyze statistics related to the average recorded temperature on the earth's surface over the last 100 years or so to better understand concerns related to global warming. Primary-level students can create simple graphs or interpret existing graphs showing how the climate has changed in their own community over time. They can be introduced to the science behind global warming, including the role that the buildup of greenhouse gases in the atmosphere is playing in climate change. In a social studies unit on weather systems, students can be asked to list and/or research the human activities that contribute to global warming. They could reflect on their own lives to ascertain how they personally contribute to the emission of greenhouse gases. Students can also research counter-arguments related to environmental issues, for example the view that global warming isn't occurring or, if it is, that humans are not the cause.

In a unit on Canada's economy, students are likely to study the natural resources (e.g., fish, trees, and oil) that Canada has in abundance. An environmental perspective can be added to this unit by tracing the history of the fisheries crisis on Canada's east coast or by having students read articles related to the overlogging debate in British Columbia. Students can be asked to weigh the benefits and costs of the overexploitation of Canada's natural resources in terms of jobs, the economy, our natural heritage, impact on the environment, and other factors. (See Chapter 15 for how to use decision-making strategies and role-playing to resolve social issues, and Chapter 16 for the values analysis approach to issue resolution.)

Activity 12-E

Imagine you are a new teacher in a British Columbia town where logging is the primary industry. The parents of many of your students work in logging and the town itself is sustained economically by jobs connected directly and indirectly to the logging industry. How would you introduce the topic of overlogging to your students? Would you even try? Pick a grade level and brainstorm a lesson idea for this topic. *Hint:* Most logging companies have very strict policies, often enforced by government regulations, that restrict overlogging. You may wish to start by having students complete a critical reading of the public relations literature published by logging companies in the area.

Outdoor Education Centres

Many school boards operate outdoor education centres that provide on-site instruction in environmental education, and nature study more generally. At these sites, visiting students variously go on a hike through the wilderness, conduct pond studies and pH tests, build birdfeeders, learn about animal tracks, or enjoy a cookout. They learn about ecosystems, native plant species, and the need to protect the wilderness. Environmental values are routinely infused into outdoor education programs in a way that emphasizes the utilitarian, scientific, ecological, and aesthetic values of the natural world. That students are in direct contact with nature as they learn about these values reinforces the knowledge, skills, and attitudes students are taught.

One chief advantage of outdoor education centres over direct instruction is that they not only put students in direct contact with nature, but also typically involve students in hands-on experiential learning led by expert staff. Field trips to outdoor education centres are also very memorable because they involve a change in the learning context (i.e., a chance for students to learn outside of school). Some field trips also involve overnight stays. For some students, a trip to a residential outdoor education centre is the first time they have been away from their parents or guardians and slept overnight somewhere other than home. On such overnight trips, students also see their teachers in a different role than in the classroom.

Outdoor education centres serve another important environmental education role. Increasing numbers of students in Canada are growing up in highly urbanized environments, especially large city centres. Many urban students have little contact with nature (save for domesticated pets and perhaps the occasional visit to a city zoo). Yet recent research indicates that sustained and intimate contact with nature is part and parcel of healthy development in childhood—especially if we wish children to grow up to be sensitive to the needs of the natural world and environmental issues more generally.[7] For many city students, that rare visit to an environmental education centre may well be the only point of contact they will have with the natural world and wildlife, save for city parks (and possibly summer camp).

Activity 12-F

Field trips that require students to be bused can also be turned on their head from an environmental point of view. Buses, like all vehicles powered by combustion engines, pollute the environment. Is busing students long distances to an outdoor education centre where they will receive instruction about environmental issues worth the environmental costs? Consider, from an environmental vantage point, the merits of busing students to field trip sites, and to schools more generally.

School Ground Naturalization

The environmental—and, just as importantly, budgetary—realities of busing students to outdoor education centres and of staffing and sustaining these centres over the long term has led some school boards to instead provide students with direct contact with nature that is much closer to school—indeed, on the school grounds itself.

A growing number of Canadian schools have embarked on **school ground naturalization** projects that endeavour, through the reintroduction of plant species that are indigenous to the local area, to return all or part of the concrete playground surrounding the school back to nature. In the last few decades, hundreds of elementary and secondary schools throughout Canada have initiated ecological restoration projects that aim to aesthetically enhance the school environment and provide quality outdoor learning experiences for students (for examples, see the Evergreen Foundation website at www.evergreen.ca). Working together, teachers, students, parents, local businesses, and community residents have designed vegetable and herb gardens, bird and butterfly habitats, prairie gardens, and woodland forests, and built outdoor amphitheatres, tree houses, and other play and learning environments to complement these naturalized spaces.

School ground naturalization projects bring nature back into the city, provide students, teachers, and local residents with opportunities for daily contact with nature, serve as living examples of developing ecosystems, provide naturalized play and learning spaces for children, and serve as immediately accessible field study centres for hands-on environmental education activities. Above all, such projects help to foster a healthy appreciation of nature and enhance a sense of community in the surrounding neighbourhood.

Naturalizing a school ground requires plenty of planning and hard work. Most schools start off small, by focusing on a small parcel of land, and only over time grow their school

Schools have created butterfly gardens, amphitheatres, and ponds (shown here) as part of their naturalized school grounds.

ground naturalization initiative into a bigger, more ambitious project. A school ground naturalization project cannot be completed overnight. Shrubs, trees, and gardens mature over successive seasons—not over a single school year—so an ecological restoration project needs to be planned and committed to over multiple years. So, too, is it critically important that teachers take full advantage of the naturalized school grounds in teaching outdoor lessons in social studies, science, language arts, and other subject areas.

Schoolwide Infusion

Naturalizing the playground surrounding the school is one thing, but some schools that aim to become model environmental schools have also considered the school building itself and all that happens inside to be of importance in teaching students about environmental issues.

At a curricular level, schoolwide infusion efforts involve teachers getting together to co-plan curriculum units and schoolwide events that have an overt environmental theme. For example, it is not uncommon in environmental schools for social studies and science teachers to work together to co-plan a weather unit that focuses in part on climate change. Similarly, when environmental issues are infused into the schoolwide instructional program, students may study the issue of climate change in social studies and science classes and then in math class analyze a set of temperature statistics that support that learning. Students may be asked to write a persuasive piece of writing in language arts class that convinces others to take the climate change issue seriously. In visual arts class, students may be asked to paint a picture of what the coastal regions of the world might look like in 50 years or so if the problems related to global warming are not addressed.

Activity 12-G

Environmental education is only one of several schoolwide themes that teachers, staff, and students working together can adopt for a school. Others include multiculturalism, anti-bullying, and peace education. Brainstorm a list of other schoolwide themes that schools could consider adopting.

The schoolwide infusion of environmental themes directly impacts on the curriculum of the school (i.e., what is taught directly to students in class)—but in schools that aspire to serve as environmental models to other schools, the tracking of the flow of resources and waste products through the school itself is also seen to represent a critical environmental learning opportunity. As all teachers know, schools (and universities) use up an enormous amount of resources each day. Paper products in particular figure prominently here (just think about the amount of photocopying that is done in the name of education), but so too do packaged goods as hundreds of students eat lunch each day in the school cafeteria.

To combat the stresses that schools themselves put on the environment, some schools have conducted **environmental audits** aiming to uncover instances where teachers, staff, and students could do more in the school to reduce their impact on the environment. An environmental audit tracks the flow of resources and waste products through the school, including paper, plastic, and other materials. An environmental audit also takes into consideration the energy-use patterns of a school; for example, whether the lights in classrooms are turned off when the rooms are not in use. For more information about environmental audits, including some strategies for conducting one, refer to the website www.greenflagschools.org.

Most schoolwide environmental audits will result in the need for change. Some environmental actions students, teachers, custodians, and other staff can take as a result of an environmental audit include reducing the amount of material usage in the school (e.g., paper); instituting a recycling program for paper and packaged goods; starting a composting program for food waste; replacing paper towel dispensers with energy-efficient air dryers; reducing the amount of chemical agents used to clean the school; turning off lights and equipment (and putting computers to sleep) when they are not in use, and so on.

Environmental audits and curricular co-planning efforts are but two ways by which environmentally conscious schools have infused the study of environmental issues into the regular and nonformal curriculum of the school. Other strategies include celebrating Earth Day (April 22), starting a student-led environment club, staging a play that has an environmental theme, honouring students who perform good environmental deeds, and (perhaps most controversially) asking students to educate their parents about the importance of recycling and other environmental topics.

Other Activities

1. Conduct an environmental audit of your school or university (or part thereof). Look for evidence of waste, inadequate recycling of paper, plastic, and other materials, and discarded litter. Consider the ways in which the amount of energy used by the school can be reduced.
2. Draw up a list of the lifestyle changes you could make (e.g., car pooling) to reduce your personal impact on the environment.

3. Brainstorm a list of five educational objectives that you believe should be addressed by any environmental education program at the elementary level. Pick one objective you have brainstormed and list three ways that objective could be fulfilled in an elementary social studies program.

Notes

1. R. Bullard, ed., *The Quest for Environmental Justice: Human Rights and the Politics of Pollution* (San Francisco: Sierra Club Books, 2005).
2. K. Warren and N. Erkal, eds. *Ecofeminism: Women, Ecology, Nature* (Bloomington: Indiana University Press, 1997).
3. T. Berry, *The Dream of the Earth* (San Francisco: Sierra Club Books, 2006).
4. R. Carson, *Silent Spring* (New York: Mariner Books,1962/2002).
5. P. Ehrlich, *The Population Bomb* (New York: Ballantine Books, 1968).
6. United Nations Intergovernmental Panel on Climate Change, *Climate Change 2007* (New York: United Nations Environment Program, 2007).
7. R. Louv, *Last Child in the Woods: Saving Our Children from Nature-Deficit Disorder* (New York: Algonquin Books, 2008).

Glossary of Key Terms

Environmental audit—A process by which the flow of energy, resources, and waste products through a school is carefully monitored in order to reduce the environmental impact of the school.

Environmental education—The study of the environment and environmental issues in schools, outdoor education centres, and other settings.

Global warming—The process by which the average surface temperature of the earth has gradually increased over the course of the last century. Global warming is predicted to continue over the next century, leading to the melting and breaking apart of glaciers, rising sea levels, more extreme weather, and other consequences.

Interdisciplinary approach—A lesson, unit, or curriculum that incorporates multiple subject areas (e.g., social studies and math). Also referred to as a cross-curricular approach.

School ground naturalization—The process of restoring an outdoor space (such as a concrete playground) to its natural ecological state through the re-introduction of plants, shrubs, and other flora and fauna.

Sustainability—A measure of the ability of the local or global environment to support life over the long term. Sustainability education refers to efforts to educate students to make ecologically sound choices that protect and sustain the environment over the long term.

CHAPTER 13

Learning in the Real World: Field Studies and Field Trips

FIELD STUDIES

Collecting data first-hand and getting a "feel" for a place are two major reasons for having students conduct field studies. Other important reasons are to help students develop specific social studies–related skills, such as map reading, and to stimulate interest in a field trip–related topic. Field studies can also act as a catalyst for further research. They should be undertaken whenever possible (e.g., whenever the budgetary realities of schools permit) because they (a) reflect what geographers and social scientists do; (b) are interesting for students; (c) provide an ideal learning situation, especially for teaching research and mapping skills; and (d) broaden students' horizons.

Activity 13-A

Field trips have to be as carefully planned as any lesson. Read the following paragraph and identify what the teacher has done properly but also what she has failed to do in planning a field trip. Then consult the Answers section.

> A teacher has organized a trip to a local industrial site. Transportation has been booked. She has visited the site and made full arrangements (e.g., tour guide, schedule, location of washrooms, and lunch facilities). Safety concerns have been addressed. Students have been given background information, a list of questions to answer, and activities to do while en route to the site and when they are actually there. Rules have been made clear to all. Parent-volunteer supervisors have been contacted. Each student has brought 25¢ for transport costs and has been told what to bring on the trip (e.g., appropriate clothing, lunch, writing materials, and medical prescriptions for those requiring them). Because all of the class's subjects are taught by this teacher, there are no timetable problems. The principal has given permission for the trip.

Once a suitable field-trip location has been identified and the logistical arrangements have been made, relevant activities must be prepared for the students. Below is a list of possible activities as well as questions that could be asked at various field-trip locations where the teaching and learning of geography are the focus. Which activities a particular class might carry out depends upon the objectives of the field trip and the abilities of the students.

1. Identify examples of different forms of land use: e.g., industrial, agricultural, residential, commercial, and recreational. Why are particular areas used for particular purposes? Is this the best use of the land in question?
2. Note different physical landform features. Locate a cliff, lake, or valley. Note the climatic conditions. How do these conditions affect the area and the people or animals living there?
3. Observe the transportation networks. Do power lines, roads, and railroads follow the best routes? Why or why not?

4. Note the location of boundaries. Where are the political boundaries? What are the reasons for their location? What other sorts of boundaries are there—property, cultural, and ethnic? How do these boundaries affect the movement of people or goods?
5. Compare house and house-lot sizes in places A and B. Are they different or similar? Why?
6. Find out the reasons for the locations of buildings, roads, and other features. Why is a particular building (e.g., industrial building, farm, or store) placed where it is?
7. Find out the history of the area. Is this an old, established area (e.g., evidence of older buildings, long-established farmsteads, established industries, etc.)? How can you tell? Why was a particular structure built? Where did the materials used in its construction come from? Do we build similar structures the same way now? Why or why not? What did the area look like 100 years ago? What changes have occurred to the natural environment over the intervening years? What changes are likely to occur in the future? Can we prevent undesirable changes? How?
8. Account for the differences in vegetation between place A and place B.
9. Identify examples of natural and human-created hazards to people, local fauna, and the environment in general. Could erosion pose a threat? Where has erosion occurred, and why has it occurred? Was it caused by natural means or for other reasons (e.g., human impact)? Could it—and should it—have been prevented? What other natural and human-created phenomena pose a hazard to the environment? Can these be prevented? How, and at what cost?
10. When studying an industry or business, find out about the site, the raw materials, the products and the markets for them, the source of power used, the transportation used, the ownership of the industry or business, and the impact it has on the environment. Find out about the workers: any health hazards they face; how much input they have into how the business or industry is operated; how they are treated (for instance, if there is evidence of discrimination on the basis of gender, ethnicity, or class); whether they are unionized; how much they earn on average; what hours they work.
11. Draw a picture of Y (e.g., building, landform feature).
12. Sketch a map of Y.
13. What do you think the area will look like in ten years' time? Will it be better or worse than it is now? Give your reasons and the criteria you used to answer this question. Draw a map showing how you would *like* the area to look in ten years' time.
14. List all the sounds you can hear, as well as the smells you can smell. Where do they come from?
15. Write descriptive words or sentences about how you feel at the site. For example, does it make you feel happy, sad, or angry?
16. At a field trip site, collect some items (if this is permissible), for example small rocks and vegetation. Label and display them for others to view. Find out the origin of the rocks and the reasons why the site is suitable for the vegetation that grows there.
17. How are people using the environment? Are they harming it in any way? Are there any indications of conservation efforts in the area?
18. Carry out an environmental appraisal. Create a score sheet similar to the one opposite. Now, posing the appropriate questions, record your observations about the area.

ENVIRONMENTAL ASSESSMENT

Location: Street Corner

Date and Time of Assessment:

+3	+2	+1	0	-1	-2	-3

Overall appearance

Architecture

Condition of natural environment (e.g., trees)

Condition of human environment (e.g., buildings)

Cleanliness (litter)

Traffic noise

Traffic danger

Traffic smell

Traffic and pedestrian controls (lights, etc.)

Ease of people movement

Ease of parking

Other______________________

There are three types of field studies:

1. **Field teaching:** This involves teaching students at a site other than the classroom (e.g., teaching a lesson on salmon at a salmon hatchery).
2. **Field inquiry:** Here students find out answers to questions at the field site. These questions could be posed by the teacher and/or by the students (e.g., at a museum: How many different types of materials were used in the construction of a pit house? or at a shopping centre: How many stores cater to women exclusively?).
3. **Field discovery:** In this type of study, students go to a site with no preconceived ideas of what to do when they get there. Rather, students and teachers use the site to generate interest in particular topics and to find out answers to student-posed questions.

Field studies of any type can be carried out in three different ways:

- On a site with clearly defined boundaries (e.g., an industry, store, farm, or village).
- Traversing areas that differ from one another (e.g., going from a valley to a hilltop; from a residential to an industrial area; from a rural to an urban area; from a low-cost to a high-cost housing area).
- From a vantage point (e.g., a tall building or hill).

In all these forms of fieldwork, students can write down the answers to questions, draw what they see, collect specimens, map the area, construct charts and graphs, capture photographs and videos, record sounds, interview people, perform scientific experiments, measure various items, count things, and so on.

FIELD TRIPS

Field trips need not require extended bus travel; the immediate community surrounding a school provides a rich source of possibilities for studying the local community. Even the school itself can serve as a "field trip" site. (Refer to the school ground naturalization section in Chapter 12 for one example.) In the following scenario, questions are raised about the geography, economics, sociology, anthropology, politics, history, aesthetics, and philosophy of a school. As you consider each question, think about the implicit assumptions you may have about schools and schooling that most people take for granted.

Questions

1. Where is the school in relation to the community? In what surroundings? Why was it built there? What does this location suggest about the relationship between the school and the community?
2. What are the architectural features of the school (both inside and outside)? What activities are encouraged by the amenities the school has (e.g., an auditorium)? What attitudes does the school building communicate through its signage, entrance way, and other features? Is there evidence that an addition has been made to the school?
3. How is space in the school used? Are there spaces in which students are not permitted to go? Are there spaces for various student activities that are determined by students (e.g., a space for skipping, for talking, for playing soccer on the playground; a space in the corridor that is used only by Grade X)? Why?
4. What kinds of special facilities does the school have? Are there rooms for specific purposes? If so, what are these purposes? What can you infer from the kinds of activities the school and community value most? How much space does each department have? Is the size of the classroom space a factor in determining how different subjects are taught? What kind of equipment is provided? Do some subjects or interests appear to have more equipment than others? Why? What does all this tell you about what is important for the school and the community?
5. How is the school decorated? Is it aesthetically pleasing? Is it comfortable? What assumptions about schools and learning does the interior space of the school reveal?
6. What are the classrooms like? What furniture is provided? Do students and teachers have the same or different furniture? Is the furniture for younger students appropriately child scaled? How is the seating arranged? What does this suggest about the kinds of teaching and learning that are carried out, and how teachers and students communicate with one another? What behaviours does the classroom seem to encourage? What does the arrangement of the students' desks suggest about the philosophy of education at work?
7. In the actual construction of the classroom, what materials were used? Where did these materials come from? Were any imported? What raw materials were used (e.g., wood and/or plastic)? How many different kinds of occupations were necessary to build the classroom? Where does the heating come from? (Take a tour of the physical plant part of the school if possible.) Where does the electricity come from? What does all this tell us about the economics and geography of the wider community? What does it tell us about the interdependence of occupations that help build a school?
8. What kinds of pictures, posters, or objects decorate the walls? What do they say? What messages do they convey? Who put them there? Are they intended to be viewed by

teachers, students, parents, and/or visitors to the school? What kinds of ideas, people, and activities does the school seem to honour? Why?

9. What rituals are performed at regular intervals in the school? What are their purposes? What values do they reflect? What kinds of symbols do they involve? What roles do people play? What cultural beliefs do these rituals transmit?
10. What activities do students undertake most often? Do males and females perform the same or different activities? Why? What do students study? For how long? What does all this tell us about what society expects students to do when they are adults?
11. How do people dress? Do teachers and students dress differently? What influences the way people dress? What materials are used to make the clothes students and teachers wear? Where do these materials come from?
12. What societal values can be inferred from the way the school is governed? Who has authority? Why? Who is involved in the decision-making processes?

Activity 13-B

With reference to your own faculty, college, or school, choose one or more of the above questions and use the following inquiry procedure:

1. Ask question(s).
2. Generate hypothesis(es).
3. Decide what data are needed.
4. Choose specific method(s) for collecting data.
5. Analyze, interpret, and evaluate the data.
6. Confirm or refute the hypothesis(es).
7. Draw conclusions.

FIELD TRIPS TO SPECIAL SITES

The types of activities that are appropriate to lead on trips to museums, historical sites, and other special places depend largely on the trip's objectives and the students' abilities. However, a few guidelines apply to most field trips:

1. Make sure the students know what the objectives are. Carry out activities to prepare students for the field trip (e.g., describe the site, tell students what to look for, have students develop hypotheses to investigate at the site). Students should be encouraged to answer the following types of questions (these are based on those presented in Chapter 10):
   - What is significant about this site (e.g., museum or art gallery)?
   - What is displayed and why is it displayed?
   - What is not displayed even though it would be relevant to the site?
   - Who chooses what to display?
   - What feelings does the site engender?
2. Choose a particular object or artifact and then state, where appropriate, what it is made of, how it is/was to be used, who made it, who used it, whether it is still used today,

what changes have occurred to its use over time, and whether the object is better or worse than comparable objects today.

3. In looking at a painting, ask whether it is an accurate representation of the subject of the painting, what could be learned about life from the painting, what the artist was trying to communicate, why it might have been painted, and how representations of the world and people have changed over time (see Chapter 19 for ideas about critically looking at images).
4. If there is an object that is unfamiliar to students, have them guess what it is.

At some sites, students can manipulate artifacts and participate in activities as they were practised in the past (e.g., visiting a one-room school as it was in the early 1900s, or living in a pioneer home).

When a field trip is over and students return to the classroom, further work should be carried out. First, letters of thanks should be written to those who helped (e.g., guides, parent volunteers, etc.). (Ask the students to contribute to this.) Second, the work done on the field trip should be compiled in the form of reports, charts, media presentations, and so on. The information collected should be discussed and interpreted so that generalizations can be formulated. If the field trip was a significant one, then students' work can be displayed for visiting parents to view. The trip should be evaluated, both by you and for purposes of student assessment, and by the students themselves in terms of what they learned through the field trip and whether they found the trip to be worthwhile. Teachers should also reflect on the field trip as a whole and consider the following questions:

- Was it well organized?
- Could it be improved next time?
- Was it the best way of imparting to students the desired information?
- Were there too many or too few activities for students to complete?
- Did the trip cover too much or too little content?
- Were there sufficient links to the social studies curriculum of your province or territory?
- Did anything go wrong? If so, how could this be avoided next time?
- Were the objectives of the trip achieved?

Other Activities

1. Choose a location that would be worthwhile for students to study. Design three activities that students could carry out at this location.
2. Design a question sheet for students to answer when visiting a museum, art gallery, or industry with which you are familiar.

Glossary of Key Terms

Field discovery—Letting students explore a site to raise their own questions and find answers.

Field inquiry—Occurs when students are guided to seek answers to questions at a site (e.g., finding out about the history of a community at a museum).

Field teaching—Teaching about something at an appropriate site (e.g., teaching about fishing on a fishing boat).

CHAPTER 14

Putting it All Together: Making Connections

If students are to learn about social studies in a meaningful way, they need to make connections between what they know and new information. Connecting information in history and geography and relating it to knowledge from other disciplines can create powerful generalizations that help students to synthesize large amounts of information. This may sound rather grandiose, but through appropriate instruction even Grade 1 students can begin to develop and understand generalizations such as these: all families have rules; people change their environments to satisfy their needs and wants; and families differ in their makeup due to a variety of factors, including a family's religion, economic status, location, and family structure (e.g., one-parent, same-sex, grandparent-led).

DEVELOPING GENERALIZATIONS

The instructional procedure outlined in this book begins with the identification of concepts necessary for the study of a particular topic or question. Students then acquire information about how these concepts can be applied through expository and/or inquiry methods. The final step in this procedure involves the development of generalizations. This instructional procedure is not the only one you can use, but it does provide an effective structure for unit planning (see Chapters 6 and 21).

Generalizations are statements about relationships between and among concepts. They summarize large bodies of information. Generalizations are useful because, once they have been verified, they make it unnecessary to carry out research in each new case that is covered by the generalization.

Several kinds of generalizations exist.[1] **Universal generalizations** cover every case to which they refer. They are true for all times and places, and therefore they may contain words such as "all," "never," and "every." Here is an example: "Urban growth increases in relation to industrial and technological developments." **Prevalence generalizations** contain terms such as "most," "the majority of," and "usually." "The majority of cities in the world suffer from air pollution" is an example here. **Probabilistic generalizations** are often identified by the word "probable," with a number attached. Gallup and other polls often state their findings as probabilistic generalizations—for example, "This poll is accurate within 2 percentage points, 19 times out of 20." Finally, there are **enumerative generalizations**, which summarize data that have actually been counted. Statements about all 30 students in a particular classroom are enumerative generalizations.

Activity 14-A

Identify the generalizations in the following passage. Answers can be found in the Answers section.

> All countries in the world have a system of government. The form of government in each country is determined by the size of the population and its history and beliefs. Where there are few people, government can be simple, whereas larger countries require more complex forms of government. All governments provide certain services to people. In most countries, the services are provided to all the people. In dictatorships, only people who support the government get services. In Canada, all people receive educational and medical services. What other services do Canadians receive?

Now that you have some understanding of what generalizations are, consider which generalizations are thought to be important for students to learn.

Activity 14-B

In the social studies curriculum guidelines for your province or territory, locate the generalizations students are supposed to learn. What sorts of generalizations are they?

We formulate generalizations through **inductive reasoning**. For example, "This A is a B, and that A is a B. Therefore, all As are Bs." Or, "Therefore, the next A will be a B." Enumerative generalizations can be verified by seeing if, in fact, all As are Bs. With other generalizations, it is usually impossible to see if every A is a B. This is why it is often said that in inductive reasoning, we "leap" from what is known to a conclusion that we cannot be *certain* is true. In our everyday lives we make a few observations about something and generalize quite reliably to all future observations. When we generalize about complex, irregular phenomena such as human behaviour, however, our generalizations have to be more tentative.

In all cases of generalization, the following criteria should be applied:

1. There are enough instances to justify the generalization.
2. The generalization fits into a larger structure of knowledge.

Here are some ways in which students can develop generalizations and begin to apply the above criteria. In primary-grade classrooms, teachers can start by collecting information from the students they teach (being careful that their privacy is not invaded), and then helping students create generalizations (e.g., we all have unique characteristics; we all share certain needs). As students become more capable of dealing with bodies of information using Taba's concept development ideas (see Chapter 6), data-retrieval charts can be used to formulate generalizations. An example follows.

DATA-RETRIEVAL CHART: NIGERIA

Climate	Landforms	Vegetation	Agriculture	Transportation
data	data	data	data	data

To encourage the formulation of generalizations, pose the following types of questions to students:

1. What is similar about all the items under the ____________ label? Can you formulate a generalization about ____________?
2. How are agricultural practices related to the climate? What general statement can we make about the relationship between climate and agriculture in Nigeria? Would this statement also be true for other countries in the world?
3. How is transportation related to the landform? What general statement can we make about the relationship between transport and landform in Nigeria? Would this statement also be true for other countries in the world?
4. What does the transportation system have to do with agriculture? What general statement can we make about the relationship between transport and agriculture in Nigeria? Would this statement also be true for other countries in the world?
5. Why is the southern area of Nigeria best for growing crops? Can we create a general statement about the relationships between climate, landscape, vegetation, and agriculture?

You can modify this chart to include other phenomena for comparative purposes. Other questions can then be asked to encourage students to make more substantial generalizations by summarizing larger bodies of information.

Location	Climate	Landforms	Vegetation	Agriculture	Transportation	Other
Nigeria	data	data	data	data	data	data
Ontario	data	data	data	data	data	data

1. How are the climates of the two places similar or different? What generalizations can you make about the climates of Nigeria and Ontario?
2. What accounts for the agricultural differences between Nigeria and Ontario? What general statement can we make?

Activity 14-C

On page 180 is a data-retrieval chart about an isolated Atlantic fishing community. The students who produced it have created maps, graphs, and pictures, and have learned how fish are caught and processed. They have written a story about life as a boy or girl in the community and have discussed the advantages and disadvantages of living in a fishing community.

DATA-RETRIEVAL CHART

Location	Climate	Jobs
Atlantic coast	Hot summer	In-shore fishers
Sheltered harbour	Cold winter with heavy rains and storms	Fish-plant workers
		Marine outfitters
Nearest town is 50 km away	Frequent fog	Dairy farmers
		Retailers
Building Materials	**Natural Environment**	**Fishing Season**
Wood	Ocean	April to October for cod and halibut
Stone	Rocky cliffs	Limited mussels, crab, lobster in season
	Beach	
	Arable land	
	Trees	
Buildings	**Unemployment**	**Transport**
Houses	40% in winter	Fishing boats
Post office	8% in summer	Pleasure boats
Fish-processing plant		Rowboats
General store		Trucks
Marine store		Cars
Church		
Elementary school		
Hotel with coffee shop		
Summer cottages		

Using the information above, answer the following questions:

1. How are jobs in the community related to the natural environment?
2. How are jobs related to the climate and unemployment rate?
3. How is the relative isolation of the community related to community services?
4. Now pose two more questions that ask, "What has ____________ got to do with ____________?" Answer these questions.

Answering the questions above will lead to the creation of enumerative generalizations about the community, such as those shown below.

Relationships:

- The trees and rocks provide building materials.
- Location on the ocean provides such jobs as fishing, marine outfitting, and tourist services.

Enumerative generalizations:

- Buildings in the community are built from materials found in the locality.
- Eighty percent of the jobs in the community are dependent upon the natural environment.

If the enumerative generalizations based on this village are true of other isolated fishing communities, then we could formulate a prevalence generalization. For example: "In isolated fishing communities in Canada, there will likely be high unemployment during the off-season because of the seasonal nature of job opportunities." To arrive at a generalization that widens this statement to include other one-industry communities (that rely on a natural resource), students would have to identify similar communities in Canada.

Students can be helped to understand how to formulate reliable generalizations from a sample of cases by carrying out the following type of activity. Give students a statement about all students in the school, for example, "Most students in the school like watching movies, TV, videos, or DVDs" or "Most students use biodegradable drink containers at lunch." Tell them that it would take far too long to ask every student about their movie and TV viewing habits or to observe all students to see if they use biodegradable drink containers. What does need to be done is to observe or ask a **representative sample.** It is important that the sample reflect all the different types of students in the school, taking into account characteristics such as age, sex, cultural background, and so on. If each class in the school is fairly representative of the entire school population, then a random sample of students from each class could be observed at lunchtime or could be asked about their TV and movie viewing habits. If each student-researcher collected data from a different sample, the results would be more reliable: the larger the sample, the more representative it is likely to be. For ideas about carrying out surveys, see Chapter 19.

Activity 14-D

Following is an incomplete web diagram showing relationships among various aspects of the fishing industry. Add further relationships to the diagram and then formulate some generalizations. Is there enough evidence to support your generalizations? Do your generalizations fit into a wider body of knowledge about resource-based industries? To verify your generalizations, ask what would happen if a particular aspect of the generalization were modified in some way. For example, "If the government placed a ban on all fishing, what might happen?" or "If the cost of oil or wood went up, what might occur?" This helps students see how everything is connected and that a modification to one link in a chain causes changes to other links. This type of web diagram is a very powerful one for helping students "see" and make generalizations about interdependence and interaction.

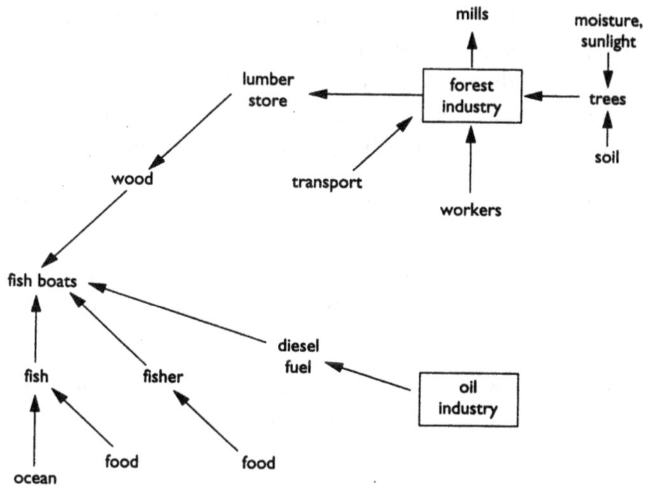

Students typically enjoy this activity and through it come to realize how complex and interconnected the world really is. For instance, a pictorial diagram showing the purchase of a chocolate bar by a student can demonstrate how this apparently simple act is related to the wider economic system and the generalization that spending on consumer goods affects the overall economy.

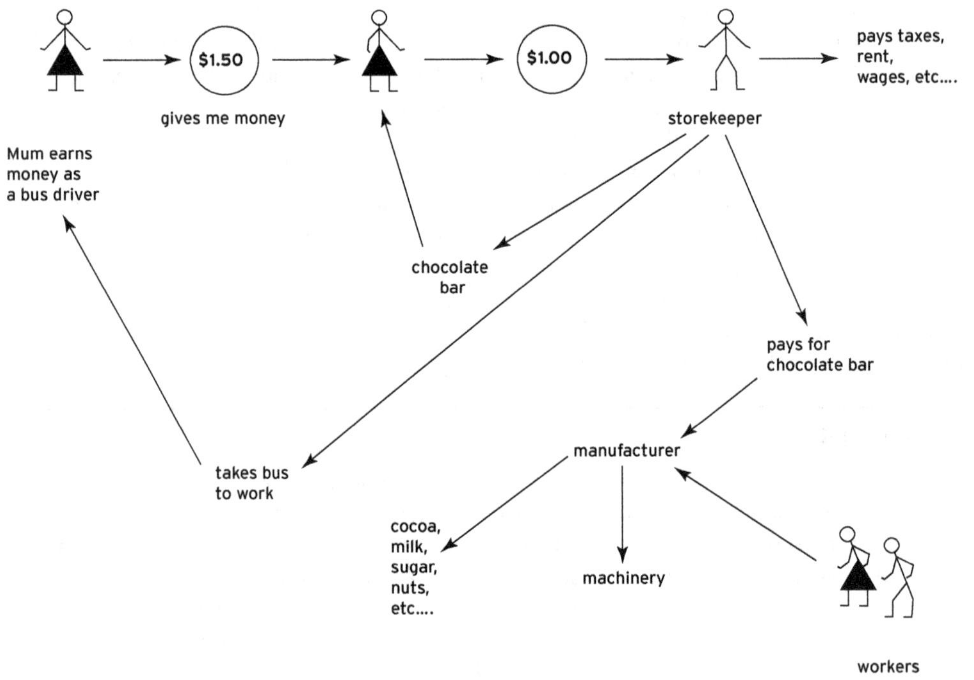

By extending this diagram, we could formulate this generalization: "All members of a society are interdependent. Individual producers of goods and services exchange things with others to get the goods and services they need to satisfy their basic wants." Further, we can ask questions that help students see cause-and-effect relationships. For example, if the cocoa bean crop fails, then the cost of a chocolate bar will likely increase. If there is more pocket money available, then more chocolate bars can be purchased; if more purchases are made, the storekeeper will, all other things being equal, make more money.

Activity 14-E

Create a web starting with an item you own. Diagram all the connections to this item. Then change one of the connections and trace the effects on all the other elements. Develop a generalization to account for the effects.

As an alternative to having students formulate their own generalizations, present students with generalizations and help them determine whether evidence exists to support these generalizations.

Activity 14-F

Here is a universal generalization:

Interaction between people and their environment influences the ways in which people meet their needs.

How would you discover if this generalization is true in your own community? If this generalization is true, then...

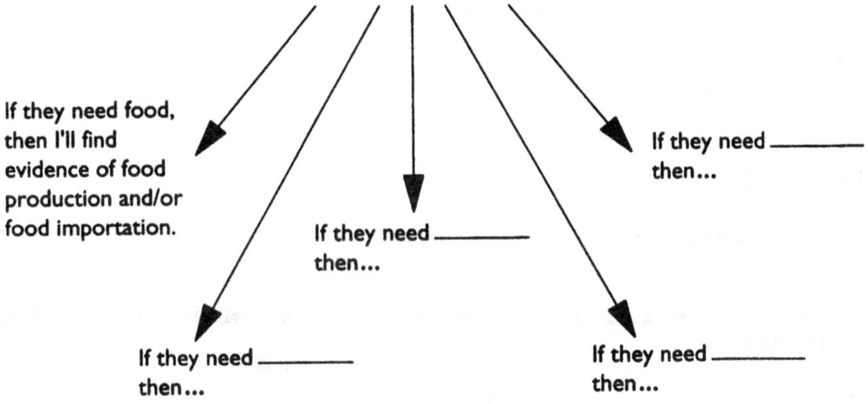

AVOIDING OVERGENERALIZATIONS

One of the most common mistakes in reasoning is overgeneralizing. We need to teach students that although we cannot possibly check the truth of every generalization we employ in our everyday lives, we have to be on our guard lest we begin to overgeneralize. This is especially important in the recognition and avoidance of stereotypes.

Activity 14-G

What generalizations are being assumed in the following? Which ones are warranted? Answers appear in the Answers section.

1. I'm going to hire recent immigrants. They'll be good workers.
2. He's a boy so he won't cry.
3. The country will change culturally and economically with the arrival of so many immigrants.
4. Because she has working-class parents, I expect she'll have problems in school.
5. I'm not going to Vancouver again in the summer. Last time I went it rained all the time.
6. He's wearing a turban so he must be from India.
7. She's a girl so she will be good at sewing.

Helping students to recognize the generalizations they make is especially important when those generalizations are not warranted. For instance, in number 4 above, it is assumed that the daughters of working-class parents have trouble in school. This is not warranted. These sorts of stereotypes can lead to prejudicial attitudes and possibly discriminatory actions. This is why it is extremely important to teach students the dangers of overgeneralization.

You can present students with examples of how overgeneralizations have created harm. For example, have a class of students research the belief held at the beginning of World War II by members of the British Columbia and federal governments that many of the Japanese living on the British Columbia coast were real or potential enemies. This belief led to the forced removal of Japanese families from their homes. Or, in researching the history of the role of women in Canada, find opportunities for students to see that throughout history women were excluded from certain roles because they were deemed to be incapable of performing them.

Other Activities

1. Develop a generalization from the following information.

THE BEDOUIN		
February	A little rain	Move herds to spring pastures.
March		Make cheese and butter for the year.
April		Shear sheep.
May	No rain	Harvest.
June		Thresh.
July		Winnow.
August		Store grain.
September		Move herds often to new pastures. Water animals daily.
October	A little rain	Plant crops.
November	Some rain	Move to central camp.
December		New animals are born.
January		

2. How would you test this generalization: "As the size of the community changes, the services within the community change"?

Note

1. R. Ennis, *Logic in Teaching* (Englewood Cliffs, NJ: Prentice-Hall, 1969), pp. 423–435.

Glossary of Key Terms

Generalizations:

Enumerative—Statements that summarize data that have been counted (e.g., "All the students in this class have English as a second language").

Prevalence—Statements that are mostly or usually true (e.g., "Most Third World countries do not have democratic forms of government").

Probabilistic—Statements about the statistical probability of an occurrence (e.g., "This poll is accurate within 2 percentage points, 19 times out of 20").

Universal—True statements for all times and places (e.g., "All people need food to survive").

Inductive reasoning—Reasoning that if this A is a B, and the next A is a B (and so on), then all As are Bs.

Representative sample—A group from an identifiable population that fairly represents the composition of that population.

Websites for Part Two

Ancient Egypt

www.ancient-egypt.org

www.ancientegypt.co.uk/menu.html

www.crystalinks.com/egypt.html

www.eyelid.co.uk

www.guardians.net/egypt

http://homepages.tcp.co.uk/~nicholson/egypt.html

www.kingtutone.com

www.pbs.org/wgbh/nova/pyramid

www.virtual-egypt.com

Ancient Greece

www.ancientgreece.com

www.arwhead.com/Greeks

www.bbc.co.uk/schools/landmarks/ancientgreece/main_menu.shtml

www.historyforkids.org/learn/greeks

www.pbs.org/empires/thegreeks

Archeology

www.archaeologica.org

Cooperative Learning

A to Z Teacher Stuff Network:
www.atozteacherstuff.com/articles/cooperative.shtml

Cooperative Learning Center:
www.co-operation.org

Jigsaws:
www.jigsaw.org

Saskatchewan Education:
http://olc.spsd.sk.ca/DE/PD/instr/strats/coop/index.html

Critical Thinking Organizations

Critical Thinking Books and Software:
www.criticalthinking.com

Richard Paul and Linder Elder's Critical Thinking Consortium:
www.criticalthinking.org

Critical Thinking on the Web:
www.austhink.org/critical

Philosophy for Children:
http://cehs.montclair.edu/academic/iapc

Philosophy for Kids Books:
http://philosophyforkids.com

First Nations

Assembly of First Nations:
www.afn.ca

Ministry of Indian and Northern Affairs Canada, Kids' Stop:
www.inac.gc.ca/ks

Geography

Discovery Channel:
www.discoverychannel.ca

Environment Canada:
www.atl.ec.gc.ca

GeoHive:
www.xist.org

National Geographic:
www.nationalgeographic.com

History

Ancient Civilizations:
www.cuneiform.org

Canada: A People's History:
http://history.cbc.ca/histicons/

Canada Aviation Museum:
www.aviation.technomuses.ca

Canadian Broadcasting Corporation Archives:
http://archives.cbc.ca

Canada's Digital Collections:
http://collections.ic.gc.ca

Canadian Heritage Information Network:
www.chin.gc.ca

Canadian Immigration Museum:
www.Pier21.ca

Canadian Museum of Civilization:
www.civilization.ca

Canadian Railroad Historical Association:
www.exporail.org

Canadian Science and Technology Museum:
www.sciencetech.technomuses.ca

Canadian War Museum:
www.warmuseum.ca

Elections Canada (History of Elections):
www.elections.ca

Historica:
www.histori.ca

History Channel:
www.history.com

Library and Archives of Canada:
www.collectionscanada.ca

McCord Museum of Canadian History:
www.mccord-museum.qc.ca

Memory Project:
www.thememoryproject.com

Parks Canada:
www.pc.gc.ca

Veterans Affairs:
www.vac-acc.gc.ca

Virtual Canadian Museums:
www.virtualmuseum.ca

Virtual Historian:
www.virtualhistorian.ca

Women in World History:
womeninworldhistory.com

Women's History:
womenshistory.about.com

Inquiry Learning

Inquiry Learning:
www.thirteen.org/edonline/concept2class/month6/webquests/index.html

Webquest Organization:
http://webquest.org/search

Maps and Mapping

Atlas of Canada:
www.atlas.gc.ca

Canadian Geographic Map Maker:
www.canadiangeographic.ca/mapping

Mapquest:
www.mapquest.com

National Geographic:
http://Plasma.nationalgeographic.com/mapmachine

University of Texas Collection of World Maps:
www.lib.utexas.edu/maps

US National Oceanographic and Atmospheric Administration:
www.ngdc.noaa.gov/ngdc.html

World History Charts:
www.hyperhistory.comwww.historychart.com

CHAPTER 15

Values and Decision Making in Social Studies

VALUES IN DECISION MAKING

Teaching requires us to make decisions about various matters, including what and how to teach, what resource materials to use, how to assess students, and what rules of behaviour students should be expected to observe and how these rules should be enforced. In these and other ways, we cannot avoid dealing with values in teaching; there is no such thing as value-free teaching or a value-neutral school. In this chapter, we focus on decision making and the social and personal values upon which teachers base their decisions. As you will see in Activity 15-A, value judgments cannot be avoided in decision making.

Activity 15-A

Read the following vignettes and decide whether the decision maker has made a good decision or a bad one. On the basis of your decisions, identify the criteria that should be used to judge (and make) decisions.

A. I decided to buy this car. I can afford it. I need a car to get to work; the bus service where I live is terrible. According to the motoring column in the local newspaper, this car has the lowest gas consumption of all the cars of its type on the market. It has all the accessories I want. It's a safe car to drive. It's my favourite colour. It's a hybrid car, so it won't pollute much. Servicing will not be a problem, as there's a service centre three blocks away that specializes in repairing this type of car. And, being a sports car, it'll suit my lifestyle.

B. I've been offered a one-year teaching position in Nigeria. I've decided to accept it, as an immediate reply was required. I would love to go to Africa; here's my golden opportunity. I haven't discussed this with my wife, who is pregnant and hates hot weather, but I'm sure there'll be good medical facilities in Nigeria and she'll get used to the heat. Anyway, I'm sure she won't want to stay in Canada on her own for a year, and when I explain to her why I've accepted the position, I'm certain she'll understand.

C. I've decided not to introduce decision making to my Grade 2 students for a number of reasons. First, my students need to learn the basics, and decision making isn't part of the basics. Second, decision making is far too difficult for my students to grasp—they'll be incapable of understanding words like "alternative" or "consequence." Third, decision making always involves controversy. I don't want parents breathing down my neck or my students getting upset because there are no right answers. And fourth, I haven't got time to introduce something new into an already overcrowded curriculum.

The following criteria should be used to evaluate decisions:

1. **The evidence used by the decision maker should be true or confirmable.** In Vignette A, the decision maker has used the local newspaper as his source of information. How reliable is this? Would *Consumer Reports* be a better source? In Vignette C there is ample evidence to suggest that children in Grade 2 can understand the terms "alternative" and "consequence." Thus, the contrary argument is not a reason to support the decision. Further, not all decisions involve controversy. If the evidence used is suspect or false, then the decision may not be a good one. This is why we emphasize intellectual standards in Chapter 8 and elsewhere.
2. **The decision maker should consider all the relevant evidence.** The decision maker in Vignette B has not considered other relevant evidence, such as housing in Nigeria, the cost of living, the salary he would receive, and especially the feelings and condition of his wife.
3. **The decision maker should consider all reasonable alternatives.** In Vignette A, the decision maker might be faulted for not considering the use of a bicycle, motorbike, or scooter to get to work. By not considering all reasonable alternatives, the decision maker might ignore the best choice.
4. **The decision maker should use concepts accurately.** In Vignette C, it could be argued that the "basics," by definition, do include decision making. If the concepts involved in the decision are not used in an accurate way, then the decision may not be justifiable.
5. **The decision maker should base his or her decisions on values that are justifiable.** In Vignette A, the decision maker appears to have satisfied his/her personal values, having considered his/her own self-interest. In Vignette B, the teacher's lack of concern for his wife is not justifiable; he has not considered the well-being of a person who will be directly affected by his decision.

In the above vignettes, the decision makers have appealed to certain values and preferences. While some decisions can be based on preferences alone, in decision-making contexts where there are serious consequences for the decision maker and/or others, the consideration and justification of all relevant values and information are required. This is where critical thinking becomes so important.

What Are Values?

All values share common characteristics. **Values** are "things" that are deemed to be of significant worth in a person's life. They guide and influence behaviour. For example, if wealth is valued, then actions are pursued to obtain it. If people value political freedom, they may try to overthrow oppressive regimes and try to persuade others to do so. Preferences, on the other hand, are expressions of taste. Unlike values, they need not be based on firm convictions, nor need they be necessarily justified. Usually, if we said that we prefer vanilla to chocolate ice cream, or apples rather than pears, no justification is necessary. (Can you think of a situation in which you would want someone to justify a food preference?) On the other hand, if we said that we preferred you to act in a certain way, then it might be legitimate to ask for justification. Smoking presents a clear case of personal taste that has emerged as a social value issue in many countries.

The values people hold can be expressed in three ways:

1. **Simple value statements:** X is good/ugly/efficient, etc.
2. **Comparative value statements:** X is better/worse/more beautiful, etc., than Y.
3. **Prescriptive value statements:** X ought to be done. People should do Y.

In justifying values, people formulate arguments in which an empirical claim about the value is linked to a value judgment. For example, if we believe that students should learn about significant events in the history of Canada, then we may decide they should learn about Louis Riel and the 1885 resistance. Our decision, written in argument form, will look like this:

> **Value premise (standard):** Students should learn about events in Canadian history that historians consider significant.
>
> **Empirical premise:** The 1885 resistance is an event in Canadian history that historians consider significant.
>
> **Value conclusion:** Therefore, students should learn about the 1885 resistance.

If we were asked why students should learn about events in Canadian history that historians consider significant, we might formulate another argument and appeal to another value. For example:

> **Value premise (standard):** Students should learn whatever is required in order to meet social studies citizenship expectations.
>
> **Empirical premise:** Learning about events in Canadian history that historians consider significant will help students meet social studies citizenship expectations.
>
> **Value conclusion:** Therefore, students should learn about events in Canadian history that historians consider significant.

This type of argument—two premises that lead logically to a conclusion—is called a **syllogism.** It has the same form as the well-known argument below. Notice, however, that in the arguments above the conclusion and the major premise are value judgments, whereas in the argument below the conclusion is an empirical claim.

> **Major premise:** All persons are mortal.
>
> **Minor premise:** Socrates is a person.
>
> **Conclusion:** Therefore, Socrates is mortal.

Activity 15-B

Fill in the conclusions for the following syllogisms. When you are through, refer to the Answers section.

1. **Value premise (standard):** Students should engage in activities that help them respect one another.

   Empirical premise: Having students work in cooperative groups will help students respect one another.

   Value conclusion: ____.

2. **Value premise (standard):** Students at age nine should learn whatever mapping skills they are capable of learning.

   Empirical premise: Students at age nine are capable of learning conventional mapping symbols.

   Value conclusion: ______________________________.

3. **Value premise (standard):** Students should come to understand whatever is necessary to become informed citizens.

   Empirical premise: Students who understand the *Canadian Charter of Rights and Freedoms* are informed citizens.

   Value conclusion: ______________________________.

Good arguments are those in which conclusions follow logically from the premises, and the premises are believable or defensible. This is why we focus on empirical and conceptual claims; value judgments are based on these. If the empirical claims are not supported, or if concepts are used inappropriately, then the value conclusions may not be justifiable.

Often, our value premises are not explicitly stated when we argue for something. We might argue that students should be engaged in group learning activities because this will encourage mutual respect, and simply take for granted that mutual respect is desirable. Or we might claim that students shouldn't damage school property because it's against the school rules, and merely assume that the school rules should be obeyed. To justify the conclusion of a value argument, we must also be able to justify the value standard in the major premise. Note how important this discussion of arguments is when we are trying to justify what and how we teach, how we evaluate student learning, and how we expect students to behave.

People can be committed to a plethora of different values. They can value justice, wealth, pleasure, beauty, equality, physical health, salvation, antiques, and so on. Some of these will be **ultimate values** and some will be **instrumental values**. If one's "ultimate" value is personal pleasure, then collecting antiques may be "instrumental" in realizing this value. These values can also be personal or social. Social values concern others and include values such as respect and justice. Of course, what one accepts as a personal value can also be a social value. What is important to note is that different **types of values** demand different justifications.

In the decision-making vignettes at the beginning of this chapter, the teacher in Vignette B clearly valued his own interests over and above the needs and feelings of his wife. In this case, **ethical values** (having to do with how people ought to be treated) were overridden by **prudential personal values** (having to do with self-interest). Simply put, moral values are *other-regarding*, whereas prudential values are *self-regarding*. Young children (and some older children as well as some adults) tend to confuse these two categories, using prudential arguments to justify a moral decision—it's OK to break the law so long as you don't get caught. In such cases decision makers use a prudential point of view when a moral one is clearly required.

We use the term **point of view** here to refer to the *kind* of value judgment being made, or the *kind* of reasons and value standards needed to justify them. Although the number of different points of view is a matter of debate, most experts in this area recognize the following points of view: **prudential, ethical, religious, aesthetic, environmental,** and

intellectual (the latter have to do with logic, reliability, and validity, which were discussed earlier in this book). Many people now place environmental values in the moral category as they believe what happens to the earth's ecosystems is a moral matter (refer to Chapter 12 for more information about this). The decision maker in Vignette A has used the aesthetic, environmental, and prudential points of view. Notice that something can be judged negatively from one point of view and positively from another.

Hundreds of opportunities exist for students to make decisions and learn and practise critical thinking. When students are given a choice of which book they will read, or what they will research, students are being asked to make decisions. In any project where research is required, students judge the quality of available resources not only on the basis of intellectual values such as accuracy and clarity, but also on aesthetic grounds. In studying Canada, students might choose a particular province in which they would like to live, or an area of the country they would like to visit. In studies of ancient civilizations, students might decide which civilization made the greatest contribution to our way of life, or which artifact of a civilization was the most significant, or which civilization had the best human rights record or treated women or children the best. In studying explorers, students could be asked to decide which explorer was the greatest, using criteria that the students had brainstormed.[1]

Why Teach Values?

Both in and out of school, students make value judgments and act on them. They make judgments about environmental concerns; they judge actions according to their conceptions of fairness; they make choices as consumers; and they hold conceptions of honesty, discrimination, justice, and so on. As they mature, students begin to make decisions and take actions within the political arena. Because the content of social studies is centred on people, moral values cannot be avoided in the classroom. How people are treated, and how they relate to their physical and social environments, are fundamentally ethical concerns.

The fact that students make value judgments, however, does not mean that such judgments will be well considered. Just as we help students deal with empirical and conceptual matters, so too must we help them to grapple with the myriad value questions that impinge on their lives, even as we foster the values that are part of the school mandate. All social studies curricula contain expectations concerning what students ought to value. For example, in Ontario, the "Values, Influences and Peers Resource Guide" states that students, "must be made aware of the set of values that Canadians from diverse backgrounds regard as essential to the well-being of society."[2] Another rationale advanced for addressing values in schools is rooted in the fact that young people are "increasingly affected by violence, social problems and lack of respect for each other."[3] Many schools have values education programs,[4] and various organizations—as well as the popular media—try to influence the values students hold.[5]

Activity 15-C

In the introduction to the social studies curriculum guidelines for your province or territory, identify the values that are to be fostered. What sorts of values are evident in the document (e.g., ethical, prudential, aesthetic, environmental, and religious)?

Not everyone agrees that it is important to help students develop the abilities necessary to make defensible value judgments. Reasons advanced for *not* focusing on teaching values in schools include the following:

a) Students may not be comfortable with discussing certain sensitive values, such as those concerned with sexuality.

b) Values taught in school may conflict with those taught at home.

c) Teachers may feel that they cannot raise certain value issues if the community has strongly entrenched views.

d) Teachers may try to indoctrinate students into accepting inappropriate values.

e) Parents may feel that the role of the school is to teach "facts," not "values."

We have to be diligent and think carefully before we introduce value-based issues into the classroom. However, as mentioned earlier, we cannot avoid values in our teaching, and we have a responsibility to help students develop those values required for responsible citizenship.

Identifying Values

How can we help students identify the values that they or others hold? One way is to use the following type of activity:

- Look at the photo below. How do you think this young boy feels in the toy airplane?
- What do you think is important to this person? What does this person value?
- Would you feel this way if you were in this situation?
- Do you think this person likes feeling this way?
- If the boy did not know that the plane had "Miss Vancouver" on the fuselage and he found out, do you think he would feel any differently?

By identifying how people feel, we can often infer what is important to them.

Other strategies can also be used to help students identify values. For example, we could ask students to analyze their classroom context and identify what is important in terms of values (e.g., respect, safety, learning, kindness, competition, etc.). Students could analyze the school rules to ascertain what values are emphasized. We could rely on values clarification activities as outlined in the next chapter. Or we could ask explicitly what students value and compile a list of their values. If we decide to carry out this activity, we should not invade the students' right to privacy. We should also consider polling students anonymously and then discussing the results in a general way, without reference to specific students. We could also use stories and have students identify the values that the story characters hold.

When studying cultural groups, students can note their values by inferring these from what people do. However, rather than emphasizing the different ways people, for example, practise religious beliefs, we can instead focus on the ways in which most cultures value some form of spirituality.

By using social studies textbooks, we can help students identify the values people hold (or historically have held): What motivated the Canadian fur traders? What values influenced the decision by the English to invade Quebec? Why did the French oppose the British?

TEACHING DECISION MAKING

Once students have identified some of the values they hold and have become aware more generally of the values involved in decision making, we can have students weigh the advantages and disadvantages of acting on any particular alternative. Many opportunities exist in the social studies curriculum (and in daily school interactions) for decision making. For example, many social studies curricula call for students to make decisions about community, provincial/territorial, Canadian, and international questions. In the classroom, students may be called upon to help make rules, or in conflict-resolution cases to decide how to resolve a problem (see the next chapter). The following **decision-making procedure** has four steps:

1. Define the problem.
2. Identify alternatives.
3. Identify and evaluate the consequences of acting on each alternative.
4. Make a decision.

This is not a lock-step model. A decision maker may consider one alternative, decide the consequences are unacceptable, and then consider another alternative until a desirable one is found.

In the first step, the situation that requires a decision presents itself (or is presented). This could be in print or pictorial form. It could arise from a current event or it could be an actual classroom or school situation that has arisen. For example, what should the class do to celebrate Christmas or Hanukkah? How can fighting be stopped on the school playground? How should the class help starving children in Darfur? The situation has to be clarified so that students understand what the problem is. Terms may have to be defined and research may have to be carried out in order to comprehend the background to the problem.

To ensure that it is a *decision-making* situation, rather than one where a mere choice would suffice, the problem has to be significant in terms of curriculum content or to the students in the class. Although the terms "choose" and "decide" are often used interchangeably, the term "decision making" will refer in this book only to significant contexts where substantial thought is required. The distinction between "choose" and "decide" can be noted in the following statements: The judge *chose* to sentence the accused to life imprisonment. The judge *decided* to sentence the accused to life imprisonment. In the second statement, it is implied that the judge thought seriously before acting, whereas the first could imply mere whim.

The second step involves generating alternative solutions. Sometimes only two alternatives exist, as in deciding whether to *renovate* a historical building or leave it *as is,* or deciding to *do something* rather than *do nothing*. In other situations, there may be several alternatives, as shown in the Incinerator Simulation Game on pages 198–199.

Sometimes, the possible alternatives will have to be generated by the decision makers. For example, if we ask students to make a decision about how to make the community a better place in which to live, it will be up to them to generate the alternatives.

In the third step, the consequences of each alternative are identified and evaluated. This will entail asking "What might happen if A is done?" and tracing the possible consequences for both the short and the long term. A good idea here is to use a web diagram or chart that shows the short-term and long-term consequences. For instance, if one possible solution for making the community a better place is the construction of a new community swimming pool, the short-term consequence may be that people will be happier and jobs will be created, but in the long term taxes may increase. In this case, a choice has to be made between immediate community satisfaction and increased long-term taxation. In the Incinerator Simulation Game, a student may have put prudential values (e.g., NIMBY—Not In My Backyard) ahead of consideration for the well-being of the entire community.

The decision-making procedure is an extremely useful one in the study of current events. Students can identify the issues and conflicts that are germane to the event, find out what alternative courses of action are proposed, generate their own alternatives, determine what they think the consequences of acting on the various alternatives will be, and arrive at their own decisions. For example, students in schools in Vancouver are involved in making decisions about environmental issues and are taking practical actions to alleviate pollution and garbage problems. This type of action is discussed at greater length in the next chapter.

Decision-Making Lesson Plan

What would make the best pet for me?[6]

Goals: Personal and social values

Strand: Interdisciplinary concern

Organizer: Problem

Objectives:

1. Students should arrive at a decision using the following procedure: (a) define the problem, (b) generate alternatives, (c) identify the consequences of each alternative, (d) evaluate the consequences.
2. Students should consider their own situations and the effects of their choices on others who live with them and in the community more generally.
3. Students should give defensible reasons for their decisions.

Tell the students that they are going to make a decision. Outline the problem by having students state what pets they have and what it feels like to take care of a pet. Discuss the benefits of having pets and any problems there are (e.g., dog bites, pets having to be looked after when the family goes away).

1. Identify the decision to be made by stating there are many pets students could have, but which one would be best?
2. Students list the pets they think are suitable. Where there is an argument about whether a pet is suitable or not, the pet is left on the list so that students can decide later. Then, either individually or in groups, they research what each pet on the list will need in terms of food, exercise, space, medical care, and accessories, and the cost of these in terms of time and money. The amount of detail and research required here will depend on the maturity of the students. For example, a visit to an animal shelter might be organized. They can consider their own family situations and make a chart showing the benefits and disadvantages of owning the pet they have initially chosen. The findings on each pet can then be shared and a large chart constructed that shows the information collected. Questions can be posed about the consequences of owning a pet. For example, if one disadvantage to owning a dog is that it might bite someone, then ask how that might be avoided. If one disadvantage to owning a cat is the need to take care of the cat when the family goes away, then ask whether a friend or neighbour might look after the cat. Each student decides on the best pet for him- or herself, and writes a sentence stating the reasons. The class results are then graphed (see Chapter 19).

If you are teaching primary-level students, you may want to engage them in the following decision-making situation. Read this story to them or, if possible, have students read it for themselves.

> Geraldine is Alice's best friend. One day Alice forgets to bring her lunch to school, and although Geraldine shares her lunch with Alice, Alice is still hungry. She asks Michelle, who has four chocolate bars, if she can have one of them. Michelle says, "No, I want them." When Michelle isn't looking, Alice takes two chocolate bars. She goes back to Geraldine and says, "I took Michelle's chocolate. She's greedy. She doesn't need four chocolate bars. Don't tell anyone." Michelle notices that her chocolate bars are missing and tells the teacher. In class, the teacher says, "Someone has taken Michelle's chocolate bars. Does anyone know who took them?" Geraldine knows that Alice took them. Should she tell the teacher?

Now, ask the following questions:

1. "What is the problem?" (Students clarify the problem.)
2. "In what ways could the problem be solved?" (Students list the possible alternatives.)
3. "With each of the solutions, who is worst off?" "What sort of harm could occur to this person?" (Students discuss the possible alternatives.)
4. "If you were the worst-off person, would it be right for you to take the proposed action?" "What would be the consequences if everyone in a similar situation acted in this way?" (Students imagine the consequences and state what they are. Students then write down their own solutions and justify them.)

Using Simulation Games to Teach Decision Making

One effective technique that helps students begin to make responsible decisions involves **simulation games.** Unlike games such as Twenty Questions or Word Bingo, simulations try to be as true to real-life events as possible. Although they cannot take the place of real situations, simulations offer students a safe environment where they can test solutions to problems and make decisions, but not suffer the actual consequences of poor decisions. Here is one simulation game in which students take on the role of a property owner and make a community decision.

Activity 15-D

Try the Incinerator Simulation Game in your class. On the map on the following page, designate a town lot for each member of the class. If there are fewer than 36 students, spread student ownership of the lots over the entire map.

BACKGROUND: The town of Actum, a small tourist resort, has a garbage problem. All of the landfill sites outside the town limits are full, and garbage must now be disposed of within the town limits. The town has been granted provincial money to build a garbage incinerator. The incinerator will have a 20-metre high chimney and will take up space equivalent to one house lot. It will have all the latest pollution reduction technology, but smoke will be emitted from the chimney which has an extremely low danger level to public health. The problem is where, within the town limits, to locate the incinerator. As there is no alternative to garbage disposal, the incinerator *must* be built.

Each individual should choose a site for the incinerator. Then hold a town meeting and decide where to locate the incinerator.

The following questions can be asked after students complete this simulation:

1. What influenced your choice for the site of the incinerator (e.g., wind direction, aesthetics, transportation routes, proximity to houses, stores, parks, and farmland)? What values did you appeal to? What point(s) of view did you adopt? Did prudential concerns outweigh concerns for the well-being of the community? What values are likely to be in conflict in this situation? Should what is best for the entire community override an individual's prudential interests?
2. How did the town decide (e.g., voting, compromise, unanimous decision of all concerned, being "ordered" by someone)? Would you want all similar decisions to be made in the same way?
3. What is the best way to make such decisions? Is there any way such decisions can be made without disadvantaging someone? If we accept a democratic form of government, do we then have to accept the fact that we will not always have our wishes acted upon?
4. If your choice was not accepted and the incinerator location is disadvantageous to you, how do you feel? As a member of a minority, could you do anything? Should you do something?
5. Should people get involved in planning their communities, or should they leave it to elected (or unelected) officials?
6. Do situations like this really occur? Where? How are they resolved?

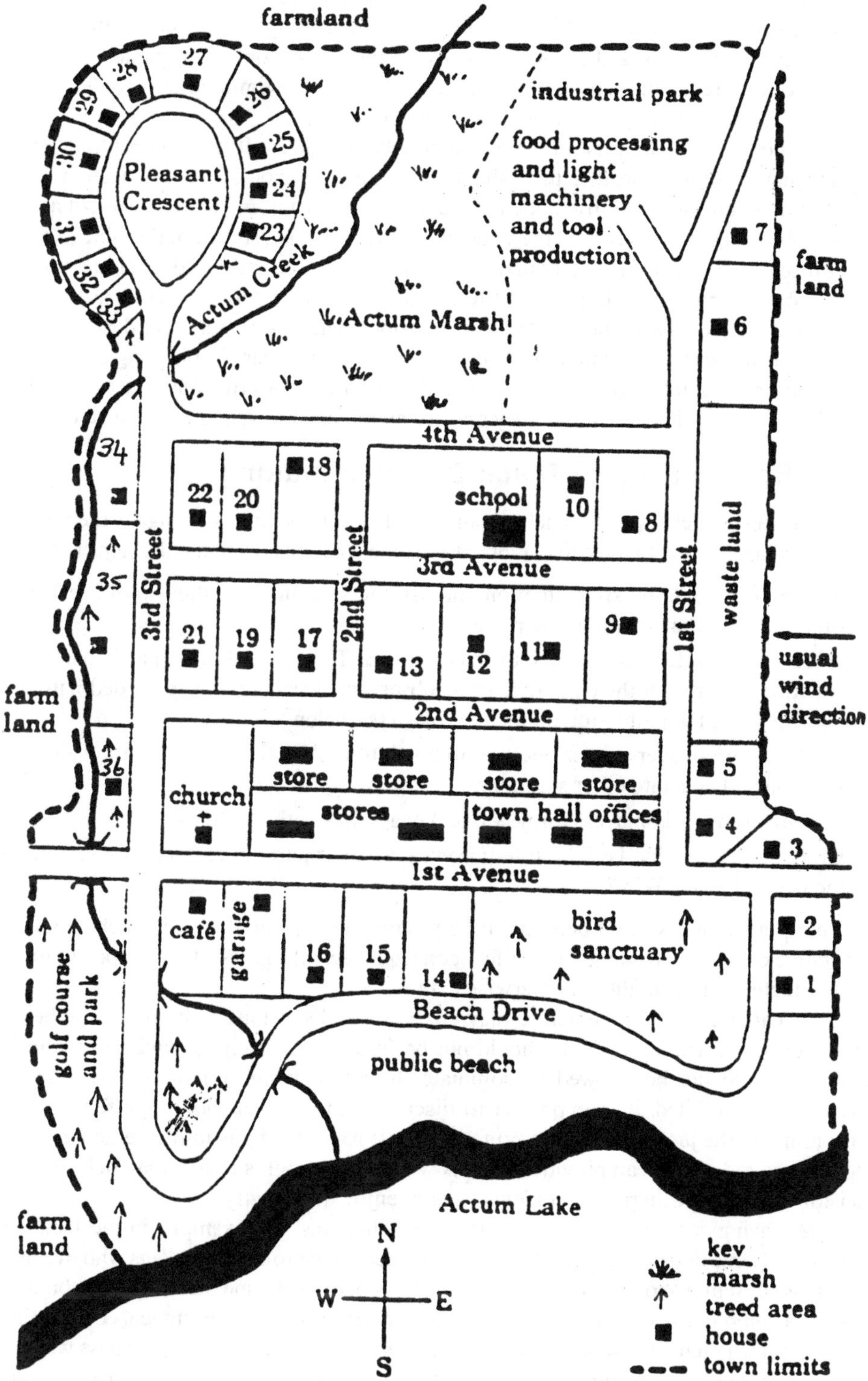
farmland
industrial park
food processing
and light
machinery
and tool
production
Pleasant
Crescent
Actum Creek
Actum Marsh
farm
land
4th Avenue
school
3rd Avenue
3rd Street
2nd Street
1st Street
waste land
usual
wind
direction
2nd Avenue
church
store
store
store
store
stores
town hall offices
1st Avenue
café
garage
bird
sanctuary
Beach Drive
golf course
and park
public beach
Actum Lake
N
W
E
S
key
marsh
treed area
house
town limits

Primary-level children can also play this game, but instead of a map use a model of the community. By actually *seeing* the incinerator, and by moving it to different sites, younger students can begin to *see* the consequences of their decisions. The game can also be adapted for different situations (e.g., where to locate a new swimming pool, industry, park, store, fire hall, community centre, ice rink, and so on).

Some possible pitfalls exist in the use of simulation games. If it is competition between students that wins the game, then there should be some discussion on the justification for this. If the game is too oversimplified, then students might get the impression that solutions to social problems are always easy. If the students can win by doing something unethical (such as taking resources away from another player), this should also be addressed. In simulations that involve role-playing, students may not always take their roles seriously. And, as alluded to above, there may be discipline problems or occasions when there is a great deal of emotion involved; such occurrences will need defusing. However, with careful planning and adequate debriefing, these pitfalls can be avoided. Simulations are a powerful way to teach particular values and foster positive attitudes. They are also extremely motivating for most students.

Using Role-Playing to Teach Decision Making

Another effective technique for teaching students decision making is to engage them in **role-playing,** which allows students to explore alternative solutions. Here are the steps to follow:[7]

1. Present a decision-making situation and ask the students how they would feel in this situation and what solutions are possible.
2. Select some students to become the role-players. They will play the participants in the situation. The rest of the class will act as observers. They are to be provided with questions to focus their attention on the role play (see below).
3. Have the role-players enact one possible solution. Ask the observers to evaluate the solution and generate other solutions.
4. Have the same role-players (or new ones) enact these other solutions.
5. Evaluate the activity. Did the role-players play their parts in realistic ways? Which is the best solution? Why?

Role-playing has several benefits. It helps students try out alternative behaviours in a safe context while avoiding "real-life" consequences. It gives them opportunities to express feelings they might not otherwise express.

Great care has to be taken in role-playing, however. Decision situations should be carefully chosen. Unwilling students should not be forced to participate, and those who love "acting" should not be allowed to dominate. In role-playing situations where negative behaviour is exhibited, it is important to discuss with the class how they felt about the behaviour and the justification (if any) for it. But if role-playing is implemented in a pedagogically sound way, it can provide students with many insights into human behaviour and decision making. Furthermore, students usually enjoy the activity.

Role-playing can be incorporated into many situations. For example, in the Incinerator Simulation Game described above, students could act out the roles of residents who live in various areas of Actum and then argue their cases for where the incinerator should be built. In a study of a community in which a "big box" retailer wishes to relocate, students could take on the roles of the potential new store's owner, a local store owner who thinks business will suffer if the new store is built, a consumer who wants more choice and cheaper merchandise, and a local resident who is concerned about the increased traffic the store will bring to the neighbourhood. When examining the forest industry in Canada or elsewhere, students could play the roles of a forest company executive who wants to clear-cut a forest, a forest worker who needs work, an environmentalist who is against clear-cutting, and a local resident who is worried about the effects of logging on her property as clear-cutting will create erosion problems. In a study of Canada, students could role-play family members who each wish to spend a summer holiday in a different province. In the section on law-related education in Chapter 17, there is an opportunity for students to take on the roles of a plaintiff, defendant, and judge. In a mock trial, students could also act as witnesses, jury members, and lawyers. Where an issue is being examined, students could be asked to play the role of a person who is opposed to their position, with the goal of developing more open-minded attitudes.

Activity 15-E

Design an activity in which a decision is required. As part of the activity, have a group of students engage in some role-taking. For example, in a unit on another culture, the students could take on the role of a member of the culture who is trying to persuade a tourist to visit the country in which he or she lives.

The questions that arise in all the above examples is, "Is there a *right* decision, and if so, what is it and why is it right?" The next chapter is devoted to a number of approaches you could take in answering these questions.

Other Activities

1. Identify the value standard in each of the following arguments. Check your responses in the Answers section.
   a) Because children are people, they should be treated with respect.
   b) Hitting a child is ethically wrong because it's a form of child abuse.
   c) Students who wear glasses in my classroom should not be given special consideration. They're not disabled.
   d) Watching TV for five hours a day is harmful to children, so they should not be allowed to do it.
2. Design a lesson plan using the decision-making procedure for a primary level class. Choose an appropriate decision-making situation and outline how you would teach the lesson.
3. Critique the following lesson on decision making and compare your critique with the one in the Answers section.

TEACHER: Today, class, we're going to help someone make a decision. Please read the story and then we'll help Alice decide what to do. [*She hands out the story to the class.*]

Sharon is Alice's best friend. They walk to school together every day. They play together at recess; they roller skate and go swimming together. Sometimes older kids tease Sharon, who wears a hearing aid because she can't hear very well. They make fun of her and whisper nasty things that she can't hear. This always upsets Sharon and that makes Alice angry. But Alice is not sure what to do when kids start teasing Sharon.

Alice's mother tells her to ignore the teasers and they'll soon stop.

Alice's father advises her to ask the teasers how they would feel if someone were teasing them.

Alice's sister tells her to go to the school principal.

Alice's brother tells her he will beat up the kids who are teasing Sharon.

TEACHER: What's Alice's problem?

STUDENT: She has to decide whether to ignore the teasing or tell the principal about it.

TEACHER: Good. Now, let's consider what Alice could do. What are her alternatives? As I write them on the blackboard, I want you to copy them down in your notebooks.

STUDENT: She could get her brother to punch out the teasers.

STUDENT: She could ignore them.

TEACHER: OK, let's not have any more. Let's see what the consequences would be if she acted on either of these.

STUDENT: Her brother might get beaten up.

TEACHER: I don't think that will happen. Her brother is much bigger then the teasers. Anyway, it's not a good idea to beat up people.

STUDENT: Her teasers might stop if they knew her brother would beat them up.

TEACHER: Do you all agree?

CLASS: Yes.

TEACHER: Would that be a good consequence?

CLASS: Yes.

TEACHER: What if she ignored the problem?

STUDENT: The teasers would get fed up and stop.

STUDENT: No, they would just keep doing it.

TEACHER: Let's take a vote. Who thinks the teasers will stop teasing Sharon? [*10 hands go up.*] Who thinks they'll keep on teasing Sharon? [*15 hands are raised.*] So, we've decided that won't work. What should Alice do?

STUDENT: She should tell her teacher and get the teacher to stop it.

TEACHER: Yes, I think that would be a good idea. So, have we decided that Alice should talk to her teacher?

CLASS: Yes.

4. Modify the Incinerator Simulation Game for a Grade 1 class to involve a decision about where to put a new park.
5. Create some decision-making vignettes for a Grade 3 class that will introduce them to the standards of good decision making.
6. Create a role-playing activity that will help students understand that different people can have different values and that these values should be taken into account in a decision-making situation.

Notes

1. For decision-making ideas framed as critical challenges, see J. Harrison, N. Smith, and I. Wright, *Critical Challenges in Social Studies for Upper Elementary Students* (Richmond, BC: The Critical Thinking Cooperative, 1999).
2. Ministry of Education Ontario, "Values, Influences and Peers Resource Guide, 1996"; www.edu.gov.on.ca/eng/document/resource/vip.html

3. Association for Living Values Education International, 2007: www.livingvalues.net (accessed February 19, 2008).
4. Rainbow School District Sudbury Ontario: www.rainbowschools.ca/programs/Characterducation/charactereducation.php (accessed February 19, 2008).
5. For example, the Olympic Committee has materials focusing on Olympic values: www.olympic.ca/EN/education/values_education.shtml (accessed February 19, 2008).
6. Although this may appear to be a matter of "mere" choice, pets can have significant consequences on family life and on the community.
7. F. Shaftel and G. Shaftel, *Role Playing in the Curriculum,* 2nd ed. (Englewood Cliffs, NJ: Prentice-Hall, 1982).

Glossary of Key Terms

Comparative value statement—Statements that evaluate the comparative worth of two or more things.

Decision-making procedure—A procedure wherein students clarify the decision to be made, generate alternatives, identify the consequences of acting on each alternative, evaluate the consequences, and make a decision.

Point of view—Used in this text to denote the type of value claim (e.g., the ethical point of view, the environmental point of view, etc.).

Prescriptive value statement—A statement that dictates what ought to be or what ought to be done.

Role-playing—An activity in which people enact a scenario by playing the characters in a given situation.

Simple value statement—A statement that evaluates the worth of something.

Simulation game—A game in which the situation is as lifelike as possible.

Syllogism—An argument in which two premises lead logically to the conclusion.

Types of values:

- **Aesthetic**—Having to do with beauty, form, and texture.
- **Environmental**—Having to do with how the natural environment is treated; now often viewed as part of the ethical domain.
- **Instrumental value**—A value that is held in order to realize some higher or ultimate value.
- **Intellectual**—Having to do with truth, logic, and/or clarity, etc.
- **Ethical**—Generally speaking, having to do with how others are treated and how disputes are resolved.
- **Prudential**—Having to do with self-interest.
- **Religious**—Having to do with a set of beliefs concerning the nature, cause, and purposes of the universe, especially as these relate to a superhuman agency or agencies; spirituality.
- **Ultimate value**—The most fundamental value; all other values are instrumental to this one.

Value—Something that is deemed important in a person's life and that motivates the person to behave in certain ways.

CHAPTER 16

Approaches to Teaching Social and Personal Values

The previous chapter argued that value judgments cannot be avoided in teaching social studies. Teachers attempt to instill values in students related to appropriate behaviour in class and on the school grounds, for example, especially in young children. Two justifications can be advanced for this. The first is that there are some values to which children must commit to ensure their own and others' continued well-being. The second justification is that young children cannot understand the often complex reasons why certain values ought to be acted upon. As well, reasoning with young children may not always be persuasive; they may need to be convinced in other ways, such as through incentives and rewards.

Children obtain their values in two basic ways. One way is through reinforcement. A child is praised for virtuous behaviour and punished for behaviour that is not acceptable. Reinforcement can take the form of exhortations, lectures, rewards, the removal of privileges, or the use of facial expressions to show approval or disapproval.

The second way children learn values is by observing and modelling behaviour. Through interaction, children "pick up" the values of their families, their peer groups, their religious affiliations, and the society in which they live. In the classroom, teachers either consciously or unconsciously exemplify acceptable values. Literature, textbooks, and the media can also exemplify values that students pick up.

You may remember that when you were at school, certain people were regarded as heroes and heroines, whereas others were viewed as villains. You may also recall the fables, parables, and stories that were read to you that were designed to teach you particular ethical lessons. Today, children's exemplars are often media stars and sports heroes, and their ethical lessons are often derived from television and other forms of popular culture.

Activity 16-A

Think back to your elementary schooling. List the names of those individuals who were regarded as the heroes and villains in the school curriculum and what their claims to fame were (e.g., Terry Fox). Now list the names of those whom *you* regarded as heroes and villains, and indicate their claims to fame. Finally, list those whom you regard as heroes today and their claims to fame. How are the three lists similar and different? Now do the same for the heroes and villains in contemporary elementary texts and stories and, separately, those in the mass media. Again, analyze the similarities and differences.

As children mature, they develop reasoning abilities and start using arguments to defend their value positions. How they argue their views depends, in the main, upon their developmental level, how they are taught, and what models of good reasoning they have.

Activity 16-B

In a group, divide up a social studies curriculum guide so that each group member analyzes approximately the same number of pages. Then identify the values that are emphasized or implied. Classify these, where possible, into ethical, prudential, aesthetic, and intellectual categories. Share your list with your peers. What values are given most emphasis?

As teachers, you might find that among members of your community there is basic agreement about certain values. Parents want their children to respect their siblings, for example; likewise, teachers want students to respect their peers in the classroom. However, other values may be controversial. Witness the recent controversy in Surrey, BC, where the school board banned elementary school books that portrayed same-sex families.

Whatever values we wish to foster, we can teach them either explicitly or by modelling good behaviour and fostering a positive classroom climate. In the latter case we can ask students to help come up with and persuade others to follow the classroom rules, have them engage in conflict resolution activities (see Chapter 18), and have them participate in activities that involve students helping other students (see Chapter 9). We can also involve students in service learning activities (see below) and social action projects (see Chapter 18).

This chapter examines various approaches to the explicit teaching of values. However, the brief summaries provided here cannot do justice to all the complexities involved in values education.

THE CHARACTER EDUCATION APPROACH

Activity 16-C

What values do you think your students ought to act upon in the classroom? Draw up a list and share it with your peers. Do they agree or disagree with the values you have listed? What reasons do they give for including the values on their list? What points of view (e.g., ethical, prudential, and aesthetic, etc.) did you and your peers use to justify your decisions?

The purpose of the **Character Education** approach is to instill in students certain values that are considered desirable. These often include virtues such as tact, honesty, perseverance, obedience, and courtesy. In a review of the virtues proposed by three experts in the area of character education, Leming[1] found that they disagreed more than they agreed. However, most character educators defend teaching certain virtues on the basis of the rise in juvenile crime, drug use, vandalism, gang wars, bullying, and the lack of respect some students show for others. It is assumed that if children are taught the "right" values, then these and other examples of "bad behaviour" will decrease. Such values may be those deemed to be universally acceptable, or they may be those shared by a society or particular group within a society. In many cases they will be enshrined in law or in a religious code of conduct.

Proponents of this approach typically regard the individual as a reactor rather than an initiator. The individual is to be taught the values thought to be desirable in much the same way as the "three Rs" were traditionally taught—directly and explicitly. Historically, the proponents of value education believed that the desired values should be instilled in children through indoctrination—initiation into fixed, doctrine-like beliefs held without a basis in evidence or consideration of alternative positions.

This approach relies on several teaching/learning strategies. All are based on behaviourism and social learning theory. One strategy is to use examples of good behaviour in literature in which characters exemplify the desired values. A story is presented that illustrates the adherence or non-adherence to a particular virtue (modelling); then students are led through questioning and discussion to arrive at the "correct" answers (reinforcement). The same intent is present when stories of heroes, heroines, and villains drawn from history are presented. In these cases, students are rarely told why they should admire the heroes and heroines or that many of them also had less-than-desirable traits. When controversial issues are taught, the Character Education approach has traditionally entailed an avoidance of presenting all sides of an issue. Students may receive evidence and arguments that support only the "right" answer; the teacher's questions about the issue are designed to lead students to this answer. Often, where the intent is to have students avoid certain actions, such as smoking or taking drugs, scare tactics are used. The student is denied any opportunity to question the evidence or the arguments presented. Or children are taught to "just say no," without consideration of why they should say no. Sometimes, the desired virtues are acted on. Students carry out **service learning**[2] in which they help out at food banks, coach ESL students, or volunteer in senior citizens' centres. However, there is debate about the efficacy of service learning.[3] Furthermore, there are two competing views about service learning. Are students engaged in service learning as an altruistic duty or are they involved in social action projects in which they try to resolve a social issue through actions such as cleaning up a polluted river or restocking a salmon stream?[4] Students may not be told why they should engage in these activities or have any choice in the matter. This does not mean by any means that these sorts of activities are not worthwhile, but set within a Character Education context the efficacy of the activities is assumed and generally not open for wide-ranging debate.

Before using this approach, we should consider several questions: (a) Who is to decide what values to instill? (b) What should be done when two acceptable values are in conflict? For example, should a woman refrain from stealing food for her children if they are starving? (c) In a multicultural classroom, how does a teacher deal with values that may conflict with those of a particular culture, or school values that conflict with parental values? A further consideration is the efficacy of this approach. If the right values are instilled in children, will children act on them? For example, there is evidence that children do not always interpret stories in the ways that are intended by an author; nor do children always act on the values that are espoused in stories or activities designed to influence them.[5] In fact, traditional approaches to sex and drug education have been found, in some cases, to increase sexual[6] and drug-taking activities,[7] and zero tolerance policies do not seem to be always effective in Canadian schools.[8] Yet we do want children to accept such virtues as responsibility, honesty, and tolerance, and we also want to warn children of the dangers of drugs, etc. We can do so when Character Education is tempered with reason, where the classroom and school climate are democratic (see Chapter 17), when rules are fair and fairly enforced, where students are involved in helping resolve conflicts[9] (see Chapter 18), and where students are treated with respect.

Every school has its own explicit or implicit Character Education program. Some provinces, such as Alberta,[10] have provincewide programs; others are run at the local or school level. Some schools use learning materials developed in the US.[11]

THE VALUES CLARIFICATION APPROACH

Rather than instilling values in students, the **Values Clarification** approach aims to help students identify their own set of values and act on them.

Activity 16-D

Below are a variety of Values Clarification activities. All are adaptations of activities proposed by Simon et al.[12] Try several of these activities and then answer the questions at the end.

1. Rank the following behaviours from the most reprehensible to the least. Give reasons for your ranking.

   a) Hitting a child who is misbehaving ___________

   b) Being sarcastic to a child ___________

   c) Ignoring a child who needs help ___________

2. On your retirement from teaching, your students present you with a scroll. If you were to write the words on this scroll, what would you like them to say? For what would you like to be remembered?

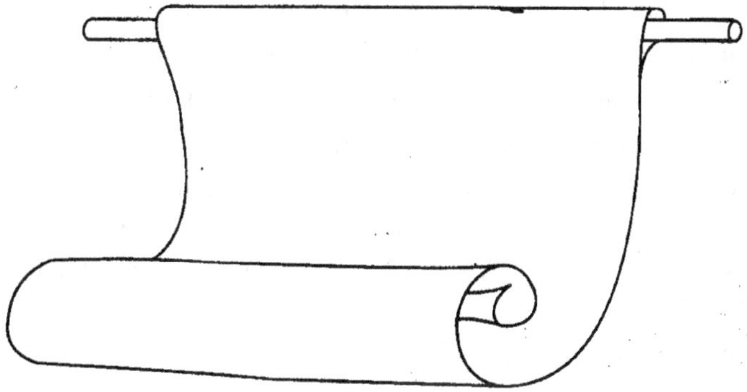

3. What is your attitude toward the use of snowmobiles in national or provincial parks? On a continuum from "banning completely" to "allowing unlimited use," where would your position lie?
4. Complete this sentence: I wish the federal government would ___________.
5. Reflect on what you have done so far this week. What made you happy? What made you upset? What are you proud of having done? Could your week have been better? How?
6. Let's suppose you expect your students to work very hard for you and to attain very high standards. Your students always do well on tests. Your principal decides to give you a class of intellectually immature students, but you like working only with better-than-average students. Your principal, however, is adamant.

   a) In what different ways might the above scenario be resolved?

   b) What might happen as a result of each solution?

   c) Which solution do you think would be best?

7. A friend of yours in a university course has copied an assignment from a student who did a similar course at another university. He or she obtained a very high mark, whereas you obtained a very low mark, despite the fact that you spent a great deal of time and effort on the assignment. Would you tell your instructor? What would be the advantages and disadvantages of telling?
8. Choose any value issue and discuss it with a group of your peers. When statements are made that positively or negatively relate to the issue, use the questions below, as appropriate, to further clarify the statement(s):
   a) Are you glad about that?
   b) What do you mean by ___________?
   c) What would be the consequences of that?
   d) Have you thought of any other possibilities?
   e) Are you going to act on that idea?

Having considered these activities, answer the following questions:

1. What do you think the aim(s) are for each of the activities above?
2. Did the activities help you to clarify your own values?
3. What procedures did you follow to arrive at answers in the activities above?
4. What types of values are found in these activities?
5. Rank the activities in terms of the importance of the value issue. Which activity focuses on the most important value(s)? Which focuses on the least important?
6. If you disagreed with a peer regarding the solution to one of the above activities, would it matter? Why or why not?
7. What would be the advantages of having a clear set of values? Would there be any disadvantages?

The Values Clarification approach is premised on four key points:

- There is a focus on students' own lives.
- There must be a non-judgmental acceptance of other students' values.
- Students must carefully consider their own values.
- There is the assumption that students who know what they value will be empowered.

According to Values Clarification theory,[13] to have a value, one must do the following:

1. *Choose freely* from alternatives after thoughtful consideration of each alternative.
2. *Prize* and cherish the choice; be happy with it and be willing to affirm the choice publicly.
3. *Act* by doing something with the choice, repeatedly, in some pattern of life.

This approach relies entirely on the individual, who decides which values are deemed to be positive and who demonstrates their adherence to them, by acting on them in their relationships with others.

This approach can be used to clarify all types of values (e.g., ethical, prudential, and aesthetic, etc.), as well as tastes and preferences. However, as preferences are a matter of personal opinion, Values Clarification can become relativistic in the manner of "Your preference is as good as my preference." Extreme proponents of Values Clarification take the view that all values are relative, but most agree with this statement made by Louis Raths:[14]

> If, for any reason, we do not want a child to choose a particular alternative, like setting fire to a house, we should let him/her know that this is not within the realm of choice.

The research evidence for the efficacy of Values Clarification is not strong.[15] Further, the use of this approach raises questions about whether values and preferences ought to be justified in the same way; whether values are, or ought to be, relative to the individual; and whether the three steps of Values Clarification always produce values that are ethically defensible.[16]

THE COGNITIVE-DEVELOPMENTAL APPROACH

Neither of the above two approaches says anything about *how students reason* about value issues. Lawrence Kohlberg[17] addresses this question in his six-stage model of ethical reasoning. In Stage 1, children reason on the basis of concerns related to reward and punishment and pleasing authority figures. In Stage 2, children serve their own needs while realizing that other children have their own interests, reasoning in effect that "I'll scratch your back if you'll scratch mine." In Stage 3, children try to live up to conventional standards of their peer group or the wider society. And in Stage 4, children show a concern with maintaining society; this is referred to as the "law and order stage." Stages 5 and 6 are generally reached only by mature adults. Stage 5 focuses on social contracts which bind people together, through collective decision making and compromise, in terms of common interests. Stage 6 focuses on universal ethical principles, often related to social justice. The stages are sequential—a person cannot skip a stage—and hierarchical, with each stage representing a qualitative improvement over the previous one and building toward the next higher stage. The reasoning at each stage is a product of both environmental and genetic stimulants. Development occurs by way of reasoning about moral dilemmas, a person's maturity, and the social milieu.

This stage-developmental theory has been integrated into moral education programs. Here is an example.[18] Students are given a story in which a young girl promises her father she won't climb trees because earlier she fell when doing so and hurt herself. Her friend's kitten is caught in a tree and she is the only one who can rescue it. Should she climb the tree to save the kitten? If she climbs the tree, she breaks a promise; if she doesn't, the owner of the kitten will be heartbroken because his mother has told him that if the kitten gets into trouble once more, the kitten will be given away.

Once the dilemma has been posed, the class is divided into groups. To ensure that conflicting opinions are well represented, each group should include students who either reason at different stages of moral reasoning or disagree on whether the girl should climb the tree. Within this approach, it is thought that if students at a given stage are exposed to arguments at the next-highest stage, they will be stimulated to begin to think at this higher level. The groups discuss their responses to the dilemma, and then state their conclusions and give reasons for them. The following questions may then be posed:

- Would it make any difference if the girl's father didn't know whether she climbed the tree?
- Would the girl's father understand if she did climb the tree?

- Should all promises be kept?
- How will the kitten's owner feel if the kitten is (is not) rescued?
- Suppose the girl doesn't like the kitten's owner. Should that make any difference to her decision?
- How would you feel if you were the girl? Or the owner of the kitten?

This approach has been criticized from the perspective that most ethical problems are not dilemmas. It is not always the case that someone will end up being disadvantaged, whatever action is taken, and there are often more than two alternative courses of action in real-life ethical problems. Further, there is evidence that children under the age of eight years old do not develop their moral reasoning by discussing dilemmas.[19] There is also the problem of having all the facts of the case presented in the dilemma. (For example, in the above moral dilemma, it is not clear what will happen to the cat if it is given away.) In real life, we often need to first uncover all the facts and evaluate them, and it is often the case that the facts are in dispute.

Feminist scholars have also criticized Kohlberg's theory for being male-oriented. (Kohlberg based his theory initially on research involving only male subjects.) These scholars claim that females tend to rely on an ethic of caring and are concerned with mutually satisfying relationships rather than with justice.[20] Many books and articles have been written about the ethic of care. The most influential proponent is Nel Noddings, who advocates for schools to act like good families. This would entail teachers modelling caring behaviour, allowing students to talk about and evaluate their relationships with others while practising care for others and their environment and affirming and encouraging others to do the same.[21]

Recent research has indicated that reasoning about ethical problems is complex and context-bound.[22] Ideally, teachers will take this complexity into account as they help students reason well about the ethical problems they face in their day-to-day lives. Relying on a variety of methodologies, rather than just one, may well be key to this.

THE VALUES ANALYSIS APPROACH

Values Analysis is based on the assumption that there are rational ways to resolve value issues. The focus is on the logic of arguments, the truth of empirical claims, the clarification of concepts, and the justifications for the value principles, rules, or standards that are used to arrive at a decision.

Here is an example: Students have been talking about the situation in Darfur, where thousands of people (as of this writing) are unable to obtain enough food or medical services to survive. The students wonder if giving aid to the people in Darfur would be a good idea. They pose the question, "Should we give aid to the people in Darfur?" They clarify the concept of "aid" by discussing examples of aid, and eventually arrive at a list of what they believe qualifies as aid (see Chapter 6 for ideas about clarifying concepts). In inquiry groups (see Chapter 9), students then draw up a list of the pros and cons of giving aid.

SHOULD WE GIVE AID TO THE PEOPLE OF DARFUR?

We Should Give Aid	We Should Not Give Aid
Giving aid will prevent starvation.	Giving aid will mean poor people in Canada won't be helped.
It'll help people who are ill and can't get medicine.	It'll result in people not helping themselves—they'll rely on aid all the time.
It'll provide schools for children.	Some children in class can't afford to give money, and they'll feel badly if everyone else does.

The students evaluate the above and other reasons for and against giving aid. Would students who cannot afford to give money feel badly when other students give? Is there evidence that aid helps people in similar situations?

The next step consists of identifying the value standards to which students have appealed. These are the standards that lie behind the reasons for giving or not giving aid: e.g., we should prevent starvation; we should help people who are ill; and we should provide schools for children. The value standards behind the reasons for *not* giving aid are that we should look after Canadians before we help others and that we should not continue to give to people who are already dependent on aid.

The final step is to "test" the value standard. This is where the Values Analysis approach differs fundamentally from the other approaches. In the Character Education approach, the standard is taken for granted if it is deemed to be socially acceptable. According to the Values Clarification approach, so long as the steps of the valuing process have been carried out, the standard is acceptable. According to the Cognitive-Developmental approach, the value standard is based on the stage of reasoning attained.

In the Values Analysis approach, the justification for the value standard or principle is judged by applying three **principle tests:**[23]

The Role-Exchange Test: When, as a child, you had hurt someone else in some way, you may remember being asked, "How would you like it if somebody did that to you?" The point of this question is to turn the tables, so to speak. If you would not want the action to be performed on you, then you should not do it to someone else. This is the basis for the Role-Exchange Test. The question, however, should be posed as "Would it be right for you in the role of the other person to do X?" It is not just a question of liking. A child may not like to go to the dentist, but it would be right for a parent to insist that the child go. These are the steps to follow:

1. Imagine what it would be like in the other person's situation and to experience the consequences of proposed actions on that person.
2. Consider whether it would be right for the other person to take the action if you were the one experiencing the consequences.
3. Decide whether it is acceptable or unacceptable to perform the action because of the consequences to the other person. This test is most powerful when the consequences to the other person are undesirable.

The Universal Consequences Test: You may also remember from your childhood being asked, when you had done something wrong, "What if everybody did that?" This question's point is that if the consequences of everybody performing a particular act would be disastrous, then *you* should not do it. In this test, the decision maker has to imagine the consequences were everyone to perform the same action for the same reasons. For example, would a motorist be justified in driving well above the speed limit were he late for an extremely important meeting? We can imagine a number of motorists wanting to use this argument as a reason, and we can also imagine the consequences if they were all to speed. Although this reason does not justify speeding, the justification offered by an ambulance driver carrying a critically ill patient might be acceptable for *every* ambulance driver in a similar situation. The steps in this test are as follows:

1. Imagine the consequences if everyone who might perform the same action for the same reason were to do so.
2. Consider whether the imagined consequences would be acceptable.
3. Conclude that the action is right if the consequences are acceptable, and then subject the decision to the other principle tests, or conclude that it is wrong if the consequences are unacceptable.

The New Cases Test: A third question that you may have been asked when you were engaged in some bad behaviour is this: "Would you do the same thing in another similar situation?" This question focuses on the presumption that people ought to be consistent in their judgments. In this test, a standard that has been accepted is applied to new, logically relevant cases. The power of the test depends on applying the standard to difficult cases. If students have said that stealing from someone in the class is wrong, it is probably ineffective to ask whether they would steal from friends, relatives, other children in the school, etc. Rather, pose a problem where stealing would lead to desirable consequences, such as saving a life. Then students must determine whether they think the principle "in no circumstances whatsoever should people steal" is justifiable or whether another principle is more acceptable, such as "people should not steal except in circumstances where a life is at stake." The latter principle would need to be tested with new cases in order to determine whether the person doing the reasoning is willing to hold to it consistently. The steps are as follows:

1. Choose a case that logically falls under the value standard being appealed to.
2. Consider whether to judge this case in the same way as the original decision was judged.
3. If the case is judged in the same way, and it is the hardest case that can be imagined, then accept the decision.

It may appear that all this is far too complex for elementary school students. Yet teachers and parents routinely ask young children, "How would you like that done to you?" "What if everybody did that?" and "If you would do that in this situation, would you do it in X situation?" These questions are the basis for the Role Exchange, Universal Consequences, and New Cases tests. Of course, elementary school students cannot necessarily apply these tests in a sophisticated way, but they can be asked to consider the consequences of their actions for other people. Even though primary-grade children will have difficulty applying the Role Exchange test—because they will believe that other people share their perspective—this does not mean that they should not consider the effects of their actions on others. By about age seven, children do realize that others can have different perspectives, and that these have to be taken into account when interpersonal decisions are made.

Activity 16-E asks you to apply the principle tests.

Activity 16-E

Read the following vignette and answer the question that follows.

> The Fraser family—a mother, a father, a three-year-old, and a five-year-old—is looking for an affordable place to rent. The parents are getting quite desperate, so when they see an advertisement for an affordable duplex they hurry over to look at it. The parents decide that it is just what they are looking for, and they tell the owner, who gets out a rental contract and starts to fill it in. He asks them if they have children. They reply that they have two. The owner tells them that they cannot rent the duplex, for he does not rent to families with children. He claims that children make too much noise and are likely to damage his property.
>
> Should the owner have the right to refuse to rent the duplex to the Fraser family?

Suppose you argue that the owner should have the right to refuse to rent the duplex because it's his property and he should have the right to do what he likes with it. The value standard is "Property owners ought to be able to do whatever they like with their own property." How would you answer the following questions?

1. Imagine you are a member of the Fraser family. Would the owner's decision be right if you were the one experiencing the consequences?
2. What would be the consequences if every property owner in the city refused to rent to couples with children because children are noisy and might damage property? Are these consequences acceptable?
3. Suppose a man comes to the owner and is told that the duplex is available for rent. The owner asks for his name and is told that it is Levin. The owner asks if he is Jewish. The man's answer is yes. The owner says he does not rent his duplex to Jews. Should the owner have the right to refuse to rent the duplex to Jews? Suppose a person in a wheelchair wanted to rent the duplex but is told by the owner that he does not rent to people who are physically challenged. Should the owner have the right to do this?
4. If you were asked to justify the principle that property owners can do whatever they please with their property, what higher principle would you use?

Suppose you were to argue that the owner should not have the right to refuse to rent to the Fraser family because that would be discriminatory. The value standard would then be "People should not have the right to discriminate." How would you answer the following questions?

1. Suppose you were the owner. Would it be right for you to experience the consequences of having renters who you believe will be noisy and will damage your property?
2. Would the consequences be desirable or undesirable if no property owners were allowed to choose their tenants?
3. Suppose two young males who have a reputation in the community for drug dealing and gang warfare wish to rent the duplex. Should the owner have the right to refuse to rent it to them?

4. If you were asked to justify the non-discrimination principle, to what higher principle might you appeal?

The Values Analysis approach demands that critical thought be applied to value questions. Difficult as it may be, it is not beyond the capabilities of students to begin to grasp some of the complexities of value reasoning. As Beck[24] says:

> While value questions are indeed complex and subtle, they are not beyond the capacity of ordinary adults and children. In fact, we all solve dozens, perhaps hundreds of value problems quite successfully every week.

Several questions can be raised about this approach: What role should emotions play in reasoning about value issues? What does one do in situations where, after applying the principle tests, there is still disagreement about the right thing to do? Is this approach appropriate in a multicultural society where there are different conceptions of what is ethically correct?

Activity 16-F

Identify a value issue in a social studies curriculum guideline or text.

a) Do you think students will find this issue significant? Is it relevant to their lives? Should it be relevant?

b) Do you think students are mature enough to make decisions about the issue?

c) If there are activities for students to carry out or questions for them to answer that are meant to help them examine or resolve the issue, evaluate them. What approach do these activities or questions seem to take? What assumptions are being made about the nature of values, how students internalize them, and how value questions ought to be resolved?

d) If there are no activities or questions, design some so that students can be helped to examine the issue and arrive at their own conclusions.

VALUES, TEACHERS, AND THE CURRICULUM

Despite the fact that all teachers are value educators, values education is a contentious issue in Canada. Few provinces have a well-thought-out policy or program. This is because, as with all curriculum decisions, politics is involved. Whatever stance a governing body takes seems to raise the ire of at least some people. Some parents do not want their children to be exposed to any form of values education, believing that it is the task of parents or the church to do this. Others want the schools to take a particular approach to values education. Teachers are caught in the middle. Yet values cannot be ignored, especially in social studies, where one of the major foci relates to how people interact with one another. It is not enough to merely identify the values people hold and the things that influence people's interactions—we must also help students make reasoned decisions about actions that affect their lives and the lives of others. Issues of violence, environmental degradation, genetic engineering, sexism, and racism confront us all. We need to learn how to deal with them, which requires that we develop particular areas of knowledge, abilities, and dispositions. Coombs[25] has described the attainments of the ethically educated person.

1. *Knowledge of what one's society regards as ethically right and wrong.* Thinking about ethical questions takes place in a society that has a moral code. Making ethical judgments is more a matter of rethinking that code than it is of devising a completely new one. Therefore, students need to know what the ethical rules of their society are and why a system of public morality is necessary. Such knowledge is gained by teaching children that there are some values, such as not killing, deceiving, or lying, which, in the main, are ethically justifiable.[26] Through activities that focus on the consequences of not having ethical rules, children come to realize that they are better off in a society that upholds such rules than one which does not. A further justification for this attainment is that we cannot stop every minute to consider the ethical acceptability of our actions. Some value judgments have to be habitual. Here character education can play a key role.

2. *Knowledge of ethical concepts such as equality, justice, stealing, cheating, lying, prejudice, discrimination, and so on.* Concepts determine how we see a situation. If shoplifting isn't viewed as "stealing," then it is unlikely to be viewed as wrong. If a situation in which a person is denied something on the basis of race, gender, or religion is not perceived as "discrimination," then it is unlikely to be regarded as unethical. Further, by grasping ethical concepts, students become more ethically sensitive. Having a profound understanding of "discrimination" will lead students to be on the lookout for evidence of it. They will also be more likely than less sensitive students to view a discriminatory situation as one of discrimination. Concept attainment activities (see Chapter 6) can be used to help students grasp key ethical concepts.

Activity 16-G

In this activity, the teacher presents students with a problem in which the application of a particular concept is fundamental to its resolution. Which of the following would qualify as an act of cheating? In which situation(s) would the action be wrong?

a) **A** looked at **B**'s quiz and copied down **B**'s answers.

b) **A** happened to see the quiz on the teacher's desk and looked at the answers. When **A** did the quiz, **A** remembered the answers he'd seen and used them.

c) **B** told **A** that he'd seen the answers on the teacher's desk and told **A** the answers. **A** used what he'd been told to answer the quiz questions.

d) To answer the quiz questions, **A** needed to remember where various countries were located. The teacher had forgotten to take the world map off the classroom wall. **A** used the map to answer the questions.

e) By mistake, the teacher gave **A** a quiz sheet on which the answers were pencilled. **A** copied the pencilled answers, then erased them.

f) **A** had missed a lot of school because of illness, but her parents insisted that she do the quiz and do well on it. So **A** wrote the information she needed on a piece of paper that she hid up her sleeve. **A** then used this information to take the quiz.

1. Is there intent to deceive in the vignettes above? Are they all cases of cheating? If not, what attribute of "cheating" is missing?

2. If a student states that a clear case of an ethical concept is X, then pose other relevant examples to see whether the student accepts these as being cases of X.
3. If a student accepts that a particular attribute of a value concept should apply, then use the Role-Exchange and Universal Consequences tests to see if the student would abide by the decision. For example, if the students say that it would be fair to cheat because everyone else does (i.e., the principle is "whatever everyone else does is acceptable"), then ask whether the consequences of holding this standard would be acceptable in all cases. Note here how important the meaning of a term is (see Chapter 6 for ideas on teaching concepts).

Activity 16-H

Design an activity that would help students clarify a particular ethical concept such as fairness. Create cases in which the concept might or might not apply so that the students are encouraged to discuss what constitutes fairness in any particular case.

3. *Ability and inclination to apply principle tests to the rules and standards used in making ethical judgments.* This includes the ability to role-take (and this requires the disposition to empathize with others), the ability to imagine the consequences if everyone who might perform a particular action actually did so, and the ability to understand what harms people, both physically and emotionally. Literature is a valuable tool here, as is the fostering of a classroom climate where students care about each other and where reason-giving is rewarded.
4. *Ability and inclination to seek all information relevant to a value question.* Too often we make judgments based on either incomplete or false information. For example, in a discussion one author held with a Grade 6 class, it was widely believed that shoplifting didn't harm anyone (the store owner had insurance, or wouldn't miss the item). These students did not realize that shoplifting created additional costs for the store owner that, ultimately, would be passed along to consumers. So, in tackling any value question, we need to collect information about the facts of the case, and about alternative solutions and the consequences of acting on them.
5. *Resolution to do what one has decided is a right action, and to refrain from doing what one has decided is wrong.* It is all very well to make decisions about what is right and wrong, but we also have to act. Thus, we should consider encouraging students to participate in social action projects (see Chapter 18) and, as teachers, we should create a classroom and school environment in which right actions are encouraged.
6. *Ability to clarify personal values using appropriate activities.* Many of the Values Clarification techniques encourage reflection on the values that are important to a person.[27] For example, the "Twenty Things You Love to Do" activity asks students to list things they love to do and then divide them into those costing money, those done alone, those done five years ago, those done daily, weekly, monthly, or yearly, and so on. Reflecting on their lists can give students an insight into what they think is of value.

Have students list their needs. What could they do without in order to survive? Extend the basic needs of food, shelter, water, and air to include basic human needs—freedom, security, self-sufficiency, respect, and happiness. What would life be like were people not to aspire to these goals? Inquire into whether people in Canada and in other parts of the world can fulfill their needs and goals. What happens when they can't? To what degree do all people require freedom, security, and so on? To what extent do individual students realize these human goals? Instruct the students to list (a) what they are free to do and whether or not they want to pursue these freedoms, and (b) what they are not free to do and the reasons why. Ask the students to identify constraints in their lives and to discuss whether these constraints are justifiable. Can or should we do anything when people's needs and goals are not being met?

To help students develop a positive self-concept, we can encourage, praise, listen to, and respect student contributions. We can also carry out activities such as "Pride Time," an activity in which students write about something they are proud of.[28]

This list of attainments raises many questions about both theory and practice. All of these attainments, however, are crucial when we focus on how to help students make decisions.

If values education is to have any effect, then we, as teachers, must exhibit the following characteristics:[29]

a) We must be perceived as possessing those traits to which teachers aspire (e.g., a high degree of subject competence and a caring attitude toward others).
b) The benefits of our modelled behaviour must be apparent.
c) The modelled behaviours must be shared by other significant people (e.g., other teachers).
d) The desired behaviours must be continually reinforced and repeated.

Other Activities

1. State how you would apply one of the approaches to values education (i.e., Character Education, Values Clarification, or Values Analysis) to the following situation:

   Jack is the star player on the school baseball team. It is mainly due to his pitching and batting that the team is in the league finals. The day before the championship game, Jack is showing off to his friends by swinging his bat around. He has been warned on two previous occasions not to do this, and he's been told he'll be punished if he's caught. Other members of Jack's class have also warned him about his bat swinging. But Jack is on top of the world because he's in the championship game. In swinging his bat around, he hits Bill on the head. Bill isn't too badly hurt, but he'll have a large bruise on his temple. The teacher sees the incident and immediately suspends Jack from the championship game. The team members circulate a petition asking the school principal to cancel Jack's suspension, allow him to play in the game, and give him some other punishment. Should Bill sign the petition?

2. Create a chart identifying the major characteristics of each of the following approaches to values education.

	Purposes	Assumptions	Teaching activities	Critique
Character Education				
Values Clarification				
Cognitive-Developmental				
Values Analysis				

3. What approach(es) are you most likely to use in your classroom? Why?

Notes

1. J. Leming, "Teaching values in social studies education: Past practices and current trends," in B. Massialas and R. Allen, *Crucial Issues in Teaching Social Studies* (Belmont, CA: Wadsworth, 1996).
2. E. Bloom, "Service learning and social studies: A natural fit," *Social Education: Middle School Learning—A Supplement* 67:4 (2003), pp. M4–M7.
3. B. Speck and S.Hoppe, *Service Learning: History, Theory and Issues* (Westport, CN: Praeger, 2004).
4. For a discussion of social action projects, see P. Clark, "All talk and no action? The place of social action in social studies," in R. Case. and P. Clark, eds., *The Canadian Social Studies Anthology* (Vancouver: Pacific Educational Press, 1999).
5. J. Leming.
6. J. Stout and F. Rivera, "Schools and sex education: Does it work?" *Pediatrics* 83 (1989), pp. 375–379.
7. E. Schapps, E. Dibartalo, J. Mortimore, C. Palley, and S. Churgin, "A review of 127 drug abuse prevention program evaluations," *Journal of Drug Issues* 11 (1981), pp. 17–43.
8. S. Cole, "Saying no to zero tolerance," *The Globe and Mail,* August 30, 2003, F6.
9. For example, the Ministry of Education Alberta has a Safe and Caring School curriculum that provides a comprehensive guide to values education: http://education.alberta.ca/teachers/safeschools.aspx (accessed February 12, 2008).
10. *Ibid.*
11. http://charactered.net (accessed February 12, 2008).
12. S. Simon, L. Howe, and H. Kirschenbaum, *Values Clarification: A Practical. Action-Directed Workbook* (New York: Warner Books, 1995).
13. L. Raths, M. Harmin, and S. Simon, *Values and Teaching,* 2nd ed. (Columbus, OH: Charles E. Merrill, 1978).
14. *Ibid.,* p. 32.
15. J. Leming, p. 153.
16. For an example of a critique, see www.catholicculture.org/library/view.cfm?renum=3512 (accessed February 25, 2008).
17. L. Kohlberg, *The Psychology of Ethical Development: The Nature and Validity of Ethical Stages* (San Francisco: Harper and Row, 1984). For a short description of Kohlberg's theory, see The Internet Encyclopedia of Philosophy, www. iep.utm.edu/m/moraldev.htm.
18. One of a series of dilemmas posed in *First Things: Values* (New York: Guidance Associates, 1979).
19. Studies in Moral Development and Education: http://tigger.uic.edu/~Inucci/MoralEd/ (accessed February 25, 2008).
20. C. Gilligan, *In a Different Voice: Psychological Theory and Women's Development* (Cambridge, MA: Harvard University Press, 1977). See also N. Noddings, *The Challenge to Care in Schools: An Alternative Approach to Education* (New York: Teachers College Press, 1992).
21. M. Smith, "Nel Noddings, the ethics of care and education," The Encyclopaedia of Informal Education, www.unfed.org/thinkers/noddings.htm, 2004, updated December 28, 2007 (accessed February 25, 2008).
22. L. Walker, C. Russel, K. Hennig, and M. Mastuba, "Reasoning about ethicality in real life ethical problems," in M. Killen and D. Hart, eds., *Ethicality in Everyday Life: Developmental Perspectives* (New York: Cambridge University Press, 1996).
23. These tests were developed by the Association for Values Education and Research at the University of British Columbia.

24. C. Beck, *Better Schools: A Values Perspective* (New York: Falmer, 1990), p. 2.

25. Adapted from J. Coombs, "Attainments of the ethically educated person," in D. Cochrane and M. Manley-Casimir, eds., *Development of Ethical Reasoning: Practical Approaches* (New York: Praeger, 1980).

26. See B. Gert, *The Ethical Rules* (New York: Harper and Row, 1966).

27. S. Simon, L. Howe, and H. Kirschenbaum, *Values Clarification: A Handbook of Practical Strategies for Teachers and Students* (New York: Hart, 1972), pp. 30–34.

28. J. Canfield and H. Wells, *100 Ways to Enhance Self-Concept in the Classroom* (Englewood Cliffs, NJ: Prentice-Hall, 1976).

29. J. Leming, p. 169.

Glossary of Key Terms

Character Education—An approach to teaching values (virtues) that relies upon the reinforcement and modelling of those values.

Cognitive-Developmental approach to ethical education—An approach to values education in which students, through discussion, are guided to reason at the next highest stage of ethical development.

Principle tests—Three tests applied to a decision to evaluate its ethical acceptability:

- **New Cases Test**—Seeing whether, in relevant similar situations, you would act in the same way as you would in the original situation. If you would not, then the decision needs to be reconsidered.
- **Role-Exchange Test**—Placing yourself in the position of the most disadvantaged person in the situation and asking whether it would be right for you, in that position, to act on your decision. If it would not be right, then the decision needs to be reconsidered.
- **Universal Consequences Test**—Seeing whether you are willing to universalize your decision in all relevant similar situations. If you are not, then the decision needs to be reconsidered.

Service learning—Activities designed to encourage students to help the disadvantaged in their community, thereby realizing the objectives of character education.

Values Analysis—An approach to values education that encourages the application of critical thinking and principle tests to issues.

Values Clarification—An approach to values education that encourages students to choose freely from alternatives after considering the consequences, prizing their choices, and acting on them.

CHAPTER 17

Values in Citizenship, Global, and Law-Related Education

The next two chapters focus on various curriculum areas that are generally considered to be a part of social studies education. In this chapter, we focus on citizenship, global, and law-related education. In Chapter 18, we focus on multicultural, human rights, gender, peace, and conflict-resolution education and First Nations, Inuit, and Métis studies.

Each of these curriculum areas rests on assumptions about how people *ought* to be treated. In **citizenship education**, we focus on how people should be governed and how people ought to act either as citizens of Canada or as citizens of the world. In **global education**, our concern is essentially with everybody on the planet. In **law-related education**, we examine the laws and rules of conduct that govern people's behaviour, who should create the laws and enforce them, and what procedures should be used to resolve disputes. All of these areas are fraught with significant value questions. Indeed, how each is conceptualized is a value question in itself. If we believe a good citizen is someone who is patriotic and always obeys the law, then what is done in the name of citizenship education will be based on this judgment. If we believe that through global education students should be encouraged to transform the world so that human rights are upheld in every country, then this value will permeate our teaching.

CITIZENSHIP EDUCATION

The primary focus in Canadian social studies is education for citizenship. (Some provinces are in the process or have implemented citizenship education programs, but mainly at the secondary level.[1]) However, educators appear to have trouble achieving any national consensus on what citizenship education should mean.[2] Other countries, such as Australia and the United Kingdom, have developed explicit citizenship education programs; even the European Union with its diversity of member countries has one. Part of the problem is that citizenship education does not lie just within the mandate of social studies; other curriculum areas also bear some responsibility, as does the whole school. And a major part of the challenge is to define citizenship education.[3] What is clear is that citizenship is a complex notion with interrelated components of national identity; a system of rights; political and civic participation; and social, cultural, and supranational belonging.[4] Each requires understanding if citizenship education is to move beyond slogans and beyond simply memorizing, for example, the three levels of government in Canada. Government, in a broad sense, is a matter of how people relate to one another in families, on the street, in places of worship, labour unions, businesses, industries, and recreational and community-organizational settings, as well as in classrooms. In all of these social contexts, notions of identity, rights, responsibilities, rules, authority, justice, and power arise. Citizenship confers a particular status on a person. It entitles that person to certain rights and privileges and, in turn, entails particular responsibilities that often manifest themselves in participation in political and civic affairs. And all of this is tied up with notions of who we are—the age-old question of Canadian identity.

It is not enough to transmit knowledge about these concepts or to inform students about politics, government, law, and the norms of society.[5] If we assume that people in a democracy have a right to make up their own minds, then students should be taught how to deal intelligently with a broad range of issues such as these:

- whether money collected from a school fundraiser should be given to the food bank or spent on a class field trip
- how to deal with bullying in the school playground
- whom to vote for as class president
- how to welcome a new student, who is a refugee, into the class

Activity 17-A

This activity could be used with elementary school students by changing the question to "What are the characteristics of a good Canadian elementary school citizen?" Your question is "What would you consider to be the essential characteristics for being a good Canadian citizen?" Share your list with others and draw on the discussion as the basis for sharpening your list.

- Is there a rule or law that covers each of the characteristics you have identified? For example, you may state that a good citizen should vote in elections, but there is no Canadian law that enforces voting.
- If there is not a law/rule that relates to one or more of your characteristics of a "good citizen," should there be? Why or why not?

Now compare the characteristics you have identified with those deemed significant for citizenship in your provincial or territorial social studies guidelines and by two of Canada's leading researchers in citizenship education.[6]

What is taught in the name of citizenship education depends largely on a teacher's philosophy of social studies (see Chapter 2). If we accept the citizenship transmission approach, then we will take a conservative view and foster the values of loyalty and participation in elections. A reflective inquiry proponent will take a more liberal view and help students learn to participate democratically in society, whereas a critical reflective approach will entail teaching students about social justice and oppression at the national and/or international levels. In the holistic approach, there is likely to be far more emphasis placed on building a classroom community that exemplifies the characteristics of good citizenship. In applying any of these conceptions, the following guidelines for citizenship education are suggested. Students should begin to:

- learn how to locate and use information about governance situations
- acquire competency in decision making
- acquire competency in communicating effectively with decision makers
- know the main structures and functions of government
- understand the function of laws and know about the main features of the *Canadian Charter of Rights and Freedoms*
- acquire competence in cooperating and working with formal and informal organizations involved in promoting one's personal interests and the interests of others

- explore the conception of Canadian identity
- act on the characteristics of good citizenship in their classrooms.

Each of these goals has to be translated into appropriate objectives. For example, in a primary class students can identify services provided by the government in their community. They can examine laws, such as traffic regulations, that directly impinge on their lives. They can become involved in decision-making situations in which their decisions are acted upon, such as choosing where to go on a field trip; deciding how to raise money for a particular school project; or deciding how to celebrate a special day (e.g., Canada Day).

Students might also be involved in "action" projects such as helping people in need, visiting people in hospitals, or collecting for charity.[7] They might even lobby for something—a crosswalk at a dangerous intersection near the school or the better treatment of zoo animals. (Both of these examples stem from actual cases in which elementary school students were involved.) Note that there is sometimes controversy about whether or not students should be involved in social action projects like these. Student maturity, the level of student commitment required to act on students' decisions, parental expectations, and institutional rules and regulations should all be carefully considered before embarking on such projects. Clark[8] provides the following criteria for judging the worth of a social action project:

1. Is it relevant for my students?
2. Is it appropriate for my school and community?
3. Does it grow out of and support the curriculum?
4. Are there adequate resources?
5. Is it worth the effort?

In the intermediate grades, students can begin to examine levels of government, how governments are formed, how representatives are elected, how governments and the judicial system function, and how laws are made and enforced. They can also continue to explore the notion of Canadian identity. They can come to understand, at a more mature level, concepts like justice, authority, rights, responsibilities, and freedom. For example, Chilcoat[9] and his co-authors developed a unit for Grade 6 students using *Yertle the Turtle* by Dr Seuss as an introduction to the issue of parental blocking of TV programs deemed inappropriate for young children. Should parents have the authority to do this? What rights should children have?

For all of these objectives, the best teaching method is actual participation. Form a classroom government; simulate different forms of government and see how students like living under them. Groups of students could represent three forms of government—a monarchy, oligarchy, and democracy—with each student taking on the role of a wealthy person, a ruler, or a labourer. Students in these roles should decide how to levy taxes according to their particular form of government. Then have all the rulers get together with the other rulers, labourers with other labourers, and wealthy persons with the other wealthy people to list the advantages and disadvantages of their form of government. Students could create and enforce classroom rules (where this is deemed appropriate) as students do not learn how to take responsibility for their actions in a system that is based solely on punishment and obedience (in such a system, they learn how not to get caught).[10] When students are involved in the formation of rules and are asked to articulate the reasons behind the rules, they are more likely to behave responsibly and democratically. This is where character education programs sometimes come up short as they tend to support the status quo and an assimilation model of social cohesion.[11]

Intermediate-level students should begin to study local, national, and world issues. Where feasible, they should become involved in events that are important to them. If social action is not appropriate, students can at least be given the opportunity to make judgments about policy questions. Here, some of the activities already mentioned can be used, such as the Incinerator game in Chapter 15.

Activity 17-B

Look at the list you developed on the characteristics of a good Canadian citizen and identify those that depend on a knowledge of government, laws, and other related information. Interview an elementary school student (e.g., a friend's child or a neighbour; be sure to obtain parental permission) and determine the level of citizenship knowledge this student has.

When research is carried out on what Canadians know about citizenship and what their attitudes are, the findings indicate a low level of knowledge and a distrust of politicians, among other findings.[12] Although interesting on its own, what teachers really need is research evidence on what their students know and what their attitudes are. Carrying out informal assessments in our own classrooms can help us identify what needs to be focused upon in the name of citizenship education.

Citizenship education is the responsibility of the whole school, but it has to be emphasized in social studies. We cannot expect students to "pick up" the requirements for good citizenship; knowledge, skills, and values have to be formally taught and practised.

GLOBAL EDUCATION

Activity 17-C

In what ways are other nations throughout the world involved in, or connected with, each of the following:

a) the room you are in now
b) the clothes you wear
c) the language you speak
d) the weather outside
e) the income tax you pay
f) the TV you watch
g) the internet sites you visit
h) the requests you receive for charitable donations
i) the food you eat

There are now about two billion TV sets and two billion cell phones in the world. In 1964 there was one TV for every 20 people. Now there is one TV for every 4 people. Cell phones were not invented until 1973 and not in common use until 1983. About one billion people have Internet access worldwide (the world population is about seven billion). In 2002, 30 000 foreign magazines were introduced into China.[13]

All these examples show that the world is becoming increasingly interdependent. As a result, social studies educators have begun to include a global perspective in the curricula they teach. However, the ways in which global education has been conceptualized have changed over the years. Richardson[14] outlines how we have moved from an imperialistic view of the world to one emphasizing the inter-reliant nature of the world, to a focus on the global environment, and more recently to one that views the world as a global market. These viewpoints mirror the current debate about global education. Some educators view global education as a means by which to enhance people's ability to compete in a global economy; some include human rights, multicultural, and environmental education under the global education umbrella; and others perceive global education as a stepping stone to world government.[15] This idea of world citizenship is especially problematic in terms of designing social studies curriculum guidelines given that Canadian educators have in a general sense had a hard time articulating what exactly to emphasize in the name of Canadian citizenship education. Despite these problems, most proponents of global education emphasize the study of world history, world systems and institutions, world cultures, and world issues. To bring the objectives of global education to fruition, educators such as Kniep[16] have proposed the following objectives:

1. Students should, through historical studies, understand the development of humankind, the rise and fall of civilizations and empires, and the causes of contemporary global problems. At the elementary school level, students should be exposed to more than just the history of Canada or Western Europe. They should also study the history of other cultures, looking at events in one part of the world in light of what was happening elsewhere. For example, in studying the first European explorers of Canada, we should emphasize the events that led to these expeditions so that students begin to understand causation and interconnectedness. If students in Canada are constructing timelines of their own or other people's lives, they should also construct a timeline showing what was occurring in other parts of the world. Further, any historical topic we are teaching should be put in a global context. If we are teaching about Ancient Greece, let's also ask what was happening in North America between the 8th and 1st centuries BC (see Chapter 10).
2. Students should understand how Canada relates to the rest of the world, and how students themselves are a part of various global economic, political, technological, and ecological systems. A start can be made by having students identify the products they use that are of foreign origin, a language they speak other than French or English, or a media or sports star they admire who is not Canadian. They can make a list of 10 words they use frequently and then find out the derivation of those words. In the intermediate grades, students can begin to understand world geographical patterns (see Chapter 11), learn about international organizations such as the United Nations, and look at the provisions of the Universal Declaration of Human Rights and the Declaration of the Rights of the Child.
3. Students should be aware of various world views—political, economic, spiritual, aesthetic, and moral. Students in the primary grades can begin to understand that although there are fundamental similarities among people, there are also some deep differences. Students in the intermediate grades can start to look for world patterns by extending the topic they are studying to the rest of the world. For example, if students are studying a country that has a predominantly Muslim population, they could identify the key

tenets of this faith and find out which other countries have large Muslim populations. One significant resource here is newspapers.[17]

4. Students should realize that their actions can contribute both to world problems and to solutions. There are several ways to show students how this works. One way is to focus on development projects sponsored by Canada and supported by Canadian charitable donations. Students could be given scenarios such as the following:

   You are a ____-year-old child. You live in ____________. The landscape looks like this: ____________. The climate is ____________. You have these tools: ____________. You have no ____________ [e.g., water supply close to where you live]. How would you cope? What skills would you need to overcome the problem?

   Students could then suggest solutions trying to see the problem through the child's eyes rather than their own.

   Students could create a decision-making chart in which they list various courses of action they could take (e.g., write letters to MPs, produce a poster for students in the school, or give money) to help alleviate a particular problem (e.g., helping people who have been devastated by an earthquake or helping alleviate starvation in Africa). Students then create a list of criteria for assessing each course of action (e.g., their abilities to act, the impact a given action would have, and the time needed to act), and discuss the pros and cons of each alternative. They finally decide what the best course(s) of action would be.

   A great way of showing how a microloan in a developing country can have a huge impact is to read students the story "One hen: How a small loan made a big difference." Here, Kojo gets a loan to buy a hen and over the years becomes a successful entrepreneur and the organizer of a charity that provides microloans in West Africa.[18]

5. Students should avoid stereotyping other people and countries, as stereotyping can lead to prejudice and discrimination. To challenge student stereotypes, teachers have to first identify them. Teachers can do this by asking students to write down what they think they know about a particular country or group of people. Where appropriate, students should then compare lists. Ask the students where they acquired their information and whether they think it is true. Then have the students find evidence for their statements. If many students share the same beliefs, they could work together as a group to accomplish this task. Once they have located enough evidence to support or reject their initial beliefs, they should present it to the rest of the class. Care should be exercised here. Teachers should first check to see whether the students have written racist or other derogatory statements. If they have, the teacher should question the student about the derivation of these statements and attempt to persuade the students that they are not justifiable because the statements are overgeneralizations or they are overtly biased. For example, one author's Grade 5 students thought that men in Papua New Guinea were "stupid" to decorate their entire bodies and stick pieces of wood through their noses. A lesson and discussion on body decoration in Canada and other parts of the world helped show students that body decoration is related to cultural mores in Papua New Guinea just as makeup, tattoos, and body piercing are related to cultural mores in Canada. To help identify stereotypes and misconceptions about women in the world with a Grade 2 class, see Merryfield and Sabedi.[19]

6. Students should understand the concept of "interdependence" as it relates to themselves and the physical and social world. This requires teachers to draw relationships between the immediate world of the student and the rest of the planet. In the elementary grades, students can begin to compare their own families and communities with those in other countries and see that people share many common needs, goals, celebrations, and problems. Students can also draw connections between themselves (the food they eat and so on) and the rest of the world. In the intermediate grades, we as teachers can discuss global issues and the role that Canada plays (and that students play) in international affairs. By studying other cultures, past and present, students can further develop such fundamental concepts as interdependence, change, conflict, scarcity, and culture.

One significant concept is **sustainable development.** Although this is usually explained as "development which meets the needs of the present without compromising the ability of future generations to meet their own needs,"[20] what qualifies as sustainable development in any particular instance is often a matter of dispute. A basic introduction to the concept, however, is relatively straightforward. Students can be made aware of the fact that many of the world's ecosystems are in danger; that the world's population is growing beyond the limits of nature's ability to support it; that 20 percent of the world's population consumes 80 percent of the world's goods; and that the gap between rich and poor nations is growing. This information can provide a background to the study of global issues, environmental education, and international development initiatives.

The following activities will help students realize the goals of global education:

1. Create webbing diagrams showing how students interact with one another and with other persons in the school. Do the same for the community in which the students live, then Canada, and eventually the world. For an example of this, continue the chocolate bar diagram in Chapter 14, linking the various phenomena to the rest of the world.
2. Have students trace the origins of the food they eat, the clothes they wear, and the toys they play with, etc. Show how all of these are dependent on the labour of workers (and, sometimes, indentured or slave workers), raw materials, transportation, and so on (in effect, a global economic system).
3. Have students trace the origins of the words they use. As well, for multicultural school communities, how many different first languages are represented in the various cultural groups of children in the school?
4. Examine social problems in Canada and have students inquire into the roles that various people, including them, will have to play if pollution or poverty is to be reduced.
5. Inquire into particular aspects of foreign aid and foreign development. How is Canada trying to help the less fortunate? Are these efforts worthwhile? Are they well designed? Are they working?
6. Inquire into particular situations in which Canadians are in need of help. Can students do anything to alleviate the suffering of their fellow citizens?
7. Examine a global problem—for example, global warming—and have students inquire into the suggested causes and solutions. Can students be part of the solution? How? When choosing problems to study, remember that the objective is not to

create the impression that students are powerless or that the problem is too complex to be resolved. Choose problems that provide a chance (should the students decide to take it) for some kind of action, even if it is only informing others about the problem.

In all the above activities, it is necessary to engender certain dispositions in students so that they move from a narrow, parochial viewpoint to a more global one.[21] These dispositions include open-mindedness, empathy, the inclination to look beyond simplistic accounts and solutions to complex problems, and the willingness to put aside (where appropriate) personal and national self-interest. Case[22] indicates three forms of bias that are significant in global education: **ethnocentrism**, where one's own culture is viewed as superior to all others; **national fanaticism**, which refers to the view that one's country's interests come before those of other countries; and **presentism**, where the concern is with the interests and well-being of people today rather than those of future generations. A global-oriented disposition, so as not to be biased, cannot be simply taught directly. It has to be modelled by teachers in the classroom and supported by the wider community.

LAW-RELATED EDUCATION

Given that social studies is concerned with the study of relationships among people and that many of these relationships are regulated by rules and laws, law-related education has an obvious role to play in the curriculum. As Cassidy[23] points out, in fact, students encounter daily legal issues: "He called me a bad name"; "Someone stole my pen." However, it is not enough to tell students that stealing is against the law. The focus should be extended to include an understanding of why we have a particular system of laws. In addition to specific content—such as statutes and regulations and how they are enacted, the court system, and the roles of judges and the police—students need to study the very idea of law and the principles that lie behind it. This will entail understanding some basic legal and moral concepts such as authority, freedom, rights, and justice. Although these concepts may already to a certain degree be familiar to students, just how these concepts are defined and applied in legal contexts will help students better understand how a legal system operates.

Understanding legal and moral concepts helps students develop the ability to determine whether a particular action is an instance of a concept under consideration. Suppose we are concerned with the concept of justice. Also suppose that a student is accused of breaking a school rule. What would constitute justice in such a situation? Should the student be given a fair hearing? Should the student be permitted to call witnesses? Should the student be deemed innocent until "convicted," and should it be up to the "authorities" to prove the student's guilt beyond a reasonable doubt? Or should the student be deemed guilty before a hearing, with the responsibility placed upon the student to prove one's innocence? This type of reasoning is common to situations in which a decision has to be made about whether a particular action falls under a particular rule or concept. So, in baseball, was X a "foul ball"? In school, was Y a case of "cheating"? (see Activity 16-G). The point of this type of activity is not to produce student lawyers. Rather, it is to help students understand our law-governed society and to reason about the complex conflicts and issues that face us all.

Law-related educational objectives can be realized not only through the direct teaching of law but also by applying a legal perspective to other social studies content. This can be carried out in numerous ways. Students can gradually learn to understand:

- how rules and laws impinge on people's lives in classrooms, in families, in communities, in industry, and in government
- how the court system operates, as well as the roles of the police, judiciary, and legislators
- what rights and freedoms Canadians have under the *Canadian Charter of Rights and Freedoms*
- such concepts as human rights, authority, power, democracy, responsibility, freedom, justice, equality, and rules
- how laws are made and what influence the public can have in making and changing the laws
- that law is closely bound up with conceptions of morality, and that laws can be changed in response to changing public views of what is immoral

Activity 17-D

You could give this activity to elementary school students, but first try it out yourself. Identify some of the statuary laws related to the following activities:

a) buying food at the supermarket
b) mailing a letter
c) having a meal at a restaurant
d) walking a dog
e) buying clothing at a local store
f) telephoning a friend
g) driving a car or riding a bicycle
h) watching TV
g) surfing the internet

If you now also identify the rules, conventions, customs, and regulations governing each of the above activities, you might be quite surprised.

There are several ways we can approach the teaching of law-related topics. Cassidy and Ferguson[24] list three approaches: (a) conceptual (focusing on concepts such as justice and authority), (b) practical (studying the impact of the law on student lives), and (c) participatory (staging mock trials and using peer mediators to resolve disputes). We can help students achieve law-related educational objectives through activities such as these:

1. Play a game in which the rules are unclear, unfair, or changed arbitrarily. Have the students sit in groups of five or six. Give one student in each group a ball. Tell the students that the first team to pass the ball around the group will win. Before any group completes this task, stop the game and tell the students that the ball must be passed with the left hand only. When group members complete this task, tell them that they are disqualified because they passed the ball clockwise (or counter-clockwise). You can now add other rules that are unclear (pass the ball vigorously) or unfair (only students

who are blue-eyed can play). By this time, the students will be thoroughly frustrated and a fruitful discussion about rules can be held.

2. Assign or read students a story where it is unclear whether a particular legal or moral concept applies. For example, was it "fair" on the school's sports day that younger students started a race 10 metres in front of older students?
3. Have students discuss cases where it is unclear whether a rule applies. For example, suppose the rule chosen is "No vehicles in the park." Could a child on a tricycle be arrested? Could an ambulance driver who enters the park to help an injured person be charged? Would the driver of the garbage truck picking up litter have to park his truck outside the park and carry out the garbage? Would a person in a wheelchair be allowed in the park? Is a wheelchair a vehicle?
4. Identify rules that directly impinge on students' lives. Identify the purpose of each rule. Ask what would happen if nobody obeyed the rule. Should there be any exceptions to the rule? Who should enforce the rule? Should there be some kind of penalty if the rule is broken? Who should decide the penalty?

Activity 17-E

Which of the following would be good classroom rules? Why? What purposes do they serve?

Nobody shall talk in class.

You should enjoy what you do in class.

Don't interrupt when someone is talking.

Keep your desk tidy.

a) Could the purposes behind the above rules be better achieved by means other than formal rules?
b) What will be the effects of the rules?
c) Identify the strengths and weaknesses of each rule:

   Is it well designed?

   Is it understandable?

   Is it clear what is expected?

   Is it fair?

   Is it designed to minimize infringement of important values?

5. Play a "desert island" game in which the class is marooned. You can decide what food and shelter are available and what the landscape and climate are like. Have the class decide what they'll need to survive, how they'll organize themselves, and what rules or laws they'll need. Or give students a list of rules and have them decide which ones would be good rules. For example:

   a) Females/males shall do all the cooking.
   b) The strongest male/female will be the leader.
   c) Everyone should be allowed to speak and vote on decisions that affect the whole society.

d) There shall be no stealing of other people's property.

e) The person who does the most work shall receive the most food.

6. Students could make up their own rules prior to any group discussion. Copies of the rules could then be distributed to the class and these could form the basis for the decision-making activity. The rules could be compared to the rights listed in the Universal Declaration of Human Rights and the *Canadian Charter of Rights and Freedoms.*

7. Hold a **mock trial**. Students can try Goldilocks for eating the bears' porridge. Assign students the following roles: judge, jury member, witness, defence lawyer, and so on.

8. Provide students with a number of scenarios in which a legal decision is required. In the following vignette, one student plays Nick, another plays Lorne, and a third is the judge who has to make a decision. Nick and Lorne argue their cases to the judge. They use the following information:

   Nick lends 10 comic books to Lorne.

   Lorne promises to return them in one week.

   Nick warns Lorne to take care of them.

   The comic books cost Nick $1 each.

   Lorne returns the comic books at the end of the week.

   Five comic books are torn and unreadable.

   Lorne says that his younger brother (age two) took the comic books from his room and tore them up. Although Lorne usually closes his bedroom door, he forgot and his younger brother got into his bedroom.

   Nick demands Lorne pay him $5 to replace the damaged comics.

   Lorne refuses to pay.

   Based on this evidence, the judge decides how this matter should be resolved.

   If there are several groups all engaged in the same situation, the judges' rulings could be compared. What were the similarities and differences and what were the reasons for these?

9. When studying other nations or cultures, whether present-day or past, have students research the legal system in that country. For example, when studying ancient Babylon, look at Hammurabi's Code. It is a fascinating vehicle for discussion, containing such laws as this one: "If a man accuses a man, and charges him with murder but cannot convict him, the accuser shall be put to death."

10. Study laws that directly impinge on students' lives. Are these laws

    a) a means of social control over antisocial behaviour?

    b) an effective means of resolving disputes?

    c) a means of providing social benefits?

    d) a means of providing guidance in daily social affairs?

It appears that young students differentiate between two kinds of rules: conventional mores (e.g., eating food with a knife and fork) and moral rules.[25] The former they view as conditional; the latter they view as absolute even if there is no law. To further develop this distinction, show pictures in which a social custom is displayed (e.g., shaking hands with someone) and ask, "Would it be all right to bow, to rub noses, or to embrace when greeting someone?" Then show pictures of scenes in which a moral rule is violated (e.g., a child hitting another) and ask, "Would it be all right to do this even if there is no rule against it?"

Other Activities

1. Look at a social studies curriculum for your province or territory and note how citizenship education is conceptualized. Then look at the rest of the curriculum document to determine where citizenship education is stressed. Do the content and activities, etc., match the conceptualization?
2. How could law-related education be related to the goals of citizenship education?
3. Design an activity that would help students realize the following objective: Students should understand how the law restricts what they are permitted to do.

Notes

1. A. Sears, "In search of good citizens," in A. Sears and I. Wright, eds. *Challenges and Prospects for Canadian Social Studies* (Vancouver: Pacific Educational Press, 2004), pp. 90–106.
2. A. Hughes and A. Sears, "Citizenship education: Canada dabbles while the world plays," *Education Canada* 46:4 (2006), pp. 6–9.
3. I. Wright, "The centrality of critical thinking in citizenship education,' *Canadian Social Studies* (2003). www.quasar.ualberta.ca/css/CSS_38_1/ARcentrality_of_critical_thinking.htm
4. F. Gagnon and M. Page, *Conceptual Framework for an Analysis of Citizenship in the Liberal Democracies*, a report to the Multiculturalism Directorate, Citizen Participation Directorate, and Strategic Research and Analysis Directorate, Department of Canadian Heritage, Government of Canada, May 1999.
5. Beck shows that 4th graders in Seattle, USA, needed to be taught how to solve problems and resolve issues before they could tackle citizenship issues. T. Beck, "If he murdered someone, he shouldn't get a lawyer: Engaging young children in civics deliberation," *Theory and Research in Social Education* 31:3 (2003), pp. 326–346.
6. Y. Hebert and L. Wilkinson, "Diversity and democratic values: Implications for public policy," in G. Richardson and D. Blade, eds., *Troubling the Canon of Citizenship Education* (New York: Peter Lang Publishing, 2006), pp. 31–41. They list self-respect, solidarity, self-reliance, valuing the earth, sense of belonging, human dignity, loyalty, sincerity, openness, civic-mindedness, valuing freedom, valuing equality (p. 35).
7. C. Chamberlin, "Citizenship as the goal of social studies: Passive knower or active doer?" *Canadian Social Studies* 26:1 (1991), pp. 23–26. Reprinted in R. Case and P. Clark, eds., *The Anthology of Social Studies, Volume 1. Issues and Strategies for Elementary Teachers* (Vancouver: Pacific Educational Press, 2008), pp. 188–196.
8. P. Clark, "All talk and no action: The place of social action in elementary social studies," in R. Case and P. Clark, eds., *The Anthology of Social Studies, Volume 1. Issues and Strategies for Elementary Teachers* (Vancouver: Pacific Educational Press, 2008), p. 198.
9. G. Chilcoat, L. Erickson, and J. Ligon, "Teaching with the use of current issues: The Canadian model," *Social Education* 66:1 (2002), Middle Level Learning Supplement Issue 13, pp. M12–M15.
10. J. Sweeney and F. Monteverde, "Creating a civic culture: Questioning classroom assumptions," in B. Massiaslas and R. Allen, eds., *Crucial Issues in Teaching Social Studies* (Belmont, CA: Wadsworth, 1996).

11. S. Winton, "Does character education really support citizenship education? Examining the claims of Ontario policy." www.umanitoba.ca/publicatons/cjeap/articles/winton.html (accessed February 27, 2008).
12. A. Sears
13. Asia Times, www.atimes.com/atimes/China/FL16Ad01.html (accessed February 28, 2008).
14. G. Richardson, "Global education and the challenge of globalization," in A. Sears and I. Wright, eds. *Challenges and Prospects for Canadian Social Studies* (Vancouver: Pacific Educational Press, 2004), pp. 138–149.
15. W. Werner, "Whither global education?" *Canadian Social Studies* 27:3 (1993), pp. 121–122.
16. W. Kniep, "Social studies within a global education," *Social Education* 53:6 (1989), pp. 399–403.
17. D. Hicks and E. Thomas, "Bringing the world into the classroom with online global newspapers," *Social Education* 67:3 (2003), pp. 134–135.
18. K. Milway, *One Hen* (www.onehen.org).
19. M. Merryfield and B. Sabedi, "A global education framework for teaching about the world's women," *Social Education* 67:1 (2003), pp. 10–16.
20. D. Roche, "The impact of sustainable development on development education," *Institute Newsletter*, Institute for the Humanities, Simon Fraser University, 5:1 (1992), pp. 15–17.
21. W. Werner and R. Case, "Themes of global education," in I. Wright and A. Sears, eds., *Trends and Issues in Canadian Social Studies* (Vancouver: Pacific Educational Press, 1997).
22. R. Case, O. Sensoy, and M. Ling, "Embedding global and multicultural perspectives," in R. Case and P. Clark, eds., *The Anthology of Social Studies, Volume 1. Issues and Strategies for Elementary Teachers* (Vancouver: Pacific Educational Press, 2008), pp. 168–169.
23. W. Cassidy, "Don't forget about law: A case for law-related education in elementary social studies," *Canadian Social Studies* 39:1, 2004. www.quasar.ualberta.ca/css/Css_39_1/ARcassidy_law_elementary_ss.htm
24. See also W. Cassidy and M. Ferguson, "Cultivating legally aware and empowered citizens," in R. Case and P. Clark, *The Anthology of Social Studies, Volume 1. Issues and Strategies for Elementary Teachers* (Vancouver: Pacific Educational Press, 2008), pp. 176–187.
25. L. Nucci, "Conceptual development in the moral and conventional domains: Implications for values education," *Review of Educational Research* 52 (1982), pp. 93–122.

Glossary of Key Terms

Citizenship education—A term used to denote a focus on how people should be governed and how people ought to act as citizens of a country or the world.

Ethnocentrism—The view that one's own culture is superior to all others.

Global education—A term used to denote a variety of different programs and approaches that focus on developing global understandings, concepts, and perspectives.

Law-related education—A term used to denote a variety of programs and approaches that focus on legal concepts, understandings, and issues.

Mock trial—A simulation of a real legal trial.

National fanaticism—The view that one's own country's interests come before all others.

Presentism—Concern with the interests and well-being of people today rather than those of future generations.

Sustainable development—Development that meets the needs of the present without compromising the ability of future generations to meet their needs.

CHAPTER 18

Multicultural, Human Rights, Gender, Peace and Conflict Resolution Education, and First Nations, Inuit, and Métis Studies

In this chapter, we continue to explore the values inherent in other curricula areas that fall under the social studies umbrella. As you will note, there is considerable overlap between multicultural and human rights education and between these and global education as outlined in the previous chapter. And all of them have to do with citizenship education in its broadest sense.

MULTICULTURAL EDUCATION

Canada's population is ethnically and culturally diverse. According to the 2001 census,[1] 5 978 875 of us identify ourselves as having English origins; 4 668 410 have French roots; 4 157 210 Scottish; 3 822 660 Irish; 2 742 765 German; 1 270 370 Italian; 1 071 060 Ukrainian; 1 094 700 Chinese; 1 000 890 North American Indian; and 713 330 identify ourselves as East Indian.

Activity 18-A

Imagine you are an elementary school child who has just moved to Canada from India. You speak a little English. What would you want to know as soon as possible about life in Canada?

The diverse population of Canada has created both problems and opportunities for educational policy-makers in Canada. For much of the 19th century, it was most provinces' educational policy to assimilate new immigrants into Canadian society. Immigrants were encouraged to cast off their cultural roots and live like "Canadians." The same Citizenship Transmission approach was used, with profound consequences, when Native children were forced into residential schools. This "eradicate differences"[2] view has been replaced in recent decades by (a) the "asserting of differences" view, wherein, for example, ethnic groups are permitted to establish their own schools; (b) the "minimize differences" view, where citizens pretend that cultural differences don't really exist—this confuses equality with equity because we deny students' unique needs;[3] and (c) the "celebrate differences" view, where each culture's unique foods, festivals, and holidays are celebrated.

Whichever view is adopted we must remember that a certain degree of assimilation must take place if society is to be able to continually renew itself. We all need to accept, for example, the basic tenets of Canadian democracy and the ethical principles that are enshrined in the *Canadian Charter of Rights and Freedoms*. This also means that we need to consider the just demands of any group.

We must remember that multiculturalism is official government policy and that discrimination on the basis of race or ethnicity is illegal in Canada. The aim in Canada is to recognize and promote the understanding that multiculturalism reflects the cultural and racial diversity of Canadian society while acknowledging the freedom of all members of Canadian society to preserve, enhance, and share their cultural heritage.[4]

Section 15 of the *Canadian Charter of Rights and Freedoms states:*

> Every individual is equal before and under the law and has the right to equal protection and equal benefit of the law without discrimination and, in particular, without discrimination based on race, national or ethnic origin, colour, religion, sex, age, or mental or physical disability.[5]

These policies seem to have borne fruit. According to Adams,[6] Canadians view multiculturalism in a positive light. Canadians tend to think that immigration is beneficial, and treat multiculturalism with pride. Today's immigrants are less likely to be residentially concentrated and are intermarrying more often. And Canadians elect more foreign-born immigrants to government than any other country. However this does not mean that we can be complacent. Racism and discrimination still exist.

With the above policies and issues in mind, educators have developed multicultural curricula (some of which include issues of sexism or are placed in a global education framework) and specific anti-racist and anti-prejudice programs for schools. Some educators differentiate between anti-racist programs and multicultural education. **Multicultural education** focuses more on learning about cultures and celebrating cultural traditions. **Anti-racist education** aims to help students understand the history and contemporary nature of discrimination, and the unequal social and power relationships in institutions and in society in general. It also aims to help students take personal or collective actions to redress inequitable practices. There is intense debate about which of the two approaches should be emphasized.[7] In our view, there is no compelling evidence at present to favour one over the other. For the purposes of this chapter, they are both considered together since both have significant contributions to make.

Banks[8] outlines four ways that multicultural education could be conceived.

1. **The Contributions Approach:** Here, ethnic heroes are added to the curriculum without changing the basic scope, sequence, or goals. This approach is easy to implement, but students do not gain a comprehensive view of the role that ethnicity plays in Canada. Rather, they see ethnicity as an addendum to Canadian history and present-day society.
2. **The Additive Approach:** Multicultural content, concepts, and perspectives are added to the curriculum without changing the basic structure. Thus, a story about the experiences of a newly arrived immigrant is incorporated into a unit on citizenship; or the history of the first Ukrainians who settled on the prairies is added to a unit on western expansion. This approach is also easy to implement but does not provide students with a rich sense of multiculturalism.
3. **The Transformation Approach:** This approach infuses the curriculum with multicultural concepts, themes, and issues. It exposes students to a variety of perspectives and provides them with a rich sense of the multicultural nature of Canada.
4. **The Social Action Approach:** This approach builds on the Transformation Approach by incorporating components that help students deal with current issues and take actions to bring about a more just society.

Activity 18-B

Given that there are various approaches to multicultural education, which approach(es) do you consider to be the best?

Reconsider your answer after carrying out the following activity. Let's say that in the community in which you teach there is a cultural minority group. Members of the group have been living in the community for 50 years and have been attempting to maintain their cultural identity. Some members of the larger community are prejudiced against them, and there have been overt acts of discrimination and harassment. Your goal is to reduce any prejudice that might exist in your class as well as teach about the minority group. Which of the following approaches would you emphasize? Why?

a) teach about the culture so students realize that the group is very different from the rest of the community
b) teach about the culture to show that the group shares the same basic needs and values as the rest of the community but has different practices
c) teach that many of the statements made about the group by some members of the community are erroneous
d) teach about the culture by going on a field trip to the group's neighbourhood so that students can have some actual first-hand experience
e) present cases in which the group was discriminated against
f) have students role-play as members of the cultural group by dressing up and dancing, etc.
g) have students read accounts of the life of the group written by the group's own members
h) teach about the contributions of the group to Canada
i) take students to the museum to see artifacts used by the culture group throughout history
j) read children's stories written by members of the cultural group
k) teach students about the nature of prejudice and why it is unjustified

Note that simply accumulating information about this cultural group is not likely to be enough to reduce the prejudice in the community. This is not to say that knowledge isn't necessary; however, multicultural education must consist of more than teaching and learning information on its own.

Although knowledge of cultures other than one's own can reduce prejudice,[9] it can also engender negative attitudes in students. If we take an outsider's perspective and compare the culture being studied with our own, we may emphasize differences rather than similarities, thereby creating an "us versus them" mentality. Even if an insider's perspective is taken—learning about the culture through the eyes of the participants—students may still judge the culture to be inferior. This perspective, however, does allow for a more realistic view because members of the culture can recount their own version of their ideals and problems. However, we must remember that the accounts we read or the speakers we listen to are not necessarily representative of all the members of the group. This is particularly significant when we teach students about First Nations people, as there are "fifty plus Aboriginal linguistic communities and cultures" in Canada.[10]

Since young children tend to judge negatively what is unfamiliar or what they find ambiguous, information can certainly help the unfamiliar become familiar and the ambiguous become clear. Children also make mistakes when defining cultural categories,[11] so reliable information will help them create categories that are more accurate and non-stereotypical. Here, presenting pictures of children from around the world, followed by discussion of these, can help students develop more sensitive attitudes.[12]

What, then, should be done? According to Aboud,[13] propositions about how children become prejudiced should guide the development of multicultural education programs. These propositions relate to specific age groups.

Propositions related to four- to seven-year-olds:

- Prejudice is based on a polarized and simple dichotomy of positive and negative emotions. Greater differentiation among emotions will reduce prejudice.
- Prejudice is based on the egocentric judgment that only one way of experiencing the world is the right one. Learning that there are many ways of being right reduces prejudice.

Propositions related to seven- to twelve-year-olds:

- Judging people on the basis of internal rather then external criteria increases with age and is inversely related to prejudice.
- Attending to between-group similarities and within-group differences increases with age and is inversely related to prejudice.
- Recognizing that one's own perspective may differ from another's and that both perspectives can be valid increases with age and facilitates the acceptance of ethnic differences.

Activity 18-C

Individually, prepare a list of such items as likes and dislikes, what you're good at, and what hobbies or interests you have. Identify your country of origin or the cultural group(s) to which you belong. Share your list with someone from another country of origin or another cultural group, and with someone who is from your own country of origin or cultural group. Does your list have anything in common with those of the two people you met with? Would you expect a member of a different cultural group to also share the same characteristics? What characteristics are you likely to share with most other cultural groups? What characteristics might differ? Do you think that you and a member of a cultural group to which you don't belong could possibly share *no* common characteristics?

Children at about three years of age begin to be aware of racial and ethnic characteristics. The type of activity above can demonstrate to older children that there are both within-group and between-group similarities and differences.

We should encourage young students to recognize a range of feelings and emotions. We should also show them that although feelings such as anger and happiness are universal, the same experiences can affect different people in different ways. (For example, what makes one person happy can make another person sad.) Children should be helped to realize that we can experience mixed emotions. One way to do this is to use examples from the students' own lives, such as "How would you feel if your best friend won the race that you wanted to win?" or "Can you be glad that you got a present from your aunt even though it wasn't exactly what you wanted?" Help your students to become aware of other universal characteristics of people. All of us are vulnerable—we can all be injured or killed. All of us are fallible—we can all make mistakes. Each of us has limited knowledge and skills; we each have conflicting desires and wants; and we all make choices. All students should be encouraged to look at people as individuals and to judge on the basis of internal rather than external criteria. Let students understand that there are as many differences within a group as there are between groups. Encourage them to see that different ways of living can be perfectly acceptable. All of Aboud's propositions have been applied to curriculum materials developed by Alternatives to Racism.[14]

Among the guidelines proposed by educators working in the area of multicultural education are the following:

1. Accentuate similarities rather than differences between people. The message to be conveyed here is not that we should all be treated the same in every respect and that any differences are aberrations. Rather, it is that we share fundamental characteristics, including certain rights, and that we all should be treated as "persons." A focus on the similarities between people can reduce children's tendencies to negatively evaluate what is different.
2. Students often tend to stereotype others. The realization that there are both within-group and between-group similarities and differences can help students avoid stereotyping, as can the following activities:
   a) Categorize people under a variety of labels in order to show that a member of a particular group can be classified in any number of ways.
   b) Where a stereotype does exist, show exceptions to that stereotype.
3. Use cooperative learning groups in which there is a cultural mix to foster positive attitudes toward members of different cultural groups. Research studies have indicated that cooperative learning can lead to the reduction of prejudice and the fostering of positive attitudes toward other cultures (see Chapter 9).
4. Help students understand the nature of prejudice and discrimination. Students should understand that prejudice is very often based on inadequate or erroneous evidence. Discrimination involves acting on prejudices so that individuals, or groups of people, are denied fair and equal treatment. These acts may consist of physical attack, verbal hostility, avoidance, and unjust treatment. Ask the students to identify examples of each of these types of behaviour and those against whom they are directed. Ask the students to write a story about an act of discrimination, identifying the feelings experienced by the people involved. Consider using puppets to enact the story. (Using puppets encourages spontaneity. Students are more willing to express themselves freely with puppets because "the puppets" are doing the talking, not the students.) Literature can also be a valuable tool. For example, reading the story of a First Nations elder in northern Manitoba and her friendship with a young boy teaches students not only about Aboriginal culture but also about friendship and trust between old and young.[15] To use this story and others effectively requires that students try to see the world through the eyes of the "other."[16] And to use literature effectively requires that books be carefully chosen. Bainbridge and her co-authors[17] provide a list of criteria that include the following: characters are authentic; members of any minority groups that are portrayed feel pride in their background; and the story increases acceptance and understanding.
5. Encourage students to learn how to reason well about empirical, conceptual, and value matters. Value judgments about other cultures are based on beliefs about those cultures as well as the value standards held by students. Principle-testing the value standards used by students (see Chapter 16) has been shown to reduce prejudicial attitudes.[18]

Activity 18-D

Avoiding mistakes in reasoning can help students avoid erroneous beliefs. In this activity, state what fallacies are being committed. Check your responses in the Answers section.

a) New immigrants are really hard-working. My next-door neighbour, who is a new immigrant, works from dawn to dusk seven days a week.

b) The unemployment rate is higher now than it was in 1960. As there are more immigrants now than there were in 1960, the high unemployment rate must be due to immigration.

c) In the past, the majority of immigrants came from Europe. Therefore, the majority of new immigrants should come from Europe.

d) In a recent poll, it was found that a majority of business executives thought that the federal government should cease giving money to cultural groups for cultural activities. We must take these important people's views seriously and stop giving money to such groups.

e) Unless we stop all immigration, Canada's economy will crumble.

f) If we allow First Nations people to govern themselves, then the Hutterites will want self-government, and soon every group will want self-government and Canada will cease to exist.

In classrooms where student self-esteem is fostered, where there is equality of opportunity, and where students are encouraged to judge others on the basis of internal rather than external characteristics, there is less likelihood of racism and prejudice. When an entire school is committed to the aims of multicultural education, and attempts are made to communicate effectively with minority parents and students, then those aims are more likely to be realized.[19]

In fact, research on classroom tolerance in the US reveals that the more tolerant students had teachers that were trusted and had classrooms where issues were discussed.[20] This approach requires that the hidden curriculum be in tune with the aims of multicultural education.[21] Teachers and administrators must also become knowledgeable about the beliefs, values, and socio-linguistic conventions of students in the school and learn how best to communicate with students and parents who belong to different cultural groups. The school is a microcosm of the larger society. If students and teachers can bring about a "society" in which diversity is accepted within a unified and cohesive "nation," then many of the aims of Canadian multiculturalism will have been achieved.

HUMAN RIGHTS EDUCATION

Activity 18-E

List the rights you think you have. Ascertain whether or not these are constitutionally guaranteed in Canada. Now list the rights elementary school children have. Compare your lists. Where a right exists for an adult but not for an elementary school child, state why you think this is so. Do children have any constitutionally guaranteed rights in Canada?

Human rights education is related implicitly and explicitly to all of the curriculum areas discussed in this and the previous chapter. Citizenship is bound up with the rights accorded members of a nation state; multiculturalism with the rights of members of cultural groups; law-related education with rights within a legal system; and global education with universal human rights.

While issues of human rights have been of concern for centuries, it was not until 1948 that the nations of the world, under the auspices of the United Nations, adopted the Universal Declaration of Human Rights. In this declaration, nations committed themselves to the advancement of such rights as equality, life, liberty, freedom of speech, education, and justice. Similarly, the UN Declaration of the Rights of the Child affirms that all children are entitled to such rights as "love and understanding and an atmosphere of affection and security, in the care and under the responsibility of their parents whenever possible," and "protection against all forms of neglect, cruelty and exploitation."

While these declarations have no legal force, the Universal Declaration of Human Rights has been influential. Its principles are evident in the *Canadian Charter of Rights and Freedoms,* which was entrenched in the Canadian constitution in 1982. However, knowing that the Universal Declaration of Human Rights exists and knowing that the *Charter of Rights and Freedoms* guarantees certain rights is not enough. Students need some understanding of why we have rights and what having certain rights entails. Thus, students should understand:

- the importance of human rights and the consequences of not having them
- the basic tenets of the Universal Declaration of Human Rights, the UN Declaration of the Rights of the Child, and the *Canadian Charter of Rights and Freedoms*
- the understanding that having rights carries with it the responsibility to uphold the rights of others

The examination of children's rights is an ideal way to study contemporary issues. Because rights cross all realms of human experience and directly concern students as individuals and as members of a definable group (i.e., children), students can easily understand their importance.

In the primary-grade classroom, activities that focus on basic human needs and goals—and the consequences of not being able to fulfill them—can help students begin to realize the importance of human rights. (It is noteworthy that young children *do* think that there are rights to which all people are entitled.[22]) Cooperative learning activities can also help students come to this realization and accept responsibility for upholding the rights of others (see Chapter 9). Students could also come to realize that they have rights in their school by determining how they are treated in school and what rights their treatment is based on and why some rights that adults have may or may not be granted to children. In the intermediate grades, students can begin a more formal examination of human rights documents and start to consider the rights of minorities, people who are physically challenged, and so on. Students could read about children in countries around the world and list what rights they have and do not have according to the UN Declaration of the Rights of the Child.[23] Students can begin to understand some of the complexities involved in resolving cases of discrimination. They can also consider foreign aid programs and how they are influenced by concerns for human rights. Furthermore, students can study problems where human rights are at issue within their own community and within Canada as a whole. In all cases, students should consider the ways in which people have acted to protect or gain human rights, and how people have organized programs to alleviate human suffering on a local, national, or international basis.[24]

Of course, all human rights education needs to occur in a classroom where rights are respected. How teachers handle disagreements between students, discuss political issues, and interact with students from different backgrounds is crucial.

Activity 18-F

Design an activity for primary-level students whereby they discover what rights they have. Design an activity whereby intermediate students discover why the right to the freedom of speech is not absolute.

GENDER ISSUES EDUCATION

Activity 18-G

Observe a social studies class in an elementary school and note patterns of gender interaction between males and males, females and females, and males and females. Also pay attention to patterns of gender interaction in your social studies college/university class. Remember to take into account the class composition and the gender of the teacher.

Sexism is a human rights issue. Issues of gender, therefore, have an important place in social studies. As well, gender education is of relevance to both males and females. For far too long females have been relegated to a minor role in social studies curricula and textbooks. Whereas there has been some improvement in the number of females and males depicted in non-traditional roles, especially in elementary textbooks, there still exists the problem of reverse stereotyping.[25] This is demonstrated in the way that females are often portrayed in textbooks as *only* being involved in traditionally male roles. There are few portrayals of women engaged in housekeeping, or girls playing with dolls, because these may be viewed as reinforcing a traditional stereotype. Further, women are often mentioned in history textbooks only because they were married to men who were famous, or they excelled in roles normally reserved for men. There has been progress but, as Noddings[26] points out, merely showing pictures of women or mentioning them doesn't move us very far toward an inclusive curriculum. She points out that "mentioning women for achievements that would go unrecognized if the subjects were male is demeaning to women and trivializes the history under examination."[27] She argues that the social studies curriculum needs to be radically altered.

Activity 18-H

The book you are reading was written by two Caucasian males. Pick a section of the book on which to perform a gender analysis. How could this section be improved in terms of the way males and females are represented? Now perform a cultural analysis on the same section of the book. How could the section be improved in terms of the way different cultural groups are represented?

Noddings argues that there should be much more emphasis placed on what we once called "private life" as contrasted with "public life." As we know, the sharp separation between the two breaks down under analysis, but the tradition that sustains the separation is still dominant.[28]

Noddings calls for an emphasis on family membership and homemaking, by which she means the study of what constitutes a home, who would count as members of a home, and why a nation is often referred to as a homeland. Like Tupper,[29] who argues that in Canada there is a male bias in conceptions of citizenship education, Noddings asserts that instead of the traditional focus on citizenship education, we need an inclusive curriculum that deals with "private" matters. Yet we see little if anything in the various social studies curriculum guidelines about care (with the possible exception of the Kindergarten curriculum and the very early primary grades). In fact, as students move from the study of the family and community, where one would expect there to be a focus on caring, to the study of large geographical regions and the history of Canada, there is more and more emphasis on the "public" sphere than on the "private."

Recognizing that females have just as much claim as males on both the public and the private spheres, how then do we address the "gender gap" in our curriculum? Several approaches can be taken.[30]

The Comparison Approach

In the **comparison approach**, the lives and accounts of women are compared with those of men. For example, the lives of pioneer women are contrasted with the accounts of pioneer life written in textbooks by male historians. Comparisons focus on both similarities and differences among a variety of voices. The strength of this approach in the elementary grades is that students learn quickly how to spot similarities and differences. However, its potential weakness is that students may see things in black and white and may not realize the complexity of human lives. Yet we can present the lives of women in their families, in their communities, in the past, and around the world and contrast these to the lives of males. And we can ask students to consider these comparisons and begin to think about questions of sexism.

The Segregated Approach

In the **segregated approach**, the study of women's experience is treated as a separate topic. So, in a community study, the roles of women are examined; in a unit on Canada, famous and not-so-famous women are in part the focus. For example, we could examine the lives of women during the Cariboo or Klondike gold rush, or the experiences of women during the expulsion of the Acadians, or the life of a farmer's wife on the prairies. The strength of this approach is that women are seen as deserving special attention; the weakness is that women are not mentioned except when they are the subject of a special topic.

The Integrated Approach

As the title suggests, in the **integrated approach** the study of women is incorporated into all aspects of the curriculum.[31] This approach gives women a central place, socializing students to the equal importance of males and females. It also has the potential to increase the self-esteem of girls in the class. However, this approach is difficult to implement because of a lack of resource materials that appropriately represent the contributions of women to history, for example. Existing textbooks, despite much improvement over the last several years, often continue to portray males as the "movers and shakers" and relegate women to sidebars.

The above approaches can be put into practice through activities such as these:

1. Ask the students to anonymously state what they like and dislike about being a boy or a girl. Compare their statements and have the students identify which things, if any, could be changed. Are their likes and dislikes things that girls or boys are "supposed to" like? In the intermediate grades, have students pretend that they are parents and state what behaviours they would expect from their sons and daughters.
2. Give students the following letter, modelled on the type one reads in a popular advice column, and have them answer it.

   Dear Abby,

   In my class, the girls get to set up the science experiments and supervise the use of the computers. We boys get to wipe tables and clean the sink. It should be the other way round. What should we do?

3. Provide students with pictures of various occupations and sports. Ask the students to state whether they would expect males or females to be more involved in these activities. For those occupations and sports the students see as being gender stratified, have them carry out research and collect evidence of both men and women engaged in the occupation or sport.

   Another idea is to ask students what they want to be when they are adults. Could both men and women carry out their chosen jobs? Are there equal opportunities in society for both genders to train for their chosen jobs? With primary school children, discuss who does what jobs in the home and whether both sexes are able to do the same jobs.
4. When discussing historical topics, ensure that the role of women is given equal consideration to that of men. For example, have students focus on the role of women in First Nations cultures; in the first European settlements; and in politics, the arts, and science. Whenever students discuss the topic of famous women (see Kirman[32]), have them role-play an interview with one of the women under study, or write a diary as if they were that person. In preparing a family history (see Chapter 10), encourage students to focus on the history of a female relative. As pointed out in Chapter 5, students can also analyze their textbook to determine the number of times women are mentioned and, just as importantly, the contexts in which they are mentioned and how they are represented. In the later grades, students could be encouraged to rewrite part of a textbook that does not adequately represent the contributions of women. For further ideas, especially on how women have been treated in the curriculum, see Tetreault.[33]
5. Read stories or biographies about women. Demonstrate to students how both "ordinary" and famous women have made a difference.[34]
6. To help students understand the role played by the media in **sex-role stereotyping**, have students watch television programs and complete the following chart.

	Women	Men	Boys	Girls
Activities carried out				
a) for fun				
b) as work in the home				
Occupations				
a) Who was in charge?				
b) Who needed help?				
What people worried about:				
What decisions people made:				

Activity 18-I

Try this activity for yourself. Watch a couple of television programs and complete the chart above. After watching the programs, what general statement can be made about how males and females are portrayed in television programs?

Ask your students to answer the following questions when they watch a specific commercial:

- To whom is the product being sold?
- Whom will the product help?
- Who was shown using the product?
- Who was talking about the product?
- What activities were males and females shown doing?
- What message was conveyed about what males and females should be like?
- What values were seen to be important to males and females?

Students can also inquire into how cartoons portray males and females. Are women and girls viewed as being weaker and more in need of protection than men and boys? Do women in the cartoons have jobs? Do they make important decisions?

Primary-level students can also discuss the portrayal of men and women in fairy tales, stories, and nursery rhymes. What roles do girls and boys play out in such tales? Who is strong? Who is weak? Would the story make equal sense if the roles were reversed, for example if a boy was scared by a spider? In the European version of *Little Red Riding Hood,* the main character is rescued from the wolf by the woodcutter. In the Chinese version, the female character, Lon Po Po, triumphs over the wolf by herself. Teachers can read stories to students in which there are strong female characters or where girls perform roles once reserved for boys. Or students could make up a story in which traditional gender roles are reversed. Telling children stories that lack gender-role stereotyping can result in less gender stereotyping by children.[35]

Gender roles are learned early in childhood and are reinforced by society. Students need models. Therefore, the school must be conscious of its role in reinforcing gender stereotypes. Teachers must be especially aware of the vital role they play in modelling non-sexist behaviour. We should ask ourselves whether:

- we seat and group students according to their gender
- we have different expectations for boys and girls
- girls and boys are allowed to participate equally in all classroom and school activities
- the roles of women in the curriculum are given equal consideration to those of men
- there is a focus on non-traditional sex roles

PEACE AND CONFLICT RESOLUTION EDUCATION

Peace education, like the other curriculum areas discussed in this chapter, is conceptualized in various ways. For some people, peace education is focused on disarmament and the avoidance of war; for others it relates to conflict resolution more generally. Peace may be seen as an ultimate goal or as a means by which to improve human rights. The organization InterPares puts it this way:

> Peace is rooted in justice. It is rooted in the principle of self-determination of all people and peoples, free of coercion, acting in their own name. Peace implies, therefore, profound respect for people, their places, their ideas, their aspirations, and their actions to realize the world they imagine. Peace means the acceptance and nurturance of diversity. It means openness to embrace others as ourselves. Peace means dialogue, within and among diverse societies and cultures.[36]

Whatever conception of peace is adopted, peace education should at least introduce students to the following sorts of questions:

a) How do students conceive of peace?
b) How do other people conceive of peace?
c) What are the benefits of peace?
d) Is preserving peace more important than fighting for liberty or security?
e) Is the use of force ever justified?
f) Can the use of force (in a particular situation) be avoided? How? Does playing with war toys or watching violent TV programs lead children to be more aggressive?
g) What causes wars? What are the effects of war?
h) Is a peaceful life possible without having basic human rights?

Students should not be required to give firm answers to all these questions; rather, they should be encouraged to think about peace as they begin to wrestle with these complex questions. The purpose of peace education is to encourage students to reflect on the value of peace, as well as the role that peace education can play in helping students and others to resolve conflicts in peaceful ways.

Activity 18-J

Given that conflicts and disagreements between elementary students occur often, how can peace education contribute to the solving of conflict between students in school? Suppose a student in your class accuses another student of stealing her ideas for an assignment.

What is at stake here? What important social studies objectives could be focused on were you to attempt to resolve the issue privately versus designing a learning situation for the class that deals with a similar situation?

One key way to encourage students to resolve their conflicts is to directly teach students conflict resolution skills. Bickmore[37] defines this as the "process of seeking to understand conflicts and their sources and to nonviolently resolve them." She describes two dimensions: the substantive one, which involves learning what conflict is all about and how it comes about, and the procedural one, focusing on the managing and resolving of conflicts and the resources required. As with any form of values education, we can explicitly teach these dimensions or we can do so indirectly. Explicit teaching involves helping students understand how conflicts occur in the family, the community, the country, and the wider world. The social studies curriculum itself entails the study of conflicts (e.g., the study of war). Topics related to conflict can also be focused on when studying multiculturalism, gender, citizenship, law, human rights, global studies, First Nations studies, environmental education, and history. In these areas, we can help students analyze conflicts in terms of how they arise, whose interests are involved, what the various interests are, what the relationships are between the people involved, and how the conflict was resolved—if it ever was. Students, where possible, can evaluate the resolution and question whether it was the best one possible. This kind of analysis is also useful in looking at current events and in resolving real problems.[38] Students can be taught to act as peer mediators who are involved in the establishment and enforcement of classroom rules. Students also learn about conflict resolution indirectly by observing how their parents, teachers, peers, and world leaders deal with conflict. Keep in mind that not all solutions to conflicts may be justifiable, so students should always be encouraged to consider the value issues involved in the solutions to the conflicts they are studying.

A simple idea is to have students identify conflict situations that they have experienced and note how they felt, what they thought, and what they did or thought of doing as the conflict was occurring. If what they felt and did was not likely to resolve the conflict, then have students consider some of the other actions they might have pursued to resolve the conflict. For example, if you are pushed, you might feel angry and push back. This could well escalate into a conflict. How could this conflict be prevented? Role-playing is another powerful strategy for teaching conflict resolution, since to deal with conflict students need to learn about other people's points of view. For example, the activity where students play the plaintiff, the defendant, and the judge (see the section on Law-Related Education in the previous chapter) can help students realize that a story can have many interpretations and that resolutions to conflicts can vary depending on whose resolution is adopted. Probably the best strategy that can help students resolve conflicts peacefully is to teach them how to be peer mediators. Bickmore[39] has carried out research in this area in Toronto and has demonstrated its effectiveness. To ensure that peer mediation helps teachers achieve social studies knowledge objectives, students should learn about the causes of conflict and some of the history of conflict resolution.[40]

FIRST NATIONS, INUIT, AND MÉTIS STUDIES

Activity 18-K

Review your province or territory's social studies guidelines and list all the topics that would be directly or indirectly relevant to understanding First Nations, Inuit, and Métis people past and present. In how many of these topics are these people, and their cultures and issues, actually mentioned?

We end this section with the first inhabitants of Canada because First Nations, Inuit, and Métis people have a unique status in Canada and so many of the questions raised and ideas presented in the last three chapters and in other chapters in this textbook pertain to how we could proceed to teach about these people.[41] How should we incorporate First Nations, Inuit, and Métis content into the curriculum? Should we treat topics about First Nations, Inuit, and Métis people as a separate subject from the rest of the social studies curriculum? Or should we incorporate First Nations, Inuit, and Métis studies wherever it is relevant? And if we do the latter, should we focus on these people's contributions as an "addendum" to Canadian history and contemporary society, or as a tightly interwoven and integrated theme that runs through most of Canadian history? Should we adopt a socio-cultural approach to First Nations, Inuit, and Métis studies by focusing on how these peoples lived in the past and what we can tell about their lives by looking at historical artifacts, Native artwork, and through visits to museums? Or should we take a more proactive approach and teach about not only their cultures, past and present, but also their treatment and mistreatment by federal and provincial governments and the church throughout history (e.g., the banning of the potlatch and the relocation of children into residential schools), as well as contemporary issues concerning land claims, self-government, poverty, and access to clean water, health care, and social services?

We should consider several guidelines:

1. When teaching about Canadian communities, ensure you include First Nations, Inuit, and Métis communities. Although these people are part of the multicultural makeup of Canada, they have a different status than do other cultures that are represented throughout Canada. The indigenous people were here long before the first European explorers and settlers arrived.
2. When teaching about a particular First Nations or Inuit culture, past or present, try to ensure that students know this is but one culture among many. This will help students to avoid overgeneralizing or stereotyping these cultures and people. Follow the guidelines on pages 233 to 238 presented for multicultural education when dealing with and preventing prejudicial attitudes.
3. When teaching about pre-contact or early post-contact cultures, also ask students to find out how these people live today.
4. When teaching about the early exploration and settlement of Canada by Europeans, ensure that students are aware of the impact (both positive and negative) of Western civilization on First Nations, Inuit, and Métis people.
5. Don't back away from controversial debates that explore whether First Nations, Inuit, and Métis people were—and still are—discriminated against and subject to unjust laws and treatment.
6. When studying contemporary First Nations, Inuit, and Métis people, consider asking students to research how they are represented in the media and in school textbooks. Here, information about the present status of First Nations, Inuit, and Métis people, The Assembly of First Nations, land claims, and especially the views of First Nations, Inuit, and Métis people should be emphasized.
7. Ensure that students read some First Nations, Inuit, and Métis stories and understand some of their beliefs.[42]

8. Try using a Talking Circle when students are discussing an issue. Orr explains how this works.[43] Students sit in a circle and an object such as a stick is passed around as each speaks.
   a) Only the person with the stick may speak.
   b) If a participant does not wish to speak, he or she passes the stick to the next person.
   c) Speakers must direct their comments to the topic being discussed. They may not comment positively or negatively about what another speaker has said.
   d) It is the responsibility of everyone in the circle to listen to the speaker.
   e) What is said in the circle stays in the circle.

Note how interrelated First Nations, Inuit, and Métis studies are with other areas such as human rights citizenship, law-related, global, gender, and multicultural education, and how interrelated all of these are. In the introduction to this chapter, we pointed out that the boundaries between the curriculum areas discussed are flexible. What is common to each is the question of how human beings ought to be treated. Whatever the specific objectives of First Nations, Inuit, and Métis studies, citizenship, multicultural, global, law-related, human rights, and peace education, they are (or should be) concerned with helping students to better understand themselves, others, and the multifaceted relationships that constitute human society in general.

Other Activities

1. State whether you agree or disagree with the following proposition and present your reasons. Share your reasons with a peer, and if you disagree with each other, argue your case. If you agree, do you share the same reasons? Which reasons do you think are most compelling?

   Distinguishing between global, human rights, multicultural, law-related, peace, citizenship, conflict resolution, and gender education is confusing. Teachers should incorporate all of these educational approaches into social studies without giving them separate labels.

2. Analyze a social studies curriculum guideline or textbook to ascertain whether any of the subjects discussed in this chapter are mentioned. If they are mentioned, what is the focus—information giving, conceptual understanding, or issue resolution, etc.?
3. Analyze an elementary school social studies textbook in terms of the representation of women. How are women depicted? What are their roles? Are they portrayed in non-traditional roles or stereotypical roles? Are women's contributions integrated into the text or do they appear as sidebars? How does their depiction differ from that of men?
4. Design an activity based on a conflict incident in which students are required to analyze the conflict, determine avenues for resolving it, and pick the most appropriate solution.

Notes

1. Statistics Canada, 2001 Census. www.statcan.ca/english/Pgdb/demo28a.htm
2. M. Varma-Joshi, "Understanding multiculturalism in the social studies classroom," in A. Sears and I. Wright, eds., *Challenges and Prospects for Canadian Social Studies* (Vancouver: Pacific Educational Press, 2004), pp. 150–163.
3. B. Beairsto and T. Carrigan, "Imperatives and possibilities for multicultural education." *Education Canada,* Spring 2004, pp. 1–5.
4. From Bill C-93, *An Act for the Preservation and Enhancement of Multiculturalism in Canada*, House of Commons, July 12, 1988.

5. *Canadian Charter of Rights and Freedoms*, Constitution Act, 1982.
6. M. Adams, *Unlikely Utopia* (Toronto: Viking, 2007).
7. J. Kehoe, "Multiculturalism in social studies," in I. Wright and A. Sears, eds., *Trends and Issues in Canadian Social Studies* (Vancouver: Pacific Educational Press, 1997).
8. J. Banks, *An Introduction to Multicultural Education*, 2nd ed. (Boston: Allyn and Bacon, 1999).
9. J. Banks, "Multicultural education: Its effects on students' racial and gender role attitudes," in J. Shaver, ed., *Handbook of Research on Social Studies Teaching and Learning* (New York: Macmillan, 1991).
10. J. Orr, "Teaching social studies for understanding First Nations issues," in A. Sears and I. Wright, eds., *Challenges and Prospects for Canadian Social Studies*, 2nd ed. (Vancouver: Pacific Educational Press, 2004).
11. N. Wyner and E. Farquhar, "Cognitive, emotional and social development: Early childhood social studies," in J. Shaver, ed., *Handbook of Research on Social Studies Teaching and Learning* (New York: Macmillan, 1991).
12. T. Linter, "A world of difference: Teaching tolerance though photos in elementary school," *The Social Studies* 96:1 (2005), pp. 34–37.
13. F. Aboud, *Children and Prejudice* (Oxford: Blackwell, 1988).
14. These include *Alternatives to Racism: New Friends* (1984); V. Bowers and D. Swanson, *More Than Meets the Eye* (1989); V. Rogers, *All the Colours of the Rainbow: A Multicultural Storybook* (1990); and V. Rogers, *Apple's Not the Only Pie: A Multicultural Storybook* (1990). All have accompanying teachers' guides and all are available from Pacific Educational Press, University of British Columbia, Vancouver, BC V6T 1Z4.
15. P. Eyvindson, *Red Parka Mary* (Winnipeg: Pemmican Publications, 1996).
16. J. Skolinck, N. Dulberg, and T. Maestre, *Through Other Eyes: Developing Empathy and Multicultural Perspectives in the Social Studies* (Toronto: Pippin, 1999).
17. J. Bainbridge, S. Pantelo, and M. Ellis, "Multicultural picture books: Perspectives from Canada," *The Social Studies* 90:4 (1999), p. 185.
18. J. Kehoe and F. Echols, "Educational approaches for combatting prejudice and racism," in S. Shapson and V. D'Oyley, eds., *Bilingual and Multicultural Education: Canadian Perspectives* (Avon, UK: Multilingual Matters, 1984).
19. J. Kehoe, *A Handbook for Enhancing the Multicultural Climate of the School* (Vancouver: Pacific Educational Press, 1983).
20. P. Avery, "Teaching tolerance: What research tells us," *Social Education* 66:5 (2002), pp. 270–275.
21. M. Varma-Joshi, p. 158.
22. L. Stone, "Intercultural and multicultural education," in V. Atwood, ed., *Elementary Social Studies: Research as Guide to Practice* (Washington, DC: National Council for the Social Studies, 1986).
23. See the Oxfam website for an example: www.oxfam.ogr.uk/education
24. Amnesty International has curriculum materials designed to focus on human rights issues. www.amnesty .ca/resource_centre/teachers.php
25. P. Clark, "Between the covers: Exposing images in social studies textbooks," in R. Case and P. Clark, eds., *The Canadian Anthology of Social Studies* (Vancouver: Pacific Educational Press, 1998).
26. N. Noddings, "Social studies and feminism," in E. Ross, ed., *The Social Studies Curriculum: Purposes, Problems and Possibilities* (New York: State University of New York, Albany, 1997).
27. *Ibid.*, p. 59.
28. *Ibid.*, p. 63.
29. J. Tupper, "The gendering of citizenship in social studies curriculum," *Canadian Social Studies* 36:3, www.quasar.ualberta.ca/css/Css_36_3/ARgendering_of_citizenship.html
30. L. Bloom and A. Ochoa, "Responding to gender equity in the social studies curriculum," in B. Massialas and R. Allen, eds., *Crucial Issues in Teaching Social Studies* (Belmont, CA: Wadsworth, 1996).

31. See M. Hickey and D. Kollerman, "Special women in my life: Strategies for writing women into the social studies curriculum," *Social Education* 70:4 (2006), pp. 190–196. See also P. Sincero and C. Woyshner, "Writing women into the curriculum," *Social Education* 67:4 (2003), pp. 218–225.

32. J. Kirman, "Women's rights in Canada: A sample unit using biographies and autobiographies in teaching history chronologically," *Social Education* 54:1 (1990), pp. 39–42.

33. M.Tetreault,"Rethinking women,gender, and the social studies,"*Social Education* 51:3(1987),pp. 170–179.

34. S. Hart, "Listening to a different voice: Using women's stories in social studies," *Canadian Social Studies* 31:2 (1997), pp. 90–92, 96.

35. J. Banks, "Multicultural education: Its effects on students' racial and gender role attitudes," in J. Shaver, ed., *Handbook of Research on Social Studies Teaching and Learning* (New York: Macmillan, 1991), p. 465.

36. InterPares, *Annual Report 2002* (Ottawa: InterPares, 2002), p. 1.

37. K. Bickmore, "Education for peacebuilding citizenship: Teaching the dimensions of conflict resolution in social studies," in A. Sears and I. Wright, eds., *Challenges and Prospects for Canadian Social Studies*, 2nd ed. (Vancouver: Pacific Educational Press, 2004).

38. For an example of a unit dealing with violence, see R. McBee, "Can controversial issues be taught in the early grades? The answer is Yes!" *Social Education* 60:1 (1996), pp. 38–41, and for one on conflict in general, see K. Bickmore, "Conflicts global and local: An elementary approach," *Social Education* 66:4 (2002), pp. 235–238.

39. K. Bickmore, "Peer mediation training and program implementation in elementary schools: Research results," *Conflict Resolution Quarterly* 20:2 (2003).

40. K. Bickmore, "Conflicts global and local: An elementary approach," *Social Education* 66:4 (2002), pp. 235–238, and K. Bickmore, "Student conflict resolution, power 'sharing' in schools, and citizenship education," *Curriculum Inquiry* 31:2 (2001), pp. 137–162.

41. Orr points out that teaching "about" First Nations people may not lead to social justice but teaching "for" First Nations people will help develop student commitment to justice and equality. J. Orr, "Teaching social studies for understanding First Nations issues," in A. Sears and I. Wright, eds., *Challenges and Prospects for Canadian Social Studies* (Vancouver: Pacific Educational Press, 2004), pp. 164–175.

42. For a list of suitable stories, see The University of Lethbridge site: www.uleth.ca/edu/edlinks/native.cfm. Also see the Department of Indian and Northern Affairs website for children: www.ainc-inac.gc.ca/ks/index-eng.asp. See also M. Caduto and J. Bruchac, *Keepers of the Earth: Native American Stories and Environmental Activities for Children* (Golden, CO: Fulcrum Publishing, 1999).

43. Orr, *op.cit,* p. 172

Glossary of Key Terms

Anti-racist education—An instructional program that is designed to help students understand the history and contemporary nature of discrimination and the unequal power relationships in society so that they will take action to bring about social justice.

Comparison approach to gender studies—Comparisons between male and female experiences, how males portray females, and vice versa.

Conflict resolution—A process of seeking to understand conflicts and their sources and to resolve them non-violently.

Human rights education—A term used to denote a variety of programs and approaches that focus on concepts, understandings, and issues related to human rights.

Integrated approach to gender studies—An approach to gender studies in which the experiences and actions of both men and women are incorporated into all facets of the curriculum.

Multicultural education—Education to develop an understanding and respect for other cultures and their contributions to society. There are four approaches:

- **Additive**—Multicultural concepts and understandings are added to the curriculum without changing the basic structure of the curriculum.
- **Contributions**—Accounts of heroes who belong to a variety of cultural groups are added to the curriculum without changing the scope, sequence, or goals of the curriculum.
- **Social action**—Strategies and skills that help students bring about a more just society are taught.
- **Transformation**—Multicultural concepts, understandings, and issues are infused into the curriculum.

Peace education—A term used to denote a variety of programs and approaches that focus on peace and conflict resolution.

Segregated approach to gender studies—The experiences and actions of women are treated as a separate topic in the curriculum.

Sex-role stereotyping—The view that only one gender can perform certain tasks or occupy particular roles.

Websites for Part Three

Citizenship Education

Centre for Canadian Studies Citizenship Education Bibliography:
www.mta.ca/faculty/arts/canadian_studies/english/about/multimedia/citizenship/index.html

Citizen Education Research Network:
http://canada.metropolis.net/research-policy/cern-pub/overview.html

First Nations, Inuit, and Métis

First Nations School Net:
www.firstnationsnt.ca

Aboriginal Canada Portal:
www.aboriginalcanada.gc.ca/acp/site.nsf/en/ao31045.htm

Assembly of First Nations:
www.afn.ca

Library and Archives Canada—The Kid's Site of Canadian Settlement:
www.collectionscanada.gc.ca/settlement/kids/index-e.html

Ministry of Education Manitoba—Aboriginal Perspectives:
www.edu.gov.mb.ca/k12/abedu/perspectives/resources.html

Ministry of Education Saskatchewan Heritage (Canada's First Peoples):
www.sasklearning.gov.sk.ca/docs/elemsoc/g5u22ess.html

Ministry of Indian and Northern Affairs Canada, Kids' Stop:
www.inac.gc.ca/ks

University of Lethbridge, First Nations, Métis, and Inuit Edlinks:
www.uleth.ca/edu/edlinks/native2.cfm?category=English%20and%20languages%20arts

Virtual Museum of Canada—Inuit History, Art and Other Traditions of the Inuit:
www.virtualmuseum.ca/English/Teacher/inuit_history.html

The Virtual Museum of Métis History and Culture:
www.metismuseum.ca/exhibits/resources

Global Education

American Forum for Global Education:
www.globaled.org

AusAID Global Education:
www.globaleducation.edna.edu.au

Canadian Hunger Foundation:
www.chf-partners.ca/

Canadian International Development Agency:
www.acdi-cida.gc.ca

Check Your Head:
www.checkyourhead.org

Facing the Future:
www.facingthefuture.org

Fair Trade:
www.transfair.ca

George Lucas Educational Foundation:
www.edutopia.org/global-education-canada-media-literacy

Global Education Network:
www.gen.com

Oxfam:
www.oxfam.ca

Statistical Information about UN Countries:
www.un.org/cyberschoolbus

United Nations:
www.unesco.org/education/index.shtml

UNICEF:
www.unicef.ca

Unitarian Service Committee of Canada:
http://usc-canada.org/resources/links/global-education-resources/

World Affairs Council:
www.world-affairs.org/classroom.html

Human Rights

Alberta Teachers Association Diversity and Human Rights:
www.teachers.ab.ca/NR/rdonlyres/D0848356-2B23-4C95-A0AD-6170484AE130/0/DEHRbrochurePD802.pdf

Amnesty International:
www.amnesty.ca

Anti-Slavery Coalition:
www.antislavery.org

Canadian Civil Liberties Association:
www.ccla.org

Child Labor Coalition:
www.stopchildlabor.org

The Child's Rights Information Network:
www.crin.org

Working Group on Girls:
www.girlsrights.org

Human Rights Education Organization:
www.hrea.org

Human Rights Resource Center:
www.hrusa.org

Save the Children:
www.savethechildren.ca

Law-Related Education

Centre for Education, Law and Society at Simon Fraser University and the Law Courts Education Society of British Columbia:
www.lawconnection.ca

Law Courts Education Society of BC:
www.lawcourtsed.ca

Public Legal Education Association of Saskatchewan:
www.plea.org

Multicultural Education

Canadian Council for Multi/Intercultural Education:
www.ccmie.com

Canadian Multicultural Education Foundation:
www.cmef.ca

Canadian Race Relations Foundation:
www.crr.ca

Community Learning Network:
www.cln.org/subject_index.html

Handbook of Research in Multicultural Education:
www.wileycanada.com

Multicultural Education Resources:
www.schoolnet.com

Skipping Stones, an International Multicultural Magazine:
www.skippingstones.org

UN High Commissioner for Refugees:
www.unhcr.org

CHAPTER 19

Where's the Information? Obtaining, Analyzing, and Evaluating Information

Students rely on information, including text, images, and sound, in order to learn more about a topic, test out hypotheses, solve problems, and study history, geography, and other subjects more generally. Similarly, teachers rely on information from a variety of different sources in order to plan their social studies units. Although texts and other books suitable for elementary school children exist (see Chapter 5), some schools are lacking in print resources while others rely on resources, such as textbooks or atlases, that are out of date or unsuitable on other grounds (e.g., they lack Canadian content). Therefore, it is often necessary to be strategic as a teacher in locating Canadian social studies–related information. Many teachers turn to books they have purchased or borrowed from the library; more recently, the internet has been enormously helpful as a source of information for learning. But there are also whole categories of additional sources of information that teachers and students can turn to. These include information published by museums, industries, government agencies, chambers of commerce, tourist bureaus, and private organizations.

In this chapter, you will find out how to access some of these sources of information. Keep in mind that what is included here is only the beginning. In the 21st century, the sources of information—as well as information itself—are constantly in flux, as old sources dry up and new sources appear. In particular, teachers should always be on the lookout for valuable information sources that exist on the local level. Often times, local sources of information are especially attuned to the local context in which you are teaching. Teachers should also feel comfortable in requesting information from others. A well-written letter, a well-placed phone call, or a personal email can go a long way in securing even a full class set of some materials (e.g., city maps) for the school.

BIBLIOGRAPHIES

There are several useful bibliographies to which you may wish to refer when looking for resource materials. Websites for some of these (and many other resources) can be found at the end of Chapter 20.

- D. Ferguson, ed., *Children's Book Review* (Detroit: Thomson Gale, 2002).
- J. Gillespie, *Best Books for Children: Preschool through Grade 6* (Westport, CN: Bowker Greenwood, 2002).
- S. Peacock, ed., *Children's Literature Review* (Detroit: Thomson Gale, 2002).
- S. Egoff and J. Saltman, *The New Republic of Childhood: A Critical Guide to Canadian Children's Literature in English* (Don Mills, ON: Oxford University Press, 1990).
- R. Jones and J. Scott, *Canadian Children's Books: A Critical Guide to Authors and Illustrators* (Don Mills, ON: Oxford University Press, 2000).

Also check *The Globe and Mail*'s Book Review section, where children's books are frequently reviewed; the National Council for the Social Studies, which publishes an annual list of Notable Children's

Trade Books; the reference section in your school and public library; and various teacher magazines that routinely advertise new books.

SCHOOL BOARDS

School boards often have teaching resource centres, and they also publish catalogues. Find out if your school district has such a centre, and locate the appropriate catalogue for social studies.

SCHOOL LIBRARIES

Libraries vary in quality and quantity of materials. Some school libraries contain not only books but also audio-visual resources (e.g., audiotapes, videotapes, pictures, and CDs) as well as files of newspaper clippings and other materials. Conduct a thorough search of the library (especially if you are new to the school) and ask the teacher-librarian, if there is one, to help you. Often, on request, teacher-librarians will collect materials on a given topic and place them in a particular location so a class of students can easily access them.

TEACHERS' ORGANIZATIONS

Teachers' organizations often produce journals and newsletters and may have professional libraries. In British Columbia, the British Columbia Teachers' Federation has a Lesson Aids Service, for example.

MUSEUMS

Museums often provide services to schools. These may include the distribution of resource materials (e.g., pictures, booklets, and pamphlets), guided tours, and workshops for teachers and students. Contact your local museum(s) to learn more about what is offered, and visit Museumlink's Canadian museums website (see the websites section at the end of Part 4).

GOVERNMENT (FEDERAL, PROVINCIAL, AND LOCAL)

Governments produce a host of documents, some of which are suitable for elementary schools. Provincial and foreign governments also have websites that can be located by keying in the name of the country or province in the search box along with the words "and government."

TELEPHONE DIRECTORIES

These are a great source of information. Use them to find contact information for industries, businesses, and services in a particular area.

MAGAZINES AND JOURNALS

The list of magazines useful for social studies is huge. Only a few are highlighted here. For children, there are *Owl* and *Chickadee* (publications of the Young Naturalist Foundation), *Highlights for Children, National Geographic World,* and *Sesame Street.* For your own professional development, the Canadian journal for social studies is called *Canadian Social Studies* (formerly *The History and Social Science Teacher*). The journal is online, and you can access it at the address listed at the end of Part 4. Many provincial teachers' organizations have social studies professional groups that publish their own journals or newsletters. The North American social studies organization is the National Council for the Social Studies (NCSS). It publishes *Social Education, Social Studies and the Young Learner,* as well as bulletins, newsletters, and other publications that you receive as a member of the NCSS. Another journal is *The Social Studies* (available from Heldref Publications, 4000 Albermarle Street NW, Washington, DC 20016).

EMBASSIES

Now that the internet is ubiquitous, the best way to learn more about other countries is to use an internet search engine to ascertain what resources are available. For example, many countries have tourist agencies that provide valuable (albeit promotional) information)

TOURIST OFFICES IN CANADA

Each province has its own tourist agency that publishes advertising material. Some provinces produce high-quality booklets, brochures, and maps. Some towns and cities also produce tourist literature. Again, an internet search will help you to find this information.

NEWSPAPERS

There is a wealth of information related to newspapers. Have students collect information on current events and, where possible, on issues directly related to the social studies topics they are studying. Try to obtain newspapers from the geographical area under discussion. A list of websites is included at the end of Part 4.[1]

Here are a few ideas for using newspapers as a teaching and learning tool.

1. Look at the advertisements. Have students prepare two lists for a week's worth of groceries for a family of three with a budget of $50 and of $100. How easy or difficult is it to feed a family within these budgets?
2. Compare the coverage of the same news story in two or more newspapers. How are they similar or different? What may account for the differences? Trace the same news story over a period of time in several newspapers. Compare the amount of space devoted to the story, the headlines used, any evidence of a positive or negative bias, and a list of empirical and value claims. Decide which of these claims are supportable. Also consider having students compare two newspapers to ascertain how much space in each is devoted to different types of stories—crime, disasters, politics—and whether the newspapers report on the same major stories in similar ways. Editorials can also be compared. The same comparisons can be applied to radio and television news.
3. Read aloud a newspaper story about a particular event and have the students draw a picture depicting it. Compare the students' pictures. What may account for the differences? If a photograph were to be taken of the event, what images would the photographer most likely wish to show? Would another photographer almost certainly choose to show the same images? Why or why not? How could a photograph influence people to think in a certain way about an event?
4. Collect pictures of prominent people. Quiz students to check for recognition.
5. Graph weather information.

6. Make up headlines for pictures. How does a particular headline influence how you feel while viewing the picture? How could the use of emotional words make a difference to your interpretation of the picture?
7. Make a class newspaper. Ask the students to choose which stories will be featured and the space that will be devoted to each. Have them give reasons for their choices.
8. Obtain newspapers from other countries and compare them. What is reported? How is a story about one's home country handled by the foreign press?

VIDEOTAPES, MOVIES, AND TELEVISION PROGRAMS

The National Film Board of Canada (NFB) website (www.nfb.ca) lists all of the movies and videos that are available for purchase by individuals and schools. The NFB also publishes a free learning resources guide.

The Canadian Broadcasting Corporation (CBC) has produced numerous programs that nicely augment the social studies curriculum. Perhaps the most notable TV series in this regard is *Canada: A People's History*, a 32-hour 2000–2001 series on the history of Canada. (Many excellent international television programs can also be found on American television, especially the Public Broadcasting System (PBS), the Learning Channel, and the History Channel.) If you tape television programs, make sure you are not breaking copyright laws should you choose to broadcast them in your classroom. Special public broadcast permission is normally required.

As many schools are now wired for cable, you can take advantage of the services provided by Cable in the Classroom (www.ciconline.org). This organization produces a quarterly publication that lists the available TV programs for a variety of networks. These programs can be taped and then used copyright-free in a classroom setting for at least a year. Programs are vetted by educators and then summarized and classified according to their subject matter. Some also come with lesson plans.

SPEAKERS AND INTERVIEWS

Many organizations will provide speakers for schools. Contact the relevant agencies to ascertain if someone is available. Sometimes, you may wish to invite someone in the community to come and talk to your class, or you may arrange for students to interview someone offsite. Parents can often be a rich source of information in interviews. Interviewing people on a particular topic is a valuable activity for students. It can teach them how to structure questions, listen carefully, collect first-hand information, and interact responsibly with others. By interviewing others, students can improve their communication and social skills.

Interviews have to be planned carefully.[2] Prior to conducting an interview, students must have amassed sufficient background information on the topic they are studying. They must also know the purpose of the interview and what types of questions to ask. Teachers should ascertain in advance that the person being interviewed is comfortable with the sorts of questions students are expected to ask and with the ways in which students are planning to record the responses (e.g., a tape recorder or written notes). When the interview is over, students should make a special effort to thank the interviewee and also send a written letter of appreciation.

OTHER SOURCES OF FREE INFORMATION

Flyers, free magazines, pamphlets, mail-order catalogues, calendars from banks and businesses, and newsletters can also serve as useful resources for teaching social studies. Collect, file, and—most importantly—organize all of the social studies materials you can.

VISUAL IMAGES

Visual images—family photos, billboard advertisements, signage, and many other types of visual media—are critical to the study of media literacy and social studies. Historians and geographers rely on visual information in their professional work, but so do many other types of social scientists. Moreover, everybody who is sighted relies on visual images due to the fact that we live in a visual culture that is rich with visual symbols and images. In teaching through the use of visual images, educators should encourage students to not just take fleeting glances at (or otherwise consume uncritically) visual media; rather, teachers should encourage students to closely "read" images, to look deeply into them, and to think critically about them. Perhaps partly because of television viewing, most children (and many adults) tend to skim pictures very quickly, failing to observe important details. Children will also tend to concentrate on what is important to them. As students become increasingly attuned to images, visual information can be used in powerful ways.[3] A good idea when introducing a new social studies topic is to strategically position pictures around the classroom and use them to raise questions about the new topic. The following activities focus attention on how pictures can be used.

Activity 19-A

How could these pictures (below and on the following page) be used to teach social studies?

Where do you think the picture above was taken? What is happening in the picture?

Look at the clothing and the ship. In what decade do you think this photo was taken? The people are watching a ship carrying Canadian soldiers sailing from Vancouver. Given the date you have just hypothesized, where might these soldiers be going? Check your response in the Answers section.

Walt Werner points out that visual images may be read in numerous ways.[4] Take another look at the picture of Bill Miner in Chapter 10. We can look at this picture through many different lenses:[5]

Empathetic: We can ask students to imagine how Miner felt as a prisoner. We could give students sentences to complete, such as, "If I were William Miner I would feel ______________."

Narrative: Students can place the photo within the context of Miner's life.

Editorial: Students can be asked: What is the photographer trying to say about Miner? Does she appear to sympathize with this train robber? Is she trying to show him as a notorious criminal?

Instrumental: We can have students look at the details in the photo to learn something about Miner and his times. What is he wearing? What are his clothes made of? With other photos we can sometimes make inferences about climate, the economy, people's lifestyles, and so on.

Iconic: Some photos have iconic status as they come to represent something significant in a culture. Although Bill Miner did not have the same status as Robin Hood, he did represent an outlaw who pulled off some daring train robberies and was regarded with a degree of awe by some people.

Oppositional and Evaluative: Students can look at other photos of Miner and compare the portrayals. They can make critical judgments about the messages they think the photographers are visually capturing.

Activity 19-B

Focus on a suitable photo in another social studies textbook (or this text) and pose questions that derive from each of the above categories. Share your questions with a peer and have him or her answer them. Discuss both the posed questions and the answers given.

Werner also recommends that students consider the viewpoint (or vantage point) of an image under study. For each photo you analyze, ask yourself: where is the viewer (or photographer) positioned and what effect does this vantage point have on the photo? For example, looking at Photo 5 in Chapter 6, we can imagine quite a different effect if the photographer had been standing off to one side. Images can also be rhetorical; cartoons are a clear example of this. Sometimes, symbols can also be used rhetorically. Can you find any photos in this text that you would consider symbolic? Sometimes images are shown in binary juxtaposition in order to display competing ideas such as old/new or developed/undeveloped. An example of this would be placing the photo of the classroom in Chapter 10 next to the photo of the classroom in Chapter 7. This intertextuality can be used with great effect. Witness the three photos of Vancouver in Chapter 10. By placing them in a particular order, we are showing you the changes that have occurred and prompting you to look at these photos through the lenses of continuity and change. When you look at these images, how do they influence the ways in which you read the printed text? Have students look at the images in a new social studies textbook they are going to read before actually reading the text. Based on their "reading" of the images, ask them what they expect the text to say.

Activity 19-C

Consider the axiom "a picture is worth a thousand words." What does this phrase mean, exactly? How can teachers demonstrate this axiom to students?

The captions that often accompany photos are also important. Werner shows us how our previous perceptions and experiences, and the context in which we view a picture and its caption, influence what we see. How does a caption affect the ways in which we look at an image? What caption would you write for a given image? For example, the photo of the students in a classroom in China (Chapter 7) has elicited captions ranging from "Happy students" to "They only smile because they are told to." Have students write captions for a given image and share them with each other. Discuss with students the similarities and differences in how they viewed the image.

Many images—especially advertisements—have a specific purpose: to persuade the viewer in some way, to sell a product, to build brand awareness and loyalty, and so on. But other types of images have other types of purposes: to move us in some way, to capture a moment of excitement, to represent a scene artistically. The bottom line is that social studies teachers should make every effort to help students think critically about the explicit and more subtle purposes of the images they see all around them.

PERFORMING A PHOTO ANALYSIS

Choose a historical photograph for this photo analysis exercise. Pick a photograph that is as high quality (and large) as possible and in which a lot of detail is revealed. Ask the students to work in pairs as they analyze the photograph. Have them look deep into the photograph, searching out its most minute detail. Have them hypothesize what might be happening around the periphery of the photograph, just out of view. For action photographs, ask students to consider what might have happened just before the photograph was taken or what might be happening immediately after. Provide students with magnifiers so they can make the most detailed study of the photograph possible. Remind students that they are using the same photo analysis techniques that historians use when they analyze old photographs of historical settings in their research.

After the students have completed the above photo analysis, ask them to perform a comparative photo analysis in which they compare and contrast two photographs, perhaps of the same setting but captured at different times, maybe even years apart. Ask students to draw up a list of similarities and differences between the photographs. Optionally, provide students with some guiding questions that direct their attention to certain themes, such as the differences in topography between two natural settings or the differences in dress between period and modern photographs of family portraits.

Activity 19-D

Select a social studies topic you are likely to teach and locate five different resources for that topic: a textbook, a novel, a video, a newspaper article, and a website. Choose one image from the resources you have collected and design an activity incorporating some of the ideas mentioned above.

COMPUTERS AND THE INTERNET

One of the most significant and pedagogically challenging changes in elementary education over the last two decades has been the introduction of computers into the classroom. There are ongoing debates in the literature as to what grade is most appropriate for computers to be introduced, how computers should be used, and whether they are even worth all the time and expense required. That said, computers are ubiquitous in our lives and revolutionary in their applications. In the 21st century, schools are generally expected to ensure that students are technologically literate. This requires that students become familiar with operating computers, utilizing popular software programs, and generally using computers as powerful technological tools that can help them to learn new information, solve problems, and present their findings to others in attractive ways (e.g., through multimedia presentations). This last sentence treats the computer as a tool, but the computer is also a technological artifact—albeit a complex one—and this should be of great interest to social studies teachers, if only for the impact that computers have on our lives and the ways in which we make sense of the world through our interactions with computers and other technologies.

Activity 19-E

Calculate how much time you spend using a computer each week. Don't consider just the personal computer you use at home or school. Also consider other types of computers, such as banking machines and public kiosks that you interact with. Now brainstorm all of the different ways in which you interact with computers, from emailing friends to taking out money from a bank machine. Rank these activities from the most to least time-consuming.

Here is a series of critical questions that social scientists and educational researchers are currently asking in relation to computers and classrooms, as well as computers and society more generally. Discuss these questions with others and pose some of them to the students you teach:[6]

1. Can computers help us to solve social problems and/or think about things in new ways? If yes, how so?
2. Do computers augment or inhibit face-to-face interaction in the classroom? Some teachers purposefully pair up students when working on computers, even if there are enough computers in the classroom for every student. Why might teachers choose to do this?
3. Does the use of computers as instructional resources augment or diminish the teacher–student relationship?
4. Can computers help at-risk and special needs students? If so, how? If not, why not?
5. Is the ease with which information can be obtained from the internet turning students into mindless information gatherers?
6. Will typing eventually supplant printing and writing as the chief means by which people communicate using text? Has it already?
7. Is computer use leading children (and adults) to read fewer books?
8. Does inequitable access to computers (also know as the "digital divide") end up broadening the gap between the rich and the poor? Between males and females? Between those who have home access to computers and those who do not?
9. Has the advent of the World Wide Web led to information control by only a few, or has the web instead democratized the information production process? (*Hint:* Read though the next chapter for one possible answer.)
10. Do elementary school students regard what they see on the screen as "the truth"?[7] Students tend to view textbooks as a source of truth. Has this belief now been transferred to information gleaned from the computer screen?
11. Is it safe for students to browse the web? How can teachers and parents protect students from inappropriate online material?
12. How much do others know about us because we use email, log on to sites that collect information about us, use credit cards to make online purchases, and/or communicate in a chat room? What privacy and security concerns should students be aware of?
13. When using information downloaded or copied from the internet, do students realize that they might be breaking copyright and intellectual property laws?

14. Will learning about other cultures via the internet overcome students' insular world views? If students engage in internet conversations with children from other countries how much will they be limited by language and other cultural beliefs? What information about, and perspectives on, their own country will they present, and what perspectives and information will they receive? Will the information be accurate and the perspectives warranted?

These questions should ideally be discussed in upper elementary classrooms. The computer, the internet, and other technologies are not benign. They are the product of human beings and institutions that sometimes have their own subtle (even hidden) agendas. Teachers and students should be wary of these agendas and critique them as best they can.

Research evidence suggests that students do learn via computer technology:[8] they are motivated to learn; their self-esteem may rise because they are in charge of their own learning; and they learn social skills such as taking turns and cooperating with others.[9] Many teachers also find that they, too, have become more productive through computer use. They can store and retrieve grades, handouts, and quizzes; post assignment information and reference material;[10] and find information for their lessons.[11]

Student Presentations

Students can use computers to type up stories, add photos and other images, and lay out reports in attractive ways. With the sophistication of desktop publishing programs and multimedia software such as Microsoft PowerPoint, text in multiple styles and sizes, graphs, audio, video, and other types of multimedia can be incorporated into stylish presentations. Be wary of students spending too much time on the *style* rather than the *substance* of a report or presentation, however. That said, the tendency to focus on style over substance is offset by research that suggests some students learn to "write" better on the computer than they do using more conventional means.[12]

Tutorial Software

Tutorial software teaches factual information, such as subject content, principles, and problem-solving strategies. Tutorials are typically organized as follows: 1) an introduction to the topic is presented and the objectives are outlined; 2) subject content is presented; and 3) a question is posed that, if answered correctly, allows the student to proceed to the next question or topic. Students can typically stop or start tutorial programs at any point, and often the student's work is saved. There are also drill programs that provide repeated practice in learning a specific rule, skill, or set of facts. Research evidence[13] suggests that computer-based instruction holds a very small advantage over other methods in teaching specific knowledge and skills. This evidence, however, is based on numerous studies whose points of reference may not be comparable. Because students learn in different ways and computer programs vary dramatically in terms of quality, it should not be assumed that computer-based instruction is more effective than other means of instruction. A varied instructional program in which students engage in a wide variety of on- and offline activities is important.

CD-ROMs and DVD-ROMs

CD-ROMs can store encyclopedic content and allow students to view and listen to multimedia, such as famous speeches, national anthems, and interactive maps. Students can also use the links that are embedded in online encyclopedias to connect bits of information. Here are some examples of CD-ROMs about Canada that teachers have found useful:

- *Cabot: The Discovery of the New World* (1997). National Research Council of Canada. St John's: Media Touch Technologies Inc.
- *Canada's Visual History* (1994). National Film Board of Canada.
- *Canadian Encyclopedia* (1998). Toronto: McClelland & Stewart.
- *Canadian Geographic Explorer Kit* (1996). Royal Canadian Geographical Society. IQ Media Holdings Corporation.
- *Canadian Visual Images* (1996). Edmonton: Arnold Publishing.
- *John Cabot* (1997). St John's: Media Touch.
- *Klondike Gold: An Interactive History* (1996). Whitehorse: Hyperborean Productions; Vancouver: Multimedia Corporation.
- *The Metis: Our People, Our Story* (2000). Gabriel Dumont Institute. Edmonton: Arnold Multimedia: Department of Canadian Heritage.
- *Parliament Hill: An Interactive Tour* (1997). Sydney, NS: Voyageur Interactive Technologies.
- *The Peopling of Atlantic Canada* (2001). Sydney, NS: Folkus Atlantic Productions (www.folkus.com).[14]
- *World Fit for Children* (2002). Ottawa: Health Canada.

Simulations and Games

Some of the most popular educational activities for students are simulations and games. These include simulations of how things "work" (e.g., how a glacier is formed and how it moves), and games such as *Battleship* and other simulation games. Some recommended educational computer games include the following:

- *Crosscountry Canada* (www.ingenuityworks.com)
- *The History Canada Game* (www.historicanada.com)
- *SimCity* (http://simcity.ea.com)

Database Programs

Students can use **database programs** to organize information so that data can be easily stored, searched, and processed. Students can search existing databases and also create their own databases—either on paper or using computer software. Examples of databases filled with content include:

- *Historica* (www.histori.ca)
- *The Canadian Encyclopedia* (www.thecanadianencyclopedia.com)

Students can also create their own databases using software such as FileMaker Pro (www.filemaker.com). Macintosh users may wish to consider iList Data (www.lakewoodstudios.com), which was developed by one of the authors of this book.

Email and Chat

One primary function of computers and the internet is to aid communication over long distances. By using electronic mail and chat software, students can communicate with their peers in other locations. For example, consider starting up a penpal relationship with a school in another country.[15]

The World Wide Web

Computers are routinely used to obtain information from the web. With the advent of the World Wide Web, students have more information at their fingertips than they will ever need. Teachers can put this information to good use through webquests (see Chapter 20).

Search engines, such as Google.com and Yahoo.com, allow teachers and students to perform internet-wide keyword searches. For example, entering the search term "Pyramids and Egypt" using the Yahoo search engine produced this list (only the first five results are listed):

- Pyramids: The Inside Story (www.pbs.org/wgbh/nova/pyramid)
- National Geographic: Egypt Pyramids—Facts, Photos, Diagrams (www.nationalgeographic.com/pyramids/pyramids.html)
- Egyptian pyramids—Wikipedia, the free encyclopedia (en.wikipedia.org/wiki/Egyptian_pyramids)
- NOVA Online/Pyramids/Explore the Pyramids (www.pbs.org/wgbh/nova/pyramid)
- Guardian's Egypt (www.guardians.net/egypt/pyramids.htm)

Activity 19-F

Look at the list above. Given the title of the site and the URL, which sites do you think would be most useful for intermediate students who are studying how the pyramids were built? Log on to the sites to ascertain whether your hypotheses were correct.

The majority of search engine references on the internet are not carefully categorized or evaluated, so students will need to either search through the list to find exactly what they are looking for or, better yet, narrow down their search results by adding additional keywords to the search query (e.g., using "and," "or," and/or "not" connectors to return a subset of results). Students also need to be able to make judgments as to what information on the internet is reliable. With written textbooks careful attention is paid to standards of accuracy, but this is not true of all websites. For this reason, students need to be taught to ask critical questions about the online information they find. They need to have some understanding of the criteria they should use to judge the reliability of the information they are browsing online. Below are some key questions that teachers and students can ask about the websites they visit.[16]

- How long has this website been in existence and how often is it updated?
- Who are the contributors to the website and what are their qualifications?
- Who is (commercially) sponsoring the website and what impact does this have on the website's content?

- What is the purpose of the website and who is the intended audience?
- How easy is it to gain access to the website and to navigate it?
- Does the website feature links to similar websites?
- Is additional software required to use the site and is this provided?
- What level of ability (e.g., reading comprehension and technical knowledge) is required to obtain information from the website?
- Has the website been evaluated by any external agency and, if so, how is it rated?
- What are the strengths and weaknesses of the website?
- Is the website attractively presented?
- Is the print size appropriate?
- Is the website's information accurate and up to date?
- Is the information biased in some way?
- Is the information logically sequenced?
- Is the information representative of the topic?
- Is the language subtly sexist or racist?
- Does the website present stereotypes? For example, are females shown pursuing activities that were once male-dominated as well as those that have been traditionally female-dominated?
- How are seniors, children, and people with special needs portrayed?
- If there are student activities at the website, are they appropriate?
- Is the material interesting?
- Do students have the necessary prerequisite knowledge and skills to use the material?
- Can students with differing abilities use the materials?

Activity 19-G

Locate a website that you think would be useful in your teaching and evaluate it using the questions listed above.

USING GRAPHS AND SURVEYS

Teachers using either expository or inquiry methods to teach history or geography can make good use of graphs and survey information. Students can also use graphs to present what they have learned and can carry out surveys to ascertain answers to questions.

If you look at nearly any newspaper or textbook, you will find graphs. Because graphs can display a great deal of information in a more understandable form than a list of numbers, they are useful as important tools in teaching social studies (e.g., young children can "see" how big numbers are and they can "see" relationships among sets of data).

Block Graphs

The simplest form of graph is a **block graph**. Young children can actually construct these graphs by using objects like wooden blocks or coloured stickers. For example, if you were to graph the information about pets discussed in Chapter 15, your graph could show Grade 1's most popular pets.

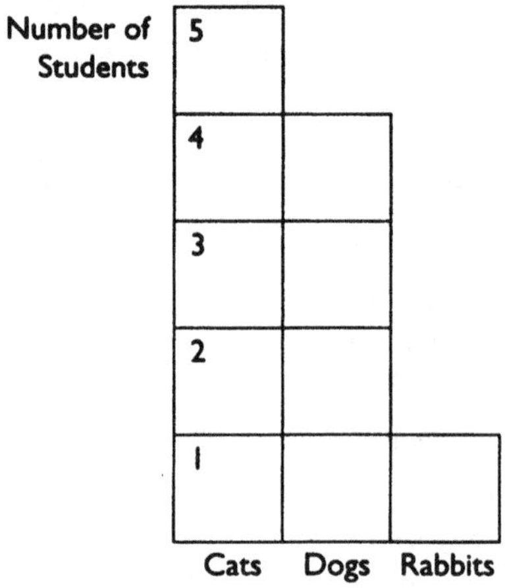

Most Popular Pets in Grade 1

Another way of building the graph is to use student names. Here is an example using the same popular pet information:

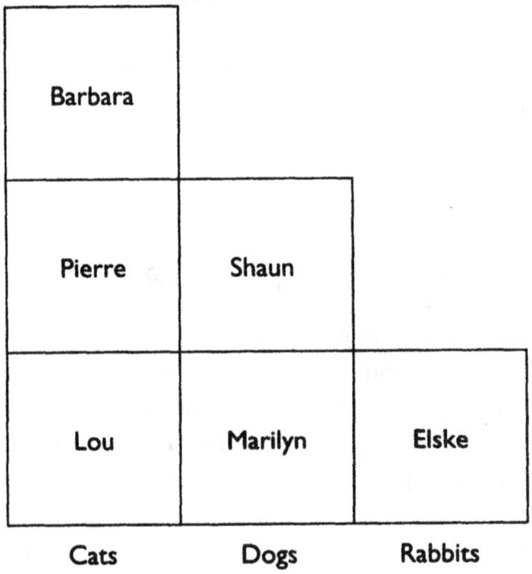

Student Choices of Most Popular Pets in Grade 1

Once students are able to make graphs and use equal intervals, they can draw the intervals or measures on graph paper with large squares.

Activity 19-H

In a group, have each member draw a graph based on the following information, each using a different scale on the population figure axis. What different impressions do you get with the different scales? If there is a large interval, do the differences between the cities seem larger than when the interval is smaller? How could advertisers or others use graphs to influence your beliefs and attitudes?

Population of metropolitan areas, 2002 (to nearest thousand):

St. John's	177 200
Halifax	363 200
Montreal	3 548 800
Toronto	5 029 900
Winnipeg	685 500
Regina	197 000
Edmonton	967 200
Vancouver	2 122 700

Line Graphs

Once children are able to "read" points on a line, **line graphs** can be introduced. The same information on a block graph can be used to show how a line graph is constructed. Here is an example using the popular pet data:

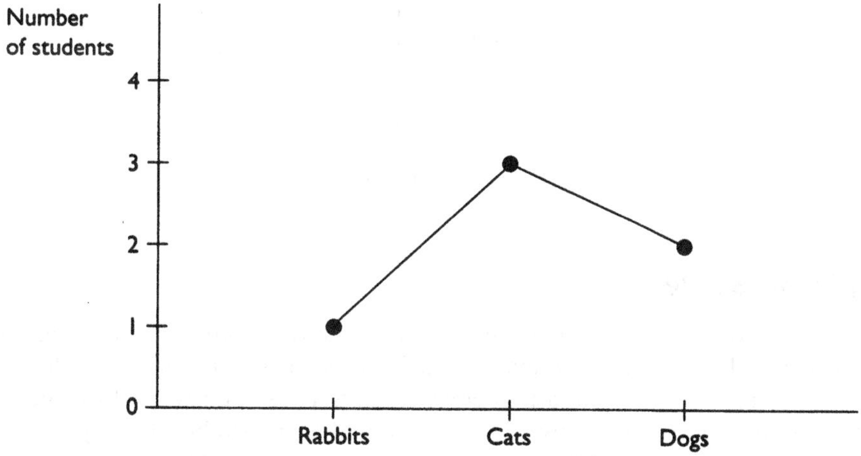

Most Popular Pets in Grade 1

Once students are able to construct graphs (look for interdisciplinary connections with math), they can learn to interpret them. Interpretation involves translating (reading) the data, as well as using data to draw inferences and create hypotheses, which can then be checked in reference to other information. Graphs can be created using any numerical data—temperatures in various cities in Canada, students' favourite television shows, population figures, results of traffic surveys, different kinds of products in a supermarket, and so on.

Circle Graphs

Circle graphs (also known as pie charts) are perhaps the most complicated types of graphs for children to comprehend, as they must first understand angles in a circle. Once they can comprehend the clock face they may be able to construct simple circle graphs, but more complicated ones may have to be left until the intermediate grades. A simple circle graph might consist of information related to how children spend their time in a 12-hour period between 8:00 a.m. and 8:00 p.m.

Complex circle graphs may show percentages. If this is done, children have to divide a 360° circle into 100 parts. Because this is fairly complex, it has to be left until ratio skills are mastered.

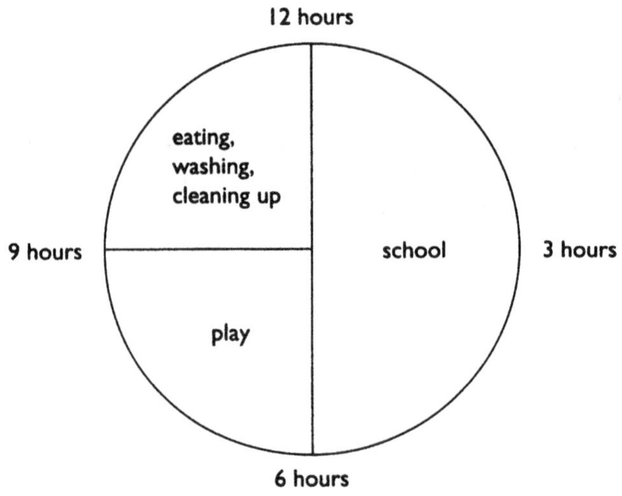

Opinion Surveys

Opinion surveys are not only an important source of existing information, but also a means of finding out new information. Surveys can be used to solicit people's opinions, beliefs, or knowledge about a particular topic. Suppose you wanted to find out more about your peers' attitudes toward the teaching of social studies. First, you would need to determine what question(s) to ask. For example, respondents could be asked an open-ended question, such as "How do you feel about teaching social studies?" Or they could be asked to choose from a list: "I feel ______________________ about teaching social studies."

happy *nervous* *frightened* *confident*

Another format that could be used is a scale.

	Strongly Agree	Agree	Undecided	Disagree	Strongly Disagree
I feel confident about teaching social studies					

Once the question(s) have been chosen and are judged to be clear and unambiguous, it is important to decide how to conduct the survey. This could be done by conducting individual interviews or by using a questionnaire. In both cases, you have to decide who is to be surveyed. If there are only a small number of potential respondents available, everyone could be questioned. However, if the population is large, you'll have to use a sample. To choose a *random sample,* you can put all the names of potential respondents in a hat and draw out as many names as you think is feasible to survey. You might also wish to find out information about the persons surveyed. For example, age might be important, or gender, or whether respondents are in the first, second, third, or fourth year of university. Once you have determined what demographic data you require, then you can solicit the permission of those being surveyed, conduct the survey, collect and classify the responses, and interpret the results.

Activity 19-I

Conduct a survey to determine the favourite TV shows, movies, books, video games, and/or hobbies of your peers. Design a questionnaire and collect, graph, and interpret the results. Design your survey to answer the following questions:

a) Do males and females differ in their entertainment preferences? Can you explain the differences or similarities?

b) Is age a significant variable in explaining entertainment preferences? Why or why not?

When students are conducting surveys, they should learn how to make sure the questions they ask are understandable and do not contain ambiguous words such as "some" and "many." They should divide complex questions into smaller, more specific ones and choose the best way of obtaining responses. After conducting the survey, they should interpret the results. Ensure that students recognize the limits of their data. For example, ensure they understand that people who volunteered to fill out their survey forms do not represent the entire population of the community being studied.

Activity 19-J

Design a lesson plan to teach students how to conduct a survey. State what the survey topic will be. Describe the steps you would follow in helping students to design a questionnaire, carry out the survey, tabulate the data, and interpret the results.

Other Activities

1. Select a book, movie, videotape, or instructional software program. Evaluate it using the questions discussed in this chapter. Is the material suitable for use in teaching social studies?

2. Select a series of visual images about one person, place, or event. Using the categories suggested by Werner, pose a number of questions that relate the images to each other. For example, if there are two pictures of the same person, then ask questions such as these: How do the images differ? How are they the same? What might account for the differences? What is the image maker trying to say in each image?
3. Locate an appropriate governmental or non-governmental organization in your area, and collect whatever information it has that would be useful in your teaching. Evaluate this information using the questions in this chapter.

Notes

1. For a list of specific sites, see D. Hicks and E. Ewing, "Bringing the world into the classroom with online global newspapers," *Social Education* 67:3 (2003), pp. 134–139.
2. A. Sears, "Enriching social studies through interviews," *History and Social Science Teacher* 25:2 (1990), pp. 95–98.
3. P. Clark, "Training the eye of the beholder: Using visual resources with elementary students," in R. Case and P. Clark, eds., *The Anthology of Social Studies, Volume 1. Issues and Strategies for Elementary Teachers* (Vancouver: Pacific Educational Press, 2008), pp. 290–305.
4. W. Werner, "Towards visual literacy," in A. Sears and I. Wright, eds., *Challenges and Prospects for Canadian Social Studies* (Vancouver: Pacific Educational Press, 2004). Also see W. Werner, "Reading visual texts," *Theory and Research in Social Education* 30:3 (2002), pp. 401–428.
5. W. Werner.
6. R. Pahl, "Digital technology and the social studies," in B. Massialas and R. Allen, eds., *Critical Issues in Teaching Social Studies* (Belmont, CA: Wadsworth, 1996).
7. C. Luke, S. De Castell, and A. Luke, "Beyond criticism: The authority of the school text," *Curriculum Inquiry* 13:2 (1983), pp. 111–127.
8. S. Gibson and R. McKay, "How research on the use of computer technology can inform the work of social studies educators," *Canadian Social Studies* 35:2 (2001). www.quasar.ualberta.ca/css/Css_35_2/research_computers_technology.htm
9. R. Pahl. See also H. Smits, "Is there a legitimate 'Luddite' response to technology in the social studies?" *Canadian Social Studies* 35:2 (2001). www.quasar.ualberta.ca/css/Css_35_2/legitimate_luddite.htm, and J. Dale, "A case against the internet," *Canadian Social Studies* 35:2 (2001). www.quasar.ualberta.ca/css/Css_35_3/FTinternet_resources.htm
10. J. Eaton, "The social studies classroom on the eve of the cyber century," *Social Education* 63:3 (1999), pp. 139–141.
11. S. Gibson, "Computer technologies as supportive tools to enhance learning in social studies," in A. Sears and I. Wright, eds., *Challenges and Prospects for Canadian Social Studies* (Vancouver: Pacific Educational Press, 2004), pp. 280–289.
12. R. Pahl.
13. S. Alessi and S. Trollip, *Computer-Based Instruction: Methods and Development,* 2nd ed. (Englewood Cliffs, NJ: Prentice-Hall, 1991).
14. For a description of this CD, see G. Reynolds, "Making Canadian history more inclusive through the multi-media: The peopling of Atlantic Canada," *Canadian Social Studies* 36:1 (2001). www.quasar.ualberta.ca/css/CSS_36_1/ARpeopling_atlantic_Canada.htm

15. C. Risinger, "Instructional strategies for the World Wide Web," *Social Education* 62:2 (1998), pp. 110–111.

16. Note that the evaluative questions posed about textbooks in Chapter 5 are also of concern here.

Glossary of Key Terms

Block graph—Data displayed in plane or three-dimensional shapes, usually squares, rectangles, or cubes.

Circle graph—Data displayed as segments of a circle. Also known as a pie chart.

Database programs—Computer programs that organize information into records and fields so that data can be easily stored, searched, and processed.

Line graph—Data displayed in line form.

CHAPTER 20

The New Media and Social Studies

In many ways, the study of social studies constitutes the study of change. As teachers, we ask students to consider the various ways in which society has changed and transformed itself throughout history. The study of geography in part explores the changing landforms, weather systems, and cultural conditions that constitute the world we live in.

Perhaps nowhere have we seen more dramatic social change than in the technologies we interact with in our daily lives. The last century has seen a veritable revolution in how children and adults learn and work, spend their leisure time, and interact with one another in society. And it is advancements and innovations in technology that have in large measure driven such changes.

Consider, for example, how the car has transformed notions of distance and speed, the design of cities, roads, and highways, and perceptions of wealth and status over the last century. What would our world look like today if the car had never been invented? Or consider the rise of the internet as a virtual social space that continually redefines work, leisure, and how we communicate and organize information with each new online innovation. How has your life been impacted by the way you interact with others using web-based technologies such as email, or popular social networking websites such as Facebook and MySpace?

Activity 20-A

Imagine a world where the World Wide Web does not exist. You only have to think back to the early 1990s to imagine such a time. Interview a family member who grew up without the internet. Ask them to reflect on how the advent of the internet has or hasn't changed their life, including how they work, learn, and have fun. As a follow-up to the interview, track the amount of time you personally spend online each day. How might you have spent that time were there no internet?

This chapter focuses on what is commonly referred to as the "new media," or sometimes **web 2.0**: blogs, wikis, and other web and computer-based technologies that organize information in new and pedagogically interesting ways.[1] The main difference between the traditional media discussed in the previous chapter and the new media discussed in this chapter is the added interactive element. When it comes to the new media, we don't just read, view, or otherwise "consume" information, as we do with, for example, newspapers and television. Rather, we respond to the information, leave our own stamp on it, or even remake the information as it is presented in its original form by rewriting it, adding to it, deleting from it, or transforming it in some other way.

The net effect of this added interactive element is to transform the means by which information is produced and consumed and, just as importantly, who has control over the information production process. Traditional media, in large measure, assume that there is a "producer" of media (a specialist, who is uniquely qualified to produce information) and a separate "consumer" of media (often a nonspecialist, who relies on the producer's specialized knowledge). The consumers of media (e.g., the subscribers to a newspaper) read the information that has been produced for them by the specialists (e.g., a group of experienced journalists).

The new media turn this relationship on its head. Everybody is potentially both a consumer and producer of the new media. Specialists and nonspecialists alike participate in the information production process. Moreover, the clear demarcation between the producer and consumer of information is dramatically scaled back. Indeed, in some cases the demarcation is totally nonexistent. This has important implications for how social scientists in the 21st century conduct their research. It also has important implications for how social studies is taught.

FROM CONSUMER TO PRODUCER

The social studies textbook you are reading right now was written by two social studies specialists, university professors who have taught social studies courses for many years. It is also a print publication that, once published, cannot be changed. Both of these facts clearly situate this textbook in the traditional media category, along with newspapers, television, billboard advertisements, and static noninteractive webpages.

Now imagine for a moment that this textbook was instead published online. Also assume that anyone who was interested (and signed up) would be permitted to contribute to the textbook. At least two things would happen. First, unless a deadline was set by the publisher, the book would never be finished and complete. Contributing authors would continually remake the textbook, making changes to the text even as others used the current version of the textbook in their social studies courses. Second, anybody would be able to contribute to the textbook, including social studies instructors, practising K–12 teachers, teacher candidates, and perhaps even parents and elementary and high school students. Each, of course, would bring a different experience of social studies to the online textbook. (A few might—intentionally or not—contribute factually incorrect information to the textbook, but other contributors would soon spot and correct that.) The textbook would essentially become an ever-changing document that was continually being remade and transformed through the efforts of many contributing authors all across Canada.

Activity 20-B

Fifteen years ago, before the popularization of the internet, the above scenario would surely have sounded like the stuff of science fiction. But the internet as a worldwide interactive telecommunications medium has in many ways democratized the information production process and made the possibility of publishing information online just a "point and click" away. Compile a two-column list of the pros and cons of opening up the information production process and having multiple authors contribute to an online social studies textbook.

One of the premises of the Web 2.0 technologies is that the information production process is enriched when it is opened up, made public, and interactive processes are utilized. These are just a few of the premises that underlie the new media technologies discussed in this chapter.

BLOGS

In its most basic form, a **blog** is similar to an online diary or journal. A blog chronicles the thoughts of one or more contributors. A blog may focus on a single topic (e.g., teaching social studies), or instead comprise a potpourri of ideas related to one's work and leisure activities, online travels, political leanings, plans for the future, and so on. Blogs are organized in reverse chronological order by posting date and typically feature a "Comments" section below each blog entry that allows readers to post their responses to specific entries and comment on the responses of others.

Some blogs are contributed to by only one person, who essentially "owns" the blog and determines whether readers are permitted to comment on the entries he or she posts. Other blogs, however, feature a community of contributors who each write entries for the blog and also comment on the entries of others.

What defines the new-media focus of blogs is the dialogue between contributors and visitors that a blog entry can generate. Far from serving as personal diaries or journals meant only for private consumption, individual and community blogs are purposefully designed to promote the public interchange of ideas. They are written to be read and commented on by others, who may in turn express agreement or disagreement with the bloggers' opinions, expand a blog entry in interesting ways, suggest resources for further information, or take the ideas expressed in a blog entry in entirely new directions.

Most blogs are updated at least weekly with new entries. Some are updated daily or even multiple times a day. Regular updates to a blog encourage visitors to return frequently. Sporadic updates dissuade visitors from returning on a regular basis (or at all). So, one of the basic challenges in maintaining a blog is to develop the discipline and routine needed to update the blog regularly. Community blogs (e.g., a class of students) have an advantage here because the onus to update the blog is on a group of contributors—not just one person—which takes the pressure off a single individual.

Getting Started with Blogs

Numerous easy-to-use online resources are available for teachers who wish to use blogs in the classroom. In addition to browsing the many educational blogs that are currently online, teachers can create and manage their own professional or class blogs hosted at dedicated blogging websites such as Blogger.com and TypePad.com. For greater security and control, school boards can instead install blogging software on the school board's network servers for exclusive access by teachers and students.

Blogs and Elementary Education

Many teachers encourage students to write journals as part of their language arts program. Interested students can instead be encouraged to maintain a blog that other students in the class can read and comment on. To keep parents abreast of what their students are studying in school, teachers can also keep their own online blog of what's going on in the class, alerting parents to upcoming events and special projects their children are currently working on.

As they experiment with blogs and learning, teachers should take advantage of opportunities to discuss with students important issues related to online privacy and the protection of personal information, undoubtedly a key social studies topic in the 21st century.

Start by asking the students to consider the differences between keeping a written private journal that is for personal use only and an online public blog that is purposefully designed for others to contribute to and comment on. Topics that may be appropriate for private journals may not be appropriate for public blogs. Students need to learn to make careful judgments about the information they post online.

Blogs and Social Studies

A community blog can effectively be used by a class of students to record and organize information related to a social studies topic they are researching in class. For specific subtopics in a unit on pioneer life, for example, students can be asked to write a series of blog entries that focus on pioneer clothing, food, transportation, and other subtopics they are learning about. By the end of the unit, the blog as a whole constitutes all the class has learned about the pioneer life topic. And because each blog entry is tagged with the name of the student who contributed it, the teacher can use the blog itself to assess each student's contributions. Students can also be encouraged to comment on the blog entries posted by others in the class. These too can be assessed by the teacher for levels of reading comprehension and critical thought.

Activity 20-C

Browse through the social studies curriculum guidelines for your province or territory. Which topics would be most suitable for a class blog? How would you go about implementing a class blog for one of these topics? What challenges might you face as you did so?

WIKIS

A **wiki** shares many elements that we commonly associate with encyclopedias, but unlike an encyclopedia it is generally not only specialists and experts who are invited to contribute to a wiki. Indeed, like blogs and unlike encyclopedias, wikis are typically public documents that invite interaction between contributors and visitors. However, unlike blogs, anyone can contribute to the main text and entries of a wiki. Visitors to a wiki are not limited to just leaving comments. Once they sign up to become contributors (even signing up may be optional), visitors can change the text in the main wiki entries themselves. They essentially become co-authors of the wiki content, similar to the scenario for an online social studies textbook that was discussed earlier in this chapter.

Many wikis exist on the web, covering all sorts of topics ranging from sports to science fiction. Most have a clear educational focus because, similar to encyclopedias, they aim to provide the most complete and accurate information possible on the specific topics they focus on.

By far the most well known (and, indeed, one of the first) wikis is Wikipedia.org, a nonprofit website that, unlike most wikis, aims over time to cover the breadth of human knowledge and the widest possible range of topics. As of this writing, Wikipedia has encyclopedic-like entries for more than two million English-language topics. (Wikipedia is also published in several other languages.) Thousands of contributors give freely of their time to contribute to, correct, and update the topic entries at the site. Anyone who visits and signs up can contribute to Wikipedia, but the changes, additions, and deletions a contributor makes are (in general) carefully tracked and vetted (and, if necessary, rolled back) by other contributors at the site.

The Wikipedia Phenomenon

On December 26, 2004, more than 175 000 people were killed in East Asia following an earthquake that triggered a massive tsunami, one of the deadliest in modern history. Nine hours after the event, a 76-word entry about the disaster appeared on Wikipedia.[2] Twenty-four hours later that entry had been edited more than 400 times and expanded to some 3000 words. Some of the first photographs of the devastation now accompanied the article, along with a chart that tabulated the casualties and graphics that explained the science behind tsunamis. Forty-eight hours after the "2004 Indian Ocean Earthquake" topic was first added to Wikipedia, the entry had been edited more than 1200 times and grown to over 6500 words. In the immediate aftermath of the tsunami, this Wikipedia entry was one of the most comprehensive online sources of information on the natural disaster.

Take a moment to get more familiar with how the exchange of ideas around a wiki entry works. Navigate to a popular (or contested) Wikipedia entry's "Discussion" page and read through the comments posted in response to the changes made to the entry over time. Identify the overriding criteria that are of most concern to those vetting the entry. The criteria for evaluating a Wikipedia entry typically include:

- *Factual accuracy*: Is the entry accurate, up to date, and long enough to do the topic justice? Is important information missing?
- *Neutrality*: Is there evidence of bias or opinion in the entry? Wikipedia is not an appropriate site for posting personal opinions or editorials about topics.
- *Original research*: Is there evidence of original research in the entry? Wikipedia is not an appropriate site for posting original research or original thought unless it has been published elsewhere in a reliable source. Content at Wikipedia must be attributed to reliable and published sources.
- *Citations*: Are there sufficient citations? Are the ideas that are cited attributed properly to respected sources of information?
- *Presentation*: Is the entry well-written and authoritative in tone? Is the introduction to the entry appropriate for the topic? Is the information that is presented well sequenced and organized into subtopics using subheadings?
- *Readability*: Can the entry be comprehended by laypeople (who are the persons most likely to be reading it)?

Also navigate to Wikipedia's "List of Policies" page and browse through the site's policies and procedures for contributors. In your opinion, has Wikipedia taken all the steps necessary to ensure the encyclopedic content at Wikipedia is as accurate and well-presented as possible? Now navigate to Wikipedia's "Schools' FAQ" page to learn more about integrating Wikipedia into the elementary instructional program.

Activity 20-D

Some university instructors do not allow the undergraduate students they teach to use Wikipedia as a reference source for the papers they submit in their university courses. They do not believe Wikipedia is accurate, scholarly, or trustworthy enough. Do you agree or disagree with this policy? Should this policy also apply to elementary and secondary school students?

Getting Started with Wikis

Numerous easy-to-use online resources are available for teachers who wish to use wikis in the classroom. Teachers can choose to create and manage a wiki that is hosted at a dedicated wiki-hosting website, such as MediaWiki.org and PBWiki.com. For greater security and control, school boards can instead install wiki software on the school board's network servers for exclusive access by teachers and students. Finally, because Wikipedia and other wiki websites encourage public participation, teachers and students can draw from and contribute content to existing wikis.

Activity 20-E

Locate a wiki entry on a social studies–related topic you plan to teach. Use the Wikipedia criteria outlined above to evaluate the entry you have chosen. Could this entry be effectively used to teach social studies to a class of elementary school students? Would the students be able to extract useful information from it? Why or why not?

Wikis and Elementary Education

A class of students can create brand-new wikis, contribute to existing wikis, or use Wikipedia and other wikis as resources for their research in social studies, science, language arts, and many other subject areas. For a specific topic the students are studying, choose a wiki website that is both pertinent and trustworthy in terms of its content. (Alternatively, restrict the webpages students can browse to a few bookmarked Wikipedia entries that you have vetted in advance.) Provide the students with a worksheet to complete and assess their reading comprehension and critical literacy skills as they pick out the main ideas in the wiki entries they are reading. Have a group of older students evaluate one or more of the contested entries at Wikipedia (contested entries are flagged at the top of the page) using the Wikipedia policies and procedures criteria noted earlier in this chapter.

Wikis provide users with a one-stop location for finding information about a specific topic on the web, but, as teachers, we also wish our students to develop research and inquiry skills related to searching, judging, and synthesizing information at various websites that bring different perspectives and expertise to a topic area. Creating a webquest is one learning strategy that teachers have found to be effective in this regard.[3] To create a **webquest**, a teacher

1. introduces the topic to be researched by students;
2. clearly defines the culminating task to be accomplished;
3. outlines the specific steps to be followed as students complete the webquest;
4. articulates how the students will be assessed; and
5. reflects on the results of the webquest.

Visit www.webquest.org for specific details on each of these steps.

Whether students are completing a webquest or doing other forms of online research, it is critical that teachers help them develop the ability to effectively judge the reliability of information they are perusing online. As they collect information, ask students to record (where possible):

1. the date the information was last updated;
2. background information about the author of the information (e.g., is he or she an expert on the topic?);
3. any outside sources of information that are cited and their reliability;
4. any evidence of overt bias or one-sidedness in the information; and
5. any other details that provide clues as to the information's reliability and validity.

Wikis and Social Studies

Creating a wiki from scratch can also serve as a helpful brainstorming exercise. Choose a topic and create a new wiki. Have a class of students collectively brainstorm all the subtopics that a complete wiki entry on the topic of pioneer life would ideally have. Insert these subtopics into a wiki you have created, and then have students work together over the course of the unit to gradually add to the wiki, watching it grow ever more comprehensive with each passing day.

Blogs vs. Wikis: What's the Difference?

One major difference between blogs and wikis is how they respectively organize and present information. The entries in blogs are nearly always presented in reverse chronological order (i.e., beginning with the most recent entry). A calendar to the side of a blog allows visitors to quickly navigate to a blog entry that was written on another day or month. A search box allows visitors to search for specific terms and keywords. A wiki, on the other hand, is organized alphabetically, similar to a dictionary or encyclopedia. Highlighted weblinks in the wiki entries themselves allow visitors to quickly navigate between related topics, similar to traditional webpages. Wikis also have prominently displayed search boxes that are used to quickly look up topics and keywords.

VIRTUAL WORLDS

Of all of the emerging internet technologies explored in this chapter, **virtual worlds** are arguably the most cutting edge and innovative, especially in terms of how they remake (and sometimes challenge) taken-for-granted patterns of social organization in the real world. Popular massively multiplayer online role-playing games (MMORGs), such as World of Warcraft, and popular virtual worlds, such as Second Life, aim in large measure to create a virtual 3D online social space where people can interact with one another, cooperate or compete, trade goods and services, and otherwise engage in everyday social practices—all in a virtual cyber-based world that exists only over a computer network.

Imagine you are moving to a new neighbourhood or joining a new community that you know very little about. The experience of getting to know the new neighbourhood and of getting to know long-time residents in the community to which you are moving is very similar to joining a virtual world. How will you present yourself to others? With whom will you first try to forge a social connection? What taken-for-granted social conventions are you expected to follow? These three questions (and no doubt many others) are just as relevant whether you are moving to a new community in the "real world" or joining an online virtual world that exists only as packets of data sent over a computer network.

Many individuals who are members of a virtual community maintain two identities—the everyday persona(s) and identity(ies) that they present to others in the real world, plus the persona(s) and identity(ies) of the character (also known as an avatar) that represents them in the virtual world to which they belong. Great care is typically taken by new members of a virtual world in creating the character that will represent them. Decisions such as the gender, ethnicity, and age of the character must be made (indeed, the character may not even be human); and, as is sometimes true in the real world, virtual characters may well be distinguishable in terms of the cultural group to which they belong by the type of clothing they wear, the hairdo they sport, or other markings. Most virtual characters also have an occupation (or craft) of some kind that determines what they spend much of their time doing in the virtual world. Just as in the real world, these two elements—what I look like and what I do—go a long way in framing the nature of the social interactions virtual characters have online.

Think about the above paragraph from the perspective of a social studies teacher. What overriding themes in the social studies curriculum are addressed by studying the experience of membership in a virtual community? Through their membership in a virtual world, we can help students to better understand the nature of social interaction, the formation of cultural identity, and the ways in which communities form and sustain themselves over time.

Activity 20-F

Virtual worlds are not the only web destinations where people invest time and energy in building up an online identity. Social networking websites, most notably Facebook.com and MySpace.com, have quickly emerged from obscurity to become some of the most popular destinations on the web, particularly for young people—including beginning teachers and upper elementary and secondary school students. Discuss the educational merits of social networking websites. Are they purely for fun and recreation or are there worthwhile pedagogical benefits to referencing Facebook and MySpace in the social studies classroom? *Hint:* Think about issues related to social identity and how we represent ourselves to others as you answer this question.

Getting Started with Virtual Worlds

There are a number of online initiatives related to virtual worlds that teachers and students may wish to tap into. Some virtual worlds, for example Webkinz (Webkinz.com), are clearly targeted to younger children, others to both children and adults. By far the most popular virtual world is Second Life (SecondLife.com). A number of schools and universities have created educational spaces in Second Life that others can visit and explore, but Second Life also hosts adult content that is inappropriate for children. The child-friendly online community known as Whyville (Whyville.net) is specifically designed for children and, just as importantly, it has a clear educational mission plus plenty of activities and resources for integrating the Whyville community into the elementary curriculum. For even younger children, Club Penguin (ClubPenguin.com) is a virtual world that was originally created by a Canadian company.

Virtual Worlds and Elementary Education

Students who are members of a virtual world can be invited to track what they do in the virtual world and to keep a diary (or blog) of their thoughts as they interact with others and engage in virtual world activities. Because time and distance are nonissues, students can meet and interact with other young people from all over the world. Whyville has a strong science mandate through its partnership with NASA and other scientific organizations. The virtual art galleries that exist in Whyville can also be visited by students and integrated into the visual arts curriculum. Finally, Second Life has a number of educational spaces that older students can safely visit. (Be sure to vet them in advance.) Second Life also routinely hosts virtual speeches, theatrical performances, and museum exhibits that students can attend. There is also a special version of Second Life for adolescents called Teen Second Life. For more virtual world activity ideas, refer to *Playing to Learn: Video Games in the Classroom,* written by one of the authors of this book.[4]

Virtual Worlds and Social Studies

In many ways, virtual worlds today function as brave new worlds—ongoing community experiments in new forms of social organization. Older students who are studying economics and trade in the real world can be challenged to track the flow of goods and services in a virtual world. They can map the topography of a virtual world in geography class, engage in a study of virtual archeology, or take on the role of architects as they design new virtual buildings in Second Life. Older students can also wrestle with the real-world ethical dilemmas posed by life in a virtual world (as, for example, some members of a virtual community push the boundaries of what is socially appropriate behaviour). For example, should the laws that govern acceptable behaviour in the real world also apply equally to the behaviour of virtual characters in virtual worlds? For that matter, should property rights and real estate law apply equally to virtual buildings and dwellings that are bought, sold, and leased in virtual worlds, even though they don't exist in the real world? Should virtual money be convertible to real-world dollars? Should virtual currency be traded on the stock exchange? Students who are in elementary school today may reasonably be expected to have to deal with legal and ethical questions such as these as they grow older, especially if virtual worlds become ever more popular, commonplace, and integrated into mainstream society as is predicted.[5]

DIGITAL VIDEO PRODUCTION

Chapter 19 touched briefly on the use of television broadcasts, movies, and other video productions in the classroom; the focus there was squarely on the classroom use of educational and commercial videos produced by movie studios, television networks, newscasters, and other professional video producers, such as the Canadian Broadcasting Corporation (CBC) and the National Film Board of Canada (NFB). Yet, in addition to viewing the professional video productions made by others, students can also create their own videos using relatively affordable digital video cameras and computer software.

Digital Video Hardware and Software Checklist

To produce a digital video in the classroom, the following equipment and software are required:

- digital video camera
- Windows or Macintosh computer
- FireWire connection or removable media card (for transferring videos from the digital video camera to the computer)
- digital video editing software (e.g., Apple iMovie or Windows MovieMaker)

The following equipment and software are recommended:

- camera tripod
- boom microphone
- document scanner
- music composition software (e.g., Apple Garageband, PG Music Band in a Box, or the open-source software Audacity (audacity.sourceforge.net))
- music and/or sound effects library
- MIDI keyboard (for creating music soundtracks)
- microphone (for adding narration)
- DVD editing software
- CD or DVD burner (for distributing videos to others)
- high-speed internet (for posting videos online)

As they produce a digital video, such as a historical documentary, have the students work through the same six stages of video production that professional moviemakers also work through:

1. *Preparation and exploration*: Students need time to learn to use the video production technology (especially the digital video camera and video editing software) without the added pressure of having to plan and carry out a full-blown digital video production. Have one group of students (the production team) learn how to use the digital video camera, tripod, and other production equipment while another group of students (the post-production team) learn to use the video editing software. Assign the two groups small, focused exercises that teach and reinforce the moviemaking skills they need to learn. Also introduce students to some basic moviemaking concepts and pre-production skills, such as storyboarding and the various types of camera shots (e.g., pans and zooms) used by professional filmmakers.
2. *Development*: Provide students with plenty of planning time to brainstorm ideas for their historical documentary, including the subject matter, sources of information, and filming locations. Where feasible, help students to brainstorm both primary and secondary sources of historical information. Encourage students to draw up a list of people they would like to interview on tape as part of the documentary. (Each of these people will first need to give their permission.) Potential interviewees may include experts on the subject itself and, in the case of recent history, witnesses to the historical

event under study. As students draw up plans for their historical documentary, it is absolutely essential that they continue to research the topic of the documentary itself. Students will require a solid understanding of their topic if the documentary is to be a success.

3. *Pre-production*: Before greenlighting (i.e., approving) their historical documentary and moving it into the pre-production phase, ask the student moviemakers to write a treatment (i.e., proposal) and also pitch their idea for a historical documentary to the rest of the class. Invite the class to provide feedback to the filmmakers. This feedback will help the filmmakers to structure and organize the scenes in their historical documentary, as, for example, they storyboard (i.e., sequence) each scene. For each storyboarded scene, the students will need to list the specific people, equipment, and props that are required. They will also need to write the narration and dialogue for the scene, and (where appropriate) scout for offsite locations to shoot. There are also a number of administrative tasks that need to be completed before the documentary can move into production. Permissions need to be secured. A budget (if applicable) needs to be approved. A shooting schedule needs to be worked out. Perhaps most importantly, the filmmaking role that each student will play needs to be agreed upon. In a historical documentary there is likely to be one or more narrators, interviewers, document collectors and scanners, researchers, and writers in addition to the requisite director(s), camera operators, and movie editors.
4. *Production*: A historical documentary will probably require both on-set and location filming. Interviews with historians and other experts are probably best conducted in the school on a constructed interview set, but the documentary will be enriched by location filming (where feasible) at the sites where the historical events under study actually occurred. Also consider filming the opening and closing narration sequences on location. Perhaps the most important rule when videotaping is to carefully log each shot that is captured in order to ease the video editing process.
5. *Post-production*: Once the raw footage has been captured, the editing begins. Students should begin by importing and cataloguing all of the footage they have captured, ensuring it is carefully organized and easy to find on the computer. A historical documentary is also likely to feature still images, scanned photographs, and other documents. These too need to be carefully catalogued. Editing and combining the video footage, still images, scanned photographs, and other media will take some time, especially for novice video editors. For longer productions, much patience and plenty of breaks are going to be needed. Most historical documentaries also require a narrated audio track plus the occasional music cue. Once the historical documentary is complete, beginning and end title credits should be inserted before the video is burned to CD or DVD or posted online.
6. *Distribution and marketing*: The final stage in the video production process is just as important as the first five stages if the students wish their historical documentary to be viewed by as many people as possible. Encourage the student filmmakers to think about a distribution plan for their documentary well in advance of the release of their video. They can burn video CDs or DVDs that can then be sold or distributed freely to others as gifts. (School-produced DVDs make for great fundraising projects.) Digital videos can also be posted online, perhaps at the school's website or at popular video hosting websites such as YouTube.com or TeacherTube.com. (Ensure the parents and guardians of every student who appears in the video have given permission for their

child to be in the video before distributing or posting a video online.) In terms of marketing, the students can design and post movie posters around the school that advertise their historical documentary. They can also compose a "radio advertisement" for broadcast over the school's public address system. For major productions, definitely consider hosting a movie premiere celebration to which other students and the filmmakers' parents and guardians are invited.

All but the most modest of movie projects move through the six stages described above. Smaller projects move quickly through them. Larger projects may require a commitment of several weeks or even months, but the rewards in viewing a completed video for the first time are well worth the effort. And the media literacy skills students learn in producing—not just viewing—a historical documentary or other type of video production are immense.

Podcasting in Schools

Podcasts are online audio or video broadcasts that listeners and viewers can subscribe to. When a new podcast is available from a source a listener or viewer subscribes to, it is automatically downloaded to the subscriber's computer or portable media player. In education, podcasts are routinely used in distance learning courses to distribute educational content to students. They can also be used by in-school teachers to augment or complement traditional classroom lessons. Students can also create their own podcasts about a subject they are studying in school, for example. The Culture Canada website maintains an up-to-date directory of Canadian podcasting links at http://podcast.culture.ca.

Digital Video Production and Elementary Education

Many students will be tempted to create a Hollywood-style action or comedy film using the video production skills they are learning in class. Encourage them to think about other genres as well. Students can create a 30-second TV commercial in which they pitch a real-life or fictional product to the rest of the class. They can dramatize a single scene from a novel they are reading in language arts class. They can videotape a school play or a dance sequence they have choreographed. They can interview each other or an expert on a subject they are studying in school. In science class, students can use stop-motion photography techniques to film a speeded-up view of a plant's growth over a couple of weeks.

Digital Video Production and Social Studies

There are also a number of video production genres that are directly relevant to social studies. Students can create a historical documentary in the style of Ken Burns or another documentary filmmaker. They can create a television newscast that reports on recent events that have occurred in the school, their local community, or the wider world. They can report on a real-world event as it happens, such as a protest march or an environmental cleanup campaign. They can film a historical "Historica Minute"–style mini-documentary (www.histori.ca/minutes) or a two-minute public service announcement for a worthy cause, or produce a persuasive video that attempts to convince other students to recycle their garbage. The public service announcement idea is a particularly good place to start since it is short and focused and there are plenty of existing public service announcements for students to draw on as examples.

MEDIA LITERACY IN THE 21ST CENTURY

This chapter began by asking readers to consider the dramatic social changes that came about during the 20th century, the direct result of the invention of the automobile. To the degree that the 20th century was defined in terms of developments in transportation (e.g., the invention of the car and airplane), it may well be rapid developments in telecommunications that come to define the changing social conditions of the 21st century. More specifically, it may be the ways in which information is collected, stored, archived, processed, shared, and communicated—increasingly in real time—that may come to frame much of the discussions related to how we learn, work, recreate, and interact with each other more generally.

The Canadian media theorist Marshall McLuhan (1911–1980) famously summed up his philosophy of media theory with the phrase "the medium is the message."[6] McLuhan meant that the medium itself—not just the content the medium communicates—plays a significant role in how information is perceived. The new-media technologies explored in this chapter—blogs, wikis, virtual worlds, social networking websites, and digital video—are all complex media that are right now being used to test out new approaches to communication and social interaction. Helping students to better understand these new technologies—and the still-to-be-invented online technologies that emerge in the decades that follow—is sure to become an important topic area for social studies as ever-increasing numbers of children and adults spend significant portions of their life learning, working, and recreating online.

Other Activities

1. Investigate the online policies and procedures that are in effect for the school board you are working for. What rules and protections are in place for students when it comes to browsing the web, emailing or chatting with one another, or posting information online?
2. Use the internet to research a) how many Canadians are currently online; and b) how this number compares to other industrialized and developing countries. What do you think the implications of these numbers are for Canada?
3. Maintain a blog that chronicles your professional growth over time as a teacher. Use the blog to reflect on your teaching successes, as well as the challenges you sometimes face. Invite other teachers to read and comment on your blog and share their own experiences.
4. Browse and then update the Wikipedia entry for a topic you are currently studying. Choose a Wikipedia entry that is too brief or otherwise in need of improvement.
5. Choose a grade level and a social studies topic. Which technology—blogs, wikis, virtual worlds, or video productions—could be most appropriately used to teach the topic? List your reasons for choosing the technology you did.
6. Imagine that a parent has asked you for advice on strategies for monitoring and protecting their children online. What specific advice would you give them?

Notes

1. D. Tapscott and A. Williams, *Wikinomics: How Mass Collaboration Changes Everything* (New York: Penguin Books, 2007).
2. W. Richardson, *Blogs, Wikis, Podcasts, and Other Powerful Web Tools for Classrooms* (Thousand Oaks, CA: Corwin Press, 2006).
3. A. Milson and P. Downey, "WebQuests: Using internet resources for cooperative inquiry," *Social Education* 65:3 (2001), p. 144. Also see P. Molebash and B. Dodge, "Kickstarting inquiry with WebQuests and web inquiry projects," *Social Education* 67:3 (2003), pp. 158–162. For an example of a webquest on ancient Greece, see C. Reid, R. Labonne, and S. Gibson, "Engaging students in problem solving using a Webquest," *Canadian Social Studies* 35:2 (2001). www.quasar.ualberta.ca/css/Css_35_2/ engaging_students_webquest.htm
4. D. Hutchison, *Playing to Learn: Video Games in the Classroom* (Portsmouth, NH: Teachers Ideas Press, 2007).
5. E. Castronova, *Synthetic Worlds: The Business and Culture of Online Games* (Chicago: University of Chicago Press, 2006).
6. M. McLuhan, *Understanding Media: The Extensions of Man* (New York: New American Library, 1964).

Glossary of Key Terms

Blog—An online diary, journal, or commentary website that is organized in reverse chronological order.

Virtual world—A computer-based simulated environment in which users interact with one another through the virtual characters that represent them.

Web 2.0—Second-generation forms of online interactivity and communication, including blogs, wikis, and social networking websites.

Webquest—A directed activity in which students read, analyze, synthesize, and evaluate information about a particular topic using various online sources of information.

Wiki—An online website that allows users to co-create, co-edit, and co-organize information related to one or more topics.

Websites for Part Four

Bibliographies

Canadian Children's Book Centre:
www.bookcentre.ca

Canadian Materials:
www.umanitoba.ca/cm/index.html

National Library of Canada:
www.nlc-bnc.ca

Journal

Canadian Social Studies (formerly *The History and Social Science Teacher*)

Lesson Plans

Alberta Social Studies Council:
www.ssc.teachers.ab.ca

British Columbia Social Studies Teachers' Association Lesson Plans:
http://bctf.ca/psas/BCSSTA/

Canadian Social Studies Lesson Plans:
www.canadaonline.about.com/cs/socialstudies/index.htm

Canadian Social Studies Supersite:
www.ualberta.ca/~jkirman

CanTeach:
www.canteach.ca/elementary/canada.html

Historica:
www.histori.ca/default.do?page=.tl_lessons

Historica Social Studies Resources (Reviewed by Teachers):
www.access.ca

Nova Scotia Social Studies Teachers' Association:
http://ssta.ednet.ns.ca

Ontario Association for Geographic and Environmental Education:
http://oagee.org

Ontario History and Social Sciences Teachers' Association:
www.ohassta.org

Media

Cable in the Classroom:
www.ciconline.org

Canadian Broadcasting Corporation:
www.cbc.ca

CBC Newsworld:
www.newsworld.cbc.ca

Infusing Technology into Alberta's New Social Studies Program:
www.wired-and-inspired.ca/ss

Media Awareness Network:
www.media-awareness.ca

National Film Board of Canada:
www.nfb.ca

SchoolNet News Network:
www.snn-rdr.ca

World Newspapers:
www.ipl.org/div/news, www.onlinenewspapers.com

Social Studies Resources (General)

Discovery Channel:
www.discoveryschool.com

National Council for the Social Studies:
www.socialstudies.org

Museumlink:
www.museumlink.com/canada

CHAPTER 21

Writing a Unit Plan

Here, we synthesize all the material covered in this book into the framework for a unit plan. We need to have a unit framework so that we, and our students, have a good sense of what the result of our teaching is supposed to be. A unit framework gives us a map of where we want to go and how we intend to get there—and without a map we can get hopelessly lost. By careful planning we can ensure we have covered the important aspects of the chosen topic, that it is organized in a logical way, and that we have considered all the relevant curriculum and instructional variables. In practice, **unit planning** is not a linear procedure. Although the rationale, objectives, subject matter, instructional activities, and assessment must all be logically related, this does not mean we have to develop a unit in this order. We could start with the desired results of a social studies assessment, determine what students do not seem to know but should know, and use the assessment instrument as the basis for planning our instruction. Or, we may determine that we really want students to learn how to use a decision-making strategy and choose the subject matter that best matches this strategy. This chapter is written on the assumption that although we often have definite plans for a particular topic, there are times when we start out with very few clear ideas.

THE CONTEXT

Choose a specific grade level and topic. With reference to the social studies curriculum guidelines, answer the following questions:

1. What does the curriculum guide suggest that students at this grade level should learn?
2. Do I think this would be relevant, interesting, significant, and worthwhile?
3. Would it be within the students' capabilities?
4. If the curriculum guide allows me to choose my own topic, is there a skill, sensitivity, concept, problem, issue, or generalization that seems especially relevant to me and/or my students—for example, a current event? If there is, can I give positive answers to the questions above?
5. What is my basic philosophy? What are my basic aims? How can I ensure they are met?

THE RATIONALE

Having chosen the topic, write down some good reasons for teaching it. You may think of other reasons as your planning becomes more specific. Here is an example for a Grade 2 unit on the **community**:

> **Topic:** The Community (Grade 2)
>
> **Rationale:** The curriculum guide suggests this topic be studied in Grade 2. Given that students interact constantly with their community, it is a significant topic. It provides opportunities for students to learn about the interactions of people and people's interactions with the environment. This knowledge can then be built upon when students learn about other communities in the world. Students can begin to realize that a community is a microcosm of the wider world, and many of the concepts that are significant in studying communities are useful in other contexts. A community study can provide the concrete experiences that young students require. Also, a variety of skills can be developed—simple mapping, graphing, interviewing, accessing and evaluating information on websites, creating projects to display student work, and so on. All these skills are significant in the further pursuit of social studies goals and

in everyday life. Students at this grade level are capable of pursuing the topic and resource materials are easily found in the community.

THE MAJOR GOALS

In broad terms, what are your goals? Will they include subject matter knowledge, information gathering and reporting skills, intellectual standards, personal and social values, and citizenship action? For example:

Goals for the Study of a Community

Subject matter knowledge: Knowledge of the community (history, geography, and people); how people meet basic needs and how they are interdependent.

Information gathering and reporting: Getting information on field trips, from guest speakers, from the internet, and by interviewing people in the community; reporting by using simple maps, displays, and charts.

Intellectual standards: Accuracy of information.

Social and personal values: Appreciation for interdependence and responsibility to maintain interdependent relationships.

THE SCOPE OF THE SUBJECT MATTER

If these broad goals do not indicate exactly what subject matter should be studied, then it may be helpful to analyze it into subtopics. Given that the topic of **interdependence** in the community is broad, what subject matter could be studied? Here, a web is useful.

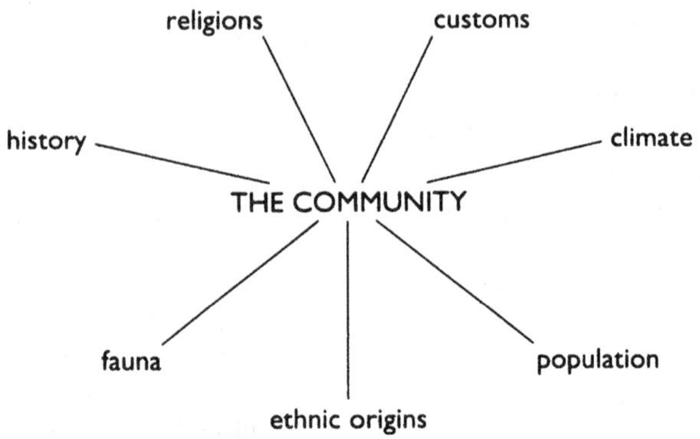

It may be impossible to study all these subtopics, so a decision has to be made as to which one(s) will be included. Rather than trying to cover everything and thereby creating a kind of hodgepodge unit, choose a focus. This may already be evident in your statement of goals. If it is not, then consider emphasizing disciplinary or interdisciplinary knowledge and organize your unit around a theme, concept, generalization, or issue, or as an inquiry, project, narrative, or problem to be solved.

Once you have identified a focus, then a rationale has to be provided for it. For example, if you decide to tackle "multiculturalism" or "pollution" as your overall topic, you have to decide what content is suitable for your particular grade or age level. If you were to select the concept of "change" as your focus, your rationale might look like the following:

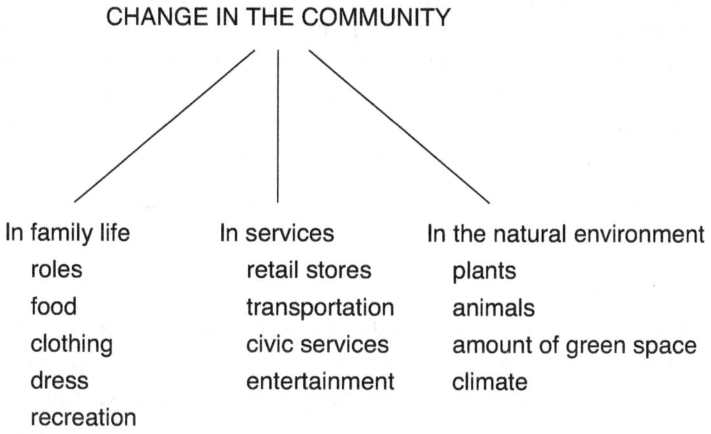

Topic: Change (Grade 3)

Rationale: Change is constant, and students should begin to consider how and why change occurs and what influence they can have on the process of change in particular contexts. Students experience change in themselves (in growth, in learning, in how they behave) and in their community (new buildings, more pollution, etc.). For this age group, both contexts are suitable vehicles through which to begin to comprehend the concept of change.

Now choose the content that will exemplify your focus. A way to focus on this is to have students decide what improvements have been made in the community since it was first established and what improvements they would like in the community in the future. For example:

Topic: Improving my community (Grade 3)

	Community in the 1900s	Community today	Future improvements
Civic services (police, firefighting, etc.)			
Schools			
Stores			
Recreation facilities			
Etc.			

THE OBJECTIVES

Throughout this exercise, more specific objectives are likely to be coming to the fore. At what stage you actually specify and articulate these objectives is a matter of judgment. Some educators like to articulate them early on; others like to state them after they have outlined a broad framework for the unit.

Once choices have been made concerning the major goals and framework for the unit, then objectives can be stated in more specific terms. For example, if the objective is "to learn what tasks the mayor of the community performs," it can be expressed as follows: "The student will correctly identify a number of tasks performed by the mayor." Suppose our topic is the history of the local community. We might write the objective as "Students will know about the history of the community." But this is too vague to be useful. If the objective is unclear, then so too will be our assessment of student learning. Thus, we need to specify objectives as clearly as possible. In the above example, we might write our objective as, "Students will research the history of the community and draw an accurate timeline listing 10 major events."

Activity 21-A

Specifying your objectives:

a) "Students will know about the geography of New Brunswick." Brainstorm three specific objectives that would relate to "knowing about the geography of New Brunswick."

b) "Students will understand the economic impact of the St. Lawrence Seaway on the provinces of Quebec and Ontario." State three specific objectives that would express this major goal in measurable terms.

c) "Students will learn about the Roman Empire." State three specific objectives that would express this major goal in measurable terms.

Having identified knowledge objectives, you are in a position to determine the information-gathering, information-processing, and information-evaluating tools necessary to attain the knowledge objectives. For example, if students are to use an atlas to find the distance between Montreal and Paris, they must locate the appropriate map and use the index and reference system to find Montreal and Paris. Then they must use the map scale and a suitable measuring instrument to ascertain the distance between the two cities. If students are to use the internet to access information, they must be able to log on to a site or use a search engine, locate relevant sites, and show that they can navigate through them, correctly index the website(s) they use in a presentation, and state why they think the website(s) they use are reliable sources of information.

Activity 21-B

For each of the following objectives, identify the information-collecting and information-processing tools the student would be practising or learning.

Objective: Using plans and pictures of Louisbourg, the student will write a description of the fortress.

Objective: Using library resources, the student will draw five means of transportation used to get from the British Columbia coast to the Cariboo goldfields in the 1860s.

Objective: In groups, students will tour the local supermarket and compose a list of jobs performed there.

Social studies is concerned not only with objectives about "knowing that" and "knowing how," but also with dispositions, sensitivities, and appreciations. These objectives are often labelled "affective" objectives. Affective objectives state how we wish students to be disposed toward something, or what we wish students to value. In the objectives above, we may wish students to *appreciate* the hardships suffered by gold miners travelling to the Cariboo goldfields. In studies of cultures or ethnic groups, we will want students to *respect* cultural differences. In decision making, we will wish students to be *willing* to consider points of view that differ from their own. In studies of disadvantaged people, we would like students to *feel empathy* for others. It is often difficult to write these objectives in specific terms. For example, we could specify that the demonstration of a positive attitude toward disadvantaged people could consist of giving money to a charitable organization, but this is only one aspect of what we might consider "a positive attitude." In the case of appreciating the hardships of gold miners, we might interpret a student's statement that "I'm glad I'm not him" as an indication the student has some appreciation for the hardships faced by others. When stating affective objectives, you should have some idea of what constitutes successful performance, even though your criteria are "subjective."

THE SEQUENCE

Having obtained a broad perspective on the scope of the unit, you can now put it into a logical sequence.

1. What kind of prior knowledge will students need to have? Do specific concepts and skills need to be taught before the unit is actually presented?
2. Would it be best to start with a topic students are familiar with or something they are not familiar with? How will I start the unit so that students are motivated? (For ideas, see the next section.)
3. Could another topic in a different subject area act as a springboard for this unit?
4. What would be a logical sequence once a starting point has been ascertained? What will my lesson sequence look like so that the major objectives are focused upon and there are a variety of instructional strategies? How will I integrate special needs students?
5. Can the unit be sequenced so that the information or skills covered relate to other subject areas?
6. How can assessments be sequenced so I can ascertain if students have achieved the major objectives?
7. How can the unit be organized so that the major findings are synthesized?

Openers

Whatever the sequence, there needs to be an opener so that students are motivated and excited about the unit. Stating "Today, class, we're going to study X; open your textbooks to page Y" is unlikely to motivate students. Below are some ideas that are designed to spark student interest.

Activity 21-C

Study the photographs that follow and answer the questions below.

a) In what country were photographs 1 to 4 taken?

b) What led you to this conclusion? What clues did you use?

c) On the basis of your experience with the photographs below, predict how well you will do in identifying photographs of the above country X from a number of photographs that may or may not be of country X.

d) Which of photos 5 to 7 are of country X? Consult the Answers section.

Why were you successful or unsuccessful in identifying these photos?

Photo 1

Photo 2

Photo 3

Photo 4

Photo 5

Photo 6

Photo 7

The above procedure is an adaptation of the **discrepant data technique**. First, we identify a stereotype that we think students hold. In this case, the stereotype was that certain scenes/objects/people are without a doubt "Canadian." Second, we reinforce this stereotype by showing pictures that fit the stereotype. Third, we introduce discrepant data that do not fit the stereotype, so that, fourth, students are led to re-examine the stereotype and formulate a new generalization.

Suppose children have stereotypic views about the continent of Africa (e.g., only black people live there, or all the people are hunters or farmers). Show the students pictures of people who live in Africa that fit the students' stereotypes and ask them, "Who are these people?" and "Where do they live?" Then, having ascertained that all the pictures are of people who live in Africa, say, "I'm going to show you some more pictures and I want you to tell me where *these* people live." Display pictures of people who live in Africa that do not fit the stereotype. If students incorrectly identify the pictures (and in our experience they will), then state that all the pictures were of people who live in Africa. The new information will have to be reinforced during your unit, as some students may be dubious. As a follow-up to this activity, it may be helpful to also show the students pictures of people from a variety of cultural backgrounds who live in the same country or community.

Another opener is to show students an object or picture of something unknown to them. Ask students to guess what the object is by asking questions that demand a *yes* or *no* answer only; i.e., the question "What is it?" is not allowed, but the question "Is it an X?" is allowed.

Activity 21-D

Using the above technique, try to ascertain from your instructor or a peer who has looked at the answer what the picture below depicts. (The answer appears in the Answers section.)

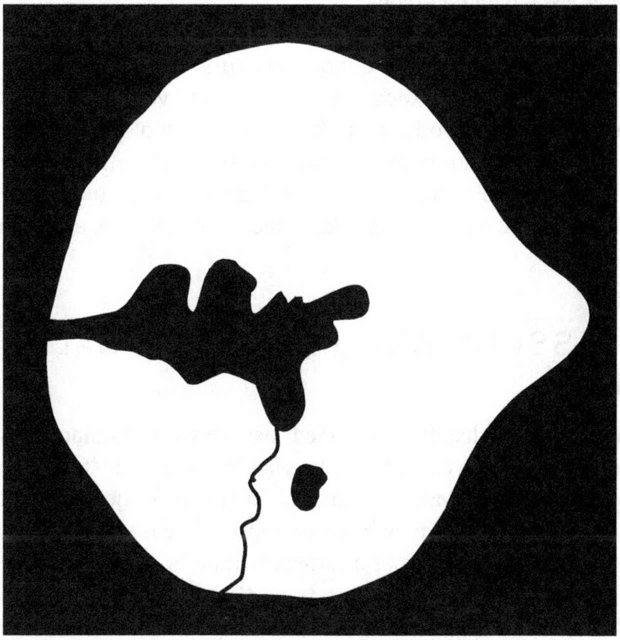

All these ideas are meant to puzzle students. The next idea can be a real puzzler if you use it when introducing a unit on culture in the intermediate grades.

Activity 21-E

Read the following passage and answer the question "Who are the Nacirema?" (The answer appears in the Answers section.)

The Nacirema[1]

The Nacirema inhabit a large area of the North American continent. Because of their belief that the human body is ugly and that its natural tendency is toward illness, everyone tries to avoid disease and ugliness by various ceremonies performed in a shrine. Every house has one or more of these shrines and people are judged to be wealthy if they have a lot of shrines in their homes.

The ceremonies performed in the shrine are private and secret. The most important thing in the shrine is a box, or chest, built into the wall. In this chest are kept many charms and magical liquids; no native believes it is possible to live without them. Most of these charms and magical liquids are obtained from medicine people who are rewarded with large gifts. However, the medicine people decide what ingredients should go into the liquid or charm by writing them down in a secret language that only medicine people and herbalists understand; it is the herbalist who, for another large gift, provides the actual charm.

Even after the charm has had its effect, it is not thrown away, but is placed in the charm box in the shrine. The charm box is, therefore, filled to overflowing, often with useless junk. The natives therefore must believe that old charms still protect them.

Beneath the charm box is a small basin. Every day each member of the family enters the shrine, bows his or her head before the charm box, mixes different sorts of holy water in the basin, and performs a washing ceremony.

There is also a mouth ceremony, when a bundle of small sticks is put in the mouth along with certain magical powders, and the bundle moved in a very specific way. Despite this magic to protect the teeth, once or twice a year the natives visit a holy mouth person. He or she, with a number of probes, prods, and sharp, pointed tools, puts the native through a painful ceremony. The native's teeth are prodded and decay is removed. Magic materials are put into holes and sometimes whole teeth are pulled out in a torturous way. All this is done because the natives believe that they will lose their friends unless they have these ceremonies performed.

SPECIFIC LESSONS AND INSTRUCTIONAL STRATEGIES

Once the sequence for a unit has been planned, we are ready to plan the specific lessons. Here, we draw upon the objectives and decide what instructional strategy or strategies will best meet each objective. If we want students to develop a framework for the unit, then an emphasis on concept development may be most appropriate (see Chapter 6). If central concepts need to be grasped, then concept attainment may be the best strategy (Chapter 6). Having students inquire into particular questions (Chapter 7) is a good way for them to learn specific information, to apply their information-gathering skills to new topics, and to develop intellectual standards (Chapter 8). Other ways could include teacher talks, using videos or DVDs, or reading stories (Chapter 5). Creating generalizations might involve the use of web diagrams (Chapters 4 and 14). Focusing on values may involve decision making and using simulation games (Chapters 15, 16, 17, and 18). For any of the above, students could present their conclusions in a variety of ways (Chapter 8).

Assessment

As a final component of a unit, we need to ascertain whether or not students have achieved the objectives (see Chapter 22). To do this, it is critically important that we go back to our objectives, state how each should be assessed, determine which ones should be formally tested, and design appropriate assessment instruments.

Example of a Unit Plan

What follows is an example of a unit plan in which the focus is on the community and the concept of **interdependence.** The unit includes a variety of lessons based upon strategies presented in previous chapters.

Topic: Community Interdependence (Grade 2)

Rationale: Interdependence is a key concept in social studies and can be explored by studying the interactions between the student and the community. By studying interdependence, students can see how their actions affect others and how the actions of others affect them. This knowledge will help them realize the interdependent and interconnected nature of the world and how they can help (or hinder) progress toward a better world.

Major Goals:

1. Subject matter knowledge: knowledge of (a) the community and how the concept of interdependence applies; and (b) the services and resources in the community and how the community interacts.
2. Information gathering and reporting: collecting information from print sources, field trips, and interviews; reporting in print and pictorial media.
3. Intellectual standards: accuracy and plausibility of inferences.
4. Social and personal values: appreciating the importance of interdependence and the responsibilities involved in maintaining it.

Scope and Sequence: Our scope is bounded by the major goals and by the abilities of the students. We have to study at least some of the people who live and work in the community and how they are interdependent. We will utilize interdisciplinary knowledge and will organize our unit around the concept of interdependence. Our sequence will be based on using the most familiar information first.

Because the school is a major focus and the teacher is an important person in the students' lives, one example of interdependence will be a study of the interactions between the students, the teachers, and the rest of the school. We would then like students to see how we are dependent on many different people and the natural environment and learn about the ways in which we interact with others. Depending on the time available, we might also look at other groups or individuals in the community and ascertain how interdependent they are. If there are a variety of cultural groups in the community, we might want to study how they maintain interdependent relationships. We could finish with students agreeing upon improvements for their community and how these improvements could benefit people's interactions with each other and with the natural environment.

Specific Objectives: This scope and focus lead to objectives that can be more specific when choices are made concerning what peoples and aspects of the natural environment are to be studied.

1 Students will describe the jobs and roles of teachers and other people in the community.
2. Students will state why these jobs and roles are important to the community and how these jobs and roles relate to the concept of interdependence.
3. Students will explore the natural environment and state how the community interacts with it. They will evaluate the ways in which the community interacts with the natural environment.
4. Students will decide on major improvements for their community.

Planning the Episodes of the Unit

We are now in a position to plan the individual episodes of the unit. We need to know the

- subtopic and/or questions
- information or resources that students will draw upon[2]
- activities students will complete
- way(s) in which students will present their information
- ways we will end the lesson
- instruments we will use to assess students, and
- opportunities for integration with other subject areas.

The following examples consist of "bites" of content that have some structural unity. It might be possible to teach a particular episode in one lesson of 30 to 45 minutes, or a particular episode might entail several lessons.

Episode 1

Topic: Perceptions of the Community

Objectives: Students will draw a map of their immediate area and be able to explain why their maps are similar to and different from other student maps. They will accurately locate their community on three different maps, including one of Canada.

Question: What does my community look like and where is it in relation to other places?

Information: Maps of the community and the province in which the community is located. Map of Canada.

Activities: Have students draw a map of either their immediate home area or their route to school. Ask students to share these with each other. Have them discuss how they feel about their community. Look at a simple map of the community and have students assess the maps they created. Have them discuss some of the similarities and differences. Why did students omit certain places depicted on the map of the community and why did they include others not shown on the map? Use other maps to show where the community is in relation to other places with which students are familiar. Have students locate their community on several different maps (of the immediate area; of the region; of the province or territory; of Canada; and, if appropriate, of the world).

Presentation: Student-drawn maps. Students' lists of how their maps are similar to/different from the actual map.

Culmination: Display student community maps and maps of the location of the community. Ensure students understand that maps differ in what they show and that their community can be located on a number of different maps.

Assessment: Evaluate each student's map and lists of similarities for accuracy. Give them a simple map of their area and have them locate their home, school, or other landmark correctly. Give them a map of Canada and have them locate their community.

Episode 2

Topic: The Community

Objectives: Students will identify the attributes of a community and correctly identify examples of community from non-examples.

Question: What is a community?

Information: Pictures and descriptions of communities and non-communities; list of attributes of a community.

Activities: Have students look at pictures and read descriptions of community (a picture of a park with many people interacting with each other—playing games, talking, etc.; a description of a high-rise apartment building where everyone knows everyone else and residents help each other out; a picture of a neighbourhood showing a community centre with a list of the services it provides and the volunteers who offer them; and a classroom where students are helping each other learn. Then have students look at pictures and read descriptions of non-communities (an apartment building where residents do not know each other and don't help each other; a group of people waiting at a bus stop—there is no interaction between them; a park with one person walking her dog on the grass and another jogging on the path). Generate a list of attributes of a community.

Presentation: Students draw a picture of a community.

Culmination: Students write a list of the attributes of "community."

Assessment: Students are given two pictures and descriptions of a community and one picture and description of a non-community. They must correctly identify them.

Episode 3

Topic: School

Objectives: Students will identify the consequences of not having to attend school and generate a list of criteria to evaluate the consequences.

Question: What would happen if you didn't have to attend school? Would the consequences be desirable or undesirable, or a mix of both?

Information: Student hypotheses. Students' or teacher's list of consequences.

Activities: Discussion. Trace the possible consequences and discuss the plausibility of each. Talk about the desirability of each consequence and what would happen to other people if the consequence actually occurred—introduce the concept of interdependence. Create a list of criteria (freedom to do whatever you like, need to be educated to get a job, etc.). Have students draw a picture of one consequence (for themselves, family, teachers, retailers, recreational facilities, etc.) and state how it would impact on other members of the community (including their parents or guardians, and any siblings) and why it would be desirable and/or undesirable.

Presentation: Class mural showing consequences and decisions about their desirability.

Culmination: Discussion about the mural and a synthesis of the consequences of not attending school.

Assessment: Assess each student's drawing to ascertain if the consequence is plausible and whether his or her reasoning about the desirability/undesirability is reasonable given the criteria generated in class.

Episode 4

Topic: Interdependence in the School

Objectives: Students will interview members of the school community and list the tasks they perform, and diagram the interactions between students, teachers, and other members of the school community in order to create a general statement about their interdependence.

Question: How are people in the school dependent upon one another?

Information: Roles of various school personnel. Jobs performed by males and females.

Activities: Interviewing. Listening to people in the school explaining what they do. Composing a list of tasks performed by school personnel and noting whether these tasks can be performed by both males and females.

Presentation: Diagram showing how students, teachers, and others interact within the school community.

Culmination: Students create a general statement about the interdependence of members of the school community.

Assessment: Use a checklist to judge students' interviewing skills. Look at the list of tasks and assess for accuracy. Assess the general statement for its accuracy.

Integration: Stories about schools.

Episode 5

The next episode would focus on other members of the community and how they are interdependent. For example, students could visit the police station, interview officers and staff, and write or draw the tasks they perform. They could then draw a web of these tasks and show how they relate—could police officers do their jobs without each other, their support staff, and the support of the community and general public? Students could create a radio interview with one student playing a police officer and the other students asking questions. Students with teacher help could create a podcast.[3] Other roles could be explored such as retail workers, City Hall staff, health care personnel, and so on. Throughout this episode students could be discovering how gender and ethnicity relate to employment and how the concept of interdependence is manifested.

Episode 6

Topic: The Local Environment

Objectives: Students will study their local environment and create a general statement about the interdependence of the community with the natural environment.

Question: How does the community interact with the natural environment?

Information: Pictures generated by both teacher and students, written descriptions, found objects that it is permissible to collect, tape or video conversations between students about their reactions on field trips, and classroom study of local areas—park, beach, forest, river, community garden, etc.

Activities: Collecting information in many forms from field trips; carrying out an environmental assessment (see Chapter 13); discussing and assessing how the community and natural environment are interdependent.

Presentation: A web diagram showing how the community interacts with its environment.

Culmination: Students use the diagram to synthesize the interactions between the community and natural environment and write a general statement.

Assessment: Field trip work is assessed for accuracy and relevance; web diagrams are checked for number of correct links and the complexity of these links—for example, does the student note that if garbage is left in a park that this can affect other park users, city staff, wildlife, pets, plants, and so on? Do students note how the river is used not only for recreational purposes but also as the source of the community's water supply?

Episode 7

Topic: Improving Our Community

Objectives: Students will identify improvements they would like in their community and will generate a list of criteria for assessing them.

Question: How could our community be improved and how could we bring about these improvements?

Information: All that has been gathered so far about the community.

Activities: Brainstorming a list of improvements to the community that students think desirable and who these would most affect; generation of a list of criteria for evaluating an improvement; groups discuss the improvements they want and present a list of prioritized improvements with accompanying arguments to the rest of the class.

Culmination: All the wished-for improvements are displayed and the class votes on a final list.

Assessment: Have students in pairs look at each others' list of improvements and using the criteria generated check all the criteria that each improvement meets.

Extending and Modifying the Plan

The unit could be extended by studying a different group (if appropriate, a First Nations or other cultural/ethnic group), noting interdependent relationships. Students could examine the history of the community noting how people interacted in the past (see Chapter 10); they could engage in a global education strategy by finding out the origin of the food they eat and other consumer goods they use (see Chapter 17); they could engage in a simulation game in which they have to decide where a new highway should be located in the community (see Chapter 15); and throughout the unit they could be using and evaluating information from numerous sources (see Chapters 19 and 20).

For various reasons, including unforeseen developments, most plans have to be modified in their actual implementation. For instance, a video may be unavailable on the day it is needed; students have to be taught (or retaught) something before the unit can continue; or (as happens frequently) students find something in the lesson very interesting and so you decide to spend more time on this topic than on the intended one.

This chapter has presented one way of unit planning—but not the only way. Students can also be involved in planning. For example, after a visit to the police station, students could pose their own questions, carry out their own research, and make a presentation. They might choose to write a poem about the police, or to find out how many police shows there are on TV. Students could read laws that affect their lives and rewrite them in language that a Grade 2 student could understand.

Activity 21-F

For this activity, choose a unit plan to work with. Answer the following questions:

1. Are the objectives, content, instruction, and evaluation procedures congruent with each other? Is each objective addressed in the teaching plan? Are students assessed on each objective?
2. Is the sequence logically presented?
3. Do the lessons focus specifically on the major concepts, or is it taken for granted that students will know what the major concepts mean?
4. Are there a variety of activities for students to carry out? Do these activities actively engage students?
5. Are there opportunities for students to work in groups? Is it assumed that students will know how to work in a group, or are there specific activities to help them do this?
6. What skills are students supposed to be able to display by the end of the unit? Is it assumed that students will develop these skills naturally, or are there specific lessons to teach them?
7. What resource materials are required? Are these provided? If not, are they readily available? Are these materials up-to-date, accurate, and written so that students are engaged with the content?
8. Do you think the unit is worth teaching? Give your reasons.

Unit Assessment

In addition to assessing how well students have achieved the objectives in the unit, it is important that teachers evaluate the unit itself, especially if they intend to teach it again. Below is a list of suggested questions:

- Was the topic worth teaching?
- Did students achieve the objectives?
- Did students find it interesting?
- Could students cope with the unit? Was it within their capabilities or too advanced or too easy?
- Were the resource materials appropriate?
- Was I interested in teaching the unit?
- Were the objectives congruent with how the unit was taught and assessed?
- Was the sequence logically presented?
- If I taught the unit again, what, if anything, would I change?

Other Activities

1. Choose a chapter from an elementary school social studies textbook and develop a unit plan outline where the organizer is a generalization.
2. Create a critical thinking unit on one of the following questions:
   a) Should children in elementary school be allowed to vote in civic elections?
   b) Who were the first people in North America and how did they get here?
   c) Whose account of the Battle of the Plains of Abraham is most reliable—the French or the English?

Notes

1. Adapted from H. Miner, "Body ritual among the Nacirema," *American Anthropologist* 58:3 (1956), pp. 503–507.
2. For a discussion on using community resources see P. Clark, "Bringing the world in: Using community resources in elementary social studies," in R. Case and P. Clark, eds., *The Anthology of Social Studies, Volume 1. Issues and Strategies for Elementary Teachers* (Vancouver: Pacific Educational Press, 2008), pp. 270–282.
3. T. Vincent and M. Van't Hooft, "For kids, by kids: Our city podcast," *Social Education* 71:3 (2007), pp. 125–127.

Glossary of Key Terms

Community—A social group of any size that usually lives in a specific locality and shares some common characteristics such as heritage, culture, religion, government, ethnicity, or occupation.

Discrepant data technique—A technique in which a stereotype is identified and reinforced; then data that do not fit the stereotype are introduced so that a new generalization is formulated.

Interdependence—A concept of interaction and interconnectedness whereby one person's (or group's) actions affect another person (or group) and vice versa.

Unit planning—Deciding on the objectives, scope, and sequence of lessons, resources, teaching and learning activities, and assessment tools that are most suitable for the teaching of a given topic.

CHAPTER 22

What Have Students Learned? Assessing and Evaluating Students

Although it is possible merely to measure and describe what students know and can do (assessment), we are also required to make judgments (evaluation). **Assessment** has to do with collecting data on student performance, and **evaluation** involves making judgments based on those data. The major role of assessment in social studies, as in all subject areas, is to ascertain whether students are realizing curriculum objectives and how well they are achieving them. Information on students' strengths and weaknesses is also needed for completing report cards, giving feedback to students, and making curriculum decisions. Student self-assessment helps students measure their own progress. Assessment and evaluation, then, are ongoing and significant processes in the classroom.

Teachers frequently use **diagnostic assessments** as a means of establishing a baseline for teaching. We assess students while they are engaged in an activity and use tests to discover what students have learned. We also want students to assess and evaluate their own progress. Thus, assessment and evaluation are key aspects in any teaching situation.

Evidence can be collected for evaluative purposes in a number of ways.[1] One of the most common is the test, whereby the student's score becomes the basis for evaluating that student. There are four basic ways of using test scores:

1. A student's score can be compared with a previous score.
2. Individual scores can be ranked from high to low.
3. A student's score can be compared using a **criterion reference** (e.g., a standard such as "Students should be able to correctly identify the latitude and longitude of places on the globe").
4. A student's score can be compared against a **norm reference**, such as an average score derived from administering the same test to other students. **Standardized tests** are an example of this type. Norms can be derived from various sizes of samples. Standardized tests may have provincial, national, or international norms.

The difference between a criterion- and a norm-referenced test is demonstrated by a driving test, which, as we will see later, is a fairly good example of an authentic assessment. Here each individual is judged by his or her ability to perform certain tasks (criterion reference); whether he or she passes or fails is not based on how many other people pass or fail (norm reference).

When we have assessment information, then we can evaluate students' progress.

Activity 22-A

a) Suppose Student A scores 73% on a social studies test. What evaluation would you make if you had this information only?

b) Suppose Student A's previous scores on social studies tests have been in the 90% range. What evaluation would you make?

c) Suppose the class average on the test is 84%. What evaluation would you make?

d) Suppose the provincial norm for the test is 68%. What evaluation would you make?

The evaluations we make are based on the evidence, which in turn is based upon our judgments about what should be assessed and how the data should be collected.

In creating our assessments, we have to use criteria.

There are two types of criteria. One type specifies in descriptive terms what to look for. Examples of **descriptive criteria** could include these: students name the capitals of each of the provinces of Canada, or give three reasons for a position on an issue, or use three sources to find out about the foundation of The Hudson's Bay Company. But these criteria do not always tell us what standards should be met. **Evaluative criteria** inform us that students should correctly name the capitals, that the three reasons are plausible and well argued, and that the three sources are relevant and accurate. "Correct," "accurate," "plausible," "relevant," and "well argued" are evaluative terms. These are general evaluative terms that, when given more specificity, become standards. So, for example, the latitude and longitude should be accurate in degrees, minutes, and seconds; the three reasons must match those of an expert in the field. In teaching students about criteria and in having them produce their *own* criteria for assessing their own and others' work, you might want to start off with descriptive criteria and introduce evaluative ones later on.

Before planning any assessment, we have to answer several questions:

1. On what should the student be assessed and evaluated: knowledge, skills, attitudes, dispositions, behaviour?
2. Why is it necessary to assess and evaluate the student on X?
3. Should *all* students be assessed and evaluated on X?
4. What is the best way of collecting information about X? Should the same information be collected from all students?
5. Who should collect the information: teachers, students, and/or outside agencies?
6. When will the information be collected: at the end of lessons or units; daily, weekly, monthly, yearly?
7. How will results be recorded?
8. How will the results be used?
9. What criterion/criteria will be used to determine success?

Answers to these questions depend upon our conception of social studies. As was pointed out in Chapter 2, those who favour the citizenship transmission conception of social studies are likely to test for the acquisition of empirical information, using "objective" tests and ranking students on the basis of their performance. Those who hold the reflective inquiry conception are likely to assess student progress vis-à-vis previous performances and to test for more than the recall of specific information. Those who adhere to the critical reflective conception are likely to use portfolio and self-assessment methods.

Activity 22-B

What is your position on assessment and evaluation? Do you agree or disagree with the following statements? Why?

a) Students should be compared with each other on any given performance.
b) Students should be tested only on "objective" criteria.
c) Students should be assessed and evaluated on knowledge, skills, and attitudes.
d) Students should be assessed and evaluated on an individual basis—improvement vis-à-vis previous performances.
e) Students should be assessed and evaluated on the basis of results from tests that have Canadian norms.
f) Students should never be tested because tests cause anxiety.
g) Students should not be tested because tests examine only for low-level knowledge and are not objective.
h) Because parents want to know how well their child is doing in relation to other children, students should be ranked.
i) Students should be assessed and evaluated on the basis of informal observations and interviews.
j) Students should be assessed and evaluated on how they tackle a problem, not on whether they get a correct answer.
k) Test results should be used only to diagnose a student's strengths or weaknesses.
l) Test results should be used only to improve instruction and the curriculum.

Once decisions have been made about the purposes and nature of assessment, decisions concerning the methods are required. As pointed out previously, one of the most common is the test or quiz. These activities can take a variety of forms, each of which needs careful planning.

You will be familiar with multiple choice, true/false, fill-the-blank, matching, and other measures. We can use these to assess students not only on their memory of specific information, but also on higher order understandings such as concepts and generalizations.

ASSESSING STUDENT UNDERSTANDING OF CONCEPTS

To test for students' knowledge of a concept, we can use the following sorts of items.

1. Give a definition of ___________.
2. Use the term ___________ correctly in a sentence.
3. From a list of definitions, select the one that correctly defines the term ___________.
4. From the following list, select those that are examples of ___________. Young students could be given cards with YES and NO printed on them and as each example is presented, students could raise the card they think represents the correct answer. In this way, we could get some information about the students' abilities.[2]
5. From the following pictures, identify the one that is an example of ___________. For instance, which of the following is a picture of an island?

6. From a number of examples, identify the concept.
7. Given a list of word pairs, identify the similarities and differences between the two terms in each pair, e.g., car/truck, nurse/doctor, farm/ranch, need/want.
8. Given a concept, identify examples and state what all the examples have in common, e.g., food, plant, continent, role.
9. Given a list of attributes, identify which ones are relevant to a given concept. For example, Law:
   a) Something you have to obey.
   b) Punishment occurs if you break it.
   c) Created by adults.
   d) Designed to protect people.
   e) Tells someone what should be done in a particular situation.
   f) Enforced by the police.
10. Make up a sentence in which the concept ____________ is used.

Activity 22-C

Design a test for students at three different grade or age levels to determine their ability to define and use one of the following concepts: power, independence, sexism, prejudice. In your view, what would qualify as an adequate understanding of your chosen concept at each of the chosen grade or age levels?

ASSESSING STUDENT UNDERSTANDING OF GENERALIZATIONS

To test for knowledge of generalizations and the ability to generalize, the following types of test items can be used.

1. Give students the following directions: Carefully study the generalization shown below. If any of the evidence below the generalization could be used to support it, indicate this by placing the letter Y (for "yes") opposite the statement. If the evidence does not support it, indicate this by placing the letter N (for "No") opposite the statement.

   Cultures change in varying degrees when they come into contact with another culture.

   a) The Native peoples of Canada were influenced by French and English fur traders.
   b) Some Australian Aborigines still maintain the same lifestyle that Aborigines practised a thousand years ago despite the influx of many Europeans.

c) European explorers of Canada ate pemmican, to which they were introduced by the Native people.
d) The first English settlers in Canada tried to live in ways to which they were accustomed.

2. Give students a number of similar cases or events and ask them to formulate a generalization:

In place A, which relies solely on fishing, there is high unemployment during the non-fishing season.

In place B, the mine is the major source of employment. In July, the mine was closed and heavy unemployment resulted.

Place C is a lumber town. When lumber prices decreased, many workers were laid off.

What generalization can be made about these three events?

Activity 22-D

Design a test item to assess student understanding of one of the following generalizations:

All families have rules.
Conflicts develop between individuals and groups when goals and expectations differ.
Contact between cultures brings changes in the social institutions within them.

We can also use multiple choice and other objective measures to test for the ability to evaluate generalizations and think critically about information.[3]

Context: Archeologists are excavating the site of an ancient Haida community on the Queen Charlotte Islands.

1. The archeologists find a stone axe. One of them says, "The Haida knew how to make stone axes." Is the archeologist correct? Why or why not?
2. The archeologists know that the Haida made clothing out of cedar bark. They examine the trees in the area and find that only small strips of bark were taken from the trees. Why might this be done?
   a) Because cedar bark is not useful.
   b) Because taking too much would damage the tree.
   c) Because taking a lot would be too much to carry.

ASSESSING STUDENT ABILITIES TO LOCATE AND ASSESS RELEVANT INFORMATION

These kinds of items can also be used to assess students in other areas. For example, the following question is designed to find out whether or not students know where to locate information:

Question: In which source would you look if you wanted weather information for Montreal today?

a) an encyclopedia
b) today's newspaper
c) a magazine about Montreal
d) an atlas

To assess other intellectual standards you could use the following sorts of items:

Suppose you want to know whether an item in the newspaper is true. What would be the best way of finding out?

1. Look at two other newspapers and the TV news and see if they told the same story.
2. Phone the newspaper office and ask the reporter if his or her account is true.
3. Look at another newspaper and see if it gave the same information.

Suppose you want to know whether a crosswalk is needed to cross the street outside the school. What would be the best way of finding out?

1. Ask your classmates whether they think a crosswalk is needed.
2. Ask the teachers whether they think a crosswalk is needed.
3. Find out from the police whether there have been any accidents on the street when children were crossing.
4. Ask parents whether they think a crosswalk is needed.

Suppose you wanted to find out whether the first people got to North America across an ice-free corridor from Siberia about 10 000 years ago. What would be the best evidence that this theory may not be true? You may choose more than one answer. Pretend all the information below is true.

1. There is evidence of human beings in South America 20 000 years ago.
2. There was only a very narrow ice-free corridor 10 000 years ago.
3. Some spear points found in the eastern United States look like ones used by people in Europe 10 000 years ago.

There are several things to remember in test construction:

1. The purpose must be clear. What exactly is it we wish to test for?
2. The test items must match the purpose of the test. If we want to find out how well students can use inquiry procedures, one of the best means would be to give them an inquiry task and assess and evaluate their performance. This sort of performance measurement, or **authentic assessment**, evaluates the way(s) in which students tackle a particular problem, not just the results of the performance.
3. We must choose the most appropriate form of test (essay, multiple choice, etc.).
4. The questions should be clear and unambiguous.
5. If we wish to rank students, the test should contain questions that will differentiate between students at the high and low ends of the scale.
6. The test should be reliable; that is, if the test were given again, students should get about the same score as they obtained the first time.
7. We must have justifiable criteria for evaluating student answers.

ASSESSING STUDENT PERFORMANCE USING CHECKLISTS

Paper-and-pencil tests are one way of collecting information about students' performance. Another way is to observe students both in and out of the classroom. As teachers, we will be constantly observing students and making decisions on the basis of our observations. By collecting observational data in a formalized way, we will obtain more reliable data.

As with all assessments, decisions have to be made about the purposes of the observation, the method, and the timing. Observations can be carried out by time sampling, in which a sequence of behaviours is recorded (e.g., how a student acts in a given period of time), or by observing a particular event, such as the behaviour of a student in a discussion group. To record these data, we will need to keep checklists. These checklists may require a *yes* or *no* for the behaviour being recorded, or they may contain a rating scale, or a space for anecdotal comments. Checklists can be **quantitative** or **qualitative**. Here is an example:

Name of Student	Uses Card Catalogue	Uses Table of Contents	Uses Index	Uses Internet

When a student is observed using the card catalogue, a check mark is put against the student's name (quantitative). You could also evaluate students' use of the card catalogue by rating their performance as *excellent, good, fair,* or *needs improvement* (qualitative).

The following type of checklist could be used if group work is to be evaluated:

	Alice	Ingrid	Lieh	Rashad	Rob
Expresses support for others					
Asks for information					
Gives help to others					
Encourages others to contribute					

When a rating scale is necessary, a checklist could be constructed as in the examples below:

GROUP WORK

Name of Student											
Enthusiastic	1	2	3	4	5	6	7	8	9	10	Unenthusiastic
Confident	1	2	3	4	5	6	7	8	9	10	Apprehensive
Responsive	1	2	3	4	5	6	7	8	9	10	Reticent
On task	1	2	3	4	5	6	7	8	9	10	Not on task
Cooperative	1	2	3	4	5	6	7	8	9	10	Uncooperative
Respectful	1	2	3	4	5	6	7	8	9	10	Disrespectful

ASSESSING STUDENT ABILITIES OF INFERRING, USING INQUIRY PROCESSES, AND MAKING ORAL PRESENTATIONS

PICTURE STUDIES

Rating Scale

1 = can do this only with prompts

2 = can do this with few prompts

3 = can do this independently

Name of student	Accurately describes what is in the picture	Generates plausible inferences from the picture
Abby	3	2
Alice	2	3

INQUIRY CHECKLIST

	Good	**Adequate**	**Causes Concern: Remedial Action Needed**
Understanding the Question	Knows what the question means. Can paraphrase the question.	Has adequate grasp of the concepts contained in the question.	Has insufficient understanding to make sense of the question.
Generating Hypotheses	Can generate several plausible hypotheses.	Can generate one or two plausible hypotheses.	Generates no hypotheses or implausible ones.

To evaluate an oral presentation, the following chart could be used.[4]

	Excellent	**Good**	**Adequate**	**Needs Help**
Content				
• is accurate				
• covers the main points				
• is detailed				
• is interesting				
Organization				
• effective introduction				
• logical sequence				
• effective ending				

	Excellent	Good	Adequate	Needs Help
Delivery				
• easily heard				
• looks at audience				
• expressive voice				

Activity 22-E

Design a checklist for a particular behaviour. Identify the specific behaviours you would observe and state why you think these are the crucial ones. State what your criteria would be for excellent performance.

These sorts of checklists, along with other techniques such as student–teacher interviews, can be used in "authentic" or performance assessment in which students are evaluated on the way(s) they perform a task. They can perform these tasks either on their own or in a group situation. During careful observation—listening to student discussion (in a group task), having students talk about what they are doing and why, and through teacher questioning—students can display what they are capable of doing in a "real" situation.[5] In a formal testing situation, students may not perform as well as they are able, so their results may not accurately reflect their competence. Although an authentic assessment tries to avoid these problems, it does have one drawback: it is time-consuming. Each student should be encouraged to judge his or her own performance. If we want students to take responsibility for their learning, then we have to provide them with opportunities to evaluate their own performances. When given the chance to assess their strengths and weaknesses, students can begin to make their own decisions about what and how they should study. They can use a self-evaluation checklist like the following:

	All the Time	Most of the Time	Occasionally	Never
I listened to others				
I shared ideas				
I worked hard				

In all the above, **rubrics** were used to evaluate student performances. Case[6] provides guidelines for developing rubrics:

1. Generate criteria.
2. Prioritize the criteria by selecting those that are most important and relevant for the purpose of the assignment.
3. Consolidate the criteria by organizing them around themes, e.g., reasoning ability, presentation, research skills, etc.
4. Set levels by deciding how many would be appropriate. Is three enough? Would five be better?

5. Select the variables to distinguish performance levels.
6. Draft intermediate descriptors.
7. Refine the rubric by checking to see if the descriptors are precise and mutually exclusive and that the levels are approximately equivalent.
8. Finalize the performance levels and attach a weight to each criterion. Where appropriate, assign a grade for each level, e.g., if a student scores 9/10 on criterion one, 3/5 for criterion two, and 18/20 on criterion three, is the final mark of 30/35 worth an A+, an A–, or something else?
9. Pilot the rubric. Try it out on a sample assignment or have your peers critique it.

USING PORTFOLIOS

A great deal of information is needed to evaluate students thoroughly. Information can be collected from test results, observations, and interviews with the student. Especially useful in this regard is a **portfolio** that contains a comprehensive collection of the student's work, including written work, photographs of projects, audio or video recordings of presentations, and self-evaluations. All these items should be collected throughout the school year. For teachers, the portfolio provides a great deal of data on which to base evaluations and diagnose instructional weaknesses. In parent–teacher interviews, the portfolio provides a picture of the kind of work the student has done over time. Confidence is fostered when students know the objective for having a portfolio and have been helped to create one.[7] Students should be encouraged to select the work they wish to include in the portfolio. They should establish their goals and decide which pieces of work best reflect those goals. A self-assessment is also useful:

Portfolio topic: ____________________

The two pieces I selected for my portfolio are ______________ and ______________.

I chose them because ____.

I do well at ____.

I could improve in ____.

I intend to improve by ____.

Students might compare their portfolios with others' so that they can evaluate their own work. They can use the portfolio to report to teachers and parents/guardians. Students can also use it as a basis for developing a plan of action for future improvements.

Evaluating student progress is only one reason for collecting data. Another reason is to help us improve our instruction. If on the basis of test results we find that students are unable to answer certain questions, then we should ask ourselves why this is so. Was the content or skill beyond the students' capabilities? In this case, the curriculum needs to be changed. Was our instruction inadequate? If so, it should be improved. Was the test item ambiguous or badly worded? In this case, we need to write better test items. Whenever test results do not measure up to our expectations, we must question them, and question the accuracy of our own expectations.

Case[8] provides a set of criteria for evaluating assessments:

a) The assessment focuses on what really matters.
b) It provides valid indications of student ability.
c) It supports student learning.
d) It uses teacher time efficiently.

Assessing and evaluating students are complex tasks. What is assessed, how information is collected, what criteria are applied, what the purposes are for the assessment, and how results are used are questions that need careful consideration.

ASSESSING STUDENT USE OF AND ABILITY IN DECISION-MAKING PROCESSES

To assess decision making, we can use the following example: The first step, clarification of the problem, can be assessed with the scenario below:

> On Saturday, Judy has been invited to (a) attend a birthday party, (b) go swimming, and (c) go to a movie. She doesn't have time to do all three, and she doesn't like swimming. What is Judy's problem?

Another item could consist of a vignette such as the following ones, in which students have to identify the decision that has to be made:

> Your class has decided to have a bake sale next Thursday. Everyone has offered to do something to help with the sale. Which of the following is the most important decision that has to be made next?
>
> a) when to have the bake sale
> b) who will buy the food at the sale
> c) whether you want to have a bake sale
> d) who will bring what food to sell
>
> Fur traders who are buying furs are deciding whether to canoe from one fur-trading post to another much farther up the river or to return to the main fort. Which of the following is the most important decision to be made?
>
> a) whether there will be enough food for the trip
> b) whether there will be enough furs to buy at the post
> c) whether the river will be rough
> d) whether the mosquitoes will make the trip really uncomfortable

Activity 22-F

Create at least one test item that would test students' ability to clarify the potential problems of "latchkey children" (children who are at home alone when they leave for school and/or when they return from school).

To test for student competency in generating alternatives, students can be presented with a particular event and asked to list as many alternatives as possible. Alternatives can be evaluated on the basis of quantity and plausibility. Here are two examples:

> Your baseball team needs new uniforms, but the team has no money. List as many ways as you can think of to get the money to buy new uniforms.

You are Simon Fraser and you are travelling down the Fraser River with three canoes when you come to a very steep canyon with very dangerous rapids. What could you do?

Activity 22-G

Create at least one test item to determine how well students can generate alternatives for solving one of the following problems: (a) too much traffic in the downtown area; (b) fighting in the school playground; (c) girls not being involved in after-school baseball because the boys make fun of them; or (d) homelessness in the community.

The following examples of items might be used to assess student ability in identifying consequences:

a) You have to decide what to do during the summer. In the left-hand column of the following chart is a list of choices. On the right is a list of the benefits you might gain from each choice. Match each choice with its *most likely gain*.

Choices	**Gains**
Taking swimming lessons	Rest
Getting a babysitting job	A healthier body
Taking art classes	Money
Relaxing at home	New skills

b) List as many consequences as you can of the following event:

If the Great Lakes dried up, then ____________.

Activity 22-H

Create at least one test item to determine if students can identify the consequences of taking the proposed courses of action in the following situation:

In order to make it safer for students to cross a busy intersection, the following proposals have been made: (a) hire a crossing guard; (b) build an overpass or underpass; (c) put in traffic lights; (d) put up warning signs for motorists; (e) give all students instructions on how to cross the road safely.

These sorts of items are fairly straightforward, and good answers are not difficult to determine. However, the criteria for determining good answers to value questions are sometimes more difficult. This does not mean that students' reasoning, or the products of their reasoning, cannot or should not be evaluated. The following type of "test" can be administered, and the teacher can use the criteria outlined below to evaluate student responses.

A vignette is presented in which someone has to make a decision that concerns other people. The following questions are then posed:

a) What decision should you make?
b) What, if any, would be the benefits to you?
c) What, if any, would be the disadvantages to you?
d) What, if any, would be the benefits to the others involved?
e) What, if any, would be the disadvantages to the others?
f) If you were the disadvantaged person, would it be right to act on the decision? Why or why not?

g) Here is a similar case. Would you make the same decision in this case? Why or why not?
h) Would you want everyone to make the same decision in this case? Why or why not?

Evaluation of responses should be based on the chart below:

Excellent	Good	Fair	Needs help
Can identify the consequences to self and others	Identifies major consequences	Identifies a few consequences	Cannot identify consequences
Has fairly clear ideas of what is in one's own best interest	Identifies what is in one's own best interest	Has difficulty identifying what is in one's own best interest	Cannot identify what is in one's own best interest
Is able to put self in the shoes of the other person and consider that person's needs, interests, and feelings	Can identify other person's needs, interests, and feelings	Can identify some of other person's needs, interests, and feelings	Cannot identify other person's needs, interests, and feelings
Can consider universal consequences of acting on the decision	Can generalize the decision to other cases	Can generalize the decision to one other case	Cannot generalize the decision
Is able to consider other similar cases and state why the decision applies or does not apply in the new cases	Can give plausible reasons the case applies or does not apply to several new cases	Can give plausible reasons the case applies or does not apply in another case	Is unable to see relevance of a new case to the one being considered
Is willing, where appropriate, to put aside prudential concerns and make decisions that do not harm others	Puts aside prudential concerns	Cannot decide whether prudential concerns outweigh moral concerns	Acts solely on prudential concerns
In group decision-making sessions, is willing to seek advice and consider the views of others in the group	Seeks advice and considers others' viewpoints in a consistent way	Occasionally considers others' viewpoints and seeks advice	Rarely, if ever, considers others' viewpoints or seeks advice

Here is an example that incorporates many of the questions posed above.[9]

In the town of Actum there is a downtown area that contains many heritage houses. A developer approaches the town council seeking permission to build a much-needed shopping centre that will revitalize the downtown area. If the shopping centre is built, the business community will be delighted. But the people who live in the heritage houses do not wish to move.

1. If the shopping centre is built, what problem would this cause?
   a) There would be too many shops.
   b) People would lose their homes.
   c) There would be too many people in the downtown area.

2. If the shopping centre is built, who will be most disadvantaged?
   a) The people who live in the heritage houses.
   b) The developer.
   c) The shoppers.
3. If the shopping centre were built, how would you feel if you were one of the people who lived in the heritage houses?
   a) Happy because you would get a new house.
   b) Unhappy because you do not want to move.
   c) Happy because you would have more stores to shop in.
   d) Unhappy because you like the furniture in your house.
4. What is the best way to make the decision?
   a) Let everyone in the town decide.
   b) Let the developer decide.
   c) Let the business people decide.

You could then pose other questions about alternative solutions to this problem and about the best solution, and ask students whether their decision would be different if the facts of the case were different. For example: Suppose the heritage houses were the only examples of this type of house left in Canada. Would this make a difference to your decision?

You can use this type of item as the basis for a **performance** or **authentic assessment.** Listen to a group of students and keep a record of their deliberations as they try to resolve the problem. Place particular emphasis on how well they define the problem, generate alternatives and consequences for proposed actions, and argue for a particular solution. In the intermediate grades, students could write a letter to the editor of their local newspaper stating how they would resolve the issue. Evaluate the letter using the criteria outlined above.

Activity 22-I

This test is for you.[10] It is designed to assess how well you would lead a class discussion on a value issue. For each example, decide which is the best question to ask.

Example 1

TEACHER: Students shouldn't take school paper home for their personal use.

STUDENT: Well, our parents pay for it, so why shouldn't we?

What should you (as teacher) say?

a) Let's take a vote. Who agrees with that and who doesn't?
b) How many of you take paper home for your personal use?
c) What would happen if the principal caught you?
d) Your parents also help pay for the video machines. Should you take them home for your personal use?

Example 2

TEACHER: Should you help other people even if it inconveniences you? Suppose a person in a wheelchair needs help getting the chair into a building and you are in a rush to get to a movie. Should you help?

STUDENT: No, the person in the wheelchair shouldn't go places where it is difficult for wheelchairs.

What should you (as teacher) say?

a) Would you think it was right if nobody helped you if you were in a wheelchair?
b) Should there be laws to make all buildings wheelchair accessible?
c) *[To another student]* Would you help?

Example 3

TEACHER: Don't walk on the running track. It's against the school rules.

STUDENT: But what harm does it do if I walk on the track?

What should you (as teacher) say?

a) I'm telling you it's against the rules.
b) But what would happen if everyone did that?
c) Are you saying it's not against school rules?
d) How would you feel if you were me?

Example 4

TEACHER: Should we allow more refugees into Canada?

STUDENT: They would take jobs away from Canadians.

What should you (as teacher) say?

a) Have you any evidence for saying that?
b) Does it matter if they take jobs away from Canadians?
c) Do you all agree that they take jobs away from Canadians?
d) Do you have any other reasons?

Example 5

TEACHER: Is it fair that Derek chose Alex for the team, and not Ian, even though Ian is the better player?

STUDENT: Yes, because Alex is Derek's brother and Alex would be upset if he wasn't chosen.

What should you (as teacher) say?

a) Do you think Ian is the better player?
b) Ian, do you think it's fair?
c) Alex, do you think it's fair?
d) Suppose Derek was in charge of surgery at a hospital and chose his brother to perform an operation even though another doctor was a much better surgeon. Would this be right?

IDENTIFYING STUDENT ATTITUDES

Wherever judgments are made, attitudes will be brought into play. As teachers, we may wish to find out what attitudes students have toward a particular person, event, or issue, and we may want to change students' attitudes. The following types of attitude measures should not be used to evaluate students. They should be used (a) to find out what individuals think so that what is taught takes into account students' attitudes and (b) to discover whether attitudes change over time. Attitude measures are administered in a pre- and posttest format. They should be anonymous so that students will be more likely to divulge their true feelings and not simply write what they think the teacher wants them to write.

Here are some examples of ways in which student attitudes can be determined.

1. On meeting a uniformed member of the police force, I feel . . .

2. Doctors are friendly.
   Strongly agree   Agree   Don't know   Disagree   Strongly disagree
3. People who work at McDonald's are . . .
   ___ hard-working ___ lazy
   ___ stupid ___ clever
   ___ wealthy ___ poor
4. Circle the words that tell what you feel about the police force:
   interesting   worthwhile   necessary
   important   exciting   dull
5. If you were to study the police force, what topics would interest you? Put a 1 against your first choice, a 2 against your second, and so on.
   ___ Police Dog Handling and Training
   ___ Police Cars
   ___ How the Police Are Trained
   ___ A Typical Day in the Life of a Police Officer
   ___ Crime Fighting
6. When I see a member of the police force, I think . . .

Activity 22-J

Create an instrument to determine students' attitudes toward one of the following: the study of Canadian history or geography, gun laws in Canada, recycling, or violence on television.

ASSESSING STUDENT SOCIAL BEHAVIOURS

One other assessment technique is to observe students' behaviours. Here we infer students' motivations, feelings, and attitudes from their speech and behaviour and note them down, either as anecdotal records or on a checklist. However, we must remember that what is in students' minds cannot be accurately identified by simple observation of their actions. We have the problem of how to determine that a given observable action is an example of a particular sensitivity, disposition, attitude, or trait. Suppose we are interested in ascertaining how respectful students are. Suppose we observe a student who appears to be hitting another child; the interpretationof that action is crucial. Is it really an act of non-respect or is the student hitting at a wasp that has landed on the other student?

We cannot observe responsibility, caring, etc. We can only infer them from certain actions. Are our inferences valid? There are three concerns here:

1. Do we have a clear concept of the trait, disposition, or attitude? Suppose a student always puts his hand up in class when he wishes to speak. Suppose he does this out of fear of punishment, or because he wants to please the teacher, or because he realizes that this rule respects the rights of others. Perhaps he does it out of habit and has forgotten the reason why he does it. Are all of these reasons examples of respect? Would we want to say that the student is a respectful person? Suppose a student considers a school rule to be a violation of her rights. Would it be responsible behaviour for her to protest against the rule?
2. How many examples of the exhibition of the trait do we need in order to say that someone is respectful or responsible? Will one example suffice?
3. To what extent do personality traits play a role in how students behave? Certainly we want students to be respectful and responsible, but an introvert may well display these traits in idiosyncratic ways. In a group project, should we assess the shy child in the same way as the outgoing child?

Thousands of studies, from before Piaget's time to the present, demonstrate that children develop in their social reasoning. Thus, a seven-year-old will keep a promise because she wants to please her parents, or because she fears punishment if she does not. A nine-year-old will keep a promise because he wants others to keep their promises to him. A thirteen-year-old will keep her promise because this is the convention of her peer group. Would we say that a thirteen-year-old who is using a seven-year-old's reasons for keeping promises is as responsible as a thirteen-year-old who appeals to developmentally appropriate reasons? That is, do we say that someone is acting in a socially acceptable way for the wrong reasons?

Clearly, we must be very careful in assessing student attitudes and sensitivities. This does not mean that assessment is impossible or that it should not be carried out. As the example below attests, we can create rubrics that can be used to assess students in a responsible way.

RESPONSIBILITY (GRADES 3 TO 4)

Poor	Moderate	Good
Rarely helps others	Sometimes helps others	Usually helps others
Needs to be reminded of classroom rules	Sometimes needs to be reminded of classroom rules	Usually follows classroom rules
Has to be told to do chores	Sometimes volunteers to do chores	Usually volunteers to do chores
Rarely completes tasks on time	Sometimes completes tasks on time	Usually completes tasks on time
Does not accept consequences for own actions	Sometimes accepts consequences for own actions	Usually accepts consequences for own actions

Other Activities

1. Choosing a grade level for each objective below, design ways of assessing student performance based on the following objectives:
   a) The student should know the names of four continents.
   b) The student should understand the concept "interdependence."
   c) The student should use a map of Canada to locate Toronto.
   d) The student should work cooperatively in a group activity.
   e) The student should state what is unique about herself/himself and what characteristics she/he shares with others.
   f) The student should give an example of a case that would support this generalization: "Technological development contributes to the nature and extent of cultural change."
   g) Given a picture and a number of statements about the picture, the student should identify which are observation statements and which are inferences.
   h) How would you find out whether students knew how to critically assess an advertisement in a newspaper? the events leading to the election of a provincial premier? how an Egyptian pyramid was built? how to use a video camera? how to conduct oneself on a field trip? how to behave in a discussion group?
   i) How would you ascertain the attitudes of Grade 6 students toward the Canadian government's immigration policy?
   j) How would you evaluate the ability of Grade 1 students to make decisions?
   k) How would you determine if Grade 3 students can put themselves into another person's role?

Notes

1. T. Fenwick and J. Parsons, "Nine modes that evaluate individual student learning in social studies," *Canadian Social Studies* 31:4 (1997), pp. 178–180.
2. J. Alleman and J. Brophy, *Current Trends and Practices in Social Studies Assessment for the Early Grades* (Silver Springs, MD: National Council for the Social Studies, 1999).
3. Adapted from C. Bognar and W. Cassidy, *Social Studies in British Columbia: Technical Report of the 1989 Social Studies Assessment* (Victoria, BC: Assessment, Examinations and Reporting Branch of the Ministry of Education, 1991).
4. P. Clark, "Escaping the typical report trap: Teaching elementary students to conduct research" in R. Case and P. Clark, eds., *The Anthology of Social Studies, Volume 1. Issues and Strategies for Elementary Teachers* (Vancouver: Pacific Educational Press, 2008), p. 117.
5. J. Myers, "Assessment and evaluation in social studies," in I. Wright and A. Sears, eds., *Trends and Issues in Canadian Social Studies* (Vancouver: Pacific Educational Press, 1997).
6. R. Case, "Building student ownership of assessment," in R. Case and P. Clark. eds., *The Anthology of Social Studies, Volume 1. Issues and Strategies for Elementary Teachers* (Vancouver: Pacific Educational Press, 2008), pp. 337–338.
7. T. Fenwick and J. Parsons, "A note on using portfolios to assess learning," *Canadian Social Studies* 33:3 (1999), pp. 90–92.
8. R. Case, "Four principles of authentic assessment," In R. Case and P. Clark, eds., *The Anthology of Social Studies, Volume 1. Issues and Strategies for Elementary Teachers* (Vancouver: Pacific Educational Press, 2008), pp. 321–327.
9. Adapted from C. Bognar and W. Cassidy.
10. Adapted from the work of the Association for Values Education and Research, University of British Columbia.

Glossary of Key Terms

Assessment—Collecting data about student performance.

Authentic assessment—Assessing students while they are actually engaged in a task, e.g., solving a problem.

Criterion reference—A standard against which a student is assessed, e.g., that the student can correctly identify the latitude and longitude of major cities in the world.

Descriptive criteria—What to look for in assessing a student's performance, e.g., that the student has written a paragraph or has used the internet to obtain information.

Diagnostic assessment—Determining what students already know and can do, in order to plan or improve instruction.

Evaluation—Making judgments on the basis of an assessment.

Evaluative criteria—The criteria that state what standards are to be met in a given performance, e.g., the student's paragraph is *coherent*, and the information obtained from the internet is *reliable* and *relevant* to the task at hand.

Norm-referenced test—A test where the standard (often numerical) is based on results from other assessments.

Performance assessment—Assessing students while they are actually engaged in a task, e.g., solving a problem.

Portfolio—A collection of student work over time.

Qualitative checklists—Checking how well a student exhibits a specific behaviour, e.g., using a rating scale.

Quantitative checklists—Checking how many times a student exhibits a specific behaviour.

Rubric—A framework of criteria for ranking student performance.

Standardized test—A test where the norms are based on provincial, national, or international results.

Answers to Activities

ACTIVITY 1-B

All the vignettes could be considered social studies activities only if the *objectives* for engaging students in the activities pertain to social studies. However, many of the vignettes may realize other goals as well. For example, creating a mural may achieve objectives in social studies and art education.

ACTIVITY 2-D

1. Citizenship Transmission
2. Reflective Inquiry (although it could be Critical Reflection)
3. Citizenship Transmission
4. Critical Reflection
5. Social Science
6. Citizenship Transmission
7. Citizenship Transmission
8. Reflective Inquiry (although it could be Critical Reflection)
9. Critical Reflection
10. Holistic

ACTIVITY 3-G

a) Vertical integration

b) Subject matter integration

c) Not integration (no central idea is pursued)

d) Personal integration

e) Whole school curriculum integration

f) Unless moves are made to link the history, geography, and First Nations studies together, this would not be an example of integration.

g) Subject matter integration. Students are synthesizing information to create generalizations.

ACTIVITY 6-B

1. Hutterite *family* (Alberta)
2. Inuit mother-and-child *family*

3. John Ware and *family*
4. Quatsino Indians at a potlatch
5. Lee Mong Kow *family* (Victoria, British Columbia)
6. Group of East Indians at North Pacific Lumber Co. (Barnet, British Columbia)

ACTIVITY 6-F

The concept is "immigrant."

ACTIVITY 6-H

The concept is "tradition." If you look at the last sentence, it sounds odd to say that watching television news every night is a "tradition" (which would be a sensible choice for all the other blanks). Watching television news on a regular basis seems to have many of the attributes of "tradition" in that it is regularly performed over some extended period of time; it is an act of persons who, in most cases, can either do it or refrain from doing it; it is usually done with full awareness of what one is doing; and one may believe that one ought to do it. However, unlike many traditions where there are sanctions applied if they are not followed, refraining from watching television news is not a punishable offence.

"Tradition" has characteristics that are similar to "custom." However, a tradition may be more robust than certain customs. It may be handed down orally and deliberately from generation to generation (whereas a custom may endure for only one generation and may not be formally taught). Tradition may be based on very strong beliefs, which, if contradicted, may seriously undermine group cohesiveness and may lead to extreme sanctions (whereas not all customs have these characteristics). Also, it sounds a bit odd to say, "X is my individual tradition that no one else practises," whereas it is normal to say, "X is my custom even though no one else practises it." Yet, words change in meaning over time, and one often hears people say that they are starting a tradition just for themselves. This usage would be incorrect if a necessary attribute of the word was that a tradition had to be passed down from generation to generation. However, in ordinary language, we may find that the words "tradition" and "custom" become almost interchangeable.

ACTIVITY 6-I

Examples of "authority" are a), b), e), f), and possibly g), depending on whether the principal really has authority to do this. Notice that in the other cases there is the exercise of power without the requisite authority.

CHAPTER 6: OTHER ACTIVITIES

The teacher has implemented Taba's Concept Development procedure well. She/he has ensured that students have 1) correctly classified items, 2) decided whether items could be classified in more than one category, and 3) created categories useful for study of the topic.

ACTIVITY 7-D

As I find many problems in using Sanders's and Bloom's taxonomies, the answers provided are, in some cases, debatable. The highest level of question is indicated.

a) Empirical Memory
b) Empirical Memory
c) Empirical Synthesis
d) Empirical Translation
e) Conceptual Memory
f) Conceptual Analysis
g) Value Evaluation
h) Value Evaluation
i) Value Evaluation
j) Empirical/Logical Analysis

If you accept the two premises in j), then logically you must accept the conclusion.

ACTIVITY 8-A

The following assumptions would be made: b), c), e), f), g), h), i), and j).

ACTIVITY 8-C

This structure is a replica of a grave house located in 'Ksan Historical Village in Hazelton, British Columbia. The village celebrates the lives of the Gitxsan people who have lived in Hazelton for centuries and still live in this area. Grave houses can be found from Alaska to Oregon. Bodies of chiefs, shamen, or other significant people were placed in the grave houses either in coffins or were buried in the ground. They were like a mausoleum in that there could be more than one coffin inside. In 1793, explorers in B.C. reported on these structures so it is assumed that they existed prior to European contact. In 'Ksan, however, there is no evidence for grave houses prior to the mid 1800s. Cremation was the common method of body disposal prior to the activities of missionaries. Emily Carr created several watercolours in Hazelton in 1912, one showing a street of grave houses and others showing individual grave houses. These paintings are housed in the British Columbia archives. Grave houses are no longer used in Hazelton. On the side of the structure is the symbol for the raven.

Sources:

G. Castile, *The Indians of Puget Sound: The Notebooks of Myron Eells* (Seattle: The University of Washington Press, 1985), pp. 334–337.

E. Gunther, *Indian Life on the Northwest Coast of North America* (Chicago: The University of Chicago Press, 1972), pp 173–174, 125.

H. Stewart, *Cedar* (Vancouver: Douglas and McIntyre, 1984), pp.74–75.

W. Suttles, ed., *Handbook of North American Indians, Volume 7, Northwest Coast* (Washington, Smithsonian Institution, 1990). pp. 191, 219, 141, 154–155, 178, 300, 332, 462–463, 465, 512, 568.

ACTIVITY 8-D

In 1818, the British government helped army personnel settle in Canada. Settlers received free transportation and some food for the first year, and privates were given 40 hectares (100 acres) of free land. According to Andrew Haydon, *Pioneer Sketches in the District of Bathurst* (Toronto: Ryerson Press, 1925, p. 64), the head of each family was entitled to receive 1 axe, 1 broadaxe, 1 mattock, 1 pickaxe, 1 spade, 1 shovel, 1 hoe, 1 scythe, 1 drawknife, 1 hammer, 1 handsaw, 2 scythe stones, 12 panes of glass, 0.5 kg (1 lb.) of putty, 5.4 kg (12 lb.) of wrought-iron nails in three sizes, 1 camp kettle, 1 bed tick, and 1 blanket.

ACTIVITY 8-F

1. Option a) is a credible source. It is up to date, relevant to the topic, and representative. It (probably) does not provide a political message (bias).
2. Option a) is representative and is a credible source. It is up to date and will have been carefully reviewed by the publisher (textbooks are not adopted by ministries of education or school boards if they do not meet certain standards). However, given that it is a textbook, the topic may not be covered in depth. *If* it is representative of the topic, the CBC documentary would be an equally appropriate source. Given a forced choice, I would opt for the textbook.

ACTIVITY 8-G

1. a) The umpire is credible. The umpire is in a position to see the event and is unbiased.
2. c) The cyclist is most reliable. The cyclist was not involved in the accident and had no conflict of interest. He/she was in a good position to see the accident and was presumably paying attention to the traffic lights.
3. a) The police used the most accurate method of measuring the skid marks.

CHAPTER 8, PAGE 96

The person described on page 96 is Kim Hunter who at the time of writing was a young woman of 11 years of age.

ACTIVITY 8-I

Primary sources are a) and d).

ACTIVITY 8-J

The inference statements are c), d), f), and h). All are plausible.

ACTIVITY 10-E

William Miner was born in 1847 in Bowling Green, Kentucky. He executed a series of robberies in the American West and was released from San Quentin prison in 1904. He came to Canada in that year and robbed a CPR train near Mission, British Columbia. On May 8, 1906, Miner and two accomplices were captured by the North West Mounted Police when they botched the robbery of a CPR train near Kamloops. He was sentenced to 25 years in the penitentiary in New Westminster, British Columbia, but escaped in August 1907. He fled to the United States and continued to carry out robberies. He died in prison in Georgia in 1913. A movie, *The Grey Fox*, was made about his life in Canada.

ACTIVITY 11-J

Tuesday at 6 a.m. London is ahead of Vancouver by eight hours.

CHAPTER 11: OTHER ACTIVITIES

The scale is incorrect. The room would be 5 km long. Further, the chair is bigger than the bed. The scale should read 1 cm: ___, not 1 cm 5 ___. If South is at the top of the room, then East and West are incorrect; if East and West are correct, then North and South are reversed. The perspective is confused; the bed, chair, and pictures are not drawn from the pilot's-eye view.

ACTIVITY 13-A

The teacher has forgotten to obtain permission from parents or legal guardians for their children to go on the field trip. This is a legal requirement and thus is obligatory before any field trip is undertaken.

ACTIVITY 14-A

Every sentence, bar the last one, is a generalization. Each one is presumed to be universally true.

ACTIVITY 14-G

The following generalizations are assumed:

1. All recent immigrants are good workers.
2. Boys don't cry.
3. Immigrants create cultural and economic change.
4. Working-class girls have problems in school.
5. It rains all the time in the summer in Vancouver.
6. People from India wear turbans.
7. Boys aren't good at sewing.

ACTIVITY 15-B

1. Value conclusion: Students should work in cooperative groups.
2. Value conclusion: Students at age nine should learn conventional map symbols.
3. Value conclusion: Students should understand the Canadian Charter of Rights and Freedoms.

CHAPTER 15: OTHER ACTIVITIES

1. a) People should be treated with respect.
   b) Child abuse is morally wrong.
   c) Students who wear glasses should not be given special consideration in school classrooms. OR: Only disabled people should receive special consideration in classrooms.
   d) Children should not be allowed to do things that are harmful to them.

3. The teacher did not implement the decision-making procedure in an appropriate way. The teacher allowed the problem to be wrongly defined; limited the number of alternatives to be considered; invented new information; held a vote when it was inappropriate (to decide whether an empirical claim concerning the teasers is true); and imposed his/her own decision on the class, cutting off any further discussion.

ACTIVITY 18-D

a) Overgeneralization. Just because one recent immigrant is hard-working does not mean that all recent immigrants will be.

b) False cause (*post hoc ergo propter hoc*). There are other reasons for the high unemployment.

c) Appeal to tradition. Just because immigrants came from Europe in the past, it does not follow that they should today.

d) Appeal to authority. Are business people experts on whether the government should give money to ethnic groups?

e) "Black or white" (either this or that). This form of argument presents an oversimplification: Canada's economy could crumble (if it were going to crumble) for a variety of reasons.

f) Slippery slope (in which it is argued that you must not accept as desirable the first event in a supposed chain of events that will lead eventually to something undesirable). In this case, you could agree to allowing Native peoples to govern themselves without agreeing to the rest.

ACTIVITY 19-A

The first photo is of the Dragon Dance in Chinatown in Vancouver. The dance is performed at special events, especially at Chinese New Year. The second photo was taken in 1918. It shows the Canadian Expeditionary Force sailing to Vladivostok, Siberia, to join with forces from the United States, Britain, France, and Japan, ostensibly to protect supplies that had been sent to Russia when Russia was allied with England and France. The real reason might have been to support the White army that was dedicated to overthrowing the Bolsheviks.

ACTIVITY 21-C

Photographs 1 to 4 were all taken in Canada: Photo 1, Quebec City; Photo 2, Vancouver; Photo 3, Toronto; Photo 4, Ottawa.

Photo 5 was taken in Beijing, China.

Photo 6 was taken in Quebec City.

Photo 7 was taken in Dr. Sun Yat-sen Gardens, Vancouver.

ACTIVITY 21-D

Map of the world as known to Europeans, 1398.

ACTIVITY 21-E

Nacirema = American (spelled backwards).

A Selected Bibliography

GENERAL CANADIAN ELEMENTARY SOCIAL STUDIES METHODS TEXTS

Case, R., and P. Clark eds.,. *The Canadian Anthology of Social Studies.* Vancouver, BC: Pacific Educational Press, 1999.

Case, R., and P. Clark, eds., *The Anthology of Social Studies, Volume 1. Issues and Strategies for Elementary Teachers* (Vancouver: Pacific Educational Press, 2008).

Gibson, S. *Teaching elementary social studies: A social constructivist approach.* Toronto: Nelson Publications, 2008.

Kirman, J. *Elementary Social Studies: Creative Classroom Ideas,* 3rd edition. Toronto: Prentice-Hall, 2002.

Sears A., and I. Wright, eds., *Challenges and Prospects for Canadian Social Studies* (Vancouver: Pacific Educational Press, 2004).

Wright I., and A. Sears, eds., *Trends and Issues in Canadian Social Studies* (Vancouver: Pacific Educational Press, 1997).

Photo Acknowledgments

'Ksan Historical Village and Museum, page 89. Used with permission.

British Columbia Archives, page 59, Image D-05832. Courtesy of Royal BC Museum, BC Archives.

City of Vancouver Archives, page 121, SGN 1586; pages 122–123, William Bros. AIR P108.1 (c. 1966), William Bros. CVA 23-12 (1973), William Bros. CVA 586 (WB40356-25) (1982); page 145, William Bros. CVA 586 (WB38829-26); page 258, MIL.P.13 N225 #1. Used with permission.

City of Whitehorse Tourism Department, page 61. Courtesy of Sheila Dodd and the City of Whitehorse.

CN Tower, page 292. Courtesy of CN Tower, Toronto, Ontario.

Evergreen Foundation, page 163 and 168. Used with permission.

Glenbow Archives, page 59. Glenbow Archives NA-263-1.

Ives Tessier/TESSIMA, page 292, Quebec City 2023K532. Courtesy of Ives Tessier/TESSIMA.

LaBar, Yvonne, page 61. Used with permission.

Library and Archives Canada, page 59, Richard Harrington/Richard Harrington fonds/PA-145006. Reproduced with permission.

Morrison, Archie, page 257. Used with permission.

National Film Board of Canada, page 59, Kryn Taconis/75-1339KC. Used with permission.

Ottawa Tourism and Convention Centre (photo from National Capital Commission), page 293. Used with permission.

Parks Canada, page 294, Louis Jacob (1988) 100/00PR-7/SPO.0001. Used with permission.

PR Services Whitehorse, page 61. Used with permission.

Vancouver Public Library, Special Collections, page 59—VPL 14082, VPL 7641; page 126—VPL 749; page 127—VPL 8371; page 194—VPL 12626. Used with permission.

Wootton, A., page 294, Dr. Sun Yat-sen Gardens, Vancouver, BC. Used with permission.

Yukon First Nations Tourism Association, page 61. Used with permission.

All other photographs by Ian Wright.

Index